THE STATE OF
BLACK AMERICA 1991

 Published by **National Urban League, Inc.**
January 1991

THE STATE OF BLACK AMERICA 1991

Editor

Janet Dewart

Copyright © National Urban League, Inc., 1991
Library of Congress Catalog Card Number 77-647469
ISBN 0-914758-13-6

Price $19.95

The cover art is "With Honors" by Synthia Saint James. "With Honors" is the fourth in the "Great Artists" series of limited edition lithographs on African Americans created for the National Urban League through a donation from the House of Seagram.

National Urban League, Inc.

The Equal Opportunity Building ▪ 500 East 62nd Street ▪ New York, New York 10021

Founded in 1910, the National Urban League is the premier social service and civil rights organization in America. The League is a nonprofit, community-based organization headquartered in New York City, with 114 affiliates in 34 states and the District of Columbia. The mission of the National Urban League is to assist African Americans in the achievement of social and economic equality. The League implements its mission through advocacy, research, program services, and bridge building.

Dedication

The sixteenth edition of *The State of Black America* is dedicated to the memory of Guichard Parris, a scholar, historian, and pioneer in communications, who created the National Urban League's Department of Public Relations in 1946 and led it for 25 years until his retirement. Mr. Parris was a trusted adviser to Lester B. Granger and Whitney M. Young, and was a major force in shaping the modern day Urban League. He worked diligently for interracial cooperation and helped break down barriers to black participation in the public relations profession. He coauthored with Lester Brooks *Blacks in the City,* the official history of the National Urban League. Mr. Parris died November 14, 1990.

TABLE OF CONTENTS

About the Authors

DERRICK BELL
Weld Professor of Law
Harvard University

Professor Derrick Bell is an expert on American racism. He has been a practitioner, an administrator, a legal teacher, a scholar, and an activist in the field of civil rights. He took an unpaid leave of absence in April, 1990, to protest the lack of diversity on Harvard Law School's faculty. He vowed not to return until the school hires and tenures a woman of color.

Professor Bell was an attorney with the Justice Department's Civil Rights Division; first assistant counsel for the NAACP Legal Defense and Educational Fund; deputy director of the Office of Civil Rights, Department of Health, Education, and Welfare; executive director of the Western Center on Law and Poverty; and former Dean of the University of Oregon Law School.

Professor Bell is the author of *Race, Racism, and American Law* (2nd ed. 1980); *Shades of Brown: New Perspectives on School Desegregation* (1980), and *And We Are Not Saved: The Elusive Quest for Racial Justice* (1987). In addition, he has published articles in dozens of law journals and lay publications.

Professor Bell earned his B.A. degree from Duquesne University and his LL.B. degree from the University of Pittsburgh. He has been awarded honorary doctor of laws degrees from Toogaloo College, Northeastern University, Mercy College, and Allegheny College.

* * * *

DR. LENNEAL J. HENDERSON
Distinguished Professor of
Government and Public Administration
University of Baltimore

Dr. Lenneal Henderson is an expert on fiscal policy. In addition to his professorship, he is a Senior Fellow in the William Donald Schaefer Center for Public Policy and a Henry C. Welcome Fellow at the University of Baltimore. Before assuming his current positions, he was Head and Professor of Political Science at the University of Tennessee-Knoxville, a senior faculty member at the Federal Institute in Charlottesville, VA, and a professor in the School of Business and Public Administration at Howard University.

Other academic accomplishments include his being a Ford Foundation, National Research Council Postdoctoral Fellow at the Johns Hopkins School of Advanced International Studies, a Kellogg National Fellow, and a Rockefeller Research Fellow.

Professor Henderson has lectured or consulted in sub-Saharan Africa, Egypt, Israel, India, Brazil, Peru, the Caribbean, the Soviet Union, and the People's Republic of China.

He has published or edited five books and numerous articles in many publications, including *The Urban League Review, The Review of Black Political Economy, The Annals, Policy Studies Journal, Howard Law Journal,* and *The Black Scholar.*

Dr. Henderson earned his Bachelor of Arts, Master of Arts, and Ph.D. degrees from the University of California, Berkeley.

* * * *

DONALD F. McHENRY
*University Research Professor of
Diplomacy and International Relations
Georgetown University*
and
President, IRC Group, Inc.

The Honorable Donald F. McHenry is renowned as an expert in foreign policy and international law and organizations.

He distinguished himself as the U.S. Permanent Representative to the United Nations during the Carter administration, representing the United States in a number of international forums, and as the U.S. negotiator on the question of Namibia. As chief U.S. Representative to the U.N., Ambassador McHenry also served as a member of President Carter's cabinet. At the time of his appointment in 1979, he was the U.S. Deputy Representative to the U.N. Security Council, a post he had held since March, 1977.

His diplomatic career began in 1963, when he joined the U.S. State Department, serving in various positions related to American foreign policy. Three years later, Ambassador McHenry received the Department's Superior Honor Award. While on leave in 1971, he was a Guest Scholar at the Brookings Institution and an International Affairs Fellow of the Council on Foreign Relations.

A director on several prestigious corporate boards, including the Coca-Cola Company, Ambassador McHenry chairs the board of trustees of Africare. He is also president of IRC Group, an international consulting firm.

Ambassador McHenry has taught at Southern Illinois, Howard, and American Universities. He is the author of *Micronesia: Trust Betrayed* (The Carnegie Endowment, 1975) and numerous articles published in professional journals and newspapers. He is a member of the Editorial Board of *Foreign Policy* magazine.

Ambassador McHenry graduated from Illinois State University in 1957; two years later, he earned his master's degree from Southern Illinois University. He has done postgraduate work at Georgetown University.

* * * *

DR. FLORETTA DUKES McKENZIE
President, The McKenzie Group

Dr. Floretta McKenzie is recognized throughout America as an expert in excellence in education. The McKenzie Group—a comprehensive educational consulting firm—offers a range of direct assistance services to both public and private organizations.

From 1981-88, Dr. McKenzie was Superintendent and Chief State School Officer for the District of Columbia Public Schools, the 21st largest school system in the nation, with an enrollment of nearly 89,000 students and an annual budget exceeding $400 million. She has served as Deputy Assistant Secretary of Education; U.S. Delegate to UNESCO; and Assistant Deputy Superintendent, Maryland State Department of Education. She was the first woman to serve with the U.S. Office of Education in the post of Deputy Commissioner.

She serves on the boards of The Acacia Group, the National Geographic Society, Boy Scouts of America, and Reading Is Fundamental (RIF), among others.

In the spring of 1990, Dr. McKenzie was a Distinguished Visiting Professor at Harvard University's Graduate School of Education.

Dr. McKenzie earned her academic credentials as follows: a B.S. degree from DC Teachers College; an M.A. degree from Howard University; and a Ph.D. degree from George Washington University. Her numerous awards and citations include five honorary doctorate degrees.

PATRICIA EVANS is a cultural anthropologist and a researcher with the McKenzie Group.

* * * *

DR. WARREN F. MILLER, JR.
Associate Director at Large
Los Alamos National Laboratory
and
E.H. and M.E. Pardee Professor
Department of Nuclear Engineering
University of California, Berkeley

Dr. Warren Miller is an eminently qualified nuclear engineer. As Associate Director at Large of the Los Alamos National Laboratory in New Mexico, he serves on the Senior Management Group, participating in strategic planning, policy formulation, and priority setting. He has laboratory-wide responsibility for administering the Institutional Supporting Research and Development

Program and for overseeing the science and technology base. He has 16 years with the prestigious agency, including seven as a member of senior management.

Dr. Miller's distinguished professorship in Nuclear Engineering at the University of California is the latest in a series of scholarly posts he has held. He was the Goebel Visiting Professor in the College of Engineering at the University of Michigan and Visiting Professor in the Department of Mechanical Engineering at Howard University, among others.

Dr. Miller has been honored as a State of New Mexico Eminent Scholar (1989), a Fellow of the American Nuclear Society (1982), and a Walter P. Murphy Fellow at Northwestern University (1969-72).

Among his active professional affiliations and memberships, Dr. Miller lists his Chairmanship of the University of Chicago Review Committee for the Engineering Physics Division, Argonne National Laboratory. A prolific author, he is one of the American Nuclear Society's Advisory Editors of *Nuclear Science and Engineering.*

Dr. Miller earned both his M.S. and Ph.D. degrees in nuclear engineering from Northwestern University, after receiving his B.S. degree in engineering sciences from the U.S. Military Academy at West Point.

* * * *

DR. GAYLE PEMBERTON
Associate Director
Afro-American Studies Program
Princeton University

Dr. Gayle Pemberton specializes in twentieth-century American fiction, American Puritan literature, and Southern and Afro-American literature and film. Before assuming her current position, she taught at several leading colleges and universities, including Columbia University, Northwestern University, Smith College, Reed College (Portland, OR), and Bowdoin College (Brunswick, ME), where she was also the Director of Minority Affairs. She has lectured widely in the United States on issues of diversity and American literature.

Dr. Pemberton is the author of *On Teaching the Minority Student: Problems and Strategies,* a monograph written for college and university faculty. She has forthcoming essays in *The Yale Review, Threepenny Review,* and *Southwest Review.*

Dr. Pemberton is from an Urban League family. She is the daughter of Muriel E. and the late Lounneer Pemberton, who was a career Leaguer working in St. Paul and Minneapolis, MN; Chicago, IL; Dayton, OH; and Kansas City, MO, where he served for 18 years as Executive Director. She is the niece of the late M. Leo Bohanon, who served his entire career with the League.

Dr. Pemberton earned her M.A. and Ph.D. degrees in English and American Literature and Language from Harvard University. She holds a B.A. degree from the University of Michigan, Ann Arbor.

DR. DIANNE M. PINDERHUGHES
*Associate Professor, Department of Political Science
and Afro-American Studies and Research Program
University of Illinois at Urbana-Champaign*

Dr. Dianne Pinderhughes is a much-sought-after lecturer on the political history of blacks and women. A prolific writer, she is the author of *Race and Ethnicity in Chicago Politics, A Reexamination of Pluralist Theory.* Dr. Pinderhughes is co-editor of *Race, Class, and the New Urban Politics,* which will be published by Chatham House.

On the faculty of the University of Illinois since 1984, Dr. Pinderhughes directed the Afro-American Studies and Research Program from 1987 to 1990. She was an Academic Advisor to the highly acclaimed "Eyes on the Prize II" television series.

Among her academic appointments are Adjunct Fellow at the Joint Center for Political and Economic Studies in Washington, DC; Guest Scholar at the Brookings Institution, also in Washington; assistant professor of government at Dartmouth College; and Postdoctoral Fellow at the University of California at Los Angeles.

Dr. Pinderhughes is active in numerous professional organizations, including the National Conference of Black Political Scientists.

She earned her academic degrees in political science—her Ph.D. and M.A. degrees from the University of Chicago, and her B.A. degree from Albertus Magnus College in New Haven (CT).

* * * *

DR. DAVID H. SWINTON
*Dean of the School of Business
Professor of Economics
Jackson State University*

Dr. David Swinton is a renowned economist and educational administrator. He is recognized as an expert in the economics of social policy and minority groups. Under his direction as Dean of Jackson State University's School of Business, Dr. Swinton has implemented a new quality assurance program to ensure that all graduates have the skills, competencies, and attitudes required for success in corporate America.

Dr. Swinton is the former Director of the Southern Center for Studies in Public Policy and Professor of Economics at Clark College in Atlanta. While at the policy center, he was the principal fund-raiser and architect of the research program.

He has also served as a Teaching Fellow at Harvard University and a lecturer at City College of New York.

Dr. Swinton has been published widely in scholarly journals. His authoritative economic analysis is a regular feature of *The State of Black America.*

Dr. Swinton earned his Ph.D. and M.A. degrees in economics from Harvard University, and his B.A. degree in economics from New York University.

DR. R. ROOSEVELT THOMAS, JR.
President/Founder
The American Institute for Managing Diversity

Dr. Roosevelt Thomas is a widely sought-after expert on managing diversity by numerous *Fortune 500* companies. The American Institute is a nonprofit applied research center and is affiliated with Morehouse College. The Institute's mission is to foster effective management of employee diversity through integrated programs of research, education/training, and management consulting. Previously, Dr. Thomas served as Dean of The Atlanta University Graduate School and Instructor at Morehouse College. He also serves as Secretary of Morehouse College.

Dr. Thomas has been a consultant for more than 18 years to numerous corporations, professional firms, nonprofit organizations, and academic institutions. He has designed and taught management workshops for executives and conducted research on the managerial and organizational practices of corporations and other organizations.

Dr. Thomas earned his Doctor of Business Administration degree in organizational behavior from Harvard University; his Master of Business Administration degree from the University of Chicago; and his Bachelor of Arts in mathematics from Morehouse College, where he was elected to Phi Beta Kappa.

* * * *

DR. TERRY M. WILLIAMS
Visiting Professor in Sociology
Yale University

Dr. Terry Williams is a social scientist and researcher specializing in drug abuse and urban policy. He has lectured in the United States and abroad on the impact of cocaine and crack-cocaine use among teenagers.

Professor Williams is the author of *The Cocaine Kids* (1989) and the seminal study *Growing Up Poor* (1985, with William Kornblum).

Dr. Williams has five books scheduled for publishing by the end of next year: *The Crackhouse* (1991), *West 42nd Street: The Bright Lights Zone* (1991, with William Kornblum), *Voices in the Street* (1992), *A Visitor's Guide to New York Con Games* (1992), and *Coming of Age in Harlem Public Housing* (1992, with William Kornblum).

He has been a consultant to private and public organizations on a wide range of issues, from developing training modules for drug abuse practitioners to devising conceptual guidelines for park planning and restoration.

Dr. Williams is the recipient of a prestigious MacArthur Foundation Grant (1988-1990). His fellowships include a National Institute on Drug Abuse Research Fellowship, an Operation Crossroads Africa Scholarship, a National Science Foundation Award, and a postdoctoral fellowship in behavioral research in drug abuse.

Dr. Williams earned his Ph.D. degree in sociology from The Graduate School and University Center (City University of New York) and his Bachelor of Arts degree, cum laude, from Richmond College (CUNY).

Dr. WILLIAM KORNBLUM is a professor of sociology at the Graduate School and University Center of the City University of New York.

Professor Kornblum received his doctorate from the University of Chicago. He is a specialist in community and urban studies and a frequent contributor to journals and magazines in the social sciences. Since 1973, he has also directed a research unit of the National Park Service housed at the CUNY Graduate School.

Black America, 1990: An Overview

John E. Jacob
President and Chief Executive Officer
National Urban League, Inc.

1990 opened with bright hopes, as freedom spread in areas of the world long shackled by bonds of dictatorship and oppression. The crumbling of Eastern European regimes and the unfreezing of South African apartheid, evidenced by the release of Nelson Mandela from prison, seemed to herald a new era of worldwide peace and prosperity.

But 1990 dragged to an end under the dark clouds of recession at home and the threat of war in the Persian Gulf.

For Black America, the year started with anticipation that the freedom surge sweeping across the world would come home to its origins, here in the United States. As the National Urban League celebrated its 80th anniversary, our hopes were high that the decade of greed and waste was ending and a new decade of progress toward racial parity would begin.

Those hopes were dashed on the rocks of fiscal austerity, continued national indifference to African-American aspirations, the veto of the Civil Rights Act of 1990, and the crisis in the Persian Gulf.

The national budget deficit appeared to preclude new domestic policy initiatives. A strategic goal of the Reagan administration was to limit government's ability to undertake social and economic programs by choking off available resources through tax cuts and higher military spending.

The success of that strategy was seen in the virtual abandonment of important job training, health, and housing programs and crippling cuts in other domestic programs. But it was most obvious in the recurring refrain that responded to virtually all proposals for government programs that would help the poor and create opportunities in the 1980s—"we can't afford to do it."

The long budget standoff between the administration and the Congress ended with the president forced to renege on his pledge of no new taxes, but the miniscule tax increase and the rosy economic predictions on which the final budget deal was based still left Washington starved for resources.

And the Persian Gulf crisis served to immunize the military from the deep spending cuts that should have been the logical outcome of the ending of the Cold War. No one wants to cut the military budget while our uniformed men and women are in harm's way, but the bulk of Pentagon spending commitments are for incredibly expensive weapons systems designed to combat the Soviet Union in the event of a European war.

The Pentagon has yet to reorder its priorities, design a force structure com-

1

mensurate with national security needs in the post-Cold War era, and reduce its budget to levels required to sustain its new mission. Many defense experts, even hawkish ones, estimate that future military budgets adequate to preserve national security objectives could be at levels about half of current expenditures. The failure to begin long-overdue military spending cuts means that the much vaunted peace dividend—savings from defense spending that could be used to meet other vital national needs—will continue to be elusive.

Despite the budget austerity, Congress did manage to shift some spending to programs that will assist the poor and children at risk. Notable were the increase in the earned income tax credit, essentially a wage subsidy for the working poor, and further income supports for below-poverty working families with children to offset private health insurance and child care costs.

Clearly, America's long-range interests will be in jeopardy unless we better prepare disadvantaged and minority people, who will be the core of the future work force, to compete in a modern economy characterized by international markets, advanced technology, and work-force requirements for high skills levels and for advanced interpersonal and communication skills.

That is why the Department of Education's attempt to bar scholarships earmarked for minority college students was a short-sighted and malicious action. Given the great disparity in family resources between white students and African Americans, and given the clear national and institutional interest in securing a more diverse student body and educated citizenry, such scholarships are an eminently desirable public policy. The net result of limiting earmarked minority scholarships would be to reduce access to higher education for minorities who are already underrepresented in higher education, exacerbating racial divisiveness, increasing black alienation, and widening the black-white gap in socioeconomic achievement.

Even conservatives long suspicious of federal programs acknowledge that minorities at risk will be a drag on the economy and on national living standards unless more is done to draw them into the mainstream. Thus, at year's end, we started hearing about new initiatives to help the poor, the so-called "new paradigm," rightly made fun of both for its verbal unwieldiness and for its naive belief that free market choices contain the answer to all that ails poor people—as if school or housing vouchers would by themselves create quality schools and housing.

At the base of such proposals is the notion that all the poor need is money. But like all half-truths, it is also half-untrue. In addition to money, many of the poor need social services, jobs, respect, and opportunities that cannot be covered by voucher or choice schemes whose effect will often be to drive up the price of apartments or medical care, leaving the poor where they started. The purveyors of the "new paradigm" have lost their chance—the pure, unalloyed free market solutions they propose should have been tried in the 1980s, in the Reagan era, when the country appeared ready for any new fad that had an antigovernmental program label on it.

The long federal budget battle left a lot of people feeling disgusted about the way government operates, and angry about the lack of accountability and responsibility in governing.

In the end, the budget that Congress passed—while not nearly good enough to solve effectively our national problems—had some important positives.

One was the simple fact of finally putting a deficit reduction program in place, something that has not been done in over a decade.

To do that, the silly "no new taxes" pledge had to be broken. It finally dawned on the administration and most congressmen that the tax cuts of the 1980s went much too far in slashing tax rates for the affluent.

Those cuts led to deep deficits, forcing cuts in essential programs. That was, of course, the hidden agenda behind the Reagan tax cuts.

The new budget's tax hikes are very small—there is good reason to support higher rates than the new 31 percent top on the wealthy.

Less positive was the array of "sin" and nuisance taxes that hit moderate income families who will now have to pay more for gas, beer, and other items.

But those excise tax hikes led to a real positive—expansion of the earned income tax credits available to the working poor. That is a wage subsidy for working families with below-poverty incomes, and such families will stand to gain at least as much as they will have to pay out in excise taxes.

But Congress does not treat all poor people alike, and the nonworking poor will not benefit from the tax credit program.

The earned income tax credit was also the vehicle for helping poor children. It will be available for below-poverty working families that buy private health insurance for their children, and for child care costs.

And after years of trying to get a strong child care bill through the Congress, it passed a block grant program for states to distribute to parents and day-care providers. While considerably short of the broader federal program needed to ensure that all children have adequate care in these days of working parents, the program does lay the groundwork for future improvements in child care policy.

Another step forward was Congress's action to extend gradually Medicaid health insurance so that all poor children will ultimately be covered by subsidized health care.

Funding for Head Start was also raised. About 40 percent of all eligible children will be able to attend Head Start classes next year, and Congress authorized future increases to allow enrollment of virtually all eligible children by 1994.

Even in the time of deficit reduction-inspired austerity, lawmakers decided to initiate or expand those progams because they know that the nation has to invest in its future.

We have neglected the education and health of our young people, and the small steps taken by the Congress in its closing days should be seen as a barely adequate down payment on the future.

Funding for the child care program, for example, will allow only a small fraction of America's 12 million working women with preschool-age children to be served.

So more must be done, and it can be done without busting a budget that still contains lots of wasteful expenditures and still leaves the military budget at astronomical levels.

It is time to stop financing multibillion dollar Cold War programs that have long outlived their usefulness and use those resources for an Urban Marshall Plan that prepares disadvantaged people to compete in a modern economy.

That is the key to national prosperity, and it is the route the next Congress should travel with the next budget.

In the 1990s, a nation recoiling from, and paying for, the excesses of the 1980s is less likely to buy proposals that look more like illustrations of free market theories in an economics book than the realities of an urban landscape starved for resources to provide the health, housing, and job training opportunities people desperately need.

And it would be helpful if Americans could understand that today's urban poverty and disorganization has powerful roots in a history of racism. Time and again, our nation has taken the path of accommodating racism rather than ending it, with the consequences we see today as discrimination still lives, stereotyping still prevails, and racially based disadvantage continues.

Perhaps the Public Broadcasting Service's documentary on the Civil War, aired during 1990, helped many Americans to understand better the roots of today's racial dilemmas. That broadcast series showed the evils of the heritage of slavery, the betrayal of the newly freed African Americans, and the centrality of race in our history. It also highlighted the terrible price exacted by the racism of the past—in this instance the extraordinary toll of lives lost and ruined in a long, bitter war.

Racism continues to extract a high price from African Americans and from the nation as a whole, even in our considerably more enlightened times, as documented by a National Urban League study issued in the summer of 1990, aptly titled, "The Price."

Unfortunately, an important opportunity to remove discriminatory barriers to maximizing all of our human resources was lost when the president vetoed the Civil Rights Act of 1990 and the Senate failed by only one vote to override the veto.

The Civil Rights Act of 1990 was urgently needed to correct several U.S. Supreme Court decisions that drilled loopholes into existing antidiscrimination laws.

In *Wards Cove Packing Co. v. Atonio*, the Reagan Court overthrew standards governing proof of discrimination in effect since the 1971 *Griggs v. Duke Power Co.* decision. The result effectively shields employers who practice subtle forms of discrimination from the consequences of their actions.

In *Patterson v. McLean Credit Union,* the Court limited nondiscrimination guarantees in the 1866 Civil Rights law to hiring, and not to such discriminatory acts as racial harassment of employees.

In *Martin v. Wilks,* the Court allowed challenges to long-standing court-approved affirmative action consent decrees for an indefinite period of time, ensuring that remedies for past discrimination will be paralyzed by continuous legal maneuvers. But in *Lorance v. AT&T Technologies, Inc.,* the Court said challenges to seniority systems that have discriminatory impacts must be filed in timely fashion and barred challenges made at a later time, when a person is directly affected. In effect, those two decisions allow white employees to challenge affirmative action programs long after they are instituted, but deny similar rights to women and minorities challenging discriminatory seniority systems.

These—and other—decisions by the Court made it necessary for the Congress to act to restore civil rights protections mangled by the Reagan Court. The urgency of this is demonstrated by the many cases now being filed in federal courts since *Martin v. Wilks,* seeking to overthrow court-ordered consent decrees that remedy proven discrimination; the many pending court cases relying on the *Griggs* principles that now face dismissal under the *Wards Cove* standards, and by the more than 200 victims of illegal discrimination whose court cases have been dismissed as a result of the *Patterson* decision.

The Civil Rights Act of 1990 would have overturned those Supreme Court decisions. The legislation was fair and equitable. It was urgently required to reverse those decisions and to protect African Americans, women, and minorities against discriminatory employment practices.

The shameful veto of the Civil Rights Act of 1990 was justified on the grounds that it would encourage employers to adopt racial hiring quotas. That claim is false.

The act specifically stated that nothing in it should be construed as requiring or encouraging quotas. Further, the act specified that a statistical shortage of women or minorities in an employer's work force could not, by itself, prove discrimination. And key negotiators for the administration publicly stated that the act was not a quota bill. Similar statements were made by major Jewish organizations, who are sensitive to the quota issue and who vigorously supported the act.

Most telling—the act would have restored the *Griggs* standards, which barred employment practices that have a disparate impact on female and minority employment opportunities, with the exception of business practices related to job performance. And in the 18 years during which the *Griggs* standards were in force, employers have not adopted quotas.

The "quota" issue was a red herring—a transparent attempt to spread a Big Lie for political reasons, and not an even remotely accurate characterization of the contents or likely effects of the act.

The administration's good faith was called into question, too, when, despite adoption of administration-backed amendments to the act that met all of its stated objections, the White House offered a new civil rights bill of its own at the eleventh hour. Essentially, that bill would have codified the very Supreme Court decisions the Congress wanted to overturn by passing the Civil Rights Act of 1990.

The administration's proposed bill included language that would imperil existing race and gender-conscious remedies for discrimination. It would have given employers a virtual license to discriminate, by allowing such practices as refusing to hire minorities because customers prefer not to deal with them, or allowing airlines or restaurants to fire female employees who marry or pass a certain age. And it was riddled with provisions that weaken antidiscrimination standards, make it difficult, if not impossible, to challenge successfully discriminatory practices, and refuse fair relief and remedies to the victims of discrimination.

Rarely has a presidential decision had so many negative consequences.

Politically, the veto thwarted the will of the large majority of Congress and undercut the president's own congressional negotiators, who succeeded in winning compromises and weakening the act. And it undermined the laudable effort of attracting African Americans to the Republican Party, a development that could have gained strength had the president built upon his reservoir of existing good will among minorities by signing the act.

Economically, the veto was a disaster—encouraging discriminatory practices at a time when our nation must encourage the maximum use of all its people to counter competitive threats from abroad and to overcome looming work-force shortages. It is a logical and economic contradiction to agree that our economy will rely more on African Americans, women, immigrants, and nonwhite minorities, and then veto a bill that would protect the groups most vulnerable to employment discrimination.

The veto was also a moral disaster, for employment discrimination—like other forms of discrimination—is a moral outrage in a society that prides itself on a heritage of justice and democracy. By pandering to the ugliest elements in our national political life, the veto was the contemporary equivalent of the Willie Horton ads of the 1988 campaign—smearing minority aspirations with codewords such as "quotas" and thereby strengthening the forces of racism typified by such demagogues as David Duke, the Klansman-turned-politician.

Further, it is unconscionable that the president would send several hundreds of thousands of young Americans—many of them women and minorities—to risk their lives in the Persian Gulf, and then veto a Civil Rights Act that would protect them against job discrimination when they return to civilian life.

The veto did not end the struggle for the Civil Rights Act. When it is reintroduced in the new Congress, the African-American community and its allies among all Americans who seek a society free of discrimination and racial disadvantage will mobilize to assure that it passes with margins wide enough to guarantee an override of another veto.

Passage of the Civil Rights Act will be a major priority for 1991, along with the Urban League's proposal for an Urban Marshall Plan for investments in rebuilding the infrastructure and in the education and job training programs needed to assure America's economic survival. Above all, Black America's objective is racial parity. While the path to that treasured goal is long and arduous, there can be no turning back, no alternative to the step-by-step progress required to attain an open, pluralistic, integrated society in which the races are equal.

The last decade of the 20th century begins with limited progress in only a few areas being made toward racial parity, as documented by *The State of Black America 1991,* which features articles by outstanding scholars. Their independent evaluations are intended to inform and to stimulate, but their views do not necessarily reflect the positions or policies of the National Urban League. Our own summation and recommendations appear at the end of this report.

This year's edition marks both a strengthening of and a departure from the kind of information for which this publication is noted. We have presented the facts, as usual, such as noted economist David Swinton's detailed analysis of the economic status of African Americans. Dr. Swinton challenges the nation to make the changes necessary to ensure that the entrenched poverty that African Americans experience in disproportionate numbers does not remain a permanent feature of American society.

This edition of *The State of Black America* also goes beyond the facts and figures to reveal more about the humanity behind the statistics. Among our departures is Professor Derrick Bell's innovative and provocative chronicle about the constitutional contradiction, based on his belief in the observation by Justice Oliver Wendell Holmes that law is more than logic; it is experience. Professor Bell further demonstrates that our society, while ideally one of laws, cannot be separated from the men and women—and their racial predispositions—who run it.

Dr. Gayle Pemberton takes us on a journey through the searing intellect of W.E.B. Du Bois to discuss intellectual bravery, spiritual optimism, and the political salvation of African Americans. She pierces the thin veil of racism that is evident in the exclusion of W.E.B. Du Bois and other African-American writers from *The Great Books.* She argues that no reasonably educated person in America can lay claim to being so without an appreciation of and a knowledge of the multicultural diversity of this country.

Sociologist Terry Williams takes us on a journey of another kind: through public housing projects in Harlem where we meet some poor teenagers and adults unlike those in most headlines: honest, hardworking, ambitious. His very personal approach is the result of extensive field study in low-income communities in New York. With his coauthor, William Kornblum, Dr. Williams underscores the need for all of us to not fall prey to stereotypes and to reach out to people who may seem different from us, but who, in reality, are very much like us. He reminds us that—whatever their social circumstances—the children in these communities are our children and that it is incumbent upon all of us to ensure their safe passage to responsible adulthood.

Inherent in these and other articles is a belief that change is possible and that an understanding of people and situations will move society toward social and economic equality.

This edition of *The State of Black America*, like past ones, contributes to the nation's awareness of the reality of life within Black America and to the decision-making process in 1991. We express our gratitude to the authors.

The Elusive Quest for Racial Justice: The Chronicle of the Constitutional Contradiction

Derrick Bell

INTRODUCTION

The news in this year's *The State of Black America* confirms the civil rights assessment made by Geneva Crenshaw, heroine of *And We Are Not Saved: The Elusive Quest for Racial Justice.*[1] Geneva Crenshaw is a fictional character who allows me to use facts with an overlay of fantasy and dialogue to uncover enduring truths.

In this Chronicle, I take the liberty of tampering with time and history to examine the original contradiction that is at the heart of blacks' difficulty in gaining legal redress. Surveying the racial scene, Geneva Crenshaw found that "we have attained all the rights we sought in law and gained none of the resources we need in life. Like the crusaders of old, we sought the holy grail of 'equal opportunity' and, having gained it in court decisions and civil rights statutes, find it transformed from the long-sought guarantee of racial equality into one more device the society can use to perpetuate the racial status quo."

The subordinate status of African Americans must be seen in context. There are familiar patterns in the painful civil rights setbacks of recent years. They replicate the society's historic willingness—particularly in times of political unease and economic distress—to sacrifice black rights to political expediency. Thus, while civil rights advocates, black and white alike, continue the struggle for racial equality, their success or failure depends less on their efforts than on whether whites decide that their status can be safeguarded by ignoring racial justice in policy-making or personal functioning.

The Constitution, the nation's fundamental law, is built on just such neglect. To dramatize the precedent-setting pattern of racial rights "set-asides," Geneva Crenshaw is transported back to Independence Hall in Philadelphia, where, in the late summer of 1887, the Constitution's Framers are putting the finishing touches on the document. Confronted with the moral significance of their decision to recognize property in slaves, they respond with arguments that, were they equally candid, might serve contemporary policymakers whose priorities continue to favor white interests over the rights of African-American people.

THE CHRONICLE OF THE CONSTITUTIONAL CONTRADICTION

At the end of a journey back millions of light-years, I found myself standing quietly at the podium of the Constitutional Convention of 1787. It was late afternoon, and hot in that late summer way that makes it pleasant to stroll down a shaded country lane, but mighty oppressive in a large, crowded meeting room, particularly one where the doors are closed and locked to ensure secrecy.

The three dozen or so convention delegates looked tired. They had doubtless been meeting all day and now, clustered in small groups, were caucusing with their state delegations. So intense were their discussions that the few men who looked my way did not seem to see me. They knew this was a closed meeting, and thus could not readily take in the appearance, on what had just been an empty platform, of a tall stranger—a stranger who was not only a woman but also, all too clearly, black.

Though I knew I was protected by extraordinary forces, my hands were wet with nervous perspiration. Then I remembered why I was there. Taking a deep breath, I picked up the gavel and quickly struck the desktop twice, hard.

"Gentlemen," I said, "My name is Geneva Crenshaw, and I appear here to you as a representative of the late twentieth century to test whether the decisions you are making today might be altered if you were to know their future disastrous effect on the nation's people, both white and black."

For perhaps ten seconds, there was a shocked silence. Then the chamber exploded with shouts, exclamations, oaths. I fear the delegates' expressions of stunned surprise did no honor to their distinguished images. A warm welcome would have been too much to expect, but their shock at my sudden presence turned into an angry commotion unrelieved by even a modicum of curiosity.

The delegates to the Constitutional Convention were, in the main, young and vigorous.[1] When I remained standing, unmoved by their strong language and dire threats, several particularly robust delegates charged toward the platform, determined to carry out the shouted orders: "Eject the Negro woman at once!"

Suddenly the hall was filled with the sound of martial music, blasting trumpets, and a deafening roll of snare drums. At the same time—as the delegates were almost upon me—a cylinder composed of thin vertical bars of red, white, and blue light descended swiftly and silently from the high ceiling, nicely encapsulating the podium and me.

The self-appointed ejection party neither slowed nor swerved, a courageous act they soon regretted. As each man reached and tried to pass through the transparent light shield, there was a loud hiss, quite like the sound that electrified bug zappers make on a warm summer evening. While not lethal, the shock each attacker received was sufficiently strong to knock him to the floor, stunned and shaking.

The injured delegates all seemed to recover quickly, except one who had tried to pierce the light shield with his sword. The weapon instantly glowed red hot and burned his hand. At that point, several delegates tried to rush out of the room either to escape or to seek help—but neither doors nor windows would open.

"Gentlemen," I repeated, but no one heard me in the turmoil of shouted orders, cries of outrage, and efforts to sound the alarm to those outside. Scanning the room, I saw a swarthy delegate cock his long pistol, aim carefully, and fire directly at me. But the ball hit the shield, ricocheted back into the room, and shattered an inkwell, splattering my intended assassin with red ink.

At that, one of the delegates, raising his hand, roared, "Silence!" and then turned to me. "Woman! Who are you and by what authority do you interrupt this gathering?"

"Gentlemen," I began, "delegates"—then paused and, with a slight smile, added, "fellow citizens, I—like some of you—am a Virginian, my forefathers having labored on the land holdings of your fellow patriot, the Honorable Thomas Jefferson. I have come to urge that, in your great work here, you not restrict the sweep of Mr. Jefferson's self-evident truths that all men are equal and endowed by the Creator with inalienable rights, including 'Life, Liberty and the pursuit of Happiness.'" It was, I thought, a clever touch to invoke the name of Thomas Jefferson who, then serving as American minister to France, was not a member of the Virginia delegation.[2] But my remark could not overcome the offense of my presence.

"How dare you insert yourself in these deliberations?" a delegate demanded.

"I dare," I said, "because slavery is an evil that Jefferson, himself a slave owner and unconvinced that Africans are equal to whites, nevertheless found involved 'a perpetual exercise of the most boisterous passions, the most unremitting despotism on the one part, and degrading submissions on the other.' Slavery, Jefferson has written, brutalizes slaver owner as well as slave and, worst of all, tends to undermine the 'only firm basis' of liberty, the conviction in the minds of the people that liberty is 'the gift of God.'[3]

"Gentlemen, it was also Thomas Jefferson who, considering the evil of slavery, wrote: 'I tremble for my country when I reflect that God is just; that his justice cannot sleep forever.'"[4]

There was a hush in the group. No one wanted to admit it, but the ambivalence on the slavery issue expressed by Jefferson obviously had meaning for at least some of those in the hall. It seemed the right moment to prove both that I was a visitor from the future and that Jefferson's troubled concern for his country had not been misplaced. In quick, broad strokes, I told them of the country's rapid growth, of how slavery had expanded rather than withered of its own accord, and finally of how its continued presence bred first suspicion and then enmity between those in the South who continued to rely on a plantation economy and those Northerners committed to industrial development using white wage workers. The entry into the Union of each new state, I explained, further dramatized the disparity between North and South.

Inevitably, the differences led to armed conflict—a civil war that, for all its bloody costs, did not settle those differences, and they remain divisive even as we celebrate our two-hundredth anniversary as one nation.

"The stark truth is that the racial grief that persists today," I ended, "originated in the slavery institutionalized in the document you are drafting. Is this, gentlemen, an achievement for which you wish to be remembered?"

Oblivious to my plea, a delegate tried what he likely considered a sympathetic approach. "Geneva, be reasonable. Go and leave us to our work. We have heard the petitions of Africans and of abolitionists speaking in their behalf. Some here are sympathetic to these pleas for freedom. Others are not. But we have debated this issue at length, and after three months of difficult negotiations, compromises have been reached, decisions made, language drafted and approved. The matter is settled. Neither you nor whatever powers have sent you here can undo what is done."

I was not to be put off so easily. "Sirs," I said, "I have come to tell you that the matter of slavery will not be settled by your compromises. And even when it is ended by armed conflict and domestic turmoil far more devastating than that you hope to avoid here, the potential evil of giving priority to property over human rights will remain. Can you not address the contradiction in your words and deeds?"

"There is no contradiction," replied another delegate. "Gouverneur Morris of Pennsylvania, the Convention's most outspoken opponent of slavery, has admitted that 'life and liberty were generally said to be of more value, than property,... [but] an accurate view of the matter would nevertheless prove that property was the main object of Society.'"[5]

"A contradiction," another delegate added, "would occur were we to follow the course you urge. We are not unaware of the moral issues raised by slavery, but we have no response to the delegate from South Carolina, General Charles Cotesworth Pinckney, who has admonished us that 'property in slaves should not be exposed to danger under a Govt. instituted for the protection of property.'"[6]

"Of what value is a government that does not secure its citizens in their persons and their property?" inquired another delegate. "Government, as Mr. Pierce Butler from South Carolina has maintained here, 'was instituted principally for the protection of property and was itself...supported by property.' Property, he reminded us, was 'the great object of government; the great cause of war; the great means of carrying it on.'[7] And the whole South Carolina delegation joined him in making clear that 'the security the Southern states want is that their negroes may not be taken from them.'"[8]

"Your deliberations here have been secret," I replied. "And yet history has revealed what you here would hide. The Southern delegates have demanded the slavery compromises as their absolute precondition to forming a new government."

"And why should it not be so?" a delegate in the rear called out. "I do not represent the Southern point of view, and yet their rigidity on the slavery issue is wholly natural, stemming as it does from the commitment of their economy to labor-intensive agriculture. We are not surprised by the determined bargaining of the Georgia and South Carolina delegations, nor distressed that our Southern colleagues, in seeking the protection they have gained, seem untroubled by doubts about the policy and morality of slavery and the slave trade."

"Then," I countered, "you are not troubled by the knowledge that this document will be defended by your Southern colleagues in the South Carolina ratification debates, by admissions that 'Negroes were our wealth, our only resource'?"[9]

"Why, in God's name," the delegate responded, "should we be troubled by the truth, candidly stated? They have said no less in these chambers. General Charles Cotesworth Pinckney has flatly stated that 'South Carolina and Georgia cannot do without slaves.' And his cousin and fellow planter, Charles Pinckney, has added, 'The blacks are the laborers, the peasants of the Southern states.'"[10]

At this, an elderly delegate arose and rapped his cane on his chair for attention. "Woman, we would have you gone from this place. But if a record be made, that record should show that the economic benefits of slavery do not accrue only to the South. Plantation states provide a market for Northern factories, and the New England shipping industry and merchants participate in the slave trade. Northern states, moreover, utilize slaves in the fields, as domestics, and even as soldiers to defend against Indian raids."[11]

I shook my head. "Here you are then! Representatives from large and small states, slave states and those that have abolished slavery, all of you protecting your property interests at the cost of your principles."

There was no response. The transparent shield protected my person, served as a language translator smoothing the differences in English usage, and provided a tranquilizing effect as it shimmered softly in the hot and humid room. Evidently, even this powerful mechanism could not bring the delegates to reassess their views on the slavery issue.

I asked, "Are you not concerned with the basic contradiction in your position: that you, who have gathered here in Philadelphia from each state in the confederacy, in fact represent and constitute major property holders? Do you not mind that your slogans of liberty and individual rights are basically guarantees that neither a strong government nor the masses will be able to interfere with your property rights and those of your class? This contradiction between what you espouse and what you here protect will be held against you by future citizens of this nation."[12]

"Unless we continue on our present course," a delegate called out, "there will be no nation whose origins can be criticized. These sessions were called because the country is teetering between anarchy and bankruptcy. The nation cannot meet its debts. And only a year ago, thousands of poor farmers in Massachusetts and elsewhere took up arms against the government."

"Indeed," I said, "I am aware of Shay's Rebellion, led by Daniel Shay, a former officer who served with distinction in the war against England. According to historians of my time, the inability of Congress to respond to Massachusetts's appeal for help provided 'the final argument to sway many Americans in favor of a stronger federal government.'[13] I understand the nature of the crisis that brings you here, but the compromises you make on the slavery issue are—"

"Young woman!" interrupted one of the older delegates. "Young woman, you say you understand. But I tell you that it is 'nearly impossible for anyone who has not been on the spot to conceive (from any description) what the delicacy and danger of our situation... [has] been. I am President of this Convention, drafted to the task against my wishes. I am here and I am ready to embrace any tolerable compromise that... [is] competent to save us from impending ruin.'"[14]

While so far I had recognized none of the delegates, the identity of this man—seated off by himself, and one of the few who had remained quiet through the bedlam that broke out after my arrival—was unmistakable.

"Thank you, General Washington," I responded. "I know that you, though a slave owner, are opposed to slavery. And yet you have said little during these meetings—to prevent, one may assume, your great prestige from unduly influencing debate. Future historians will say of your silence that you recognize that for you to throw the weight of your opinion against slavery might so hearten the opponents of the system, while discouraging its proponents, as to destroy all hope of compromise. This would prevent the formation of the Union, and the Union, for you, is essential."[15]

"I will not respond to these presumptions," said General Washington, "but I will tell you now what I will say to others at a later time. There are in the new form some things, I will readily acknowledge, that never did, and I am persuaded never will, obtain my cordial approbation; but I did then conceive, and do now most firmly believe, that in the aggregate it is the best constitution that can be obtained at this epoch, and that this, or a dissolution, awaits our choice, and is the only alternative."[16]

"Do you recognize," I asked, "that in order to gain unity among yourselves, your slavery compromises sacrifice freedom for the Africans who live amongst you and work for you? Such sacrifices of the rights of one group of human beings will, unless arrested here, become a difficult-to-break pattern in the nation's politics."[17]

"Did you not listen to the general?" This man, I decided, must be James Madison. As the delegates calmed down, he had returned to a prominent seat in the front of the room directly in front of the podium. It was from this vantage point that he took notes of the proceedings which, when finally released in 1840, became the best record of the Convention.[18]

"I expect," Madison went on, "that many will question why I have agreed to the Constitution. And, like General Washington, I will answer: 'because I thought it safe to the liberties of the people, and the best that could be obtained from the jarring interests of States, and the miscellaneous opinions of Politicians; and because experience has proved that the real danger to America & to liberty lies in the defect of *energy & stability* in the present establishments of the United States.'"[19]

"Do not think," added a delegate from Massachusetts, "that this Convention has come easily to its conclusions on the matter that concerns you. Gouverneur Morris from Pennsylvania has said to us in the strongest terms: 'Domestic slavery is the most prominent feature in the aristocratic countenance of the proposed Constitution.'[20] He warned again and again that 'the people of Pennsylvania will never agree to a representation of Negroes.'[21]

"Many of us shared Mr. Morris's concern about basing apportionment on slaves as insisted by the Southern delegates. I recall with great sympathy his questions:

> Upon what principle is it that the slaves shall be computed in the representation? Are they men? Then make them citizens & let them vote? Are they property? Why then is no other property included?. . .
> The admission of slaves into the Representation when fairly explained comes to this: that the inhabitant of Georgia and South Carolina who goes to the Coast of Africa, and in defiance of the most sacred laws of humanity tears away his fellow creatures from their dearest connections & damns them to the most cruel bondages, shall have more votes in a Govt. instituted for protection of the rights of mankind, then the Citizen of Pa or N. Jersey who views with a laudable horror, so nefarious a practice.[22]

"I tell you, woman, this Convention was not unmoved at these words of Mr. Morris's only a few weeks ago."

"Even so," I said, "the Convention has acquiesced when representatives of the Southern states adamantly insisted that the proposed new government not interfere with their property in slaves. And is it not so that, beyond a few speeches, the representatives of the Northern states have been, at best, ambivalent on the issue?"

"And why not?" interjected another delegate. "Slavery has provided the wealth that made independence possible. The profits from slavery funded the Revolution. It cannot be denied. At the time of the Revolution, the goods for which the United States demanded freedom were produced in very large measure by slave labor. Desperately needing assistance from other countries, we purchased this aid from France with tobacco produced mainly by slave labor.[23] The nation's economic well-being depended on the institution, and its preservation is essential if the Constitution we are drafting is to be more than a useless document. At least, that is how we view the crisis we face."

To pierce the delegates' adamant front, I called on the oratorical talents that have, in the twentieth century, won me both praise and courtroom battles: "The real crisis you face should not be resolved by your recognition of slavery, an evil whose immorality will pollute the nation as it now stains your document. Despite your resort to euphemisms like *persons* to keep out of the Constitution such words as *slave* and *slavery*, you cannot evade the consequences of the ten different provisions you have placed in the Constitution for the purpose of protecting property in slaves.*

"Woman!" a delegate shouted from the rear of the room. "Explain to us how you, a black, have gotten free of your chains and gained the audacity to come here and teach white men anything."

I smiled, recognizing the eternal question. "Audacity," I replied, "is an antidote to your arrogance. Be assured: my knowledge, despite my race, is far greater than yours."

"But if my race and audacity offend you, then listen to your contemporaries who have opposed slavery in most moving terms. With all due respect, there are few in this company whose insight exceeds that of Abigail Adams who wrote to her husband, John, during the Revolutionary War: 'I wish most sincerely there was not a slave in the province; it always appeared a most iniquitous scheme to me to fight ourselves for what we are daily robbing and plundering from those who have as good a right to freedom as we have.'[25] Mrs. Adams's wish is, as you know, shared by many influential Americans who denounce slavery as a corrupting and morally unjustifiable practice.[26]

"Gentlemen," I continued, "how can you disagree with the view of the Maryland delegate Luther Martin that the slave trade and three-fifths compromises 'ought to be considered as a solemn mockery of, and insult to that God whose protection we had then implored, and...who views with equal eye the poor African slave and his American master'? I can tell you that Mr.

---

*The historian William Wiecek has listed the following direct and indirect accommodations to slavery contained in the Constitution:

1. Article 1, Section 2: representatives in the House were apportioned among the states on the basis of population, computed by counting all free persons and three-fifths of the slaves (the "federal number," or "three-fifths" clause);
2. Article I, Section 2, and Article I, Section 9: two clauses requiring, redundantly, that direct taxes (including capitations) be apportioned among the states on the foregoing basis, the purpose being to prevent Congress from laying a head tax on slaves to encourage their emancipation;
3. Article I, Section 9: Congress was prohibited from abolishing the international slave trade to the United States before 1808;
4. Article IV, Section 2: the states were prohibited from emancipating fugitive slaves, who were to be returned on demand of the master;
5. Article I, Section 8: Congress empowered to provide for calling up the states' militias to suppress insurrections, including slave uprisings;
6. Article IV, Section 4: the federal government was obliged to protect the states against domestic violence, including slave insurrections;
7. Article V: the provisions of Article I, Section 9, clauses 1 and 4 (pertaining to the slave trade and direct taxes) were made unamendable;
8. Article I, Section 9, and Article I, Section 10: these two clauses prohibited the federal government and the states from taxing exports, one purpose being to prevent them from taxing slavery indirectly by taxing the exported product of slave labor.[24]

Martin will not only abandon these deliberations and refuse to sign the Constitution but also oppose its ratification in Maryland. And further, he will, in his opposition, expose the deal of the committee on which he served, under which New England states agreed to give the slave trade a twenty-year immunity from federal restrictions in exchange for Southern votes to eliminate restrictions on navigation acts. What is more, he will write that, to the rest of the world, it must appear 'absurd and disgraceful to the last degree, that we should *except* from the exercise of that power [to regulate commerce], the *only branch of commerce* which is *unjustifiable in its nature,* and *contrary* to the rights of *mankind.*'"[27]

"Again, woman," a Northern delegate assured me, "we have heard and considered all those who oppose slavery. Despite the remonstrations of the abolitionists—of whom few, I must add, believe Negroes to be the equal of white men, and even fewer would want the blacks to remain in this land were slavery abandoned—we have acted as we believe the situation demands."

"I cannot believe," I said, "that even a sincere belief in the superiority of the white race should suffice to condone so blatant a contradiction of your hallowed ideals."

"It should be apparent by now," said the delegate who had shot at me, but had now recovered his composure and shed his ink-stained coat, "that we do not care what you think. Furthermore, if your people actually had the sensitivity of real human beings, you would realize "that you are not wanted here and would have the decency to leave."

"I will not leave!" I said steadily, and waited while the delegates conferred.

Finally, a delegate responded to my challenge. "You have, by now, heard enough to realize that we have not lightly reached the compromises on slavery you so deplore. Perhaps we, with the responsibility of forming a radically new government in perilous times, see more clearly than is possible for you in hindsight that the unavoidable cost of our labors will be the need to accept and live with what you call a contradiction."

The delegate had gotten to his feet, and was walking slowly toward me as he spoke. "This contradiction is not lost on us. Surely we know, even though we are at pains not to mention it, that we have sacrificed the rights of some in the belief that this involuntary forfeiture is necessary to secure the rights for others in a society espousing, as its basic principle, the liberty of all."

He was standing directly in front of the shield now, ignoring its gentle hum, disregarding its known danger. "It grieves me," he continued, "that your presence here confirms my worst fears about the harm done to your people because the Constitution, while claiming to speak in an unequivocal voice, in fact promises freedom to whites and condemns blacks to slavery. But what alternative do we have? Unless we here frame a constitution that can first gain our signatures and then win ratification by the states, we shall soon have no nation. For better or worse, slavery has been the backbone of our economy, the source of much of our wealth. It was condoned in the colonies and recognized in the Articles of Confederation. The majority of the delegates to this convention own slaves and must have that right protected if they and their states are to be included in the new government."

He paused and then asked, more out of frustraton than defiance, "What better compromise on this issue can you offer than that which has been fashioned over so many hours of heated debate?"

The room was silent. The delegate, his statement made, his question presented, turned and walked slowly back to his seat. A few from his state touched his hand as he passed. Then all eyes turned to me.

I thanked the delegate for his question and then said, "The processes by which Northern states are even now abolishing slavery are known to you all.[28] What is lacking here is not legislative skill but the courage to recognize the evil of holding blacks in slavery—an evil that would be quickly and universally condemned were the subjects of bondage members of the Caucasian race. You fear that unless the slavery of blacks is recognized and given protection, the nation will not survive. And my message is that the compromises you are making here mean that the nation's survival will always be in doubt. For now in my own day, after two hundred years and despite bloody wars and the earnest efforts of committed people, the racial contradiction you sanction in this document remains and threatens to tear this country apart."

"Mr. Chairman," said a delegate near the podium whose accent indicated that he was from the deep South, "this discussion grows tiresome and I resent to my very soul the presence in our midst of this offspring of slaves. If she accurately predicts the future fate of her race in this country, then our protection of slave property, which we deem essential for our survival, is easier to justify than in some later time when, as she implies, negroes remain subjugated even without the threats we face."

"Hear! Hear!" shouted a few delegates. "Bravo, Colonel!"

"It's all hypocrisy!" the Colonel shouted, his arms flailing the air, "sheer hypocrisy! Our Northern colleagues bemoan slavery while profiting from it as much as we in the South, meanwhile avoiding its costs and dangers. And our friends from Virginia, where slavery began, urge the end of importation— not out of humanitarian motivations, as their speeches suggest, but because they have sufficient slaves, and expect the value of their property will increase if further imports are barred.

"Mr. George Mason, of the Virginia delegation, in his speech opposing the continued importation of slaves expressed fear that, if not barred, the people of Western lands, already crying for slaves, could get them through South Carolina and Georgia. He moans that: 'Slavery discourages arts & manufacturers. The poor despise labor when performed by slaves. They prevent the immigration of Whites, who really enrich & strengthen a Country. They produce the most pernicious effect on manners.' Furthermore, according to Mr.

Mason, 'every master of slaves is born a petty tyrant. They bring the judgment of heaven on a Country... [and] by an inevitable chain of causes & effects providence punishes national sins, by national calamities.'[29]

"This, Mr. Chairman, is nothing but hypocrisy or, worse, ignorance of history. We speak easily today of liberty, but the rise of liberty and equality in this country has been accompanied by the rise of slavery.[30] The negress who has seized our podium by diabolical force charges that we hold blacks slaves because we view them as inferior. Inferior in every way they surely are, but they were not slaves when Virginia was a new colony 150 years ago. Or, at least, their status was hardly worse than the luckless white indentured servants brought here from debtors' prisons and the poverty-ridden streets of England. Neither slave nor servant lived very long in that harsh, fever-ridden clime."

The Colonel, so close to the podium, steadfastly refused to speak to me or even to acknowledge my presence.

"In the beginning," he went on, "life was harsh, but the coming of tobacco to Virginia in 1617 turned a struggling colony into a place where great wealth could be made relatively quickly. To cultivate the labor-intense crop, large numbers of mainly white, male servants, indentured to their masters for a period of years, were imported. Blacks, too, were brought to the colony, both as slaves and as servants. They generally worked, ate, and slept with the white servants.

"As the years passed, more and more servants lived to gain their freedom, despite the practice of extending terms for any offense, large or small. They soon became a growing, poverty-stricken class, some of whom resigned themselves to working for wages; others preferred a meager living on dangerous frontier land or a hand-to-mouth existence, roaming from one county to another, renting a bit of land here, squatting on some there, dodging the tax collector, drinking, quarreling, stealing hogs, and enticing servants to run away with them."

"It is not extraordinary to suggest that the planters and those who governed Virginia were caught in a dilemma—a dilemma more like the contradiction we are accused of building into the Constitution than may at first meet the eye. They needed workers to maintain production in their fields, but young men were soon rebellious, without either land of their own or women, who were not seen as fit to work the fields. Moreover, the young workers were armed and had to be armed to repel attacks from Indians by land and from privateers and petty-thieving pirates by sea.

"The worst fears of Virginia's leaders were realized when, in 1676, a group of these former servants returned from a fruitless expedition against the Indians to attack their rulers in what was called Bacon's Rebellion. Governor William Berkeley bemoaned his lot in terms that defined the problem: 'How miserable that man is that Governes a People where six parts of seaven at least are Poore Endebted Discontented and Armed.'[31]

"The solution came naturally and without decision. The planters purchased more slaves and imported fewer English servants. Slaves were more expensive initially, but their terms did not end, and their owners gained the benefits of the slaves' offspring. Africans, easily identified by color, could not hope to run away without being caught. The fear of pain and death could be and was substituted for the extension of terms as an incentive to force the slaves to work. They were not armed and could be held in chains.

"The fear of slave revolts increased as reliance on slavery grew and racial antipathy became more apparent. But this danger, while real, was less than that from restive and armed freedmen. Slaves did not have rising expectations, and no one told them they had rights. They had lost their freedom. Moreover, a woman could be made to work and have children every two years, thereby adding to the income of her master. Thus, many more women than indentured servants were imported.

"A free society divided between large landholders and small was much less riven by antagonisms than one divided between landholders and landless, masterless men. With the freedmen's expectations, sobriety, and status restored, he was no longer a man to be feared. That fact, together with the presence of a growing mass of alien slaves, tended to draw the white settlers closer together and to reduce the importance of the class difference between yeoman farmer and large plantation owner.

"Racial fears tended to lessen the economic and political differences between rich and poor whites. And as royal officials and tax collectors became more oppressive, both groups joined forces in protesting the import taxes on tobacco which provided income for the high and the low. The rich began to look to their less wealthy neighbors for political support against the English government and in local elections.

"Wealthy whites, of course, retained all their former prerogatives, but the creation of a black subclass enabled poor whites to identify with and support the policies of the upper class. With the safe economic advantage provided by their slaves, large landowners were willing to grant poor whites a larger role in the political process."

"So, Colonel," I interrupted, "you are saying that slavery for blacks not only provided wealth for rich whites but, paradoxically, led also to greater freedom for poor whites. One of our twentieth-century historians, Edmund Morgan, has explained this paradox of slave owners espousing freedom and liberty:

> Aristocrats could more safely preach equality in a slave society than in a free one. Slaves did not become leveling mobs, because their owners would see to it that they had no chance to. The apostrophes to equality were not addressed to them. And because Virginia's labor force was composed mainly of slaves, who had been isolated by race and removed from the political equation, the remaining free laborers and tenant farmers were too few in number to constitute a serious threat to the superiority of the men who assured them of their equality.[32]

"In effect," I concluded, "what I call a contradiction here was deemed a solution then. Slavery enabled the rich to keep their lands, arrested discontent and repression of other Englishmen, strengthened their rights and nourished their attachment to liberty. But the solution, as Professor Morgan said, 'put an end to the process of turning Africans into Englishmen. The rights of Englishmen were preserved by destroying the rights of Africans.'"[33]

"Do you charge that our belief in individual liberty is feigned?" demanded a Virginian, outraged.

"It was Professor Morgan's point," I replied, "not that 'a belief in republican equality had to rest on slavery, but only that in Virginia (and probably in other southern colonies) it did. The most ardent American republicans were Virginians, and their ardor was not unrelated to their power over the men and women they held in bondage.'"[34]

And now, for the first time, the Colonel looked at me, amazed. "My thoughts on this slavery matter have confounded my mind for many years, and yet you summarize them in a few paragraphs. I must, after all, thank you." He walked back to his seat in a daze, neither commended nor condemned by his colleagues. Most, indeed, were deep in thought—but for a few delegates I noticed trying desperately to signal to passersby in the street. But I could not attend to them: my time, I knew, must be growing short.

"The Colonel," I began again, "has performed a valuable service. He has delineated the advantages of slavery as an institution in this country. And your lengthy debates here are but prelude to the struggles that will follow your incorporation of this moral evil into the nation's basic law."

"Woman! We implore you to allow us to continue our work. While we may be inconsistent about the Negro problem, we are convinced that this is the only way open to us. You asked that we let your people go. We cannot do that and still preserve the potential of this nation for good—a potential that requires us to recognize here and now what later generations may condemn as evil. And as we talk I wonder—are the problems of race in your time equally paradoxical?"

I longed to continue the debate, but never got the chance. Apparently someone outside had finally understood the delegates' signals for help, and had summoned the local militia. Hearing some commotion beyond the window, I turned to see a small cannon being rolled up, pointing straight at me. Then, in quick succession, the cannoneer lighted the fuse; the delegates dived under their desks; the cannon fired; and, with an ear-splitting roar, the cannonball broke against the light shield and splintered, leaving me and the shield intact.

I knew then my mission was over, and I returned to the twentieth century convinced that no one could have prevented the Framers from including provisions protecting property in slaves in the Constitution.

———————

Despite decisions that today are readily condemned as unconscionable, America hails the men who drafted the Constitution as heroes. Their slavery decisions are rationalized as the regrettable but necessary actions by men who were burdened by any number of serious differences that had to be compromised to save their months of work, their fortunes, and their country. If they believed, as they had every reason to do, that the country's survival required the economic advantage provided by the slave system, then for them the conclusion was clear. The continued enslavement of Africans must be recognized, rationalized, and protected in the country's basic law. The grave crisis they faced posed a seemingly insuperable barrier to infusing their rhetoric about freedom and rights with a vision that would give meaning and substance to their words for the slaves who represented one-fifth of the population and, finally, for themselves.

The necessary question is whether the Framers set in motion an economic-political outcome to racial issues that is beyond any known power to halt or even alter? The Constitution's Framers saw Africans as slaves, and used that lowly status to convince themselves that they were condemning an inferior race. The rationale for the Framers' decision is consistent with those of the country's contemporary leaders who have every reason to know that black people are not inferior, and yet they seem no less determined to maintain racial dominance— even if this obsessive conduct destroys the country.

Throughout *And We Are Not Saved,* Geneva Crenshaw uses her allegorical chronicles to examine the myriad of contradictions that constitute American racism. "Racism," she warns, "is not a group of bad white people whose discriminatory propensities can be controlled by well-written civil rights laws, vigorously enforced. We underestimate when we do not entirely ignore the fact that there is a deeply held belief in white superiority that serves as a key, regulative force in an otherwise fragile and dangerously divided society. Indeed, it is difficult to think of another characteristic of societal functioning that has retained its viability and its value to social stability from the very beginning of the American experience down to the present day. Slavery and segregation are gone, but most whites continue to expect the society to recognize an unspoken but no less vested property right in their 'whiteness.'"

With Professor Tilden LeMelle, Geneva doubts "whether a society in which racism has been internalized and institutionalized to the point of being an essential and inherently functioning component of that society—a culture from whose inception racial discrimination has been a regulative force for maintaining stability and growth and for maximizing other cultural values— whether such a society *of itself* can even legislate (let alone enforce) public policy to combat racial discrimination..."[35]

Rather than predict success, Geneva advocates continued struggle. Speaking to civil rights advocates, she expresses her conviction "that the goal of a just society for all is morally correct, strategically necessary, and tactically sound. The barriers we face, though high, are not insuperable." She encouraged her audience: "Be of good cheer. Our forebears survived the most virulent slavery the world has ever known. We will survive contemporary conservatism. Already our faith and perseverance have rewarded us with insight that affirms our humanity. We know that life is to be lived, and not always simply enjoyed; that there is joy as well as pain in struggle; and that even in a society corrupted by its wealth, forgetful of its precepts, and cursed with the conviction that money rather than morality is the mainstay of existence, there is satisfaction in the knowledge that we are not the oppressors, and have committed our lives to fighting the oppression of ourselves as well as of others.

"Finally," Geneva urged, "let us find solace and strength in the recognition that black people are neither the first nor the only group whose age-old struggle for freedom still continues and is worth engaging in, even if it never results in total liberty and opportunity. Both history and experience tell us that each new victory over injustice both removes a barrier to racial equality and reveals another obstacle that we must, in turn, grapple with and—eventually—overcome. For just as emancipation did not really free the slaves, and Lincoln's order was but a prerequisite, the necessary first step in a process that will likely continue as long as there are among us human beings who, for whatever reason, choose to hold other human beings in their power.

"Let us, then, rejoice in the memory of the 'many thousands gone,' those men and women before us who have brought us this far along the way. Let us be worthy of their courage and endurance, as of our own hopes, our own efforts. And, finally, let us take up their legacy of faith and carry it forward into the future for the sake not alone of ourselves and our children but of all human beings of whatever race or color or creed."

The Economic Status of African Americans: "Permanent" Poverty and Inequality

David H. Swinton, Ph.D.

INTRODUCTION

This latest review of the economic status of African Americans reveals that the pattern of persisting economic disadvantage continues. The long recovery in progress since the recession of 1982 has had little impact on the intensity of racial inequality in economic life. Indeed, by many measures, even though we are at the peak of the longest recovery in the last five decades, the degree of racial inequality is higher as we begin the 1990s than at any other time in the last 20 years.

Moreover, recent evidence suggests that we are about to enter another period of economic slowdown. If this downturn has an impact similar to the last few recessions, African Americans will bear a disproportionate share of its hardships. Moreover, they will not regain all of the lost ground in the subsequent recovery. Thus, the long-run impact will be further erosion in the already disadvantaged economic status of blacks.

A similar story has been told in all of the previous issues of *The State of Black America*. The inequalities in economic status have been documented each year. In our annual analysis of data on income, labor market status, and wealth ownership, we have repeatedly made two points. First, the absolute and relative economic status of African Americans is too low. Both in absolute terms and in comparison to white Americans, blacks have high unemployment rates, low rates of employment, inferior occupational distributions, and low wages and earnings. Blacks have low incomes and high poverty rates. They own little wealth and small amounts of business property. Second, no significant progress is being made to improve the status of blacks and to close the gaps. Thus, the disparities in all the above-mentioned measures of economic status have persisted at roughly the same level for the last two decades, and many indicators of inequality have even drifted upwards during this period.

This 1991 report unfortunately has much the same findings as in previous reports. The economic state of African Americans continues to be unhealthy. Their incomes are too low, their poverty rates are too high, and both remain very unequal, as we will once again see in great detail. Their labor market status shows no sign of improving. Indeed, the employment statistics from the second half of 1990 show a noticeable downturn in the labor market position of blacks, corresponding to the recent economic slowdown of the American economy. We also

25

have the latest data on business ownership, which reveal that the miniscule participation in ownership has persisted. In short, the findings in this year's analysis mirrors the results reported in each of the annual reports for the last decade.

The consistency of these results for the last decade leads to one inescapable conclusion. *The disadvantaged economic status of the African-American population is a permanent feature of the American economy.* The permanence of this disadvantaged status implies that it is perpetuated by the normal operations of the American economy. Thus, in the absence of strong and consistent intervention, we can project continued poverty and inequality as the permanent economic status of the African-American population.

To be sure, there will be fluctuations in the absolute and relative status of blacks across the business cycle. Moreover, long-range secular growth might produce small improvements in the absolute position of African Americans. However, if present trends continue, these changes will all be relatively minor, and the dominant trend in the economic status of African Americans will be the permanence of absolute and relative economic deprivation.

The major purpose of these annual reports is to present and discuss the latest available data on the economic status of blacks. This task will be taken up in the next section of the paper, where the latest available data on income, labor markets, and ownership will be added to the accumulated statistics of the last two decades to support the conclusions stated above. The data will provide clear and overwhelming evidence that the absolute and relative economic deprivation of African Americans has been a permanent feature of the American economy during this period. Moreover, the discussion of trends will reveal no sign that the extensive racial inequality in American economic life is ameliorating.

After we complete the discussion of trends and patterns, we will provide some discussion of the reasons for the permanent poverty and inequality experienced by the African-American population. The primary hypothesis to be advanced has been presented in these pages before. Namely, the low and unequal economic status of African Americans is the legacy of the accumulated economic disadvantages of this group. In particular, we will argue that black economic disadvantages merely reflect their low levels of ownership of human capital and wealth, and the low level of ownership and/or control of business and other important economic institutions. As a result, African Americans have lacked the internal resources and cohesion to change their own situation. The American economic system has lacked the incentives to bring about the change. Thus, laissez faire policies have resulted in the perpetuation of the disadvantaged economic status of blacks.

As is customary, our concluding section will provide a brief look at prospects for ending the permanency of economic disadvantage for African Americans. The argument of this concluding section will also be a familiar refrain. In particular, we will argue that prospects for racial equality will depend on the ability of the society to provide strong and consistent interventions to eliminate the African-American disadvantages of ownership and power.

REVIEW OF THE FACTS — RECENT TRENDS IN AFRICAN-AMERICAN ECONOMIC STATUS

Our review of the facts will rely primarily on data collected and published by the U.S. Bureau of the Census or the Bureau of Labor Statistics. For the most part, the data cited here are all readily available to the general public in various published reports. The data come from monthly or annual surveys of households, for the most part, and are generally based on samples. Thus, the data are subject to small year-to-year random fluctuations, due to sampling variability. However, for the most part, these fluctuations are small relative to the gaps and patterns we discuss and do not need to be mentioned here. We have adopted a number of standard conventions to make the discussion as clear and meaningful as possible.

First, since our primary interest is on trends for the African-American population taken as a whole, we generally employ the median or mean or some other measure of central tendency to discuss each indicator of economic status. This does not imply that we are not aware of within-group variability. However, this within-group variability must be averaged out in order to assess overall group progress or status. Moreover, we do look at other aspects of the distribution where this is clearly useful in understanding the overall trend.

Second, our discussion is in terms of averages, proportions, or per capita figures in order to make the measures of black status comparable to corresponding measures of white status in view of the widely different population sizes.

Third, we will generally convert the money measurements to inflation-adjusted dollars in order to improve the comparability of the various indicators over time. Thus, most of our dollar measurements are converted to 1989 CPI-U adjusted dollars.

Finally, our tables generally only show selected years since 1970. In most cases, 1970, 1978, 1980, 1982, and several of the latest years are used. These data are adequate to convey the general pattern that existed since 1970. We use 1970 and 1980 because they are the first years in the decade. The year 1978 generally is the peak year for the 1970s business cycle. The year 1982 is the trough year for the recession of the early 1980s. Recent years are used to provide information concerning the latest trends. However, our discussion is generally based on analysis of the complete data set for the indicators and time periods under review.

One final preliminary point: We will make frequent use of an index of inequality to compare the relative status of blacks and whites. For the most part, this index is simply the ratio of the black indicator to the white indicator. The index is usually shown in the accompanying tables under a column labeled B/W.

The form may be either a percentage or a decimal. If the index is a percentage, it takes a value of 100 when equality is attained, and if it is a decimal, it would have a value of 1 if equality is attained. A value greater than 1 or 100 means that the black value is greater than the white value and vice versa for values less than 1 or 100. For negative indicators such as unemployment or poverty rates, values greater than 1 or 100 show black disadvantage and white advantage, while values less than 1 or 100 show black advantage and white disadvantage. For positive status indicators such as income or ownership rates, values greater than 1 or 100 show black advantage and white disadvantage, while the opposite holds for values less than 1 or 100. The further the deviation from 1, the greater the inequality. Finally, in some cases, we will display "gaps." These measures usually indicate the distance between the current position of blacks and what would be required to have racial equality.

Per Capita and Aggregate Income

The first indicators that we will examine are per capita and aggregate income. Income obviously measures the potential ability of the community to provide for its needs. The aggregate income is a measure of the overall size of the African-American economic potential. However, per capita income, which divides the aggregate income by the population to get the average income available for each person, is a better measure of the well-being of the black population. Moreover, since per capita income adjusts for population size, the per capita income of African and white Americans is more directly comparable.

The data for these indicators are displayed in Table 1. First, it is apparent that both aggregate and per capita income rose between 1988 and 1989 for both blacks and whites. However, the rate of increase was somewhat slower than it has been for the last few years. For example, while black aggregate income rose by 5.7

Table 1
Per Capita Income, Aggregate Income,
and Income Gaps, Selected Years 1970–1989
(1989$)

| | Aggregate Black Income | Per Capita Income | | | Parity Gap | |
		Black	White	B/W	Per Capita	Aggregate
1989	$266 Billion	$8,747	$14,896	0.587	$6,149	$186 Billion
1988	259 Billion	8,670	14,566	0.595	5,896	176 Billion
1987	245 Billion	8,345	14,346	0.582	6,001	177 Billion
1986	236 Billion	8,154	13,975	0.583	5,821	168 Billion
1982	188 Billion	6,887	12,242	0.563	5,355	146 Billion
1978	192 Billion	7,672	12,927	0.593	5,255	132 Billion
1970	138 Billion	5,973	10,719	0.557	4,746	110 Billion

Source: U.S. Department of Commerce, Bureau of the Census, *Money Income and Poverty Status in 1989,* Table 17. Calculations of aggregates and gaps were done by the author.

percent between 1987 and 1988, it rose by only 2.7 percent between 1988 and 1989. Similarly, black per capita income rose by 3.9 percent between 1987 and 1988, versus 0.9 percent between 1989 and 1990. This slower rate of increase in income undoubtedly is related to the emerging economic slowdown. We can anticipate that the rate of growth of black income between 1989 and 1990 will be even slower.

As is obvious from the table, aggregate and per capita incomes for both blacks and whites have increased rather steadily since the recession of 1982. The increase in per capita income has been steadier than the increases in any of the other income indicators. The increase has been brought about by an increase in the proportion of the population that is of working age and a significant increase in the proportion of working women. For example, the proportion of African Americans 15 years and older increased from 63.9 percent to 72.1 percent of the population between 1970 and 1989, while the corresponding proportions for whites increased from 64.2 to 79.0 percent. Per capita income growth has thus been caused more by a greater work effort than by an improvement in the productivity of each worker. The growth in per capita income, thus, overstates the real improvement in social well-being because it ignores the sacrifice of leisure time, and it also ignores the foregone services of nonworking women.

The more important point for our purposes is that the degree of racial inequality has not improved since the 1970s. In fact, the index of equality is slightly lower at the end of the 1980s than it was at the end of the 1970s. The index in 1989 stood at 0.587, slightly lower than the 0.595 index of 1988. Thus, 1989 black per capita income of $8,747 was only about 59 percent of white per capita income of $14,896. The important point, however, is that the index of inequality is within two percentage points of this number every year except 1970. Thus, this degree of relative inequality appears to be a permanent feature of the American economy. The ratio rises slightly in good times and declines slightly in bad times, but it generally fluctuates in a narrow band between .55 and .60.

This three-fifths rule is very consistent for most other income indicators, as we will see. The fact that blacks receive only three-fifths as much income per person as whites creates enormous income gaps. In 1989, blacks had an income deficit equal to $6,149 for every man, woman, and child. In the aggregate, the income of the African-American population was $186 billion short of the income required for parity.

The permanency of the income deficits is seen in the fact that both the per capita and aggregate income gaps have risen right in step with the increase of per capita income. The per capita gap has risen by $1,403 since 1970, while the aggregate gap has risen by 76 billion dollars over the past 20 years.

These tremendous income deficits have enormous implications for the capacity of the African-American community to remain viable and competitive in American society. Many of the social pathologies, such as family deterioration, high crime rates, low educational attainment, and excessive death rates, are undoubtedly related to the huge income deficits.

Median Income of Persons

More insight into the permanency of the per capita income gap can be obtained by examining the income trends from the perspective of individual income recipients. The data in Tables 2 and 3 will let us do this. Table 2 contains data relating to the percentage of males and females who are income recipients by race. This table also provides a time series on the ratio of males to females by race. Table 3 contains data on median incomes of persons by race and sex along with the inequality index. These data are presented separately by sex because there are sex differences in income recipiency, in addition to race differences. To isolate the racial impact, we must therefore compare black males to white males and black females to white females.

Table 2
Percent of Persons With Income and Ratio of Males to Females,
1970–1989, by Race and Sex

| | Percent with Earnings | | | | Ratio of | |
| | Males | | Females | | Males to Females | |
	B	W	B	W	B	W
1989	88.5	96.1	88.4	92.2	83.1	93.4
1988	87.8	96.2	88.1	92.2	83.2	93.1
1987	87.8	96.0	87.1	92.1	82.9	93.0
1986	87.5	95.6	85.8	91.1	82.7	93.0
1985	87.3	95.6	85.3	90.6	82.7	93.0
1984	85.9	95.6	85.3	90.7	82.4	92.5
1983	84.4	95.2	83.5	89.8	82.4	92.5
1982	83.2	95.2	83.5	89.5	81.9	92.5
1981	86.6	97.1	84.0	89.9	82.0	91.0
1980	87.4	95.8	83.3	89.6	81.9	92.0
1979	87.9	96.3	84.4	89.7	82.0	92.3
1978	85.6	94.3	80.4	81.3	82.3	92.5
1977	84.1	93.7	78.1	74.6	83.2	92.4
1976	84.0	93.4	75.8	73.1	83.4	92.4
1975	84.0	92.8	75.2	71.9	83.3	92.2
1974	85.4	93.4	74.9	71.0	83.0	92.3
1973	86.2	93.3	73.7	68.8	83.9	92.1
1972	83.9	92.6	72.8	66.7	83.6	91.8
1971	85.6	92.4	73.0	65.4	83.5	91.9
1970	86.0	92.8	72.7	65.8	84.5	91.6

Source: U.S. Bureau of the Census, Current Population Reports, Series P-60, No. 168, *Money Income and Poverty Status of Families and Persons in the United States: 1989* (Advance data from the March 1990 Current Population Survey), U.S. Government Printing Office, Washington, DC, 1990.

First, the most important point about the data is that a smaller proportion of both the black male and female population than the white working age population received income each year since 1978. This has also apparently become a permanent feature of the American economy. Black males have had smaller proportions receiving income every year since 1970. In 1989, the percentage of the black male population receiving income at 88.5 percent was roughly 92 percent of the portion of the white male working age population that received income (96.1 percent). The proportion of both black and white males receiving income is up slightly since the early 1970s. All else being equal, this would lead to higher overall per capita incomes. The smaller proportion of black males with income translates into lower male contributions to black per capita income.

Black females had higher proportions of their working age population with incomes than did white females before 1978, and have had lower proportions with incomes since 1978. This factor would have increased the black/white income gap all, other things being equal. This change is a result of the rapid shift in the role of white women in the work force.

The changing role of women has resulted in substantial increases in the percentage of women of both races receiving income since the early 1970s. The proportion of white women receiving income was about 40 percent higher in 1989 at 92.2 percent than it was in 1970 at 65.8 percent, while the proportion of black women receiving income increased by about 20 percent, from 72.7 to 88.4 percent over the same period. Note also that the proportion of women income recipients of both races has converged to the proportion of male income recipients. Indeed, in 1989, the black female proportion almost equaled the black male proportion, while the white female proportion was only slightly less than the white male proportion. The greater proportion of women income recipients would have made a substantial contribution to increasing per capita income, all other factors being equal.

The final column in the table shows the ratio of males to females by race. In 1989, the ratio was significantly lower for blacks, at 83.1 percent, than it was for whites. The black ratio has been significantly lower throughout the period. Moreover, the relative gap has increased since the ratio has increased over the period for whites and declined slightly for blacks. The relative scarcity of black males, thus, appears to be another of the permanent features of inequality. Moreover, the situation may be getting slightly worse. There is, in any case, no indication that the situation will improve.

The lower male-to-female ratio for blacks means that there are fewer black males proportionately to contribute to black community income. This is a serious problem. In 1989, there were approximately 1.2 million fewer black males of working age than there would have been if the black and white proportions were equal. These shortages have a significant impact on the black male contribution to black community per capita and aggregate income, causing both to be significantly lower.

The data in Table 3 display the median income of persons by race and sex from 1970 to 1989. As can be seen, 1989 median income fell slightly for both black and white males from the 1988 levels. However, the incomes of both black and white males were up considerably from the depression lows of 1981 to 1983. Both black and white male median incomes were significantly lower during the 1980s than during the 1970s. The average median incomes for black and white males during the 1980s were $11,994 and $19,994, respectively, versus $13,341 and $22,121, during the 1970s. Even in 1989 both groups had lower incomes than at any point during the 1970s. All else being equal, the decline in median income for males would have lowered per capita income.

The table also makes it apparent that black male incomes are considerably lower than white male incomes. During 1989, this pattern continued, as the

Table 3
Median Income of Persons by Race and Sex
1970 to 1989 (in Constant Dollars)

	B Males	W Males	B/W	B Females	W Females	B/W
1989	12,609	20,863	60.4	7,875	9,812	80.3
1988	12,624	20,921	60.3	7,703	9,542	80.7
1987	12,242	20,636	59.3	7,585	9,286	81.7
1986	12,244	20,433	59.9	7,429	8,780	84.6
1985	12,409	19,719	62.9	7,234	8,478	85.3
1984	11,276	19,653	57.4	7,356	8,293	88.7
1983	11,230	19,203	58.5	6,933	8,114	85.4
1982	11,357	18,951	59.9	6,763	7,667	88.2
1981	11,597	19,502	59.5	6,688	7,529	88.8
1980	12,052	20,057	60.1	6,892	7,445	92.6
Decade Avg.	11,964	19,994	59.8	7,246	8,495	85.3
1979	13,010	21,017	61.9	6,829	7,503	91.0
1978	13,049	21,782	59.9	7,050	7,830	90.0
1977	12,875	21,696	59.3	7,070	8,187	86.4
1976	13,039	21,655	60.2	7,405	7,858	94.2
1975	12,815	21,435	59.8	7,161	7,883	90.1
1974	13,798	22,210	62.0	7,078	7,840	90.3
1973	14,280	23,607	60.5	7,116	7,884	90.3
1972	14,040	23,180	60.6	7,250	7,760	93.4
1971	13,214	22,158	59.6	6,567	7,495	87.6
1970	13,285	22,406	59.3	6,593	7,242	91.0
Decade Avg.	13,341	22,121	60.3	7,012	7,748	90.5

Source: U.S. Bureau of the Census, Current Population Reports, Series P-60, No. 168, *Money Income and Poverty Status of Families and Persons in the United States: 1989* (Advance data from the March 1990 Current Population Survey), U.S. Government Printing Office, Washington, DC, 1990.

$12,609 median income of black males was only 60.4 percent of the white male median income. Throughout the last two decades, black male income fluctuated between 57 and 63 percent of white male income. This is another instance of the three-fifths rule. Relative inequality may have even increased slightly during the 1980s. The mean index of inequality for the 1980s was 59.8, and for the 1970s, was 60.3. Thus, low and unequal black male incomes appear to be another permanent feature of the American economy.

Female median incomes actually increased between 1988 and 1989. Indeed, the incomes of both black and white females have generally increased during the 1980s, and are higher at the end of the decade than they were at any point during the 1970s. The decade average is higher for both groups during the 1980s than for the 1970s. However, the high incomes at the end of the decade are more impressive than the average. The median income of black females in 1989 of $7,875 was 19.4 percent higher than the $6,593 that existed in 1970. White female income expanded even faster, by 35.5 percent, from $7,242 in 1970 to $9,812 in 1989. These increases in female income would have increased per capita incomes. The increases in female incomes have been more than enough to offset the declines in male incomes.

However, the data also make it clear that black female income is lower than white female income. In 1989, the median income of black females was only 80.3 percent as much as the income of white females. Indeed as the data show, such inequality persisted throughout the period. In fact, the degree of inequality increased substantially and was much higher during the 1980s than during the 1970s. The average ratio of black to white female income was 90.5 percent during the 1970s, compared to the 80.3 percent that existed in 1989. Thus, not only does racial inequality in the incomes of females appear to be a permanent feature, but also the extent of inequality appears to be rapidly increasing. The inequality of black and white female incomes also contributes to the per capita and aggregate income gaps.

We are now in a position to discuss more fully some of the sources of black income inequality. First, as indicated, black males have considerably lower incomes than white males. Black male income provides $4,676 per capita for the black community, which is only about 47.4 percent of the $9,862 per capita income provided by white males. The difference between black and white male contributions is $5,186. Thus, inequality in black male income accounts for 84.3 percent of black and white income inequality. Lower income contributions from males cost blacks 157.6 billion dollars in 1989.

The inequality resulted from a variety of sources. The problem of missing black males cost blacks $579 per person, and $17.6 billion in the aggregate. This accounted for 11.2 percent of the male disparity, and 9.4 percent of the overall disparity. The lower percentage of black males with incomes cost blacks $401 per capita, and $12.2 billion in the aggregate. This factor accounted for 7.7 percent of the male gap and 6.5 percent of the overall gap. The problem of lower mean income for blacks with incomes is the major cause of male income inequality. This factor by itself accounted for a disparity of $3,112 per person, and $94.6 billion in the aggregate. Lower mean incomes accounted for 60 percent of the male disparity, and 50.6 percent of the overall disparity. The interaction of the first three factors accounted for another $738 per person and $22.4 billion in the aggregate. The interaction of these factors accounted for 6.9 percent of the male gap, and 5.8 percent of the overall gap. Finally, the lower overall black population above and beyond the missing males creates another loss of $356 per person in the African-American community, and $10.8 billion in the aggregate. This factor accounts for 6.9 percent of the gap, due to lower black male incomes, and 5.8 percent of the overall gap.

The per capita contribution of black female incomes is $4,071, which is 81.9 percent of the white female contribution of $5,036. Inequality between females lowers black aggregate income by $29.3 billion, or $965 per person. This accounts for 15.7 percent of the overall gap in black per capita and aggregate income.

The female disparity arises from lower mean earnings for black females and lower proportions of black females with earnings. The lower proportion of females with earnings cost blacks $174 per person, and $5.3 billion in the aggregate. This accounted for 18 percent of the gap, due to lower female earnings and 2.8 percent of the overall gap. The lower mean income resulted in a loss of $585 per person and $17.8 billion overall. Thus, lower mean earnings accounted for 60 percent of the female gap as it did for males. This factor accounted for 9.5 percent of the overall gap. The interaction of these two factors cost $27 per person of $0.8 billion overall. Only 2.8 percent of the female gap and 0.4 percent of the overall gap are accounted for by this factor. Again, the final factor is the lower proportion of working age black females to the total population. This factor cost blacks $179 per person and $5.4 billion in the aggregate. This smaller working-age population accounts for 18.5 percent of the gap in female incomes, and 2.9 percent of the overall income discrepancy.

These factors provide an initial classification of the factors generating the large permanent income gaps that we have discussed. The missing males and the lower populations of working age blacks are population factors. Together, they account for 18.1 percent of the overall gap. In the short run, little can be done about these factors. Socioeconomic conditions over the past years have resulted in these smaller populations. Thus, these demographic factors limit the possibilities for black income equality in the short run.

The smaller proportions with incomes are both demographic and nondemographic. This factor for males and females accounts for another 9.3 percent of the disparity. The underlying cause of this is unequal opportunity and the age distribution of the two working age populations. The unequal opportunity could be corrected more easily than the age distribution.

The biggest factor for males and females, as we have seen, is the unequal incomes of black male and female income recipients. This factor is caused primarily by unequal opportunities. These unequal opportunities could be due to discrimination and/or lower productivity. While we will not provide a complete analysis of the underlying causes of the persisting and permanent nature of racial inequality in economic life, we will discuss the nature of the inequality in economic opportunities in greater detail below. But first, we will look at income from the perspective of families, followed by a brief review of poverty statistics.

Family Income

Table 4 contains data on median family income for the last two decades. Family income data provide information that supplements the personal and per capita income data already reviewed. These data provide information on how the income of the black population is allocated to black families. Since the family is still the primary unit for raising children, these statistics are sometimes considered a better index of the well-being of the population.

Table 4
Median Family Income
Selected Years
(1989$)

| | Median Family Income | | | B/W | Aggregate |
	Black	White	B/W	Gap	Gap
1989	20,209	35,975	0.562	15,766	$127 Billion
1988	20,260	35,549	0.570	15,289	116 Billion
1987	20,091	35,350	0.568	15,259	116 Billion
1986	19,917	34,857	0.571	14,940	109 Billion
1985	19,344	33,595	0.576	14,251	104 Billion
1982	17,473	31,614	0.553	14,141	95 Billion
1980	19,073	32,692	0.583	13,619	87 Billion
1978	20,690	34,933	0.592	14,243	84 Billion
1970	20,067	32,713	0.613	12,646	64 Billion

Source: U.S Bureau of the Census, *Money Income and Poverty Status: 1989,*
    Table 8. Calculations of aggregates and gaps done by the author.

A review of the family income data in Table 4 reveals that the per capita income figures actually provide an overly optimistic picture of recent trends in the economic position of the African-American population. Family income for African Americans has not exhibited the steady rise over the last two decades that characterized per capita income. Indeed, median black family income fell slightly between 1988 and 1989, from $20,260 to $20,209. Overall, median black family income has been substantially lower in the 1980s than it was during the 1970s. Even during 1989, black family income had failed to regain the peak level of $20,690 obtained in 1978. In fact, the 1970s peak median family income was never equaled during the 1980s. Indeed, for most years of the 1980s, the median income of black families was below the level obtained in 1970. Thus, the absolute poverty of black families appears to be a permanent feature.

The other permanent feature of the data in Table 4 is the consistent inequality of black family income. In 1989, the median black family income of $20,209 was only 56.2 percent of the median white family income. The parity index had even fallen slightly from its 1988 level. In 1989, the median black family had $15,766 less than the median white family. In the aggregate, black families had a family income deficit of $127 billion, which was up from $116 billion in 1988.

The general trend over the last two decades has been a slight upward drift in racial inequality in family income. The index of equality was higher in seven out of ten years of the 1970s than it was during any year of the 1980s. In fact, inequality—as measured by the parity index—was nine percent greater in 1989 than it was in 1970. The ratio of black to white median family income ranged between 55 and 58 percent during the 1980s, and ranged between 57 and 62 percent during the 1970s. Inequality thus not only appears to be permanent, but it also appears to be increasing.

The gap between black and white median family income during 1989 was $3,120 higher than it was in 1970, and $1,523 higher than it was during 1978. Indeed, while median black family income still has not regained the peak levels of the late 1970s, median white family income has caught and passed these levels. The parity gaps thus steadily rose throughout the 1980s. The 1989 aggregate gap of $127 billion was almost double the 1970 aggregate gap of $64 billion, and $43 billion more than the 1978 aggregate gap of $84 billion. Thus, it is clear that the income position of black families deteriorated in both absolute and relative terms during the 1980s, at least by the median income measure.

The inadequate and unequal incomes of black families have important implications for the viability of these family units. This limited family income is a direct consequence of the limited incomes of black males and females. Low family incomes do not bode well for the ability of African-American families to provide properly for their children. Low incomes may also have a direct bearing on family formation and stability. These factors also have a direct impact of reducing future prospects for African Americans. Thus, the current low family income contributes to the permanency of inequality and poverty for African Americans.

Tables 5 and 6 provide further insight into black family income, by taking a look at the distribution of family income. Table 5 provides data on the distribution of families across selected income ranges in constant 1989 dollars. This table makes it clear that trends discussed for median family income did not hold for all black families. Indeed, while the median income during 1989 was lower than it was during the 1970s, the proportion of African-American families receiving incomes in the highest range actually increased during the 1980s. If 1978 is compared to 1989, the percent of black families with incomes $35,000 to $50,000 increased from 23.3 to 27.5 percent. The proportion with incomes greater than $50,000 increased by 38 percent, from 10.0 to 13.8 percent. Thus, despite the decline in median family income, a significant proportion of black families clearly gained higher family incomes during the 1980s. Moreover, the greatest part of this gain was movement into the more than $50,000 category.

The median income declined because, while the top quarter of the distribution may have been making progress, the bottom half was sliding backwards. Table 5 also shows that the proportion of blacks receiving very low income actually increased. The percentage receiving income less than $5,000 also increased by 38 percent, to 11.2 percent in 1989, compared to 8.1 percent during 1978. Thus, the growth in the very lowest incomes almost exactly matched the increase in the very highest incomes. Moreover, the situation that existed in 1989 was the most favorable for the decade.

The middle half of the distribution thus shrank between 1978 and 1989. While many families exited this group for higher status, many families within the group lost position and moved to lower income levels. Thus, it is clear that the bottom moved down for black families during the 1980s, while simultaneously the top moved up.

The data in Table 5 also make it clear that white families suffered much less erosion at the bottom, although there was some expansion in the lowest income class. However, while the proportion of black families receiving incomes less than $5,000 was 40 percent higher in 1989 than it was in 1978, the proportion of white families receiving such low incomes increased by only eight percent on a much smaller base. Thus, while black families were 3.4 times more likely to be in the lowest income category in 1978, they were 4.3 times more likely to be in the lowest income category in 1989. Inequality thus increased significantly by this measure as well.

The proportion of whites receiving higher incomes also grew at a faster rate than the proportion of blacks. Thus, while the percent of blacks receiving incomes of $50,000 or more increased by 38 percent, the white increase was 46 percent on a larger base. Whites were 2.1 times as likely to have incomes in this range during 1978, and about 2.2 times more likely during 1989.

Thus, racial inequality increased across the income distribution. Blacks fell into deep poverty at a faster rate and rose to upper-middle class status at a significantly slower rate. The parity gaps in 1989 were very large. If parity had existed, there would have been 642,000 fewer black families with incomes under

Table 5
Percentage of Black Families
Receiving Incomes in Selected Ranges

	1989		1988		1978		1970	
	Black	White	Black	White	Black	White	Black	White
Under $5,000	11.2	2.6	11.9	3.0	8.1	2.4	8.4	2.3
Less Than $10,000	25.9	7.7	27.3	8.5	25.4	8.5	24.6	8.0
$10,000–34,999	46.5	40.7	46.7	43.2	51.2	47.7	56.3	45.4
$35,000–$50,000	27.5	51.6	25.9	48.4	23.3	43.8	19.2	46.6
More Than $50,000	13.8	30.9	12.6	27.4	10.0	21.1	6.7	23.2

Note: Totals will not equal 100.00 due to overlap of categories.

Source: U.S. Department of Commerce, Bureau of the Census, *Money Income and Poverty Status in the U.S.: 1989*, Table 8.

$5,000, and 1,360,000 fewer families with incomes under $10,000. At the upper end, if parity had existed, there would have been about 1.3 million more families in the $50,000 and over bracket.

The conclusions stated above are further substantiated by the data displayed in Table 6. Although the income position of the lowest three quintiles actually improved slightly in 1989 in comparison to 1988, the improvements were very small. Moreover, they do not alter one very apparent fact from the information displayed in Table 6. Namely, there has been an erosion in the constant dollar incomes of the bottom three quintiles during the 1980s in comparison to 1970 and 1980. The proportionate decline was greatest in the lowest quintiles. Thus, income at the upper limit for the poorest families in 1989 was $1,639 lower than it was during 1970, and $1,069 lower than it was during 1980. Income at the upper limit for the second quintile was $480 lower than it was in 1980, and $1,282 lower than it was in 1970. Even at the third quintile, although 1989 income was higher than it was in 1970, it was still slightly lower than it was in 1980. Thus, it is clear that the incomes of the lowest two-thirds of black families have deteriorated substantially.

Table 6
Family Income at Selected Positions of the Income Distribution:
1970, 1980, 1989 (In 1989$)

1989	Black	White	B/W
Lowest Fifth	$ 7,868	$17,938	0.439
Second	15,500	29,888	0.519
Third	26,054	42,450	0.614
Fourth	41,956	61,039	0.687
Top 5%	69,545	101,354	0.686

1980	Black	White	B/W
Lowest Fifth	$ 8,937	$17,050	0.524
Second	15,980	27,802	0.575
Third	26,274	38,413	0.684
Fourth	40,401	53,366	0.757
Top 5%	65,427	83,215	0.786

1970	Black	White	B/W
Lowest Fifth	$ 9,507	$17,594	0.540
Second	16,782	27,917	0.601
Third	25,272	37,400	0.676
Fourth	37,428	50,959	0.734
Top 5%	59,249	79,723	0.743

Source: U.S. Department of Commerce, Bureau of the Census, *Money Income and Poverty Status: 1989,* Table 5.

It is also apparent from the table that the income of the fourth quintile and the top five percent have both risen, relative to their 1970 and 1980 levels. Thus, as suggested above, while the absolute income of the bottom has fallen, the absolute income of the top has risen. These trends have increased income inequality among African Americans.

Equally apparent from the data in Table 6 is the fact that racial inequality has persisted at all levels of the income distribution throughout the period. Racial inequality as measured by the parity index is greatest at the bottom of the distribution. African-American families in the lowest quintile had an upper limit that was only 43.9 percent of the upper limit for white families in the bottom quintile of the white distribution. The parity index for the second and third quintiles is only 51.9 percent and 61.4 percent, respectively. At the fourth quintile, the parity index reaches 68.7 percent before declining slightly to 68.6 percent at the lower limit of the top five percent. Thus, poorer blacks continue to be relatively poorer in comparison to poorer whites than are better off blacks in comparison to better off whites.

The most important conclusion, however, is that the unequal status of blacks at all positions of the black income distribution appears to be a permanent feature of the American economy. Moreover, not only is there no evidence of a reduction of inequality at any position of the income distribution, but also the available evidence indicates that the inequality has worsened throughout the income distribution.

The income problems of black families exist in every region of the country. As the information in Table 7 shows, even though there are regional variations in African-American median family income, black incomes are relatively low and unequal in all regions. In 1989, median family income for African Americans ranged from a low of $18,301 in the Midwest to a high of $25,670 in the West. Median black family income was $25,391 in the Northeast and $19,029 in the South. It is interesting to note that median family income declined slightly for blacks between 1988 and 1989 in all regions except the South. In view of the economic slowdown in 1990, we can expect constant dollar income to decline again for 1990.

Income inequality is marked in all regions as well. In 1989, the parity index ranged from a low of 51.1 percent in the Midwest to a high of 71.0 percent in the West. In the Northeast, median family income for African Americans was 61.9 percent of median family income for white Americans. The South was the second most unequal region with an index of 57.8. Between 1988 and 1989, inequality by this measure increased in the Northeast and the West, declined in the South, and declined very slightly in the Midwest.

The regional trends in absolute income and the degree of inequality, however, have been different among the several regions during the 1980s. During the 1970s, blacks had their highest and most equal income in the Midwest. However, during the 1980s, the Midwest became the region with the lowest

Table 7
Median Family Income by Regions
(in 1989$)

	NORTHEAST				MIDWEST		
	Black	White	B/W		Black	White	B/W
1989	$25,391	$40,990	0.619		$18,301	$35,789	0.511
1988	25,718	39,467	0.652		18,342	35,958	0.510
1987	22,611	38,611	0.586		18,321	35,154	0.521
1986	23,660	37,781	0.626		19,669	34,567	0.569
1982	18,786	32,914	0.571		15,776	31,572	0.500
1978	21,993	35,354	0.622		25,801	35,879	0.719
1970	24,869	34,995	0.711		24,690	33,616	0.734

	SOUTH				WEST		
	Black	White	B/W		Black	White	B/W
1989	$19,029	$32,939	0.578		$25,670	$36,144	0.710
1988	18,985	33,601	0.565		27,132	35,152	0.772
1987	18,394	33,005	0.557		22,555	35,549	0.634
1986	16,632	29,439	0.565		25,093	35,549	0.706
1982	17,531	31,101	0.564		25,831	34,092	0.758
1978	18,563	32,309	0.575		20,375	35,530	0.573
1970	16,718	29,560	0.566		25,596	33,214	0.771

Source: David Swinton, "The Economic Status of Blacks," in Janet Dewart (ed.), *The State of Black America 1990.* New York: National Urban League, 1990, page 32, Table 5; and U.S. Department of Commerce, Bureau of the Census, *Money Income & Poverty Status in the U.S.: 1989,* pp. 31–34, Table 7.

income and the greatest racial inequality. In fact, the incomes of blacks in the Midwest fell more sharply and recovered less than in any other region. The Midwest is the only region where the median family income for blacks at the end of the 1980s was still substantially lower than median family income was during the 1970s. Racial inequality also increased most sharply in the Midwest. The parity index typically stood above 70 throughout the 1970s but had declined to 51.1 percent by 1989.

Black income has traditionally been lowest and most unequal in the South. However, there was modest improvement in black income by 1989, which pushed the South ahead of the Midwest. Inequality remained about constant in the South over the last two decades, although there may have been a slight increase in inequality for the 1980s taken as a whole. The increase in inequality in the Midwest has resulted in the South moving ahead of the Midwest in terms of inequality as well.

Blacks tend to have their highest incomes and degree of equality in the Northeast and the West. During the 1980s, the absolute level of black median family income increased in both of these regions, and, by the end of the decade, had reached levels that surpassed the peaks of the 1970s. Inequality, however, generally was higher in the Northeast during the 1980s than during the 1970s because white income grew at a faster pace. Year-to-year fluctuations in the values in the West are subject to higher sampling variability, so we hesitate to comment on the trends in that region. However, taken as a whole, it would appear that inequality held at about the same level or may have declined slightly.

The most important point made by the data is that inequality has remained at a high level in each of the regions during the last two decades. It is clear that inequality increased significantly in the Midwest and the Northeast during the 1980s. Thus, racial inequality in income appears to be a permanent feature of the economic situation faced by black families in each region of the country.

Trends in Black Poverty

We will complete our examination of the income status of the black population by reviewing the latest data on poverty rates. These rates are intended to capture that portion of the population whose incomes are too low to provide for an adequate standard of living. The poverty level is based on an index developed by the Social Security Administration in 1964 and revised in 1969 and 1980. Poverty thresholds are defined for each family size. The poverty thresholds for three- and four-person families in 1989 were $9,885 and $12,675, respectively.

The data in Table 8 provide information on three different poverty rates for selected years of the last two decades. The first panel covers the poverty rate for all black persons. This rate covers individuals living within a family as well as individuals who are not living as part of a family. Thus, this panel provides the broadest measure of black poverty. As can be seen, the black poverty rate is very high by this measure. There were about 9.3 million black persons living in poverty during 1989. This was equal to about 30.7 percent of the black population. Thus, about one of every three black persons lived in a poverty situation. In general, black poverty during the 1980s had been at a slightly higher rate than it was during the 1970s. However, black poverty rates for all persons at the end of the decade had come close to the lowest points of the 1970s. Although the rate was lower, the absolute number of persons in poverty was considerably above the 1970s level. Thus, high levels of black poverty also appear to be a permanent feature of the American economy.

The table also makes it apparent that black poverty rates are substantially higher than white poverty rates. The ratio of black-to-white poverty rates was 3.07 at the end of the decade. Thus, blacks were over three times more likely to have income below the poverty level than whites during 1989. This three-to-one rule generally held throughout the period. However, white poverty rates

Table 8
Poverty Rates for Selected Years

Total Persons

	Number of Persons in Poverty*		Percent			Persons' Poverty Gap
	Black	White	Black	White	B/W	
1989	9,305	20,788	30.7	10.0	3.07	6.3 Million
1988	9,356	20,715	31.3	10.1	3.10	6.3 Million
1987	9,520	21,195	32.4	10.4	3.12	6.5 Million
1986	8,983	22,183	31.1	11.0	2.83	5.8 Million
1982	9,697	23,517	35.6	12.0	2.97	6.4 Million
1978	7,625	16,259	30.6	8.7	3.52	5.5 Million
1970	7,548	17,484	33.5	9.9	3.38	5.5 Million

With Related Children Under 18 In Families

	Number of Children in Poverty*		Percent			Children's Poverty Gap
	Black	White	Black	White	B/W	
1989	4,257	7,164	43.2	14.1	3.06	2.9 Million
1988	4,148	7,095	42.8	14.0	3.06	2.8 Million
1987	4,234	7,398	44.4	14.7	3.02	2.8 Million
1986	4,037	7,714	42.7	15.3	2.79	2.6 Million
1982	4,388	8,282	47.3	16.5	2.87	2.9 Million
1978	3,781	5,674	41.2	11.0	3.75	2.9 Million
1970	3,922	6,138	41.5	10.5	3.95	2.9 Million

Female-Headed Families

	Number of Families in Poverty*		Percent			Families' Poverty Gap
	Black	White	Black	White	B/W	
1989	1,524	1,852	46.5	25.4	1.83	691 Thousand
1988	1,579	1,945	49.0	26.5	1.85	725 Thousand
1987	1,577	1,961	51.1	26.9	1.90	747 Thousand
1986	1,488	2,041	52.9	27.9	1.90	742 Thousand
1982	1,538	1,813	57.4	28.7	2.00	785 Thousand
1978	1,208	1,319	53.1	24.9	2.13	673 Thousand
1970	834	1,102	58.8	31.4	1.87	421 Thousand

In 1000's.

Source: U.S. Department of Commerce, Bureau of the Census, *Money Income and Poverty Status: 1989*, Tables 19, 20, and 21.

.sed somewhat faster than black poverty during the 1980s. Thus, there _ a slight decline in relative poverty by this measure. However, the most significant point is that the level still remained above three-to-one by the end of the decade. Thus, glaring racial inequality in the total poverty rates appears to be another permanent feature of the American economy. In 1989, the poverty gap was 6.3 million additional blacks in poverty. The poverty gap during the 1980s was generally higher than during the 1970s.

The second panel of Table 8 contains data on the poverty level of black children. In 1989, the poverty rate for black children was 43.2 percent. This meant that 43 out of every 100 black children were in poor families. In total, there were 4,257,000 poor black children in 1989. The poverty rates for children were generally slightly higher during the 1980s than they were during the 1970s.

Racial inequality in the rates of poverty for children is also very high. In 1989, black children were 3.06 times as likely as white children to be poor. Racial inequality as measured by the parity index declined slightly from the 1970s level, as the much lower poverty rates of whites increased at a faster rate.

In 1989, the poverty rate differential created a children's poverty gap of 2.9 million black children. This gap has held fairly steady over the last two decades. High and unequal levels of poverty for black children also appears to be a permanent feature of the American economy.

The final panel of Table 8 displays data on the poverty rates of female-headed families. Female-headed families of both races had very high rates of poverty. However, the high rates of poverty are of particular importance to the black population because they have a much higher proportion of their families in the female-headed category. In 1989, 47 percent of black and 13 percent of white families were headed by females. Thus, black families were over 3.6 times as likely to be headed by females. This high rate of female headship is both a consequence and a cause of black economic disadvantage.

In any case, during 1989, 1.5 million black female-headed families were poor. This was 46.5 percent of all black female-headed families. However, the table makes it clear that the poverty rate among black female-headed families declined fairly consistently, except for recession periods, over the last two decades. At the same time, the number of female-headed families has increased. This reflects the continued growth in the proportion of families within the black community headed by females.

Racial inequality is also rather glaring for female-headed families. The parity index is just a little under 2 for the 1980s. However, because the rate of poverty is so high, this still represents a substantial gap. In 1989, for example, the differences between the poverty rates for black and white female-headed families was 21.1 percentage points. This produced a parity gap for female-headed families of 691,000 excess families in poverty for blacks. High poverty rates and racial inequality once again appear to be a permanent feature.

As was the case with income, there are regional variations in the poverty rate. The data on poverty rates by regions are shown in Table 9. As can be seen, black poverty is high in all regions. In 1989, the range was from a low of 23.5 percent in the West to a high of 36.4 percent in the Midwest. Thus, as one might suspect, the regional pattern of poverty rates corresponds to the regional pattern of income. The Midwest has generally become the region where blacks have their highest poverty rates. Indeed, poverty rates for blacks in the Midwest were 40 to 50 percent higher in the 1980s than they were during the 1970s. Racial inequality has also shot up for blacks in this region. At the end of the 1980s, black poverty rates were running four times higher than white poverty rates. This degree of racial inequality is unprecedented in any other region.

Table 9
Poverty Rates for Regions: Selected Years

| | NORTHEAST | | | MIDWEST | | |
	Black	White	B/W	Black	White	B/W
1989	24.7	8.0	3.09	36.4	9.0	4.04
1988	22.9	8.4	2.73	34.8	8.7	4.00
1987	28.8	8.9	3.24	36.6	9.9	3.70
1986	24.0	8.9	2.70	34.5	10.6	3.25
1984	32.2	10.7	3.01	37.9	11.5	3.30
1978	29.1	8.2	3.55	24.8	7.4	3.35
1970	20.0	7.7	2.60	25.7	8.9	2.89

| | SOUTH | | | WEST | | |
	Black	White	B/W	Black	White	B/W
1989	31.6	11.4	2.77	23.5	11.3	2.08
1988	34.3	11.6	2.96	23.6	11.3	2.09
1987	34.5	11.5	3.00	24.3	11.5	2.11
1986	33.6	11.8	2.85	21.7	12.3	1.76
1984	33.6	12.0	2.80	26.6	11.8	2.25
1978	34.1	10.2	3.34	26.1	8.9	2.93
1970	42.6	12.4	3.44	20.4	10.6	1.92

Source: U.S. Department of Commerce, Bureau of the Census, *Money Income and Poverty Status...: 1987, 1988, 1989;* Current Population Reports, Series P-60, *Characteristics of the Population Below Poverty, 1984, 1978.*

Poverty rates in the Northeast and the Midwest on the whole may have been slightly higher during the 1980s than during the 1970s. In both regions, the degree of inequality fluctuated, as measured by the parity index, but hovered around the same level. Blacks had about three times the poverty rates of whites in the Northeast and about two times the poverty rates of whites in the West. Thus, although inequality was lower in these two regions than it was in th Midwest, it was still pronounced.

During the 1980s, poverty rates in the South were generally around one-thir of the population, except for the recession of the early 1980s. The poverty rat in the South, thus, was slightly lower than it was in the Midwest. Howeve white poverty was a little higher in the South, so relative inequality was les than in the Midwest. In general, the ratio of black-to-white poverty in th South was around three-to-one. In any case, it is apparent that poverty rate were high and unequal for blacks in all regions.

Sources of Income Inequality

Income is derived from a number of sources. The low and unequal income of blacks can exist only if blacks receive low and unequal incomes from som of the various sources. Information on black income by source is shown i Tables 10 and 11. As we have already discussed, the black population may hav lower incomes than whites for two reasons. First, a smaller proportion of th black population may have income than whites; second, blacks who have in come may receive lower incomes than whites who receive income. Table 10 con tains information on these two factors for each source.

Table 10
Per Capita Income and Aggregate Per Capita Income Gaps
By Source of Income
1988

	Black Per Capita	White Per Capita	B/W Mean Incom
Earnings	63.9	70.3	0.75
Wage & Salary	62.3	65.1	0.76
Nonfarm Self-Empl.	2.4	6.9	0.60
Farm Self-Empl.	—	1.0	N/A
Property	27.2	62.1	0.35
Transfer & All Other[1]	N/A	N/A	N/A
Soc. Sec. & RR	15.4	19.1	0.81
Public Asst.	8.1	1.6	0.96
Ret. & Annuities	4.1	7.7	0.86
TOTAL	87.9	94.1	0.70

[1]Includes Soc. Sec. or Railroad Ret. Income, Pub. Asst. or Welfare pmts., Suppl. Se Income, Ret./Annuities, Veterans' pmts., Unempl. and Worker's Comp., Alimony, et

Source: Calculated by the author from data in U.S. Department of Commerce, U.S Bureau of the Census, *Money Income of Households, Families, and Person.* Unpublished data, 1990.

The data in the first two columns display the percentage of blacks that received each type of income in 1988. As can be seen, smaller proportions of blacks received each type of income except public assistance income. Equality was greatest in wage and salary income. In 1988, 62.3 percent of the black and 65.1 percent of the white working-age populations had some wage and salary earnings. Smaller proportions of both groups received income from self-employment, but the black rate of 2.4 percent was much smaller than the 6.9 percent of whites who had this type of income. Blacks also had a big disadvantage in the receipt of property income. Only 27.2 percent of blacks as compared to 62.1 percent of whites received property income. Earned transfers were also received unequally. Only 15.4 percent of blacks compared to 19.1 percent of whites received Social Security income, while 4.1 percent of blacks and 7.7 percent of whites received private retirement income. Need based, public assistance income was the only category that blacks had a higher recipiency rate than whites. Fully 8.1 percent of blacks and only 1.6 percent of whites relied on this type of income. This basic pattern in income recipiency has existed since 1970.

The last column in Table 10 contains the ratio of black-to-white mean incomes for those who received income in each category. It is apparent from the data that black income recipients had lower mean incomes in every category. Blacks who worked for wages and salaries had mean incomes that were 76 percent of the means for whites. Blacks who were self-employed had 0 percent of the incomes of whites. The smaller number of blacks who received income from property, on average, received only 35 percent as much income as whites. The transfer income categories were most equal with the ratio of means ranging between 81 and 96 percent.

Thus, blacks got a double disadvantage from each income source. They had smaller proportions of their populations receiving each type of earned income and smaller mean incomes for those who did receive incomes. Moreover, as we have seen, the disadvantage was greater than the data in Table 10 imply because these data do not take into account the missing males and the smaller proportions of working-age persons.

The impacts of these disadvantages on the per capita contributions of each income source are shown in Table 11. Several things are apparent from this table. First, wages are by far the most important source of income for both blacks and whites. Blacks received $6,627.57, or about 81 percent of their per capita income, from wages in 1988, and whites received $10,056.81, or 73 percent of their per capita income, from wages. Second, transfer income is the second most important source for both groups. However, black receipts of $1,228 are relatively more important for blacks, accounting for 15 percent of black income, while white receipts of $1,733 account for only about 13 percent of white income. Third, the property-related income categories, self-employment and property income, are much more important for whites. Whites derived

Table 11
Per Capita Income and Aggregate and Per Capita Income Gaps
By Source of Income
1988

	Black Per Capita	White Per Capita	B/W	Per Capita Gap	Aggregate Gap*	% of Gap
Earnings	$6,782.36	$10,963.62	0.619	$4,181.26	$126.8 Billion	75.0%
Wage & Salary	$6,627.57	$10,056.81	0.659	$3,429.24	104.0 Billion	61.5%
Nonfarm Self-Emp.	$ 156.27	$ 827.86	0.189	671.59	20.4 Billion	12.1%
Farm Self-Empl.	—	$ 88.48				
Property	$ 145.64	$ 1,037.34	0.140	891.71	27.0 Billion	16.0%
Transfer & All Other[1]	$1,228.20	$ 1,732.91	0.709	504.71	15.3 Billion	9.0%
Soc. Sec. & RR	$ 489.01	$ 822.08	0.595	333.08	10.1 Billion	6.0%
Public Asst.	$ 167.37	$ 37.73	4.436	- 129.64	- 3.9 Billion	-2.3%
Ret. & Annuities	$ 205.06	$ 488.38	0.420	283.32	8.6 Billion	5.1%
TOTAL	$8,156.19	$13,733.87	0.594	5,577.67	$169.1 Billion	100.0%

[1]Includes Soc. Sec. or Railroad Ret. Income, Pub. Asst., or Welfare pymts., Suppl. Sec. Income, Ret./Annuities, Veterans' pymts., Unempl. and Worker's Comp., Alimony, etc.

*Aggregate gap is = per capita gap * 1988 black population.

Source: Calculated by the author from data in U.S. Department of Commerce, U.S. Bureau of the Census, *Money Income of Households, Families, and Persons.* Unpublished data, 1990.

about $1,958—or a little over 14 percent of their income — from this source, while blacks derived only about $302 per capita, or four percent of their income from this source.

It is also apparent that blacks received lower per capita income from all of the major sources. Inequality among the earned income categories was least for wages and salaries, where black per capita income was 65.9 percent of white per capita income. Inequality is very marked in self-employment and property income. Blacks received about 18.9 percent as much per capita income from nonfarm self-employment, and only 14 percent as much from property sources. Black per capita income from Social Security was about 60 percent as large as white per capita income, and per capita income from private pensions and annuities was about 42 percent of white per capita income. Only from welfare did blacks receive more income per capita. Black per capita income from welfare was almost four and one-half times white per capita income from welfare.

The contribution of each source to the overall inequality gap is shown in the last three columns. The absolute dollar gaps due to each source are shown under the columns headed per capita and aggregate gaps. Obviously, wages were the biggest generators of inequality. In 1988, the per capita loss from wage and salary inequality was $3,429 per black person, and the aggregate loss to the black population was about $104 billion. Inequality in labor market income, thus, accounted for 61.5 percent of the income inequality. Lower property income created a $27 billion loss, and accounted for 16 percent of the gap. The lower levels of self-employment income resulted in another $20.4 billion loss, which explained 12.1 percent of the gap. Another $18.7 billion, or 11.1 percent of the gap, was accounted for by Social Security and retirement incomes. The excess black welfare income actually reduced the gap by 2.3 percent, or 3.9 billion dollars. The total excess welfare was, thus, about 75 times smaller than black losses from the inequality in other sources.

The pattern of inequality revealed in Table 11 has been fairly constant over the past two decades. There have been minor fluctuations, but the relative importance of the various sources have held. The absolute contribution of welfare income to reducing the gap declined significantly over the last decade. In 1980, for example, welfare income reduced the gap by 5.27 percent—more than two times the contribution that this income source made during 1989.

A CLOSER LOOK AT THE POSITION OF BLACKS IN THE LABOR MARKET

As the last section has made clear, the lower labor market income is the most important cause of the overall income inequality experienced by blacks. It is, therefore, important to explore the labor market position of blacks more closely. The next nine tables will help us explore the labor market position of blacks.

ꝛles 12 and 13 contain data on the employment proportions for blacks. Ɪꝛ Ɪe 12 contains the data for the most recent time period, and Table 13 contains the historical data. The employment proportion measures the proportion of the working-age population that had employment during the referenced

Table 12
Civilian Employment—Population Ratio
By Race, Sex, and Age
1990

Total Population

	Black	White	B/W
November	55.5	63.1	0.880
October	55.7	63.5	0.877
September	55.4	63.7	0.870
August	55.3	63.5	0.871
July	55.7	63.7	0.874
June	56.7	63.9	0.887

Men (20 and over)

	Black	White	B/W
November	65.9	74.6	0.883
October	65.8	74.8	0.880
September	65.3	75.0	0.871
August	65.4	74.9	0.873
July	65.9	74.9	0.880
June	67.1	75.1	0.893

Women (20 and over)

	Black	White	B/W
November	53.3	54.7	0.974
October	53.5	55.1	0.971
September	53.4	55.3	0.966
August	53.7	55.5	0.968
July	53.8	55.6	0.968
June	54.6	55.6	0.982

Both Sexes (16 to 19 years)

	Black	White	B/W
November	25.3	48.5	0.522
October	25.8	49.0	0.527
September	25.9	49.3	0.525
August	22.8	46.4	0.491
July	24.1	48.4	0.498
June	25.6	49.7	0.515

Source: Bureau of Labor Statistics, *Employment Situation: November 1990.* News Release, Table A-3, December, 1990.

time period. This number does not take into account the nature of the employment or the amount of employment. Thus, those who work on low-wage jobs and those who work part-time are counted equally with those who work full-time on high-wage jobs. This feature of the statistics overstates the employment position of blacks because they are more likely to have involuntary part-time employment and are also more likely to be unemployed. With these caveats in mind, we can turn to reviewing the data.

It is apparent from the latest data in Table 12 that employment rates declined over the last six months. This decline in employment rates impacted all three demographic groups and reflected the fact that the economy slowed down over the last half of 1990. If the slowdown persists, we can expect the situation for blacks to worsen significantly over the next year. As it stands, the annual average rate of employment for 1990 will be significantly below the 1989 level. The November employment population rate for blacks of 55.5 percent was significantly below the 1989 annual rate of 56.9 percent.

The data show clearly that blacks have disadvantaged employment rates. Overall the employment population ratio for the total black population had fallen to 55.5 for November, while the white rate was 63.1. Thus, blacks are currently only about 88 percent as likely to be employed as are whites. As noted, the relative disparity has increased as the slowdown has progressed. The November parity index of .880 was significantly below the 1989 parity index of .892.

This disparity in employment rates is particularly noteworthy for black males over 20 and for black teenagers of both sexes. Only 65.9 percent of adult black men were employed in November, compared to 74.6 percent of white males. Thus, adult black men, or about 88 percent, are as likely to be employed as adult white men. The current employment rate of black men is down considerably from the 70.0 that existed in 1989, and the parity index is also below the .928 that existed in 1989.

In November, only 25.3 percent of black teenagers were employed, compared to 48.5 percent of white teenagers. The employment rates for both groups have declined from the 1989 levels of 28.7 percent for blacks and 51.6 percent for whites. Black teenagers in the recent data have been about half as likely as white teenagers to be employed. The parity index for November of 52.2 percent was significantly below the 1989 average of 55.6 percent.

The employment rates of adult black women are closer to equality. However, the employment rates of black women have fallen more in the recent slowdown. Indeed, while the employment rates of black women have been below their 1989 average of 54.6 percent since July, the employment rate for white women has remained above its 1989 average of 54.9 percent. Thus, in the latest data, adult black women are slightly less likely to be employed than adult white women. The November parity index was .974, which is less than the 1989 parity index of .995.

Table 13
Civilian Employment—Population Ratio
By Race, Sex, and Age
Selected Years

Total Population

	Black	White	B/W
1990*	56.5	63.7	0.887
1989	56.9	63.8	0.892
1988	56.3	63.1	0.892
1987	55.6	62.3	0.892
1982	49.4	58.8	0.840
1978	53.6	60.0	0.893
1970	53.7	57.4	0.936

Men (20 and over)

	Black	White	B/W
1990*	66.2	75.1	0.881
1989	70.0	75.4	0.928
1988	67.0	75.1	0.892
1987	66.4	74.7	0.889
1982	61.4	73.0	0.841
1978	69.1	77.2	0.895
1972	73.0	79.0	0.924

Women (20 and over)

	Black	White	B/W
1990*	54.6	55.4	0.986
1989	54.6	54.9	0.995
1988	53.9	54.0	0.998
1987	53.0	53.1	0.998
1982	47.5	48.4	0.981
1978	49.3	46.1	1.069
1972	46.5	40.6	1.145

Both Sexes (16 to 19 years)

	Black	White	B/W
1990*	27.2	50.0	0.544
1989	28.7	51.6	0.556
1988	27.5	51.0	0.539
1987	27.1	49.4	0.549
1982	19.0	45.8	0.415
1978	25.2	52.4	0.481
1972	25.2	46.4	0.543

*Note: 1990 data represent average of first three quarters.

Source: Bureau of Labor Statistics, *Handbook of Labor Statistics, June 1985,* pp. 46 and 47. *Employment and Earnings, January, 1990 and October, 1990,* Table A-44.

As the data in Table 13 show, the basic pattern discussed above for adult males and teenagers has existed for the past two decades. The employment rates of these two demographic categories have been relatively low and unequal. Overall, the employment proportions for black male adults may have been slightly lower during the decade of the 1980s, and the degree of inequality as measured by the parity index may have been slightly greater. However, the variation has been in a narrow band. In most years, black men over 20 have been slightly less than 90 percent as likely to be employed as white males over 20. Generally speaking, 25 percent—plus or minus a few percentage points—of black teenagers have been employed on average throughout the period except during recession troughs. This has generally been about half of the white teen-aged employment rate, which has generally hovered around 50 percent. The persistency of this pattern for adult men and teenagers suggests that it is a permanent feature of the American economy.

The pattern for adult black women has been somewhat different. Up until the 1980s, adult black women generally had higher employment rates than adult white women. In 1972, for example, black women over 20 were 14.5 percent more likely to be employed than white women over 20. This favorable differential was a reflection of significantly higher participation rates among black women. However, as the role of women in our society has changed, the participation rates of white women over 20 have increased. Although black women have maintained a slightly higher participation advantage, their higher unemployment rates enabled white women to gain higher employment rates. Throughout the 1980s, white women had a slight advantage in overall employment rates. If white female participation continues to increase, we can expect to see an increasing inequality gap between black and white women.

The gaps in employment proportions have significant impacts on the black employment level. The current gap implies that blacks have a 1.6 million job deficit compared to the level of employment required for parity. Black men over 20 have a job shortage of 736,000 jobs, black women over 20 have a job gap of 150,000 jobs, and black teenagers suffer from a gap of 500,000 jobs. The remainder of the overall shortage is due to demographic factors. These employment shortfalls play a major role in generating the observed wage and salary income differences.

The data in Table 14 provide information on the employment population ratios by region for 1989. First, the basic pattern within each region mirrors the national pattern. The employment rates for blacks were low and unequal in all regions. It is also the case that teenagers were the most disadvantaged group, followed by adult males in all regions, while black women over 20 have more nearly equal rates of employment with white women.

There is, however, one outstanding regional difference. As we might expect from the income discussion, blacks were most severely disadvantaged in the Midwest. In this region, the employment population for the total black

Table 14
Employment Population
By Region (1989)

	Total Black	Total White	B/W	Black Male	White Male	B/W	Black Female	White Female	B/W	Black 16–19	White 16–19	B/W
Northeast	57.0	62.5	0.912	62.3	73.0	0.853	52.8	53.2	0.992	25.9	48.8	0.531
Midwest	51.9	65.6	0.791	56.7	75.0	0.756	48.0	56.8	0.845	27.4	58.2	0.471
South	58.1	62.6	0.928	64.6	72.8	0.887	52.7	53.3	0.989	30.0	48.2	0.622
West	60.4	64.6	0.935	66.2	74.2	0.892	55.4	55.4	1.000	30.0	51.1	0.587

Source: U.S. Department of Labor, Bureau of Labor Statistics, *Geographic Profile of Employment and Unemployment, 1989*, Table 1.

population was only 51.9 percent. This was significantly below all of the other regions. Moreover, the low employment rates were experienced primarily by adult black workers. The employment population rate for adult black males was only 56.7 percent, and for black women over 20, it was only 48 percent. The employment population proportions for both adult groups in the Midwest were significantly lower than those for blacks over 20 in the other three regions. Black teenagers had an employment proportion of 27.4 percent in 1989, which was slightly higher than that of teenagers in the Northeast and slightly lower than the employment proportions of teenagers in the South and the West.

The degree of racial inequality for blacks was higher in the Midwest than in the other three regions. While the employment rates of blacks were the lowest of the three regions, the employment population ratios for all three white demographic groups were higher in the Midwest than they were in any of the other three regions. Thus, the spread between the ratios of blacks and whites were greatest in the Midwest. The inequality index for the total black population in the Midwest was 79.1 percent, while this index was not less than 91.2 percent in any of the other regions. Similar differences existed with respect to the individual demographic categories.

In any case, racial inequality in employment proportions existed in all regions. The degree of inequality was relatively similar for regions outside of the Midwest. In 1989, blacks were only 91.2 to 93.5 percent as likely to be employed as whites in the other regions. This pattern of inequality has persisted across the last two decades, with the general trend noted in the discussion of the national data.

Finally, Table 15 contains 1989 data on employment population rates for standard metropolitan statistical areas (SMSAs) with large black populations. As can be seen, there was considerable variation in the absolute and relative employment rates of blacks across different cities. It is noteworthy that in eight out of 43 SMSAs, the parity index was greater than 1, indicating higher employment rates among blacks. This outcome was influenced by demographic factors such as the relative age distributions, and economic factors such as the degree of tightness in the local labor market. However, in most cases, the employment population ratio for blacks was less than it was for whites.

There was also a wide range in the employment proportions of blacks—from 31.4 percent in Buffalo to 72.2 percent in Dallas. The range for whites was much narrower and higher, ranging from 55.4 percent in New York to 73.8 percent in the Washington, DC SMSA. Again, it comes as no surprise that the greatest absolute and relative inequality was found in the major cities of the Midwest. Once again, whites were doing about as well in the Midwest as in the other regions, but blacks were doing substantially worse.

Table 15
Employment to Population Ratio for Selected SMSAs by Race, 1989

Metro Area	Black Emp/Pop Ratio	White Emp/Pop Ratio	B/W
Dallas-Ft. Worth, TX	72.2	71.1	1.015
Washington, DC	71.7	73.8	.972
Nassau-Suffolk, NY	71.7	64.1	1.109
Fort Lauderdale, FL	70.2	57.0	1.232
Charlotte, NC	69.3	69.9	.991
Rochester, NY	68.6	66.3	1.035
Atlanta, GA	67.6	71.7	.943
Kansas City, KS	67.6	69.1	.978
San Diego, CA	67.3	64.0	1.052
Hartford, CT	66.2	70.7	.936
Providence, RI	65.6	66.3	.989
Riverside, CA	65.0	61.1	1.064
Phoenix, AZ	64.8	65.3	.992
Tampa-St. Petersburg, FL	64.6	57.7	1.120
Houston, TX	64.2	68.0	.944
Newark, NJ	63.9	64.5	.991
Columbus, OH	62.9	65.7	.957
Bergen-Passaic, NJ	62.8	62.9	.998
San Antonio, TX	61.7	57.5	1.073
Seattle, WA	60.9	71.5	.852
Los Angeles, CA	60.7	64.2	.945
Baltimore, MD	60.2	66.0	.912
Oakland, CA	60.0	66.3	.905
Boston, MA	59.2	67.8	.873
Indianapolis, IN	57.8	71.4	.810
Denver-Boulder, CO	57.0	70.2	.812
Miami, FL	56.9	60.7	.937
Sacramento, CA	56.5	62.7	.901
Norfolk, VA	56.0	64.9	.863
Philadelphia, PA	55.5	64.0	.867
Memphis, TN	55.1	60.8	.906
St. Louis, MO	53.5	64.3	.832
San Francisco, CA	52.8	68.8	.767
New York, NY	52.6	55.4	.949
Dayton, OH	52.4	61.8	.848
Cincinnati, OH	51.9	67.9	.764
Louisville, KY	50.6	65.4	.774
New Orleans, LA	50.0	59.3	.843
Chicago, IL	49.9	68.3	.731
Milwaukee, WI	49.2	69.7	.706
Pittsburgh, PA	48.0	56.0	.857
Cleveland, OH	46.0	64.7	.711
Oklahoma City, OK	45.6	67.8	.673
Detroit, MI	43.8	64.3	.681
Buffalo-Niagara Falls, NY	31.4	60.7	.517

Source: Bureau of Labor Statistics, *Geographic Profile of Employment & Unemployment, 1989,* Table 23.

Unemployment Rates

The next four tables contain data on the unemployment rates of blacks by demographic category. The most recent data on unemployment rates are contained in Table 16. As can be seen, unemployment has drifted upwards for all groups since mid-year. The November unemployment rate for all blacks was 12.4 percent, which is a full percentage point above the 1989 average of 11.4 percent. The November rate was higher for all black demographic categories than it was earlier in 1990 and 1989.

Racial inequality in November also was high for all demographic groups. Unlike the case with employment rates, black women experienced about as much inequality in unemployment as did black men. The November rate of 11.5 percent for black men was about 2.5 times the corresponding white male rate of 4.6 percent. The slightly lower unemployment rate for black females of 10.2 percent was nonetheless 2.3 times the white rate—an inequality index only slightly lower than the black male inequality rate. Black teenage unemployment in November was 35.8 percent, which was 2.6 times the white rate of 13.8 percent. We can expect the unemployment rates of blacks to rise faster than the white rates over the next few quarters if the slowdown continues.

The historical data for unemployment rates are shown in Table 17. Unemployment rates for black men and women have been very high throughout the period. These unemployment rates increased significantly after the mid-1970s (all data not shown in the table). During the 1980s, unemployment for black adults was significantly higher than it was during the 1970s. The 1989 unemployment rates of 10 percent for black males and 9.8 percent for black females were the lowest for the decade. Unemployment remained high for black teenagers as well. However, the rate was already very high during the 1970s.

Equally as striking was the high degree of racial inequality revealed by the data. The population overall and each demographic category have unemployment rates that were twice the corresponding white rates throughout the period. However, the degree of inequality generally increased over time. During the 1970s, for the most part, the parity index was close to 2.0 to 1. During the 1980s, these disparity indexes generally fluctuated around the 2.5 to 1 level. This was a significant increase in inequality.

Table 18 contains data on the regional distribution of unemployment rates. The table makes it clear that black unemployment rates were higher than white unemployment rates in every region of the country. The rates ranged from 9.8 percent in the Northeast to 15.4 percent in the Midwest for the total population. Each demographic category also had high rates in each region. Black men over 20 had unemployment rates that ranged from a low of 10 percent in the South to 16.4 percent in the Midwest. The lowest rate for adult black women was 8.5 percent in the Northeast, and the highest rate again was

Table 16
Unemployment Rates By Sex, Race, and Age
Selected Years

Total Population

	Black	White	B/W
November	12.4	5.4	2.30
October	11.8	4.9	2.41
September	12.1	4.8	2.52
August	11.8	4.8	2.46
July	11.3	4.6	2.46
June	10.4	4.5	2.31

Men (20 and Over)

	Black	White	B/W
November	11.5	4.6	2.50
October	11.3	4.4	2.57
September	11.8	4.3	2.74
August	10.6	4.3	2.47
July	10.7	4.1	2.61
June	9.4	4.1	2.29

Women (20 and Over)

	Black	White	B/W
November	10.2	4.4	2.32
October	9.7	4.2	2.31
September	10.3	4.2	2.45
August	9.9	4.2	2.36
July	9.4	4.0	2.35
June	8.9	3.9	2.28

Both Sexes (16 to 19 Years)

	Black	White	B/W
November	35.8	13.8	2.59
October	31.8	13.9	2.29
September	28.9	13.9	2.08
August	36.7	14.5	2.53
July	31.8	13.7	2.32
June	31.4	12.2	2.57

Source: Bureau of Labor Statistics, *Employment Situation: November, 1990.* News Release, Table A-3, December, 1990.

in the Midwest at 14.4 percent. Black teenagers experienced a low rate of 28.9 percent in the West and a high rate of 36.5 percent in the Midwest. These data confirm once again that the Midwest has become the most disadvantaged region for blacks.

Inequality was also pronounced in all regions during 1989 for all demographic groups. This is indicated by the B/W column for each category. This parity ranged from 2.0 to 3.6. Thus, the black unemployment rate was

Table 17
Unemployment Rates By Sex, Race, and Age
Selected Years

Total Population

	Black	White	B/W
1990	11.0	4.7	2.34
1989	11.4	4.5	2.53
1988	11.7	4.7	2.49
1987	13.0	5.3	2.45
1982	18.9	8.6	2.20
1978	12.8	5.2	2.46
1972	10.4	5.1	2.04

Men (20 and Over)

	Black	White	B/W
1990	10.1	4.2	2.40
1989	10.0	3.9	2.56
1988	10.1	4.1	2.46
1987	11.1	4.8	2.31
1982	17.8	7.8	2.28
1978	9.3	3.7	2.51
1972	7.0	3.6	1.94

Women (20 and Over)

	Black	White	B/W
1990	9.4	4.0	2.35
1989	9.8	4.0	2.45
1988	10.4	4.1	2.54
1987	11.6	4.6	2.52
1982	15.4	7.3	2.11
1978	11.2	5.2	2.15
1972	9.0	4.9	1.84

Both Sexes (16 to 19 Years)

	Black	White	B/W
1990	29.6	13.3	2.23
1989	32.4	12.7	2.55
1988	32.5	13.1	2.48
1987	33.4	13.3	2.51
1982	34.7	14.4	2.41
1978	48.0	20.4	2.35
1972	35.4	14.2	2.49

Note: 1990 data represent average of first three quarters.

Source: Bureau of Labor Statistics, *Handbook of Labor Statistics, June, 1985,* pp. 69, 71, 72, and 73. *Employment and Earnings, January, 1989.*

Table 18
Unemployment Rates by Region
(1989)

	Total Black	Total White	B/W	Black Male	White Male	B/W	Black Female	White Female	B/W	Black 16–19	White 16–19	B/W
Northeast	9.8	3.9	2.51	11.2	4.1	2.73	8.5	3.7	2.30	29.6	11.3	2.62
Midwest	15.4	4.4	3.50	16.4	4.5	3.64	14.4	4.4	3.27	36.5	11.6	3.15
South	10.7	4.6	2.33	10.0	4.4	2.27	11.4	4.8	2.38	32.0	13.4	2.39
West	10.6	5.0	2.12	11.2	4.9	2.29	10.0	5.1	1.96	28.9	14.4	2.01

Source: U.S. Department of Labor, Bureau of Labor Statistics, *Geographic Profile of Employment and Unemployment, 1990.*

Table 19
Unemployment Rates for Selected SMSAs
By Race, 1989

Metro Area	Black Unemp Rate	White Unemp Rate	B/W
Nassau-Suffolk, NY	4.8	3.2	1.500
Washington, DC	5.1	2.0	2.550
Rochester, NY	5.3	3.4	1.559
Charlotte, NC	6.2	2.4	2.583
Providence, RI	6.4	4.1	1.561
Columbus, OH	6.8	4.4	1.545
Memphis, TN	7.5	3.0	2.500
Phoenix, AZ	7.6	4.5	1.689
Bergen-Passaic, NJ	7.7	3.3	2.333
Oakland, CA	7.9	3.7	2.135
Riverside, CA	8.0	3.9	2.051
Philadelphia, PA	8.2	2.9	2.828
Atlanta, GA	8.4	3.3	2.545
Louisville, KY	8.4	4.5	1.867
Fort Lauderdale, FL	8.5	4.4	1.932
Los Angeles, CA	8.8	5.2	1.692
Newark, NJ	9.3	3.6	2.583
Boston, MA	9.3	3.3	2.793
Baltimore, MD	10.0	3.2	3.125
Dallas-Ft. Worth, TX	10.1	4.8	2.104
Hartford, CT	10.2	2.9	3.517
San Antonio, TX	10.4	9.2	1.130
Dayton, OH	10.6	4.1	2.585
Kansas City, KS	10.7	5.1	2.098
Sacramento, CA	10.8	4.9	2.204
San Francisco, CA	10.9	3.2	3.406
Denver-Boulder, CO	11.3	4.1	2.756
New Orleans, LA	11.3	3.6	3.139
New York, NY	11.4	5.0	2.280
San Diego, CA	11.7	4.5	2.600
Indianapolis, IN	11.7	3.9	3.000
Tampa-St. Petersburg, FL	12.5	4.3	2.907
Houston, TX	12.7	5.0	2.540
Pittsburgh, PA	12.7	4.7	2.702
Seattle, WA	12.8	4.4	2.909
Norfolk, VA	13.3	4.2	3.167
Miami, FL	13.4	5.6	2.393
Cincinnati, OH	13.6	3.2	4.250
St. Louis, MO	14.7	3.4	4.324
Oklahoma City, OK	15.4	3.1	4.968
Detroit, MI	16.5	5.7	2.895
Cleveland, OH	17.3	3.6	4.806
Chicago, IL	17.5	3.8	4.605
Milwaukee, WI	20.1	3.8	5.289
Buffalo-Niagara Falls, NY	24.0	5.2	4.615

Source: Bureau of Labor Statistics, *Geographic Profile of Employment & Unemployment, 1989,* Table 23.

double the white rate in the best case, and in the worse case, it was 3.6 times the white rate. Once again, the highest inequality was in the Midwest for all of the demographic categories. For each group, the index of inequality in the Midwest was greater than three to one. The level of inequality was at record levels in the Midwest throughout the 1980s.

Finally, Table 19 provides data on unemployment rates in the larger SMSAs during 1989. Black unemployment was high in most places. Twenty-seven SMSAs had black unemployment rates greater than 10 percent, and six had unemployment rates greater than 15 percent. Two places, Buffalo-Niagara Falls and Milwaukee, had unemployment rates for blacks that were above 20 percent. There were only three SMSAs in which black unemployment rates were less than six percent, while all of the SMSAs except San Antonio had white unemployment rates less than six percent.

It is apparent that, in the case of unemployment rates, blacks had significantly higher unemployment rates in every SMSA. There was no area that blacks had lower unemployment rates than whites. Of the 45 places included in the table, only nine had unemployment rates less than twice the white rates. At the other extreme, seven places had unemployment rates four times the white rates and one place—Milwaukee—had an unemployment rate that was over five times as high as the white rate of 3.8 percent.

The data in the previous four tables make it clear that black unemployment rates are high and unequal throughout the country. This has important implications for black income. The current excess unemployment for labor force participants cost blacks over 900,000 jobs. The unemployment indicator does not take into account the lower participation, part-time workers or discouraged workers. Therefore, this indicator understates the black unemployment disadvantage. In any case, although the absolute disparity fluctuated from year to year, the relative disparity persisted throughout the period and, thus, appears to be permanent.

Occupation and Wages

Tables 20 and 21 provide data on black occupational distribution and wage rates. Obviously, in addition to the level of employment, black earnings depend on the type of job and the wages received. The data in Table 20 show that both black males and females had unfavorable occupational distributions in 1989. The five top-paying occupational categories for males were professional, managerial, sales, technicians, and craft. As can be seen from the table, these are the occupations in which the proportions of blacks employed were relatively low. Employed black males were only about half as likely as white males to be employed in managerial, sales, or professional occupations, and only about three-quarters as likely to be employed as technicians or craft workers. On the other hand, black males were employed at much higher rates

Table 20
Occupational Distribution of Employed Workers, 1989

	Male			Female		
	Black	White	B/W	Black	White	B/W
Exec., Admin., & Managerial	6.7	14.7	0.456	7.4	11.6	0.638
Professional	6.3	12.4	0.508	10.8	15.3	0.706
Technicians & Related Support	2.2	2.9	0.759	3.6	3.2	1.125
Sales Occupations	5.8	11.7	0.496	9.4	13.6	0.691
Administrative Support	9.0	5.3	1.698	25.9	28.2	0.918
Private Households	0.1	0.1	1.000	3.5	1.3	2.692
Protective Service	4.6	2.4	1.917	0.9	0.5	1.800
Other Service	13.6	6.1	2.230	22.8	14.5	1.572
Precision Pro., Craft & Repair	15.5	20.2	0.767	2.4	2.2	1.091
Mach. Operators, Assem., & Insp.	10.7	7.3	1.466	9.6	5.8	1.655
Trans. and Materials Movers	11.2	6.6	1.697	1.1	0.8	1.375
Handlers, Cleaners, Helpers, Labor	10.9	5.8	1.879	2.3	1.6	1.437
Farming, Forestry, and Fishing	3.5	4.6	0.761	0.4	1.2	0.333

Source: U.S. Department of Labor, Bureau of Labor Statistics, *Employment and Earnings, January, 1989.*

in the five lowest-paying occupational categories. The impact of these disparities are such that black males have a good-job gap of 1.5 million jobs.

The situation was similar for females, although the degree of inequality was somewhat less. Black females were underrepresented in the four high-paid largely female occupations of sales, professionals, managerial, and administrative support. They were overrepresented in the lower-paid, less prestigious occupations of service workers, operators, and household workers. The net impact of the female underrepresentation is more than a 900,000+ good-job gap.

The occupational disadvantages have been consistent since the early 1970s. These figures also only take into account the employed blacks and are based only on broad occupational categories. However, blacks had unfavorable distributions across sub-occupations within the broad categories. Thus, the data in Table 20 understate the black occupational disadvantage. This poor occupational distribution has a big bearing on the lower labor market income of blacks.

Table 21 provides information on the wage rates received by black workers. This information adds one more piece of evidence that the disadvantages that blacks experience are permanent features of the American economy. The table provides information for full-time wage and salary workers. Blacks' median

Table 21
Median Weekly Earnings of Full-Time Wage and Salary Workers
By Race and Sex, 1979–1989

Total

	Black	White	B/W
1989	$319	$409	0.78
1988	314	394	0.80
1987	301	383	0.79
1986	302	383	0.79
1985	292	374	0.78
1984	290	371	0.78
1983	291	363	0.80
1982	288	358	0.80
1981	291	361	0.81
1980	283	361	0.78
1979	311	385	0.81

Males

	Black	White	B/W
1989	$348	$482	0.72
1988	347	465	0.75
1987	326	450	0.72
1986	329	449	0.73
1985	322	441	0.73
1984	333	441	0.76
1983	338	448	0.75
1982	325	435	0.75
1981	326	435	0.75
1980	335	436	0.77
1979	351	467	0.75

Females

	Black	White	B/W
1989	$301	$334	0.90
1988	288	318	0.91
1987	275	307	0.90
1986	272	305	0.89
1985	267	298	0.90
1984	265	289	0.92
1983	261	287	0.91
1982	249	283	0.88
1981	252	271	0.93
1980	250	277	0.90
1979	258	281	0.92

Source: Bureau of Labor Statistics, *Handbook of Labor Statistics, June, 1985,* p. 94.
Employment and Earnings, January, 1986–90.

weekly earnings were $319 in 1989, which was modestly higher than the level for 1979. Thus, the aggregate wage regained much of the ground lost since the recession of 1982. However, wages were still somewhat lower than the levels that existed in the 1970s. The earnings for black males of $348 in 1989 were still below the 1979 wage of $351. However, the earnings of black females rose considerably since 1979 from $258 to $301.

All black wages were lower than corresponding white wages in each year. The median wage for black males in 1989 was only 72 percent of the median white male wage. Inequality has been increasing for black males since the mid-1970s. The median wage for black females was 90 percent of the white female median during 1989. Wage equality was therefore greater between females. However, the current ratio is still below the levels that existed during the second half of the 1970s. Thus, wage inequality has been increasing for black females as well. The unequal wages cost black full-time workers an estimated $84 billion in 1989.

CAUSES OF INCOME INEQUALITY

Causation may be discussed at two levels. At the first level, one may look for those factors that are proximate causes of lower income recipiency of blacks. As has been noted, the proximate causes may be divided into those that help determine the number of blacks available to receive income and those that determine the amount of income that they receive. In general, the first set of factors is demographic. We have already identified two of these as the proportion of the population that is of working age and the number of missing males. We have also estimated the impact of these factors on existing income inequality, so we will not pay much more attention to these two demographic factors in our discussion of proximate causes. However, some other demographic factors will be noted.

The second set of proximate causes has been identified as those that determine the number and quality of black opportunities to receive income. On the one hand, the opportunities will depend on the relative ability of blacks to contribute to the economy. This in turn depends on their relative ownership of human and nonhuman capital. On the other hand, black opportunities to employ their resources will depend on the extent of discrimination. This in turn depends on the distribution of power.

At a deeper level, a discussion of causation must not only be concerned with the impact of black/white differences in demographic factors, capital ownership, and discrimination, but also will have to explain these differences. Obviously, this deeper level of understanding is required in order to project future prospects for racial equality or to devise policies or strategies to end inequality.

A complete treatment of causation is obviously beyond the scope of this paper. What we intend to do first is to look at some of the demographic and

Table 22
Median Income of Households by Select Characteristics and Race, 1989

	Percent of All Households		Median Income		B/W
	B	W	B	W	
Place of Residence					
All Households	100.0	100.0	18,083	30,406	59.5
Nonfarm Residence	99.8	98.0	18,119	30,442	59.5
In Central Cities of Lge Metro	41.1	16.4	17,325	29,061	59.6
Outside Central Cities of Lge Metro	18.9	30.9	29,725	39,257	75.7
Inside Central Cities Small	16.5	11.6	16,275	26,587	61.2
Outside Central Cities Small	7.5	17.4	18,482	31,082	59.5
Nonmetropolitan Area	15.9	23.7	12,130	23,611	51.4
Region of Residence					
Northeast	17.8	20.9	21,563	34,225	63.0
Midwest	20.0	25.4	16,514	29,948	55.1
South	53.6	32.6	16,788	27,887	60.2
West	8.6	21.1	23,288	31,406	74.2
Type of Household					
Married-Couple Family	35.8	58.6	30,833	39,328	78.4
Single-Female H/H Fam.	31.2	9.1	12,170	20,164	60.4
Single-Male H/H Fam.	4.3	2.9	20,044	32,218	62.2
Female-Headed Nonfam.	16.2	17.0	8,944	14,205	63.0
Male-Headed Nonfam.	12.5	12.4	14,737	23,799	61.9
Age of Householder					
15 to 24	6.89	3.96	6,488	18,941	34.25
25 to 34	27.24	21.76	16,849	32,804	51.36
35 to 44	26.10	25.02	28,245	41,688	67.82
45 to 54	15.89	17.84	29,212	48,122	60.70
55 to 64	12.10	14.39	22,582	39,505	57.16
65 to 74	7.60	11.50	16,828	25,805	65.21
75 +	4.18	5.54	12,638	19,999	63.19
Number Persons in H/H					
One	24.9	24.8	9,451	15,384	61.4
Two	25.9	33.3	18,721	31,037	60.3
Three	19.5	16.9	21,049	38,298	55.0
Four	14.8	15.5	26,246	42,103	62.3
Five	8.2	6.4	24,963	41,131	60.7
Six	3.9	2.0	20,288	39,550	51.3
Seven or More	2.8	1.1	21,534	38,108	56.5

This table continues on next page.

Table 22 *(continued)*
Median Income of Households by Select Characteristics and Race, 1989

	Percent of All Households		Median Income		B/W
	B	W	B	W	
Number of Earners					
No	24.1	20.7	5,707	11,900	48.0
One	38.5	32.4	16,532	25,254	65.5
Two	28.4	35.8	31,977	41,032	77.9
Three	6.8	7.9	43,176	52,321	82.5
Four or More	2.1	3.1	54,164	66,113	81.9
Work Experience					
Worked	66.1	72.8	25,093	36,775	68.2
Worked YRFT	45.2	54.1	30,114	41,066	73.3
Did Not Work	32.7	26.4	7,059	14,341	49.2
Educational Attainment of Householder					
Less Than 4 Yrs. H.S.	35.1	21.8	9,788	15,964	61.3
4 Yrs. H.S. & 1 to 2 Yrs. College	53.5	54.6	21,383	30,512	70.1
4 Yrs. or More College	11.3	23.6	37,958	48,862	77.7

Source: U.S. Bureau of the Census, Current Population Reports,Series, P-60, No. 168, *Money Income and Poverty Status in the United States: 1989* (Advance data from the March 1990 Current Population Survey), U.S. Government Printing Office, Washington, DC, 1990.

capital differences between the African-American and white populations. In examining these differences, we will be interested in the extent to which these differences can account for existing racial disparities. Having considered the impact of the characteristic differences, we will be in a position to speculate about the impact of discrimination. However, our method will be simplistic; we will provide only suggestive answers. In the concluding section, we will return to take up the deeper issues and discuss the permanent disparity hypothesis and its implications for policy.

The Impact of Differences in Selected Socio-Demographic Characteristics

Table 22 contains a variety of information about selected characteristics of black and white households for 1989. The first panel in this table contains information on the distribution of the two populations across different types of places of residence. As can be seen, the black and white distributions differ. Blacks are more likely to live in central cities, metropolitan areas, and large metropolitan areas than are whites. Whites are more likely than blacks to live on farms, in nonmetropolitan areas, in suburbs, and in small metropolitan areas. Obviously, since this pattern is partially self-selected, each group must find its best advantages with its choices, given existing situations.

We can note that black incomes were higher in large metropolitan areas than in smaller places, and they were larger in metropolitan than in nonmetropolitan areas. Thus, the distribution of blacks across different-sized places corresponded to their income differences. Blacks had higher incomes in the suburbs than in the cities. The differential was very large in the large metropolitan areas. However, the fact that significantly more blacks lived in the central cities suggests that causation probably runs from high income to suburban residence rather than from suburban residence to high income.

In any case, black incomes were lower than white incomes in all places of residence. The differential was greatest in the nonmetropolitan areas, where blacks received only 51.4 percent of white income. The suburbs of the large metropolitan areas had the greatest income inequality as well as the highest absolute income. The income inequality and absolute income in all other places were relatively close to each other.

There is little reason to suspect that place of residence is an important factor in generating the income inequality experienced by blacks. A rough estimate of the impact of the distribution has been obtained by estimating the impact that having the same residence distribution or the same incomes as whites would have on the parity gap. This calculation suggests that only about nine percent of the gap could be attributed to the pattern of black location. In other words, if black locations were changed to match the white distribution, but blacks continued to earn what they currently do in each location, this would eliminate at most only nine percent of the earnings disparity. On the other hand, the calculations suggest that if blacks did as well as whites in each location, 90 percent of the gap would be eliminated without any relocation. This suggests that the problem of unequal opportunities at each location is much more important than the existing locational differences.

The second panel shows the distribution of households by region of residence. We have already discussed income differences across regions. We note here that blacks were distributed differently across the regions. A much larger proportion of blacks was located in the South, and a much smaller proportion in the West. Modest differences in proportions existed in the other two regions.

A calculation to look at the impact of the regional differences in location, all else being equal, indicates that little of the gap, only about six percent, could be attributed directly to differences in regional distributions. The calculation again suggests that if blacks did as well as whites in each region, over 92 percent of the disparity gap would close.

The third panel shows the distribution of black households by household type. As is well known, there are significant differences between the white and black distributions. As can be seen from the table, the main difference is that blacks had fewer married-couple families and many more female-headed families. Married-couple and male-headed households of both races generally had higher incomes. The degree of equality was highest among married-couple families.

It is important to recognize that the causal link between the black/white differential in marital status and the black/white differential in income is not established. The differential in the rate of stable two-parent families may be as much a consequence as a cause of the income disparity. In any case, our rough estimate suggests that the maximum contribution of this factor would be 34 percent of the differential. The estimate also shows that roughly 70 percent of the differential could be eliminated by equalizing incomes within the existing distribution of household types. While 34 percent of the differential is significant, it is still worthy of note that the impact of unequal opportunities is much stronger.

The next panel of Table 22 provides data on the age distributions of the two populations. As is well known, the black population is considerably younger than the white population. This is revealed in the table by the fact that blacks had larger proportions in the three youngest age categories and smaller proportions in the remaining categories. It is also apparent that black incomes were lower than white incomes in all categories. The lowest absolute and relative incomes were for the very youngest households.

Surprisingly, the estimate of the impact of the age distribution suggests that this factor accounts for very little of the differences in income. The results suggest that a maximum of 2.1 percent of the disparity can be due to this factor. The estimates also suggest that almost 97 percent of the disparity could be removed if blacks at each age level fared as well as whites.

The next panel deals with household size. As can be seen, blacks and whites had equal proportions of one-person households. Blacks had smaller proportions of two- and four-person households, and larger proportions of all other size categories. Income for both groups tended to rise to the four-person household and decrease after that point. Blacks had lower incomes at all family sizes; the differentials are not marked.

Our estimate suggests that household size does not contribute anything to the existing disparities. In fact, the estimate suggests that the existing household size distribution has a small favorable impact. The calculation implies that black income would be reduced by four percent if blacks had the white household size distribution. Blacks would have higher incomes than whites if blacks fared as well as whites at each household size.

The next panel looks at the distribution of households by number of earners. Black households tended to have a smaller number of earners than white households. This is shown by the larger proportions at the one- and two-worker categories and the smaller proportions at all other categories. As was the case with all other characteristics, blacks received lower income at each category. However, the differential declined as the number of earners increased.

This factor has a significant impact on the disparity. The estimate suggests that almost 22 percent of the disparity could be due to lower numbers of workers per household. On the other hand, 80 percent of the disparity could be eliminated by equal earnings within each number of earners category. Moreover, since the number of earners may be more related to opportunities than anything else, it follows that the opportunity factor is far more significant than the characteristic difference.

The final of these demographic or social factors is the work experience of the households. Blacks were less likely to have worked and less likely to have worked year-round full-time when they did work. This is evident from the labor market statistics reviewed previously. Blacks received lower income in each category. However, the degree of equality increased as the work experience increased. The calculation suggests that the lower work experience factor could account for about one percent of the disparity. The unequal incomes within work experience categories accounted for about 89 percent of the differential.

The upshot of this discussion is that there are many differences between the black and the white community. However, blacks have unequal opportunities, regardless of their characteristics. The existing differences in demographic and social characteristics are related to the income disparity. However, it is doubtful if they explain much of the existing economic disparity between blacks and whites. It is clear that an unequal outcome for each characteristic is by far the most important cause of existing racial disparities.

THE IMPACT OF DIFFERENCES IN CAPITAL OWNERSHIP

As we suggested above, the primary cause of differences in opportunities excluding discrimination is differences in capital ownership. The opportunity to earn various types of income is related to differences in the ownership of human and nonhuman capital. Labor market wage and salary income differentials might be caused by differences in human capital ownership.

The last panel of Table 22 provides some summary data on differences in educational distributions. As can be seen, blacks in general had less education than whites. Smaller proportions of blacks completed four or more years of college (11.3 versus 23.6 percent), and larger proportions dropped out before completing high school (35.1 versus 21.8 percent). Roughly, the same proportions completed high school or fewer than four years of college. Incomes for blacks and whites increased with educational levels. Racial inequality also declined as educational level increased. However, even with four years of college, black households had only 77.7 percent as much income as similarly educated white households.

The rough estimation method employed earlier suggests that educational differences could account for 29 percent of the income disparity. Differences

Table 23
Wealth Ownership 1984
(1989$)

	Black Mean	White Mean	Black %	White %	B/W	Black Aggregate*	White Aggregate*	Aggregate Gap*
Net Worth	$24,168	$103,081	100.00	100.00	23.45	$229,813	$7,766,444	$695,808
Interest Earning at Financial Institutions	3,743	20,137	43.80	75.40	10.80	15,590	1,143,952	128,787
Regular Checking	715	1,131	32.00	56.90	35.56	2,176	48,474	3,942
Stock & Mutual Funds	3,359	33,067	5.40	22.00	2.49	1,725	548,099	67,451
Equity in Business	40,593	77,008	4.00	14.00	15.06	15,440	812,278	87,077
Equity in Motor Vehicle	4,115	6,814	65.00	85.50	44.34	25,431	454,362	31,913
Equity in Home	35,718	62,016	43.80	67.30	37.47	148,762	3,144,555	248,111
Equity in Rental Property	45,542	88,155	6.60	10.10	33.75	28,582	670,827	56,083
Other Real Estate	17,221	41,901	3.30	10.90	12.43	5,404	344,198	38,037
U.S. Savings Bond	657	3,133	7.40	16.10	9.63	462	38,005	4,334
IRA or Keogh	4,109	10,802	5.10	21.40	9.06	1,992	174,168	19,989

*in millions

Source: U.S. Department of Commerce, Bureau of the Census, *Household Wealth and Asset Ownership: 1984*, Tables 1 and 3.

in earnings within educational categories could account for about 66 percent of the disparity. Obviously our calculation is rough, but it suggests that much progress could be made if blacks at each educational level were treated more equally.

Property receipts are influenced by the ownership of nonhuman wealth. Table 23 provides the latest data available on wealth ownership. These data clearly show the black disadvantage in wealth ownership. The mean wealth ownership for black households was $24,168, or only 23.45 percent of the mean holdings for whites. The black disadvantage is generated by two factors. First, blacks owned fewer of each type of asset, as indicated by the data in the means column. Second, fewer blacks owned each type of wealth, as indicated by the data in the percent column. For example, 43.8 percent of blacks owned interest-earning assets at financial institutions compared to 75.4 percent of whites. The ratio of black per capita to white per capita holdings is shown under the B/W column. In this case, blacks owned about 10.8 percent of the interest-earning assets at financial institutions that whites owned.

These ownership gaps add up to huge disparities in black wealth holdings. Overall, blacks had a $695 billion shortfall in their wealth ownership. The disparities for each type of wealth holding are shown in the table.

These large disparities in wealth ownership probably fully explain the gap in property income. These disparities also suggest that blacks have relatively little economic power and are thus susceptible to discrimination by groups who own significant amounts of wealth.

Table 24 provides even more dramatic evidence of the limited power of blacks. This table contains business ownership data. Business ownership may contribute directly to self-employment and property income.

These are new data from the recently released *Survey of Minority-Owned Businesses*. The survey reports business ownership as of 1987. The first two columns show black receipts and total business receipts in the U.S. economy. As can be seen, the black-owned business sector contributed a miniscule amount to the American economy. In 1987, the total receipts were 10.8 trillion dollars, and black-owned businesses generated receipts of only 21.6 billion dollars. The contributions of black businesses per black person were only 1.6 percent of the per capita contributions of all American businesses. Black businesses generated $1.299 trillion less in receipts than would have been required for business ownership parity.

In terms of the number of firms owned, ignoring differences in size, blacks fared a little better. Blacks owned 424,000 firms, while there were 17,526,000 firms in the American economy. Black per capita firm ownership was 19.8 percent of the total per capita firm ownership. The total firm ownership gap was 1,713,000 firms.

The rest of the table provides information on business ownership by major industry category. As can be seen, black ownership by the receipts measure was

Table 24

Total Receipts (in Billions of 1989$) and Number of Firms (1,000's) in 1987 by Industry

	Black Receipts	Total Receipts	B/T**	Receipt Gap	Black Firms	Total Firms	B/T**	Firm Gap
Total	21.6	$10,828	0.016	$1,299	424	17,526	0.198	1,713
Construction	2.5	561	0.037	66	37	560	0.539	32
Manufacturing	1.1	2,899	0.003	353	8	642	0.102	70
Transportation and Public Utilities	1.7	827	0.017	99	37	735	0.412	53
Wholesale Trade	1.4	1,335	0.009	161	6	641	0.070	73
Retail Trade	6.4	1,641	0.032	194	66	2,658	0.204	258
Finance, Insurance, and Real Estate	0.9	1,652	0.004	201	27	1,426	0.155	147
Selected Services	6.7	907	0.060	104	210	7,095	0.242	656
Other Industries*	0.9	1,006	0.007	122	34	3,769	0.075	425

Note: 1987 dollars were converted to 1989 dollars using CPI-U.

*Includes Agriculture, Mining, and industries not elsewhere classified.

**This is black receipts or firms per capita divided by the complement for total per capita. Black population in 1987: 29,417,000; total population in 1987: 241,187,000.

Source: U.S. Department of Commerce, Bureau of the Census, *Survey of Minority-Owned Businesses: Black, 1987,* and *The Statistical Abstract of the United States, 1990,* Table 859, p. 521.

73

limited in all industries. The best performances were in construction, retail trade, and selected services. The worst performances were in manufacturing, finance, wholesale trade, and other industries. With respect to the number of firms owned, blacks were closest to parity in construction, transportation and public utilities, selected services, and retail trade. They were furthest away in wholesale trade, other industries, manufacturing, and finance.

In any case, the evidence is clear that black business ownership is extremely limited. Thus, blacks would be expected to earn limited amounts of income from self-employment. They also would have limited power and influence over business decisions. They will, thus, be susceptible to discrimination.

CONCLUSION

This paper has presented substantial information showing that blacks have a low and unequal economic status. We have argued that this disadvantaged economic status appears to be a permanent feature of the American economy. Black economic disadvantage appears to be generated by a number of factors. We have argued that demographic and social differences play a role. However, we have also suggested that differences in opportunities are more important generators of inequality than differences in characteristics of the two populations. Moreover, the differences in opportunities are generated by differences in human and nonhuman capital ownership and discrimination. The susceptibility of blacks to discrimination is, in turn, caused by their limited ownership and power. Thus, the proximate causes of black economic inequality are disadvantaged demographic characteristics, unfavorable social characteristics, limited human capital, limited ownership of wealth, limited ownership and control of businesses, and limited political power.

Obviously this paper cannot sort through the relative importance of this list of causes. However, from the perspective of the permanent inequality hypothesis, this is not necessary. The important question is what impact does the "business as usual" operation of the American economy have on these factors? If the economy could be counted on to reduce the black disadvantages automatically, then the inequality and poverty would not be permanent. On the other hand, if the normal operations of the American economy tended to perpetuate or exacerbate the causative factors, then we could be sure that the inequality would be permanent sans intervention.

The record obviously supports the permanent poverty and inequality hypothesis. The constancy of the absolute and relative status of blacks over the last 20 years cannot be a mere accident. It is apparent that systemic factors built into the economy perpetuate black disadvantage. Why? Primarily because the system will automatically perpetuate the inequality in the relative ownership, demographic, and social factors. The constancy of these causative factors will not only directly generate inequality, but will also perpetuate the group's susceptibility to discrimination.

A moment's reflection ought to convince one of the truth of these propositions. First, it is apparent that the ability to increase capital ownership in this country is an increasing function of current income and wealth. The more income and wealth one has, the more one can create future wealth. Thus, those groups who are currently disadvantaged must be disadvantaged in the future.

The demographic and social factors are unfavorable primarily because of unfavorable initial conditions. Thus, the continuation of unfavorable conditions will result in the continued generation of unfavorable demographic and social characteristics. The disadvantaged, therefore, are caught in a vicious cycle in which disadvantage begets additional disadvantage.

In short, since the future value of the factors that determine the degree of inequality are determined by the current distribution of advantage, the current unfavorable distributions guarantee future disadvantage.

The upshot of all this is that we cannot expect the normal operation of the system to ever produce an end to racial inequality in American economic life. Thus, if racial inequality is to end, then there must be direct intervention to eliminate the aforementioned disadvantages. In particular, the disadvantages in ownership, power, and current economic position must be eliminated if racial inequality is to end.

How can this be accomplished? The answer is that blacks must obtain sufficient surplus funds to eliminate the disadvantages in ownership of human and nonhuman capital and power. The possibility of obtaining the required surpluses through internal community sacrifice is nil in the absence of compelling political power. Thus, the only viable option is a program of reparations. A constructive and well-designed program of reparations will bring an end once and for all to racial inequality. No other strategy can work unless it eliminates the inherited disadvantages of ownership and power. Any strategy that accomplishes this without creating a separate black nation would have to be a form of reparations.

We can conclude that, in the absence of reparations, the racial inequality that currently characterizes the African-American population will continue indefinitely, as long as the current economic system is in place.

* * * * *

ACKNOWLEDGMENTS

The author would like to thank Bill Powell for his excellent research assistance and Bridget Jones for her expert secretarial assistance. Needless to say, the views expressed here are those of the author, who takes complete responsibility for the content of this paper.

Budgets, Taxes, and Politics:
Options for the
African-American Community

Lenneal J. Henderson, Ph.D.

The issue has been framed as: "How big is the 'peace dividend'?" and, in effect, "How can I get mine?" These are issues that the budget and political system must treat.

Budget of the United States Government
Fiscal Year 1991

Governments exist to provide to people valuable services that businesses or individuals are unwilling or unable to provide independently.

John L. Mikesell, *Fiscal Administration*

INTRODUCTION

African Americans continue to have a monumental stake in the politics and economics of government budgets and taxes. Given the disproportionately large dependency of African Americans on government for a variety of income transfer programs, education, Medicare, Medicaid and other health-oriented programs, housing, business development, transportation, employment, and other essentials, fiscal policy—the public financial transactions of government—can enhance or depress, accelerate or slow the African-American community.

And yet, the 1991 budget and 1992 budget debates are characterized by more and more diverse financial demands on the federal, state, and local governments. As of July, 1990, the Bush administration had volunteered inflation-adjusted defense-spending reductions of about $3 billion, while congressional Democrats sought cuts from $15.5 to $13 billion,[1] first steps in the implementation of a "peace dividend" following the reduction of tensions between the U.S. and the U.S.S.R. and democratization of Eastern Europe. However, the Iraqi invasion of Kuwait on August 2, 1990, and the massive mobilization and deployment of U.S. troops to Saudi Arabia to quell Iraqi leader Saddam Hussein all but put on hold peace dividend discussions.

Moreover, the federal government is allocating billions of dollars to address savings and loan (S&Ls) institutions and insolvent banks. By 1986, S&Ls started to collapse at an alarming rate—517 thrifts closed between 1980 and 1988. With liabilities of $100 billion in excess of assets, the Federal Savings and Loan Insurance

77

Corporation (FSLIC) depleted its funds. Its insurance obligations passed to the Federal Deposit Insurance Corporation (FDIC), and a new agency, the Resolution Trust Corporation (RTC), was established to dispose of approximately $400 billion of insolvent thrift assets. The government dealt with 205 insolvent S&Ls in 1988 alone. Government estimates suggest that $400 billion could be spent bailing out S&Ls over the coming years.[2]

In addition, the combination of dramatic and sweeping political changes in Eastern Europe, Central and South America, and global economic recession places great pressure on the U.S. government to be financially responsive, if not preferential, to thousands of persons within, and departing from, these nations.

The message for African Americans is simple: remain politically active, vigilant, and well-informed on fiscal policy, or be placed further back in the budget line behind other "priorities." The task of vigilance is a complex and difficult one, for fiscal decisions are quite broad. Mikesell, for example, describes fiscal policy as inclusive of the budget cycle, taxes, charges and fees, administration of the government debt, bonds, procurement policy, public enterprise, and the creation and use of various trust accounts earmarked for specific purposes.[3]

In many respects, fiscal policy combines past, present, and future policy practices and issues. It asks how much the past allocation patterns should guide present (usually current fiscal year) allocation options. Simultaneously, it ponders and struggles over the short- and long-term consequences of selecting one financial option over the other. It debates one method of using budgets and taxes to respond to social priorities over another. Thus, historical, contemporary, and future policies toward blacks are reflected in the nature of fiscal policies adopted by government, whether blacks are explicitly or implicitly the focal point of such policies.[4] This process is further complicated by various equity and equality issues and the national economics and financial woes that undergird budgetary and tax decisions.

Such complications imply five interrelated essential points about the relationship between fiscal policies and black economic and political aspirations.

First, blacks continue to be disproportionately dependent upon public finance in order to advance their economic and political agenda. This fiscal dependence assumes three dimensions: (a) the generic or macroeconomic level of dependency; (b) the institutional level of dependency; and (c) the household level of dependency. These three interdependent levels are shared by other socioeconomically disadvantaged populations in the U.S.[5]

Second, the politics and economics of deficit reduction and tax policies continue to pose severe challenges for African Americans. Deficit reduction is often employed as a justification for federal budget rescissions, deferrals, reprogramming, or deprogramming. The 1990 budget summit agreement and eventual deficit reduction package represented some of the most acrimonious, intense, and difficult budget and tax negotiations ever. Voters expressed their dismay with both the process and product of these negotiations in the 1990 elections, particularly at the state and local levels.[6]

Third, continued shifting of financial and public policy responsibility from the federal to state and local governments challenges black elected officials, who are more numerous at these levels. Black mayors are particularly vulnerable to fiscal stress.[7]

Fourth, African Americans have a direct and continuing stake in the fiscal policies about defense, banking, savings and loans, public works, nonprofit, public sector, and other major institutions in America. Not only must African Americans continue to pursue civil rights, housing, employment, education, health care, and other primary agendas, but they must also relate to the fiscal policies that affect lending institutions, hospitals, local and state governments, strategic large and small businesses, nonprofit organizations, and other institutions upon whom African Americans are directly or indirectly dependent.[8]

Finally, the methodology of economic, social, and political development pursued by African Americans should incorporate a fiscal component: a plan for acquiring, allocating, and leveraging fiscal resources so as to reduce excessive dependence on government. While vigorously seeking to change national, state, and local fiscal priorities through such mechanisms as lobbying, the courts, and mass media exposure of presidential budget and tax postures, blacks should extend their use of fiscal impact assessments as part of their arsenal for addressing and transcending the new fiscal ethics.

Consequently, the Congressional Black Caucus, in its *Quality of Life, Fiscal 1991 Alternative Budget*, argues that "a nation's values and concern for social and economic justice are measured by the fiscal priorities established in its national budget."[9] The League of United Latin American Citizens (LULAC) has repeatedly warned tax experts that the failure to incorporate large numbers of unemployed and underemployed Hispanic citizens and aliens represents not only a fiscal failure but also a moral failure. The rapidly rising number of women entering the work force who are subject to rising taxes without benefit of adequate child and eldercare for those whom they work makes a loud statement about value priorities and not just fiscal dynamics.[10]

THE CURRENT DEPENDENCY OF BLACKS ON FISCAL POLICIES

Paradoxically, blacks are simultaneously dependent on federal, state, and local governments for most of their household and institutional financial resources and regressively subjected to most taxing and revenue policies. It is essential to emphasize that "dependency" is not used pejoratively in this context. Many of America's largest corporate, nonprofit, and educational institutions are substantially, if not predominantly, dependent upon public budgets or tax breaks.[11]

However, of the more than 300,000 businesses owned and operated by black entrepreneurs, more than 90 percent of them supply or provide services to government. Fewer than 50 percent of all other enterprises are as dependent on the

79

government dollar.[12] Black households are more than twice as dependent on some form of federal, state, or local transfer payment; subsidy; public assistance; or Aid to Families with Dependent Children as other households. A black student in any college or university is almost three times as likely to receive government support as the predominant support for tuition and room and board as other students. Black men and women in the correctional institutions of the nation represent far more than their demographic representation in the population as a whole. Moreover, as Persons, Walton, and other experts on black elected officials point out, black elected officials usually serve the state or in jurisdictions containing large numbers of impoverished, poorly housed populations with health care, day care, education, employment, and infrastructural needs that severely strain city, county, or state budgetary resources.[13] Given advancing rates of poverty, homelessness, health care deficiencies, and other social maladies, the dependency of the needy on government will increase.

The Civil Rights, antipoverty, feminist, and other movements in the '50s, '60s, and '70s thrust an ethic of social responsiveness upon fiscal decision-makers unprecedented even during the Great Depression. Through the Manpower Development and Training Act of 1962, the Economic Opportunity Act of 1964, the Cities Demonstration and Metropolitan Development Act of 1966, and other policies, the alleviation of poverty was placed higher on the public policy agenda than ever before. The result was a great redistributive impulse: a desire to reallocate the financial resources of the nation through fiscal policy. Walton has pointed out that federal outlays for civil rights regulatory activities increased from $900,000 in 1969 to $3.5 billion in 1976.[14] Also in 1976, the Small Business Act of 1958 was amended to create federal set-aside programs for minority businesses through what has become known as the 8(a) program.

Although it is common to be concerned primarily about those government programs earmarked specifically for blacks and other "target groups," the other levels of dependency must also be discussed. First, like all Americans, blacks are dependent upon government for "public goods." Support for national defense, the space program, research and development, law enforcement, parks and recreation, streets, highways, and bridges represent a generic or macroeconomic level of public goods and services depended upon by all Americans. While blacks may receive inadequate quantities or qualities of these goods and services, they are public in the broadest sense of the term and are supported by a variety of public spending and revenue-generating schemes such as corporate and individual income taxes, property taxes, sales taxes, excise taxes, trust funds, and user fees.

Such generic spending, however, may affect black Americans in particular. This is because black Americans may depend disproportionately on key components of generic-level spending not evident in other groups of citizens. For example, when recommendations are made for across-the-board reductions in military installations, weapons systems, or research and development, blacks employed as civilians or enlisted in the armed services may suffer more than others because

they are represented more in the employment at military inst.
others.[15] When President Nixon decided to close or reduce 274 mi\
tions in 1974, many blacks lost jobs or were transferred to lower-p
installations within or near cities like Philadelphia, Boston, and Sa
Oakland. Military spending does create jobs: each $1 billion reduc   ._ . cn-
tagon outlays affects 38,000 U.S. workers.[16]

Moreover, the so-called "peace dividend" expected to result from reductions
in military outlays in response to democratization in Eastern Europe and the
U.S.S.R. has yet to materialize. Not only has the crisis precipitated by Iraq's invasion of Kuwait stalled discussions of major defense reductions, but also no one
knows if deep or far-ranging reductions in military spending will be possible after
the resolution of the Iraqi-Kuwaiti crisis. Prior to that crisis, Defense Secretary
Dick Cheney instructed the services to consider reductions of up to $180 billion
for fiscal years 1992-94.[17] In addition, indirect macroeconomic effects from
reduced military spending, such as the decline in demand for electronic parts,
vehicles, aircraft, and other goods and services produced for defense by the private
sector can exacerbate economic conditions in metropolitan areas with substantial black populations.

A second point about the generic level of dependency is its *intergovernmental
nature*. Federal defense, education, space, and infrastructural spending is so inextricably intertwined with fiscal decisions of states, cities, and counties that
any political or economic strategy involving public finance must consider its
intergovernmental dimensions. Table 1 illustrates the impact of federal defense
spending for goods, services, and research and development on selected
metropolitan areas.

Moreover, in addition to defense, *infrastructure*—the nation's systems of roads,
bridges, tunnels, water systems, transit systems, highways, airports, gas mains,
and other public works—is in terrible disrepair. Estimates for infrastructural
restoration range from $50 billion to $3 trillion dollars over the next 10 years.[18]
While federal leadership is essential, an intergovernmental response is imperative,
as Table 2 suggests. All Americans, including African Americans, are impeded
by poor infrastructural conditions. And poorer infrastructural conditions in the
African-American community are a glaring reality.

A third point about the generic level of fiscal policy is its frequent lack of racial
sensitivity. For example, the Tax Reform Act of 1986 is income-based rather than
racially-based. The Earned Income Tax Credit (EITC) provides tax assistance to
low-income working families to support their children. The assistance is provided
without regard to family size, penalizing black and Hispanic families with larger
family sizes.[19] Nor were Gramm-Rudman-Hollings sequesters sensitive to their
adverse impacts on predominantly black institutions such as the District of Columbia government.[20]

Consequently, an analysis of the generic level of fiscal dependency is essential
to overall black economic and political development. It facilitates the interface

Table 1
Department of Defense Share of Spending on Goods,
Services, and Research and Development (Excludes Military Payroll)

	Share of Total Spending	Share of R & D Spending
Los Angeles*–Long Beach	7.2%	19.7%
Washington, DC*–MD–VA	4.2	5.4
Norfolk–Virginia Beach–Newport News*	4.2	0.0
St. Louis–E. St. Louis, IL*	3.8	1.1
Nassau–Suffolk, NY	3.0	4.5
Boston	3.1	9.1
San Jose, CA	2.7	4.5
Philadelphia*–NJ	2.2	1.5
Fort Worth–Arlington, TX	2.1	2.4
Anaheim–Santa Ana, CA	2.1	3.7
Seattle*	1.7	3.9
Dallas	1.6	1.6
Denver*	1.5	7.8

*Cities with African-American or Hispanic-American mayors.

Source: Adapted from the Bruton Center for Developmental Studies, The University of Texas at Dallas, 1989.

between black and other populations at the intersection of broad use of public goods and services. Although its distributional effects on blacks vary, its objectives may be found in broad statements about national, state, or local public needs.

A fourth level of black fiscal dependency exists at the institutional level. Black schools, hospitals, churches, fraternal organizations, professional and occupational organizations, charitable and community-based organizations, and municipalities and counties depend disproportionately on public finance. This dependence reflects the ever-increasing needs of black individuals and households for goods and services beyond the reach of black incomes or inadequately provided by the marketplace.

This level of dependency includes "targeted" or "earmarked" public programs aimed at black institutional development. Black institutions are supported in order to generate more black educational, career, employment, or business opportunity. Several examples of these programs illustrate the point. The Small Business Administration's (SBA) Office of Minority and Small Business manages the 8(a) minority set-aside program. Of more than 400,000 minority-owned firms, just over 3,000 (Table 3) participate in the sheltered market reserved for them that consists of work for various federal agencies. Through federal offices of "small and disadvantaged business utilization," the 8(a) program has generated millions of dollars for minority firms that could not have been generated in the competitive marketplace.

[In millions of dollars, except percent. Represents expenditures from own funds, excluding intergovernmental grants.]

Level and Type of Expenditure	Total	Highways	Airports	Mass Transit	Water Resources	Water Supply	Solid Waste
Current Dollars							
1980: Total	78,211	33,869	5,048	8,564	6,282	10,286	3,347
Federal	25,688	9,490	3,139	3,453	3,735	4,720	—
State	18,483	15,121	275	1,208	1,369	188	—
Local	34,404	9,258	1,635	3,902	1,178	5,378	3,347
Percent: Capital Expenditures	49.8	57.3	32.6	32.6	51.3	64.8	12.7
Operations and Maintenance	50.2	42.7	67.4	67.4	48.7	35.2	87.3
1987: Total	124,652	52,547	8,814	15,122	7,731	15,265	6,463
Federal	28,891	13,547	4,856	3,340	3,551	3,320	—
State	29,489	23,570	386	2,641	2,384	400	—
Local	66,272	15,503	3,572	9,142	1,785	11,545	6,463
Percent: Capital Expenditures	42.2	53.8	36.0	22.2	35.2	50.5	16.4
Operations and Maintenance	57.8	46.2	64.0	77.8	64.8	49.5	83.6
Constant (1984) Dollars							
1980: Total	96,483	41,618	6,296	7,746	12,588	13,390	4,221
Federal	31,159	11,395	3,925	4,576	5,659	1,380	—
State	22,899	18,745	341	1,475	234	400	—
Local	42,426	11,477	2,030	4,917	6,694	11,610	4,221
Percent: Capital Expenditures	48.3	55.8	31.4	31.4	63.5	42.7	12.0
Operations and Maintenance	51.7	44.1	68.6	68.6	36.5	57.3	88.0
1987: Total	113,886	48,207	8,032	13,743	13,987	17,032	5,844
Federal	26,773	12,574	4,426	3,086	3,102	327	—
State	26,886	21,495	352	2,418	365	98	—
Local	60,228	14,138	3,254	8,240	10,521	16,607	5,844
Percent: Capital Expenditures	43.2	54.8	36.9	22.9	51.5	34.9	16.9
Operations and Maintenance	56.8	45.2	63.1	77.1	48.5	65.1	83.1

— Represents zero.

Source: Apogee Research, Inc., Bethesda, MD; unpublished data compiled from the Public Works Data Base.

Table 3
Number of Minority Firms Participating in SBA's 8(a) Program, 1985–1989

Year	Number of Participating Firms
1985	2,977
1986	3,188
1987	2,990
1988	2,946
1989	3,297
1990	2,500

Source: Small Business Administration, Office of Minority and Small Business Files, 1989.

Another example of a targeted federal program is the U.S. Department of the National Energy Act of 1978.[21] The Office of Minority Economic Impact (OMEI) provides a comprehensive program of socioeconomic research on the impacts of energy prices, supplies, and policies on minorities; assistance to minority institutions of higher learning on research and development opportunities in the Department of Energy; a Minority Energy Information Clearinghouse, and a Comprehensive Business and Community Development Program.[22] Moreover, OMEI collaborates with Argonne National Laboratory on the economics of household energy consumption and expenditures and with a variety of African- and Hispanic-American-oriented colleges and universities. Although small in both budget and staff (Table 4), OMEI is pivotal in both its monitoring of energy policies for minority impacts and its bordering of opportunities within DOE for a variety of nonwhite institutions. The monies reflected in these "minority programs" are minimal, but the impact on the financial well-being and development of the institutions they assist is substantial.

The last level of public financial dependency is quite direct. Black households are sensitive to minute changes in the financial disposition of either black institu-

Table 4
Budget of the Office of Minority Economic Impact,
U.S. Department of Energy, 1985–1989

Year	Budget (In Millions of Dollars)
1985	$2.4
1986	2.6
1987	2.8
1988	3.8
1989	4.1
1990	3.9*
1991	3.5

*Reflects Gramm-Rudman-Hollings sequester.

Source: U.S. Department of Energy, Office of Minority Economic Impact.

tions or generic fiscal policies. Taken together, Gramm-Rudman-Hollings, its 1987 amendments, the 1990 deficit reduction packages, and the Tax Reform Act of 1986 are <u>fiscally regressive for black</u> households. What minor benefits the Tax Reform Act provided to the poorest black households were eliminated by real-dollar budget-deficit reductions and changes in both generic and targeted federal programs.[23] Socioeconomic retrogression in inner-city and poor rural black communities are unfortunately correlated with declines in the levels of federal, state, and local spending in *black communities.*

THE 1991 BUDGET SUMMIT AGREEMENT

Given the levels of financial dependency of African Americans on public finance and the politics of estimating, formulating, adopting, and implementing a budget and tax package, key provisions of the 1991 summit agreement are emphasized.

The Budget Provisions

First, in contrast to the original summit proposals of September, 1990, final budget legislation adopted by Congress on October 27, 1990, was generally progressive.[24] To reach a deficit reduction target of nearly $500 billion over the next five fiscal years, reductions in entitlement programs and defense spending were enacted together with increases in federal user fees for government services, a variety of tax increases, and reductions of interest payments on the national debt.[25]

Funding reductions for defense are significantly offset by incremental funding for Operation Desert Shield in the Persian Gulf. The deployment of 450,000 troops to Saudi Arabia, almost one-third of which are African Americans, and the uncertainty of the timelines and parameters of the conflict between Iraq and the U.S. also make uncertain both the eventual level of expenditures for the Operation and their impact on other components of the budget.

Second, more than half of the $41 billion in deficit reductions for the 1991 Fiscal Year (FY) will be generated by direct spending reductions. Entitlement programs will be reduced by nearly $10 billion. User fees for a variety of federal services will be increased by nearly one billion dollars. Entitlement programs are particularly significant to African Americans. These are programs mandated by statute that require the payment of benefits to any person or unit of government that meets the eligibility requirements established.[26] These include Food Stamps, Aid to Families with Dependent Children (AFDC), nutrition programs, housing programs, veteran's benefits, Social Security benefits, worker's compensation, and Medicare. African-American participation in these programs ranges from 22.7 percent of the Social Security beneficiaries to 53 percent of AFDC recipients.

Real-dollar deficit reduction, while important to overall fiscal control, is at least a three-dimensional hardship on African-American beneficiaries: (a) the reductions occur in an economic recession and exacerbate near-crisis conditions, particularly in African-American urban neighborhoods and rural settlements; (b) reductions ignore accelerating needs in African-American communities, even when documented through means-testing; and (c) reduction in net disposable income in the African-American community is a negative economic multiplier; that is, landlords, businesses, churches, local governments, and other institutions dependent upon the purchasing power of blacks experience aggregate revenue reductions. These revenue reductions may significantly affect their continued capacity to provide goods and services to African Americans.[27]

TAX PROVISIONS

Almost $18 billion in deficit reduction in FY 1991 is generated by revenue increases, principally tax increases. These provisions represent a reversal of the general, "no new taxes" pledge by the Bush administration. They raise taxes for most income earners. Tax increases by income group are described in Tables 5 and 6. Although those earning incomes of over $200,000 will experience a 6.3 percent increase in taxes and are 46 percent of the total, tax increases are fairly well distributed among other income groups. Net increases in taxes over the next five years total $137 billion.

In addition, there are five major excise tax provisions in the new statute. These include a five-cents-a-gallon increase in gasoline taxes; increases in cigarette taxes from 16 cents a pack to 20 cents a pack in 1991 and 24 cents a pack in 1993; increase in alcohol taxes; and increase in airport and aviation excise taxes, including an increase from eight percent to 10 percent in the tax on airline tickets. The tem-

Table 5
Percent Change in Federal Taxes

Income Level	Final Package	Summit Agreement	House	Senate
Less than $10,000	−2.0%*	7.6%	−1.3%	0.0%*
$10,000–20,000	3.2	1.9	−1.6	−2.3
$20,000–30,000	1.8	3.3	1.0	2.7
$30,000–40,000	2.0	2.9	1.0	2.8
$40,000–50,000	2.0	2.9	0.8	2.8
$50,000–75,000	1.5	1.8	1.4	1.9
$75,000–100,000	2.1	2.1	1.5	2.5
$100,000–200,000	2.3	1.9	0.7	3.5
$200,000 and over	6.3	1.7	7.4	3.7

*Includes child care bill with approximately $12 billion in tax credits primarily for working families with children and incomes under $20,000.

Source: Center on Budget and Policy Priorities calculations, based on data from the Joint Committee on Taxation.

Table 6
How Much of the Tax Increase
Is Borne by Various Income Groups

Income Category	Final Package*	Summit Agreement	House	Senate*
Under $50,000	19%	57%	11%	34%
$50,000–100,000	22	22	22	24
$100,000–200,000	13	10	5	18
$200,000 and over	46	11	63	24

*Includes effects of the tax provisions of the child care bill.

Source: Center on Budget and Policy Priorities calculations, based on data from the Joint Committee on Taxation.

porary three percent excise tax on telephone service now becomes permanent under the law.[28]

In contrast to the income tax provision, these taxes are generally *regressive,* in contrast to the more progressive budgetary provisions (Table 7). Given the documented tendency of poorer and larger African-American families to use older, larger, less fuel-efficient vehicles, the gasoline tax will have a disproportionately higher impact on them than their Hispanic and white counterparts.[29]

"Sin taxes" on cigarettes and alcohol will also tend to impact disproportionately on African Americans. Despite vigorous efforts to discourage smoking and drinking in African-American communities, these taxes will also adversely affect small business establishments serving African Americans.

However, the positive structure of the revenue side of this enactment is best expressed in the new Earned Income Tax Credit (EITC) (Table 8). The EITC is a tax credit available to working families with children that have incomes below about $20,000. For the tax year 1990, the income cutoff is $20,264; for the tax year 1991, it will be about $21,000. The credit is "refundable." If an eligible family earns too little income to owe federal income tax, or if the amount of the credit exceeds the income tax owed by the family, the Internal Revenue Service will send the family a check.[30]

TOWARDS AN ETHICAL FISCAL STRATEGY

It is essential to maintain both the values implied in the struggle of nonwhite and poor Americans seeking fiscal alternatives and the related criteria for good fiscal policies. At a minimum, good fiscal policies include the principles of productivity, equity, and elasticity. A *productive* fiscal policy generates sufficient revenues to meet governmental needs on the tax side and makes investments in human needs, economic development, and defense on the spending side. If tax policies fail to generate adequate revenue, more public monies must be spent on borrowing, with a subsequent effect on interest rates and economic growth. An

Table 7
Deficit Reduction in Final Budgt Legislation
(in billions of dollars)

	FY 1991	FY 91–95
Non-entitlement programs		
Domestic	—}	
International	—}	182.4*
Defense	9.8}	
Entitlements and User Fees	10.4	99.0
Entitlements	9.7	92.1
User Fees	0.7	6.9
IRS Initiative	3.0	9.4
Tax and receipt measures	17.6	137.2
Interest payments	1.6	68.4
Total deficit reduction	42.6	496.3

*In FY 1994 and FY 1995, there would be one overall spending ceiling for all non-entitlement programs, including both defense and nondefense programs. This issue is explained in Chapter III. Totals do not add due to rounding.

Source: Center on Budget and Policy Priorities, 1990.

equitable fiscal policy is fair to both taxpayers and to specific public constituencies benefiting from public expenditures. In tax policy, economists refer to two kinds of equity—horizontal and vertical. Horizontal equity means that taxpayers who have the same amounts of income should be taxed at the same rate. Vertical equity implies that wealthier people should pay more taxes than poorer people. A related principle is that tax policies should be progressive: taxes increase as income increases. Proportional principles of taxation increase taxes in exact and direct proportion to increases in income. Regressive taxes impose greater burdens on taxpayers least able to pay, or taxes increase and income decreases.[31]

Although traditionally applied to taxes, notions of progressivity, proportionality, and regressivity also have a budgetary counterpart. Fiscal policies that tend to benefit the least needy and deprive the most needy are budgetarily regressive. Generally, Gramm-Rudman-Hollings (GRH) is regressive in its impacts on blacks and Hispanics because it utilizes budget bases that were already retrenched before 1985 as baselines for GRH-mandated cuts and because needs continue to rise as funding levels decline.

Finally, the principle of *elasticity* suggests that the fiscal system be flexible enough to address its revenue and spending needs, regardless of macroeconomic changes in economic conditions. Taxes and spending contribute to the stabilization of the economy as well as to the stability of socioeconomic components of society.

As the *Congressional Black Caucus Quality of Life, Alternative 1991 Budget* and work by organizations such as the Center on Budget Priorities point out,

Table 8
The New EITC Benefit Structure

Tax Year	Family With One Child		Family With Two or More Children		Supplemental Credit For Families with a Child under age one	
	Credit Percentage	Maximum Benefit	Credit Percentage	Maximum Benefit	Credit Percentage	Maximum Benefit
1990	14% of first $6,810	$953	14% of first $6,810	$953	—	—
1991	16.7% of first $7,140	1,192	17.3% of first $7,140	1,235	5% of first $7,440	$357
1992	17.6% of first $7,440	1,309	18.4% of first $7,760	1,369	5% of first $7,760	372
1993	18.5% of first $7,760	1,436	19.5% of first $7,760	1,513	5% of first $7,760	388
1994	23% of first $8,090	1,861	25% of first $8,090	2,023	5% of first $8,090	405

Note: Dollar amounts for 1991 and beyond are based on current Congressional Budget Office estimates of inflation (using the consumer price index). Precise dollar amounts may vary when inflation estimates are revised.

Source: Center on Budget and Policy Priorities, 1990.

when GRH and Tax Reform are considered together, they tend to be fiscally regressive for black and Hispanic households, individuals, and institutions. Strict enforcement of the 1990 deficit reduction provisions, particularly of the EITC objectives, is generally progressive for low-income families and households.

Moreover, in considering the ethics of good fiscal policy, it is also essential to consider the reciprocal relationship between households and institutions. Institutions like charitable organizations; businesses; advocacy organizations; municipal, county, and state governments; trade unions; and others provide essential services to their members and constituencies. Conversely, these institutions are profoundly affected. Similarly, if fiscal policies damage institutions, households suffer.

Consequently, the ethical budget holds as its principal mission not only responsiveness to black economic and political needs in the United States, but also economic and political empowerment. It is aimed at a redistribution of resources that only temporarily charges more affluent members for subsidies so that the less affluent eventually become more affluent. Human capital is as essential as physical capital. And long-term investments in human capital development are perceived as realizing multiple returns to society that will more than pay for themselves.

SUMMARY AND CONCLUSIONS

African Americans are substantially and uniquely dependent upon government. Increasingly, other groups and institutions in America are becoming dependent upon government budgets for their very survival: groups such as farmers, the disabled, immigrants, the homeless, and AIDS victims; and institutions such as state and local governments, lending institutions, transitional foreign governments, and declining manufacturing industries. Consequently, African Americans are competing with an increasingly diverse constellation of budgetary needy while available budget dollars at all levels of government continue to shrink.

The anticipated availability of additional federal budget dollars through "peace dividend" defense budget reductions has been eclipsed by Operation Desert Shield in the Persian Gulf and longer-term uncertainty about the permanency of democratization in Eastern Europe and the Soviet Union. An increasingly expensive banking and savings-and-loan crisis threatens to overwhelm other domestic budgetary and financial needs. Moreover, the economic recession signals greater demand for shrinking federal, state, and local dollars.

The result of these combined developments is a clouded set of budgetary scenarios for African Americans. Equity issues pour from the controversies over the president's veto of civil rights legislation, an Assistant Secretary of Education's thwarted effort to prohibit the award of scholarships to nonwhite students, and exponential increases in the number of young black men killed or wounded in inner-city, drug-related warfare. African-American budgetary dependency has increased as these controversies sweep America. Entire African-American communities dangle on the edges of total economic and social anarchy and instability.

In response, the politics of federal deficit reduction temporarily shut down government and made no effective response to any particular group or institutional need. After a greatly flawed September budget summit, negotiators combined $18 billion in new revenue generation and nearly $23 billion in spending reductions for FY 1991 to generate a $41 billion deficit reduction package.

Major budgetary reductions are scheduled for social entitlement and defense programs. African Americans are inextricably intertwined in both of these spending areas. Reduced entitlements not only erode the value of Food Stamp, AFDC, Medicare, and other entitlement dollars, but are also nonresponsive to increases in need resulting from the economic recession. Moreover, tax provisions, particularly the earned income tax credit, but are generally progressive at the income tax level but generally regressive at the excise tax level. Consequently, the new fiscal package is only partially responsive to the fiscal principles of productivity, equity, and elasticity.

What economic and political strategy implications do these fiscal ethics have for African Americans? How can African Americans favorably influence the establishment of fiscal priorities at the federal, state, and local levels of government?

First, the struggle to attain equity and financial choice for blacks, Hispanics, women, and the poor should escalate. Majority Americans have as great a stake in the outcome of the moral struggle as do those that need. The ultimate financial and moral beneficiaries of this struggle are the majority businesses, educational institutions, and public agencies, because the poor buy from them.

Second, African Americans should increasingly monitor local, state, and federal fiscal activity, particularly given the combined budget reduction and tax provisions of the 1990 deficit reduction statute. Priority areas for monitoring include:

(a) Assess spending and taxing policies, proposals, and plans for the current and potential impacts they may have on the needy;

(b) Analyze procurement and contracting practices to determine whether, and to what extent, small, minority, and women-owned business utilization plans are in place; and

(c) Where privatization occurs or is proposed, ensure transitional plans contain mandates for private owners to continue inclusion of the needy.

Third, expanded use of formal policy and impact assessments should be used by African-American organizations to advance the need of the poor in legislative hearings, public rule-making, and regulatory processes and judicial proceedings.

All of these points underscore the need for African-American policy advocates to acquire, utilize, and work carefully with experts. Policy expertise comes from many disciplines and is the major weapon of interests whose ethical preferences prevail in policy. The new fiscal imperatives are therefore best met by a new and more effective use of expertise.

POLICY RECOMMENDATIONS

Given the budgetary constraints now experienced by the federal, state, and local governments and the general malaise and morass of problems facing lending institutions, African Americans risk, at best, fiscal indifference. Traditional policy approaches to the resolution of obstinate socioeconomic and institutional problems in African-American communities will be largely ignored by fiscal decision-makers without visible financial and socioeconomic paybacks to the nation. The budgetary emphasis on cost-benefit analysis, self-financing, and revenue-generating policy options leaves little room for expansion of income transfer or subsidy policies.

Consequently, several major recommendations are offered. First, maximal policy coordination and integration is imperative. Too much of the federal dollar is wasted by the failure to interrelate anti-drug and education, education and child/family support, child-family support to employment, employment to housing, housing to transportation, and other existing programs. Although too frequently characterized as a service-delivery problem, policy coordination is an inherent problem in policy design that results in billions of dollars being wasted. Given the close association of African-American communities with many federal programs, blacks are often blamed for what are essentially federal budget and bureaucratic decisions.

Second, better intergovernmental fiscal coordination is essential. Given the declining outlays of federal support to state and local governments coincident with sharp increases in the number of African-American state and local elected officials, better coordination of federal, state, and local roles would greatly enhance limited fiscal resources.

Third, human capital-oriented fiscal policies are essential. Given the increasing infrastructural and environmental needs of American cities, the adverse impact of these needs on the economic competitiveness of America, and the increasingly large and socially disconnected inner-city labor pools evident in major U.S. cities, an *Urban Marshall Plan* should be initiated immediately by Congress and the White House. Just as was the case of the original Marshall Plan following World War II (a $13 billion investment in the rebuilding and recovery of ravaged European cities and industries), U.S. cities require such an investment to rebuild and reconstruct entire urban communities; to build or maintain roads, bridges, tunnels, water systems and other infrastructures; and to abate continued damage to urban, rural, and wilderness areas. An Urban Marshall Plan would utilize and cultivate the human resources and small and minority business development in African-American communities at all levels to build and rebuild America. Such a revitalization plan would stimulate short-term and contribute to longer-term economic growth, and enhanced growth in the gross national product (GNP) will make a significant and continuous contribution to deficit reduction. Seed funding of an Urban Marshall Plan would come from federal asset sales, reclamation of government-owned houses and buildings, and sales of assets from failed or failing lending institutions. An Urban Marshall Plan implemented in the African-American community would enrich, enliven, and enhance African Americans who, in turn, would enrich, enliven, and enhance America.

Education Strategies for the '90s

Floretta Dukes McKenzie, Ph.D.
with
Patricia Evans

HISTORICAL AND CONTEXTUAL ANTECEDENTS OF THE AMERICAN EDUCATIONAL DILEMMA

American civilization has reached a period of profound spiritual crisis coupled with a serious economic quandary facing many African Americans and other minority group members. The recessionary spiral of dwindling resources, job layoffs, and escalating prices of consumer goods accompanies a climate where violence is extolled, the rich transgressors of our laws receive token or no sentences, and the drug market has been tailor-made for amassing amazing profits at all levels of the supply and demand chain. Such problems are not new to American civilization, but the virulence of the current outbreak seems particularly ominous for the future of young black persons. Systemic problems that we are confronting today display their intensity and severity generally in the lives of those citizens with the least amount of power to avoid those problems. Black children, especially those from the lower middle class and underclass, are victims of all that has gone wrong with our country. Without a conscientious, systematic mobilization of community supports for these children's needs, a whole generation of young black persons will not survive with the skills necessary in the 21st century. African-American leaders must set the stage for setting "clear national, state, city, community, and personal goals for child. . .development, and invest whatever leadership, commitment, time, money, and sustained effort that are needed to achieve them."[1]

Wide disparities in academic achievement exist between African-American children and their white, or Anglo-American, counterparts; African-American children in greater proportion face the more distressing issues of homelessness, drug abuse and its effects, teen pregnancy, poor health, and crime. The shortage of staff, shrinking pool of qualified black teachers, decaying urban infrastructures, and abandonment of black and minority children to ill-maintained, antiquated, substandard, or unrepaired school facilities without basic instructional materials are not part of the particular educational dilemmas facing more affluent or Anglo-American children.[2]

This litany of problems in urban and suburban schools serving low-income minority children schools is frequently repeated and unfortunately has not changed over the last few decades: it includes illiteracy, teenage pregnancies, and fragmented home situations. The cataclysmic "crack" epidemic, coupled with the availability of an alarming arsenal of automatic weaponry, its sensually numbing and economically detrimental effect upon all who have the requisite cash to purchase, would have been a crushing new obstacle for our communities, even if the logistical aspects of the cocaine distribution system had not targeted young minority males as the most profitable and legally defensible [reprehensible] modus operandi.

"Between 1979 and 1988 the proportion of American children living in poverty grew by 23 percent. One in five American children lives in poverty."[3] "One half million children drop out of school in the United States each year (author emphasis). Poor teenagers are three times more likely than other teens to drop out and are four times more likely to have below-average basic skills."[4] Thirty percent of the ninth graders in America fail to complete high school.[5] School failures are not just an African-American dilemma: mathematic achievement of American eighth grade students was lower than Japan, Hungary, and England, and eight other countries.[6]

That children are the victims of this societal decline is not news. Statistics on child welfare and educational attainment have demonstrated for decades the effect of systemic problems on the attainment of low-income and minority children. These problems are striking African-American children in disproportionate numbers. The chance of being poor is four in nine for African-American children and one in two for children raised by a single parent.[7] The children who inhabit the inner cities of America are primarily black and poor; it is these children who are most in jeopardy of disenfranchisement from the American dream of a quality education and subsequent upward mobility. The inner-city child is most probably a child of a child of a child.[8] Many African-American and other minority group single-parent families are trapped in a desolating cycle of developmental, educational, and socioeconomic impairment as a result of children raising children.

But the socioeconomic disasters of the late eighties and early nineties are influencing the lives of all low-income children, not just African American, but also Hispanic, Native American, and Caucasian. These problems affect those children without the safety nets of earlier generations. Extended families and greater community cohesiveness prevailed throughout this country, including urban Black America, until recently. The rising wave of violence in many inner cities threatens to blanket community spirit with fear. That stray bullets and street robberies could destroy the connections among urban families is a major obstacle to fostering resurgences of community vigor.

The structural inequalities of the American economic system are prison walls for young people without marketable skills and, minimally, a high school diploma. "The earnings of men younger than 30 have dropped sharply since 1973. When your men make very low wages, young couples are far less likely to get married. Since 1973 young men's marriage rates have declined by one third, *and the proportion of births that were out of wedlock doubled* (author emphasis)."[9] Single-parent households are on a dramatic upswing in all age and ethnic groups. While there have always been many single-parent households, what has changed is that there are less extended familial ties that help mitigate against the missing parent as well as the daily stresses and economic vagaries of raising children alone.

Research supports what common experience has shown us; that is many African-American families are "consanguineal" (built around "blood relatives")[10] as opposed to "conjugal" (built around the marital pair). Niara Sudarkasa points out that while conjugality is not unimportant in African families, consanguineal kin groups have traditionally formed the nucleus of continuity and the economic focal point. Even during slavery such relations continued. Traditional African principles underlying family relations are *"respect, restraint, responsibility, and reciprocity."*[11] Furthermore, such extended familial groups *"did not originate in America in response to the adverse socioeconomic and political circumstances in which blacks found themselves. . .,*[but rather] the groups originated in Africa."[12] Racist ideology often has interpreted black family patterns based on deficit or other models that are not in any informed relationship to the reality of the people that are being described. The African-American extended family pattern has been somewhat shifted from its natural course by contemporary events; cultural differences from the majority American family practice should no longer serve as a barrier to revitalizing this important and creative African-American institution.

As our nation's schools wrestle with these issues, educators are forced to come to the conclusion that this time is like no other in terms of addressing such severe impediments to educational access and success. Conscientious educational leaders, especially African-American, Native American, and Hispanic educational leaders, will have to assume tiring legal and policy struggles at the state and federal levels. Educators with minority group concerns will have to come together and be of many minds and one heart. They must assure that the values advocated in our schools are the values we wish to transmit, rather than the historically biased, albeit acceptable as "core Western culture," Calvinistic, and Eurocentric messages that the far right and well-meaning conservatives have injected into every major textbook in the country and into every course of study required for graduation credits or college acceptance.

Our teachers in the inner cities have substantially fewer financial resources and face greater levels of students' needs; they must endure the shadowy climate of violence that pervades American cities in these most recent years, after a decade of supply-side economics.

Our children are resilient, however. Educators' assertions that any child can learn is not outdated. The data show that we have not reached all of the children; but, a cadre of good teachers can reach all of the children. In order to address students' needs, things will have to change from business as usual within school bureaucracies; schools will have to garner all the support they can *in their communities.*

Based on our knowledge of how people learn about their world and our research on children's behavior in school, the entire community can begin to examine how best to address the serious problems which are before us. Ethnicity in a multicultural society is a very potent force in our children's educational process. It is important at this point to discuss aspects of this critical issue for our children's successful education and participation in the socioeconomic life of America.

MISEDUCATION IN BLACK AMERICA

Young black males: a special dilemma?

In recent months, the newspapers and electronic media have been filled with reports about newer strategies to address the special problems of young black men and boys. Jawanza Kunjufu's companion volumes on the "conspiracy to destroy Black boys"[13] are widely cited in the lay community. He reminds us that "it is considerably easier to educate, which is a one-step process, than it is to re-educate, which is a two-step process."[14] His data are substantiated by work of African-American anthropologists who have observed our schools and by educational and developmental psychologists who generally concur that different cultural groups and the two genders may have differing learning styles.

Speaking of "black boys," Kunjufu asserts that "primary divisions sing and recite louder and seem much happier than the intermediate and upper [elementary] divisions,"[15] where the fourth grade and older boys begin to "tune out." Most African-American educators and parents can identify with his observation that there is a downward spiral in the achievement of black boys beginning around third grade.[16] School-tolerated or encouraged behaviors are "those that are more natural for girls"[17]—a finding corroborated by developmental psychology assessments and ethnographic analyses of educational settings. Kunjufu asserts that [African-American] "Male seasoning" has become a dehumanization process designed to create man "with no feelings and compassion for. . .children, women, or brothers."[18]

Hawkins' 1986 study of the variation in imprisonment rates among black and white males documents some facts already known to most African Americans— the black rate of imprisonment. In one southern state, when population differences are accounted for statistically, the number of black men incarcerated was 4.5 times that of whites. His data further show that the differences are even more dramatic in other parts of the country: 10.7 in Connecticut, 12.7 in Massachusetts and Maryland, 13 in New Jersey, 15 in Illinois, 13 in Michigan, and eight in California.

This overrepresentation of black males in our criminal justice system is well known to black Americans, and it does help to give cause to ponder Kunjufu's only slightly paranoid assertion.[19]

OVERCOMING RACISM: FOSTERING A HOLISTIC EDUCATION AND MULTICULTURAL UNDERSTANDING

The undereducation of black children does not exist in a void: the school is not an isolated social institution. "The crisis in education is also a crisis in democratic citizenship."[20] The crisis in education is also a crisis in each community across the vast expanse of America, including Puerto Rico. The crisis in education is also a crisis in each family, especially in the African-American family where none escapes some unhappy connection with the powers that be.

The black community must assure that "the transformations taking place in the American economy and the proposals for [national] school reform that promote a narrow view of 'excellence' devoid of social justice concerns for black youth and their families" are not foisted upon urban schools.

> If proposals for core curricula or a national curriculum are adopted, these reforms would be implemented without input from the black community, it is clearly in danger of being locked out of the new economic arrangements that will structure U.S. society well into the 21st century. We must respond forcefully to the myopic perceptions that perpetuate the black underclass.[21]

Indeed, any curricular changes will affect not just an underclass, but *most black families,* perhaps excluding the handful of extremely rich who can alleviate their own families' potentially malevolent experiences with the wider social system.

While it is neither prudent nor wise to reject any movement towards a national curriculum, it is most important for black Americans to assure that African-American history and other contributions of Africa to America's progress not be given short shrift.

> The hard fact is that what we call "world history," in most cases, is only the history of Europe and its relationship to non-European people. The Western [European and European-American] academic community, in general, is not yet willing to acknowledge that the world did not wait in darkness for Europeans to bring the light. The history of Africa [and African "civilization"] was already old when Europe was born.[22]

Frances Fitzgerald's important work on the American textbook, *America Revised,* clearly articulates curriculum and text revisions with national policy and current ideas in the dominant cultural milieu, which may or may not give adequate coverage to minority concerns. In fact, she points out the difficulty in adequately portraying the Native American's perspective in any authorized majority culture text since the world views of each group are almost diametrically opposed.

> Current texts represent the United States as a multiracial society to the extent that they include some materials on all the large racial and ethnic groups, and that their photographs show people of all colors. . .and suggest that even white Americans come from different ethnic backgrounds. . . .[T]he texts also describe certain of the 'problems' that minorities have faced in the United

States.... But it's on the subject of these 'problems' that the texts are still confused. They have succeeded in including all groups, but they have not succeeded in treating them all equally. There is, for instance, a remarkable disparity between their treatment of European ethnic groups and their treatment of all other ethnic minorities.[23]

The press for cultural pluralism in schools is particularly critical for African Americans and a subject that requires not a little thought. The press to substituting Afrocentric education for Eurocentric education will result in the same distortions that the biased Eurocentric focus of American education has foisted upon so many for so many generations. Reparations for the past cannot be extracted through fallacious actions. Only a holistic, richly-developed multicultural approach to the issue of humankind will allow the flexibility to maintain an African focus where such is appropriate. The necessity of assuming a meaningful incorporation of the African-American and other voices into the classrooms all over America must be the goal, without being trapped into performing an oppositional action and media sideshow, and without recognizing the consequences for students if they are again unnaturally hampered by rigid, culturally prescribed ethnic and racial representations.

STRUCTURAL IMPEDIMENTS

America's social structures can be characterized by the pervasive institutional racism of the "longue duree."[24] The late renowned anthropologist, St. Clair Drake, described institutional racism as "situations where, although *there may not be deliberate intent to act in an unfavorable, discriminatory fashion* [emphasis added], the objective result of various actions is reinforcement of subordination and control over a racial group and an inequitable distribution of power and prestige."[25] Drake also discussed the notion of *metaracism,* which he ascribes to South African, Bantu scholar psychiatrist, Noel Chabani Manganyi: "with the disappearance of these structures [social political institutions existing to support racism and racist behavior], the metaracist, sleeker in his ways, . . . may very well continue to be afflicted with unconscious racist fantasies that have survived the changes in manifest social organization."[26,27] Drake's compelling central premise is that transcultural color symbolism and preference differences *"affect social interaction, social structure, and psychological states," that the designation of some people as black relegates them to "an inferior position in socioeconomic hierarchies," thereby having a profound affect on both individuals and groups.*[28]

Cognitive science and anthropological studies of cultural models in language and thought underscore that dominant cultural models are presupposed or taken-for-granted views of the world "that are widely shared (although not necessarily to the exclusion of other, alternative models) by the members of a society and play an enormous role in their understanding of that world and their behavior in it."[29] It is important to note that a critical mental task to decoding the world is examining multiple models, often simultaneously. Most minority group members are already adept at this, as they hold in mind the dominant cultural model and their own cultural model; the task often requires concurrent and discordant nonverbal and verbal behavior. For example, "A waiter bent on getting a good tip, for instance, might be attempting to provide customers with swift, faultless service, silently anticipating their requests before these can be voiced, while at the same time keeping up a line of niceties and flattery."[30]

Clearly, an ideology of social hierarchy is etched in American society, the implications of which cannot be ignored or dismissed in that such an ideology justifies the nearly birth-ascribed nature of structural inequality[31] for the majority of African Americans. This ideological component pervades each public institution in this country and can only be changed through sustained insistence on a more holistic world view at the core of our educational values.

Child development research often has overlooked the historical, social, cultural, and structural factors influencing schools and their wider community.[32] Luckily, there is an emerging body of literature from recent research that can cut through the haze of Anglo-American hegemony to get at the real questions of rearing and educating millions of minority children across all of African-, Hispanic-, Asian-, Native-, and Anglo-America. It should be noted that when "as a group, children. . .experience disproportionate school failure *despite individual ability*,"[33] there are cultural and structural impediments that must be addressed and further, "prevailing intervention strategies seek to adapt these children to school environments that themselves reinforce structural inequality."[34] Therefore, in order to assure more effective education, approaches toward school reform cannot ignore cultural, social, and structural aspects of the greater community.

Finally, Piaget views the transmission of culture as an important mission of schools: "regarding the transmission of collective values, it becomes ever more obvious that the various activities of man form an indissoluble whole. . . . It must bring the concept to an idea of the history of civilization in the widest sense of the term, and not only pertaining to the political and military events of history (rather the causes of related collective events than the consequences thereof). . .this 'general culture' has much to gain by re-entrenching itself in reality and by being based on interaction between various aspects of social living; in short, by discovering and studying man such as he is and has always been, and *not only as scholarly tradition has taught that he was*"(emphasis added).[35] Piaget's statement, which is part of his commentary on the United Nations' 1948 declaration of the right to education, undergirds the notion of a multicultural or holistic approach to education in a pluralistic society such as the United States.

The United Nations has affirmed, Piaget asserts, the basic human right to an ethical and intellectual education that in turn implies "more than a right to acquire a knowledge or to listen and more than an obligation to obey: it is a question of a right to forge certain precious spiritual tools in everyone, which requires a specific social environment, not made exclusively of submissiveness."[36] Education should enable the student to develop "normally, in accord with all the potential he possesses"; Piaget posits a parallel obligation for society to transform individual potential "into useful and effective fulfillment."[37] But in order to accomplish this fulfilling educational experience, only a holistic, multicultural, internationally focused education will suffice.

It has become clear that

> [an] international education cannot be restricted to adding one more course to the ordinary courses that will simply bear on present . . . institutions or even on the ideal that they represent and defend. First of all, it is the entire teaching that must become international, not only history, geography, and living languages, but also literature and science, where the common efforts of the whole human race, as well as the role of social and technical conflicts, are too often neglected.[38]

OUR CHILDREN

Recent research on black children and stress gives cause for encouragement, given the seeming weight of the Eurocentric bias in American life. Margaret Beale Spencer's research found that,

> With increased awareness of the world around them, . . . children come to understand the personal intricacies of their racial identity. When they are about seven years old, black children begin to perceive a discrepancy between the devalued status of blacks and their own sense of self-worth. . . . Black children are distracted from studying by their attempts to solve the disturbing issue of racial identity. . . . Just as strong gender identity provides children with a defined sense of themselves, as [Eric] Erikson found, so strong racial identity proves to be a positive force for black children during their critical grade-school years: it counterbalances the stress they naturally live with as minorities in the United States.[39]

Preschool-age children already understand the dominant cultural and aesthetic hegemony, but their differences from it generally do not disturb them at that point. Adolescent children get another jolt when the structural limitations of a supply-side capitalist state economy with rampant multinational free enterprise makes its regional and structural limitations apparent.

Low-income minority children reach our schools in a state of distress from a psychological and developmental perspective. Spencer's research performed on black school children in Atlanta (adolescents, preschool, and school-age children) [to measure the aftermath of the "extraordinary tension in that city" during the time when the Atlanta "serial murders" occurred] showed less impact than a single traumatic effect of a single community disaster [where a busload of white schoolchildren was kidnapped]. The urban black children showed more resilience and very few other behavioral changes.[40, 41] The researcher concluded that, by growing up in environments in which they were already "'at risk,' the Atlanta children, . . . had learned to handle fear" and further, "black children showed some resilience to additional stress." However, Spencer placed an important caveat: "relative to the *academic performance* of many minority group children, one must also question the school-related costs of psychological adaptation responses to chronic status-related stress."[42]

Dr. James Comer's work at Yale has examined this issue from an organizational perspective. He also contends that black families have a great deal of stress: "A disproportionate number of black families experience above-average economic and social stresses."[43] His data substantiate a growing body of research; he finds that

> Many kindergarten-aged children do compensate for their underdevelopment; they respond to academic teaching and make significant progress. By the third grade, the nature of learning becomes more abstract and underdevelopment along the intellectual pathway again created a significant learning problem. At the same time such children develop a capacity to place themselves in the social scheme of things—different from other children, school people, better-off neighbors. . . . The combination of academic underdevelopment and a sense of not belonging can cause a number of children to lose their interest in meeting the school task. But again, many respond to teaching and catch up, only to turn away again as apparent social and economic opportunity limitations outside of school begin to become apparent at around 15 or 16 years of age.[44]

STRATEGIES FOR CHANGE: RANGE OF SUGGESTIONS FROM PROFESSIONAL EDUCATORS TO GRASSROOTS COMMUNITY SPOKESMEN

Dr. James Comer has devised and implemented a program in several cities to address the problems of low-income African-American youth. His plan includes a four-pronged intervention: school and other support personnel form teams that address issues about management, mental health problems, and curricular and staff development. Parental involvement includes strategies to support a positive climate in the school, training parents about school expectations, and general school activities.[45]

Like the research of Baratz and Baratz two decades earlier and Ron Edmonds over 10 years ago,[46] Comer asserts that "it is clear. . .that low-income children or children from families under social, economic, and racial stress conditions can learn at an acceptable level" and that "school staff must understand child development, be able to respond to underdevelopment, and support and advance adequate development."[47]

Planning for the meshing of the various programs and services must be systematic to address the complexity of problems facing the schools today rather than merely relying on the "natural way" that schools operated in the past. All levels of the school community must be incorporated into a cohesive educational system.

The Committee on Policy for Racial Justice has recommendations for "progressive educational reform"—involving black parents in the educational process, with schools welcoming parental participation; striving to make schools less impersonal; developing closer ties between school and social services agencies; recruiting more black teachers; developing sensitive and precise testing procedures for the diagnosis of students' abilities and needs; abandoning rigid systems of tracking and ability groups; expanding the curriculum to reflect the lives and interests of black and other minority children; and providing adequate funding for Head Start and Chapter 1. The frame of reference for these changes in public educational strategies is that effective education must lead to effective participation in the economy. *All segments of the black community must assume a greater responsibility for the education of black youth;* and the improvement of public education must be the principal objective of the black community in the next decade.[48] Such an ambitious program of improving our educational system is not impossible. What seems to underlie the entire thrust of suggestions for school reform are two critical aspects: curricular reforms to reflect the multicultural nature of American society and the involvement of parents and community in school programs.

The solution is to "get involved...; every parent, child care worker, educator, ...and citizen concerned about helping children should know what investments in children are needed."[49]

MORAL VACUUM: THE AMERICAN DILEMMA

All children need educational settings that can build their self-esteem, identify and develop their natural talents, instill pride, and convey high expectations about academic performance and career options. Our children have been born into an age of conspicuous consumption; they are indeed "living in a material world." Nearly each one of us has indulged ourselves with the myriad of consumer goods, the disposables that litter our planet. Is it any wonder that our children are mimicking such values? Our participation in this consumerism leads to urban teenage male violence over $300 leather jackets and $150 superstar athletic shoes. Kunjufu's *Countering the Conspiracy to Destroy Black Boys, Vol. II,* articulates a community view about parental involvement and modeling different value systems. He underscores a moral dilemma in our American dream: "Parents [are] being annoyed at their children for not possessing drive and enthusiasm despite being given everything. [Yet common sense tells us that] parents who give everything...do not help their children...that is, the parents] who buy their sons [or daughters] expensive gym shoes, stereos, and leather bags."[50] Teachers and educators have long recognized the destructive nature of rampant consumerism in low-income communities.

Projections are that by the year 2000, only five percent of the teachers in public schools will be black; how ironic is such a decline in minority teachers at a time when minority student enrollment will be continuing to increase, and without drastic turnabouts, academic achievement of black and other minority students may still fall far short of parity with their white classmates. The devastating shortage of qualified minority teachers will demonstrate itself most chillingly in our inability to fill the affective needs of young black students and to provide the types of role models that low-income students from dysfunctional families desperately need. The dominant culture's failure to accede to legitimate demands for culturally relevant materials within a context of a multicultural framework will prove a disaster. Howard Zinn, a renowned historian, on a recent television appearance, commented that no history is completely objective. Children are perceptive commentators on what they perceive as inaccuracies in school accounts of historical and cultural events. We cannot continue to portray Europe as the sole wellspring of American life, nor can we educate children without regard for the skills that they require for earning a living.

Equally important is the necessity of attracting men into the teaching profession, especially black male teachers, in settings where there are boys with single-parent families and low income. We must help provide male role models for African-American youth in single-family, female-headed households. This is not an ascription of blame, but rather a pragmatic strategy to address the particularly insidious psychological stress of American existence on African-American boys and girls and the psychopathological concomitants to contemporary socioeconomic realities of ethnic and racial uneasiness. There must be more and varied adult male role models brought into our schools and special attention accorded to the male socialization process. Issues of gender differences should not be ignored nor allowed to become embroiled in battles staged about Anglo-American cultural hegemony and social structure.

The changing demographics of American culture are reflected first in the black community, but are increasing in other segments of the greater community. There are more young, single parents with inadequate incomes rearing children; there is less extended family nearby and accessible when children need the help. Kunjufu also suggests that educators, parents, and communities make every effort to reduce "street time." "Children cannot raise themselves, and parents should not allow television or the streets to try."[51] Single parents cannot assume the entire burden for raising their children; the experience is too fraught with anxiety and tension for children and parent, which leads to family stress and conflict. Social networks and community support must be mobilized for both parents and children. Support networks must be developed so that overstressed parents, especially single parents, can enroll their child in organized and adequately supervised community-based activities such as soccer, gymnastics, homework and academic centers, carpentry, and musical groups. These will foster the redevelopment of communities to support the activities of the schools.

City and state governments will have to continue to offer and coordinate programs and services for young people. But they, too, must be held to higher standards. Community strategies that cannot succeed, such as repressive police measures, should be countered with mobilization efforts to provide constructive after-school activities and family supports. Problematic issues in the national educational arena should be confronted directly.

W.E.B. Du Bois's words from over a half-century ago are still as true today as they were then—"The *community* must be able to take hold of its individuals and give them such a social heritage, such present social teachings, and such compelling social customs as will force them along the lines of progress, and not into the great forests of death."[52] Human "growth must be led; it must be guided by ideals. . . [Perhaps the] ideal of *poverty*. . .we cannot all be wealthy. . .a simple healthy life on limited income is the only responsible ideal of civilized folk. . .the ideal of work—not idleness, not dawdling, but hard continuous effort at something worth doing, by a man supremely interested in doing it, who knows how it ought to be done and is willing to take infinite pains doing it."[53] These are the spiritual messages that must be shared within the larger educational community to address the inadequacies of the chilling American socioeconomic environment.

Teenagers must be especially bombarded with positive messages to keep their attention sparked and to prepare them for the very complex and unfair world of work that they will enter. They must be presented with the opportunity to forge several options for themselves that they can continue to develop through hard work after public schooling is over. A number of communities has experimented with mentor programs and corporate linkages with schools. These types of programs can provide the adult role modeling as well as the concrete assistance that so many young people need. Educational and community leaders must address the parallel issues of postsecondary vocational and higher education.

PARENTAL AND COMMUNITY INVOLVEMENT: STRATEGIES THAT WORK

Parental involvement is so critical to supporting the activities of the school. We know that those parents who get involved and contribute in a tangible way to their children's academic and social development absolutely increase their children's chances for success in school. Piaget states that the "synthesis between the family and the school"[54] is crucial to real improvement of schools through fostering mutual informational exchanges beneficial to the child as well as serving as the potential source of a transformed pedagogy.

Studies repeatedly tell us characteristics of families that support the development of reading and writing skills in children from low-income homes":

> 1. Literacy is part of the social world in which the children live. 2. Due to the flexibility of the social arrangements, the children encounter print in various situations with family members and friends. 3. The parents expect the children

to succeed. Failure is not an option. 4. There is a strong determination on the part of the parent(s) to do everything they can to ensure that the children received a good education. 5. The parents are knowledgeable about school practices and procedures and they can talk about the ways in which their children are being taught to read and write in school. 6. Homework is an integral part of everyday life.[55]

Schools must work with parents to help them help their children. Modeling behavior and providing a cogent "cultural model, whether invoked to persuade another or to order one's own inner experience, motivates behavior."[56] Parents want to know specific strategies or approaches they can use with their children. Teachers must sometimes patiently show parents what they already know that can help their own children. Wealthier and middle-class parents regularly consult with schools, oftentimes for particular strategies to complement classroom or other activities. Many parents who are "highly literate" are not "educated" in the traditional sense and may feel embarrassed about seeking out such direct guidance in terms of home-based activities. Schools must help the parents by welcoming them and initiating contacts that are not merely threatening incursions from governmental agents in times of trouble.

What are the indicators of successful community strategies? They are found in many cities and communities that grapple with global issues of economic changes and employment, of poverty engendered by shifting economic practices, poverty, and homelessness both at home and outside of the United States, utilizing technology for positive purposes and influences on family and community systems. Therefore, for future directions, it is imperative to forge our African-American communities into child-focused environments, studying what has been successful in similar circumstances, and to assume a prominent national advocacy role in terms of federal and state educational legislation and policy.

School improvement strategies require the mobilization of external resources as well as the actual aspects of school system philosophy, management, curriculum, and services.[57] But experts point out that "public support cannot be maintained for long if nothing changes."[58] We know that a good principal can make a school come to life if conditions are fortunate; only strong educational leadership can mobilize the necessary ingredients for assuring a successful community mobilization to improve its schools.

Experience around the country indicates that the superintendent of schools "is the essential link between schools and community,"[59] playing a "broad and demanding role as a political leader and coalition maker"; good superintendents assure continuity by "imbuing younger staff with the principles of their strategy and otherwise prepare for succession."[60] They increase the amount and flow of information within the system as well as to the public, maintain close linkages with principals and schools, and model the behavior of their top assistants through exemplary behavior.[61]

Mobilization activities for communities in support of improved public educational services should involve parents, community leaders, community doers, talented resourceful people, organizational affiliates, grassroots people who are often "acted upon," youth leaders, school personnel, persons employed or operating businesses in the community, church leaders, and corporate leaders. Resources should be obtained from each group in consonance with its ability to contribute; for example, churches might provide space, corporations might donate equipment, colleges might provide consultants, and community members might provide child care for parents attending meetings.[62] Community groups must determine for themselves which are the critical priorities within their region.

The Rand Corporation's study of six cities' community mobilization illustrated clearly how the interaction of school, business, and civic leaders are pivotal in rekindling interest and enthusiasm for school reform.[63] Success in community mobilization requires certain attributes: *consensus* on a general mission, at least one staff member, clearly stated goals, fund-raising machinery, issue-research capability, a public dissemination program, skillful negotiators, and monitoring of governmental and educational institutional programs.

The business and community leadership are critical components toward school improvement; they "possess the funds, technical resources, staff, and motivation that, properly focused, can make a major difference in the schools."[64] The business community can be approached by a superintendent through capitalizing on its awareness of the importance of a qualified labor force as well as appealing to its community responsibility to contribute to the general quality of life in a particular city or area.

Editor's Note: Rochester, New York, is an excellent case in point of this public-private partnership that Dr. MacKenzie is referring to here. See David Wirschem's "Community Mobilization for Education in Rochester, New York: A Case Study," in the Appendices section of this book.

NATIONAL STRATEGY

Just as approaches to community mobilization are necessary, there needs to be continued vigilance at the national level that assures advocacy for urban educational resources and increased public awareness of the social, economic, political, and spiritual health of the United States, especially as it impacts upon children and education. This includes vigilance of the legislative process as well as the ability to become involved in any national discussions of curriculum standardization to assure that the needs of all minority children are met. Additionally, it means developing electronic databases and information clearinghouses for institutions as well as funding researchers, setting forth a minority research agenda, facilitating a researcher network for persons involved in minority and urban educational research projects, and monitoring research that helps document African-American and other minority needs in areas related to education. Finally, it means that national forums will have to be convened periodically to discuss pertinent issues, and speakers will have to become available to disseminate information about minority and urban educational concerns, as well as the identification of a cadre of recognized experts who can provide a national voice for promoting African-American interests in educational issues and proposed reforms. There needs to be a forum immediately on the implications of, and strategies to change, the vanishing African-American presence in postsecondary educational institutions.

Our challenge is the future of our children and the health of our communities and the entire nation. We must "recognize that America's ideals, future, and fate are as inextricably intertwined with the fate of its poor and nonwhite children as with its privileged and white ones. We must love our children more than we fear each other."[65]

Developing Untapped Talent:
A National Call
For African-American Technologists

Warren F. Miller, Jr., Ph.D.

INTRODUCTION

As we enter the last decade of the millennium, statistical indices indicate that Black America continues to lag behind the country as a whole in several very key aspects. The legacy of racism remains alive and persists despite the struggles of many to eradicate it. The National Urban League's Racial Parity Index (RPI), which attempts to compare the status of the African-American community with that of the white community with respect to various measures, is one convenient way to express this inequality.[1] With an RPI of 100 indicating full parity, in 1989 the index stood at 47, a drop from 51.2 in 1967. The League extensively analyzed the time spans required to reach parity in various categories, assuming no change in prevailing trends. For example, the estimates were that 54 years are required to reach parity in executive and managerial jobs, 169 years in poverty rates, and 73 years in average income for male adults.

As discouraging as these numbers are, there appears to be one important area where the gap may be narrowing, at least at a comparatively more reasonable rate. Parity in high school graduation rates could be reached in 16 years. This estimate implies that there might be some hope that college and university attendance and completion rates correspondingly could be improved in the reasonably near term. Following this line of reasoning, a higher rate of university completion could eventually eliminate the gaps in jobs, income, and poverty rates. A major focus of this article is the education gap, specifically in the quantitative subjects, and the relationships between this gap and the hope for major improvements in the economic life of Black America as well as the country as a whole.

The quantitative disciplines (e.g., mathematics, science, and engineering) involve skills needed to develop new technologies for industrial applications and consumer consumption. New jobs added in the United States will increasingly be in the high technology-related areas,[2] putting a premium on mathematics and science education. If the U.S. is to retain its economic position in comparison to other countries in an increasingly economically competitive world, a key ingredient will be educating its people in the quantitative subjects. What does the future hold for the supply of quantitatively skilled workers? How are African Americans doing in quantitative areas, and what are their prospects for the future? What actions are being taken or need to be initiated to strengthen black participation in science and engineering? Issues emerging from these questions and other related ones provide the focus for this article. For the sake of specificity, the focus is on engineering, because of its more direct relationship to new technology development and economic competitiveness. Remember, however, that the roots of engineering are in the general quantitative subjects of science and mathematics.

Before proceeding, it is important to note that articles arguing for increased black involvement in area X or field Y abound. An attempt is made here to argue convincingly that engineering is an area of fundamental importance, since long-term economic survival of the country and, specifically, of the African-American community, is directly linked to the availability of a large, technically trained work force.

BLACKS IN TECHNOLOGY: PAST AND PRESENT

Some of the historical black heroes of science are well known to the broader community, including botanist George Washington Carver, mathematician Benjamin Banneker, and chemist Percy Julian.[3] The contributions of these researchers and educators are even more remarkable considering the interactive way in which natural science research is usually carried out. Typically, scientists conducting research addressing similar issues stay in close communication, frequently attending the same key technical conferences. During the periods in which the above-mentioned black scientists and others like them worked, the mores of the times disallowed their participation in these interactive circles to any appreciable extent. Yet, working virtually alone, they left unforgettable marks on the history of science.

Lesser known are the past black giants of technology—the early-day inventors and the predecessors of today's black engineers. These include Jan Matzeliger, who invented the shoe-lasting machine; Elijah McCoy, who developed the first successful approach to automatic lubrication (the expression "the Real McCoy" referred to the high quality of McCoy's machines); and Garrett Morgan, who invented the traffic light signal as well as the gas mask.[4]

A particular testimony to the greatness of the human spirit was Granville T. Woods (1856-1910). Born in Columbus, Ohio, Woods was fortunate enough at an early age to be selected apprentice in a machine shop that repaired railroad equipment. Almost immediately, he became fascinated with electricity and studied every book and article on the subject he could find. Over the first three decades of his life, he frequently moved to cities that offered a possibility of employment and further technical training. Yet racial prejudice frustrated any significant advancement he could make within the engineering community. In 1884, virtually out of frustration, he opened his own shop in Cincinnati. From the very beginning, the Woods Electric Company made a major impact. His irst patent was received early that year for a steam boiler furnace. His subsequent inventions included an improved telephone, a railway telegraph to allow communication between moving trains and a fixed station, railway braking devices, and a railway safety system to prevent train collisions. According to the January 14, 1886, issue of the *American Catholic Tribune,* "Granville T. Woods, he greatest colored inventor in the history of the race, and equal, if not superior, o any inventor in the country, is destined to revolutionize the mode of street ar transit."[5] And revolutionize it he did!

The number of black inventors of the past is not large; on the other hand, t is amazing that there are any examples at all, given the obstacles they faced when attempting the classic routes available to the larger, majority community. For the white budding inventor at the turn of this century, it was not unusual or him to be exposed to technology through tinkering with machinery in his father's garage or barn. His teachers with scientific training and experience would encourage him in the classroom. In many cases, a relative would be technically oriented. An apprentice position often was available for this up-and-coming engineer.

In contrast, in the black community, technical role models were virtually nonexistent. Opportunities to tinker with equipment were indeed scarce. Engineering positions were basically absent. This bleak situation was substantially brightened in 1925, when a small group of black engineers and technicians held a meeting in Chicago that led to the formation of the National Technical Association, providing for information exchanges among blacks in science, engineering, and architecture. The Association is still thriving today and continuing to fulfill the charter of its founding fathers.[6]

This abbreviated history of black technical contributions establishes the legacy on which today's practicing African-American engineers continue to build. Current outstanding contributions include George Carruthers' development of the Far Ultraviolet Camera for the Apollo 16 mission of the National Aeronautics and Space Administration; Otis Boykin's work in electronic devices for heart stimulation; and Marc Hannah's developments in computer graphics.[7]

Despite the specific accomplishments noted here, Black America remains seriously behind White America in achieving parity in the overall development of technology. This assessment may be gleaned from several perspectives: early expression of interest in science and engineering among precollege students; participation in quantitative majors in colleges and universities; graduation rates in technical majors; and participation in the nation's engineering ranks.

Early interest in mathematics, science, and engineering is crucial to attracting and retaining high school students in these disciplines. Figure 1 represents data[8] emerging from the analysis of approximately four million American students who were high school sophomores in 1977. Their progress was monitored for 10 years. Already, as tenth graders, the percentage expressing interest in quantitative fields was small—about 18 percent. The trends at later times

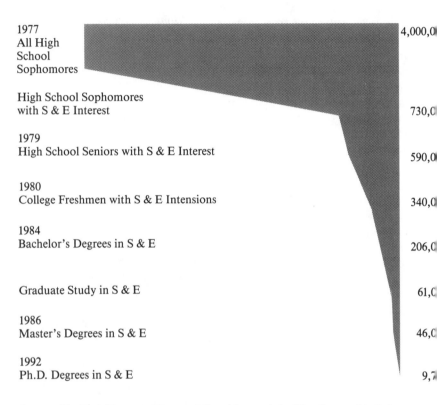

Figure 1
Science and Engineering (S & E) Pipeline,
from High School through Ph.D. Degree

1977 All High School Sophomores	4,000,0
High School Sophomores with S & E Interest	730,0
1979 High School Seniors with S & E Interest	590,0
1980 College Freshmen with S & E Intensions	340,0
1984 Bachelor's Degrees in S & E	206,0
Graduate Study in S & E	61,0
1986 Master's Degrees in S & E	46,0
1992 Ph.D. Degrees in S & E	9,7

Source: The Task Force on Women, Minorities, and the Handicapped in Science
and Technology.

all pointed markedly away from quantitative subjects. The number that hoped
to earn the Ph.D. degree and serve as the researchers and university faculty of
the future is quite small, comprising less than a quarter of one percent of the
original cohort. Such a small percentage emerging from this and later classes
could not meet the nation's needs for the future.[9]

A figure analogous to Figure 1, focused on minority students, would show
an even more negative result. For example, whereas 18 percent of the general
population of sophomores expressed quantitative interests, only 10 percent of
the female and minority students did so.[10] This disparity in interest in quantitative fields did not seem to be surmounted in subsequent years. Figure 2, for

Figure 2
Bachelor Degrees and Freshman Enrollments:
African Americans, 1970–1989

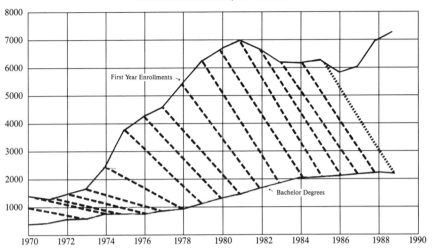

Source: Engineering Manpower Commission.

example, depicts the fall semester college freshmen enrollment in engineering over a 20-year period.[11] The percentage of African Americans among entering engineering students increased significantly during the '70s but then became stagnant—in the range of six percent—until about 1987. The startling 15 percent improvement in enrollments the next year (1988) and continued progress last year are encouraging, but it is too early to tell if a significant and long-term upward trend has begun. Nevertheless, in enrollments, engineering is approaching the point where it receives its proportionate share of black students. In 1988, for example, the African-American participation depicted in Figure 2 represented 7.5 percent of the total engineering enrollment.[12] This compares to an overall nine-percent representation of African Americans among college students that year.[13]

Engineering is actually doing worse among blacks than these numbers might indicate when one considers college retention rates. Although these rates have slightly improved recently, retention of black engineering students needs substantial attention. The percentage of bachelor's degrees earned by blacks in the past two decades is depicted in Table 1.[14] Since approximately three percent of all engineering bachelor's degrees are earned by blacks, the retention rate for black engineering students is approximately one-half that of the general engineering student population.

As the degree level increases, the retention situation worsens. In 1989, 2.24 percent of all engineering master's degrees and 1.14 percent of all engineering doc-

Table 1
Minority Engineering Graduates Over Time:
Bachelor's Degrees, 1970–1989

| | | Underrepresented Minorities: | | | | | | | | | |
| | Total B.S. Degrees | African Americans | | Hispanics | | Native Americans | | Subtotal | | Asian Americans | |
Year		Number	Percent	Number	Percent	Number	Percent	Number	Percent	Number	Percent
1970	41,069	378	0.92%	N/A	—	N/A	—	N/A	—	N/A	—
1971	41,291	407	0.99	N/A	—	N/A	—	N/A	—	N/A	—
1972	41,919	579	1.38	N/A	—	N/A	—	N/A	—	N/A	—
1973	40,950	574	1.40	721	1.76%	36	0.09%	1,331	3.25%	568	1.39%
1974	38,574	743	1.93	636	1.65	32	0.08	1,411	3.66	957	2.48
1975	35,217	734	2.08	685	1.95	44	0.12	1,463	4.15	883	2.51
1976	34,810	777	2.23	658	1.89	41	0.12	1,476	4.24	1,074	3.09
1977	36,722	844	2.30	658	1.79	36	0.10	1,538	4.19	1,146	3.12
1978	42,669	894	2.10	734	1.72	37	0.09	1,665	3.90	1,195	2.80
1979	48,373	1,076	2.22	808	1.67	59	0.12	1,943	4.02	1,532	3.17
1980	53,518	1,320	2.47	1,003	1.87	60	0.11	2,383	4.45	1,922	3.59
1981	56,993	1,445	2.54	1,193	2.09	90	0.16	2,728	4.79	2,267	3.98
1982	61,242	1,644	2.68	1,270	2.07	91	0.15	3,005	4.91	2,577	4.21
1983	65,971	1,862	2.82	1,534	2.33	97	0.15	3,493	5.29	3,098	4.70
1984	70,743	2,022	2.86	1,683	2.38	112	0.16	3,817	5.40	3,609	5.10
1985	71,564	2,043	2.85	1,731	2.42	109	0.15	3,883	5.43	4,276	5.98
1986	71,540	2,114	2.95	1,864	2.61	129	0.18	4,107	5.74	4,805	6.72
1987	69,171	2,182	3.15	1,840	2.66	149	0.22	4,171	6.03	5,056	7.31
1988	65,102	2,211	3.40	1,920	2.95	187	0.29	4,318	6.63	5,591	8.59
1989	62,572	2,122	3.39	1,996	3.19	192	0.31	4,310	6.89	5,873	9.39

Source: Engineering Manpower Commission.

toral degrees were awarded to African Americans.[15] Further, of the 1,805,000 employed engineers in the U.S. in 1988, 68,600 were African Americans, of which only 31,497 (1.7 percent of the total) had engineering degrees.[16]

Of those who teach engineering in our colleges and universities, black participation is even smaller. Of 21,600 doctoral engineering faculty in the U.S., approximately 200 (0.9 percent) are African Americans.[17] In order not to cloud the stark reality in percentages, some specific numbers tell the tale more directly. Twelve blacks received doctorates in engineering in 1987—three in chemical engineering, two in mechanical engineering, and none in the very large and dynamic field of electrical engineering. In the past 11 years, only nine African-American women have received doctorates in engineering.[18]

To summarize, the early interest of black students in quantitative fields seems to be even lower, on the average, than is the interest of the general student population. Even though the percentage of black freshmen selecting engineering is not grossly lower than their representation among the college population (7.5 percent vs. nine percent), retention in engineering is a serious problem and remains, at the undergraduate level, at about one-half the retention rate of the general population. Black representation drops dramatically at the higher degree levels, and their representation among professional engineers and doctorate-level engineering faculty is abysmal.

There have been several studies of the situation faced by minority scientists and engineers. The National Action Council for Minorities in Engineering (NACME) recently undertook a study to try to understand engineering attrition among underrepresented minorities.[19] The results indicate that some key obstacles exist that impact on the probability of success of minority engineering students. The lack of minority role models, principally engineering faculty, has been identified as a significant impediment to a satisfactory comfort level and, presumably, to success in completing the engineering program. The results also seem to indicate, however, that nonminority faculty can have a positive influence on minority student performance, depending upon how helpful they are perceived to be.

Insufficient financial aid emerges as another key obstacle. Though not directly emerging from the NACME study, it seems logical that combining full participation in a rigorous engineering curriculum and a demanding outside job is unworkable, rendering financial aid even more important for students in the quantitative disciplines.

The final primary obstacle to increased black participation is the required adjustment from secondary school to a university setting. At predominantly white campuses, many blacks have the added burden of adjusting to a new cultural environment. Almost half of the students surveyed reported having special problems as minorities.

The NACME study did not take specific account of the historically black colleges and universities (HBCUs). If engineering programs are ranked according to the production of blacks with bachelor's degrees, the top five in 1988 were

HBCUs: North Carolina A&T State University—112 degrees; Howard University—92 degrees; Tuskegee Institute—83 degrees; Prairie View A&M University—81 degrees; and Southern University—75 degrees. Of the 2,211 bachelor's degrees awarded to black engineers that year, 22 percent were awarded by HBCUs.[20] Further, the increase in black engineering freshmen that has recently occurred is especially strong at HBCUs.[21] It is clear that the availability of black faculty role models, outstanding student peers, and the increased comfort level afforded by the HBCUs make these institutions increasingly attractive to some of the best black undergraduates.[22] Any strategy for increasing African-American participation in engineering must make full use of the capabilities of these institutions.

In sum, the numbers of blacks in engineering have increased dramatically over the past 20 years. However, parity has yet to be reached, and there are signs that progress has slowed. Although the numbers of blacks expressing interest in quantitative areas are lower than the general population, an even greater problem seems to be retention of those black students that do express such interest as college freshmen. As discouraging as these data are, the situation provides opportunities for aggressive intervention. Returning to an earlier observation, a comparatively short time is projected for blacks to achieve parity in high school graduation rates. As will be discussed more fully below, rapidly achieving improvement of these graduation rates, attracting larger numbers of black students to engineering, and retaining them through degree completion relate directly to improving the economic performance and well-being of the country.

THE INCREASING DEMAND FOR AFRICAN-AMERICAN ENGINEERS

It is well known that the position of the United States economy has declined relative to that of some of its competitors, particularly in the Far East and Europe.[23] In some areas, the U.S. has competed quite well in terms of balance of trade. Agriculture is a notable example where it enjoys a sizable and positive balance with the remainder of the world. On the other hand, in one important area where American performance has historically been excellent, the trends are quite disturbing. The U.S. has seen a sizable positive trade position in high technology (e.g., consumer electronics) erode remarkably quickly.[24] Growth in gross national product and corresponding improvements in the standard of living are increasingly tied to the development and commercialization of new technologies.[25] This was even true in the past: from 1929 to 1969, almost 45 percent of the increases in U.S. productivity were due to technological innovation as compared to other factors such as better resource allocation.[26] Japan, in particular, has demonstrated an uncanny ability to market inexpensive, yet quality, high-technology products in record time. Its success is largely attributable to its highly educated and literate work force.[27] Japan is challenging the U.S. for technological and economic leadership for the 1990s and into the next millennium.

In much of the latter half of this century, Japan and other Asian countries have focused on innovation for commercial applications, while engineering innovation in the U.S. has focused largely on defense applications and space technologies. America has used much of the capabilities of its technical work force to create a military capability second to none. The U.S. defense capability is not so formidable because of mere size, but because of its effectiveness in war fighting. Aircraft, tanks, ships, and other defense machinery reflect the philosophy of favoring first-rate technology over large numbers of military personnel. This approach has been remarkably successful in establishing an effective military with minimum manpower requirements. Similarly, the exploits of the U.S. space program in the past half-century are legendary, including the remarkable achievement of a manned moon landing. Accomplishments in space required outstanding technological innovations. Space and defense programs did result in some spinoff technologies that were commercialized for civilian applications.

Nevertheless, while the U.S. technology infrastructure was significantly directed towards space and defense, Japan and other emerging economic giants were focusing on increasing their high-technology commercial market share. To counter this trend in the next decade, the U.S. must significantly direct its engineering capability toward economic competitiveness as the Cold War declines, and economic—as opposed to military—competition becomes more dominant in the world. This can be done while retaining a strong defense capability and a reasonable program of space science and exploration.

Examples of industrially related technologies for new emphasis include computer technology and robotics for both domestic consumption and export. These technologies are extremely important in a country such as the U.S., in which the cost of labor is comparatively high. Therefore, to reduce the cost of high-quality, manufactured goods, automation becomes most important. New computer-component technology promises to revolutionize the way we create, manipulate, transfer, and understand information. Miniaturization of electronics and reduction in costs could soon result in a supercomputer of the 1980s being readily available in the typical workplace. Networking advances can electronically connect locations to allow easy, rapid, and massive communication capabilities throughout the United States. Wholesale changes in lifestyle are possible, including flexible work hours, allowing one to complete one's workday at home while in constant communication with the workplace. The related technology of robotics, which requires refined and miniaturized computer circuits for effective use, will increasingly free humans from the drudgery of manual labor, doing the job more accurately and more cheaply. These future directions are not just possible; they will be imperatives if America is to compete effectively on a worldwide scale.

But how do African Americans prepare for such a world when those manual jobs that will be replaced are largely theirs? How does Black America compete for these "high-tech" jobs? Part of the answer has to be a revolutionary increase in the technical literacy of the black community, beginning with a massive improvement in the number of black engineers.

As persuasive as is the argument for more black engineers to meet the challenge of economic competitiveness, there is more to the story. Other challenges the engineering community in the U.S. will face in the next few years beyond defense, space exploration, and economic competitiveness include energy requirements, environmental improvement needs, and required improvements in health care.

America imports approximately 50 percent of its oil, a large portion of which comes from the Persian Gulf region. The Iraq conflict of 1990 is the most recent example of a series of incidents that has threatened, and can continue to threaten, the U.S. oil supply. New technologies to provide alternative energy supplies and reduce demand are sorely needed. On the energy supply side of the equation, advanced approaches to improve the effectiveness and to reduce the cost of oil recovery from domestic wells could provide tremendous advantages. An example of such a technology is a new, extremely sensitive seismic instrument designed to provide detailed maps of the fracture fields in oil reservoirs.[28] Such maps could greatly assist oil companies in better understanding the distribution of oil pockets underground and in developing a strategy for drilling and pumping oil from reservoirs. Another example is emerging technology that simulates on a computer the process of pushing oil from a reservoir, using a pressurized secondary fluid, such as water. Computer modeling could allow an oil company to optimize fluid type and flow pressures without expensive field operations. Examples of emerging technologies designed to reduce the demand for oil include electric automobiles; automotive engines designed to use alternative liquid fuels, such as methanol or ethanol; and advanced electricity production technologies using geothermal, solar, wind, and nuclear energy sources.[29]

Improving the environment has been an important issue on the national agenda for at least two decades, but recent developments have increased its urgency. Air quality in some cities has not improved at the rate previously predicted and desired. Acid rain, resulting largely from emissions from burning coal to produce electricity in power plants, causes damage to plants and materials. Recent analyses and observations indicate that large-scale burning of fossil fuels (e.g., coal and gasoline), produces gases such as carbon dioxide in such large quantities that the balance of heat on the earth's surface is impacted, and long-term changes in the earth's climate can potentially occur. Significant average temperature increases on the surface of the earth, for example, could cause unpredictable and potentially disastrous increases in the sea level, endangering man-made structures on shorelines as well as causing droughts in regions of high agricultural output in the central U.S. Technological innovation is also needed to develop more efficient transportation approaches and electricity production alternatives to reduce dramatically effluents to protect the environment.[30]

In the area of health care, technology has contributed dramatically over the past century. Artificial organs, radiation therapy sources, and diagnostic technologies using laser and X-ray sources are just a few contributions of technology to medicine. The future challenges to medical care continue to require inventions. To help reduce the spiraling cost of health care, inexpensive and nonintrusive diagnostic technologies are needed to replace present approaches. To improve appreciably the understanding and treatment of many genetic diseases, advanced instrumentation is needed to allow detailed analysis of the human genetic material, allowing identification of anomalies. The recent announcement of a laser-based instrument that can detect genetic material at its most fundamental level is an exciting step in this direction.[31]

The urgent need for advanced technologies is not just in the industrialized countries but also throughout the world. For example, in sub-Saharan Africa, a major need exists for drought-resistant crops. A challenge to biotechnology is to develop strains of grains that can thrive in this region to alleviate the suffering due to almost continuous food shortages. Advanced sensors, usually satellite based, can be developed and used to better understand the changes in climate and vegetation over time in such regions, allowing the development of more effective intervention strategies.

The challenges facing society are formidable and require substantial contributions from the engineering community. Recognizing this, industry provides good salaries for engineers. For example, focusing on the bachelor's degree level and engineering graduates in the industrial sector, salaries range from $28,000 to $36,000 immediately after graduation, with a median level of $31,600. Year after year, engineering graduates at the bachelor degree level lead the professions in beginning salaries. At mid-career, it is not unusual for these engineers to earn salaries exceeding $75,000 annually.[32]

The need for engineering creativity is immense. Who will fill the need for the future? As the data previously provided indicate, the traditional source of engineering talent in the United States has been the white male. Yet, demographic data indicate that this source cannot be depended upon to satisfy future needs. While 74 percent of the country's students, ages five to 17, were white in 1982, projections indicate that only 53 percent will be white 30 years from now.[33] White males will comprise only 32 percent of the new entrants to the labor force during the interval 1988-2000.[34] Estimates are that African Americans will provide 13 percent of these new entrants during that period—a percentage that is projected to grow thereafter. While this is happening, estimates are that 25 to 30 percent more engineers will be needed in the United States.[35]

To exacerbate even further the situation, the nation's science and engineering university faculty is aging dramatically. In 1979, a little over 25 percent of such faculty were above 50 years of age. In 1987, almost 35 percent were above 50.[36] If the U.S. is to keep from falling into decline, African Americans must increasingly fill the existing and future needs for engineering manpower.

A REVIEW OF THE OBSTACLES

The case for increased black participation in engineering is extremely persuasive. The obstacles to obtaining those increased numbers over the next decade, however, are substantial. Major obstacles that have been discussed by a wide range of scholars (see footnote 8) include the negative influences that discourage large-scale black advancements in many disciplines and professions, not only in engineering. These include high rates of crime and drug usage as well as low quality, on the average, of elementary and secondary schools in the inner cities.

One major obstacle that is more specific to engineering, however, is that fewer than two percent of all practicing engineers are African Americans with engineering degrees, resulting in few role models. Compounding this problem is the fact that science and invention are not always positively portrayed in the mass media, which greatly influence the views of impressionable youngsters beginning to develop attitudes that will sway future career choices. Detectives, private investigators, musicians, athletes, etc., are portrayed as heroes to youngsters, while scientists and engineers are too often portrayed either as sinister characters or, perhaps even worse, as on the fringes of normality.

For black engineering students, another formidable obstacle previously discussed is financial assistance. Engineering is clearly one of the more demanding curricula at both the undergraduate and graduate levels. The notion of full-time employment while engaged in education is problematic in engineering.

Finally, the adjustment faced by many students, from predominantly black high schools to predominantly white university settings, can cause severe cultural adjustment problems.

WHAT IS BEING DONE?

There is little doubt that intervention is needed to strengthen African-American participation in engineering; many programs are in place, led by universities, by the private sector, by government, and by private citizens in their communities.

Innovative university programs abound. The University of California, Berkeley (UCB), for example, has a comprehensive Center for Underrepresented Engineering Students, which includes a Minority Engineering Program focused on support for undergraduate engineering students. Graduation data indicate that this program has met with some success in that the number of black engineers earning a bachelor's degree increased from seven in 1985 to 19 in 1988. However, as an indication of how far there is to go, these numbers are from UCB engineering graduating classes of 707 in 1985 and 768 in 1988.[37] The Minority Engineering Program Office at the University of Michigan conducts a multifaceted program that includes a summer freshman experience, weekend visits to campus by prospective students, an "adopt a school" program that establishes special relationships with specific middle and secondary schools throughout the country, and an internship/job placement effort. Again, although the total numbers are small, Michigan has been successful in increasing its black engineering enrollment by more than 50 percent in just two years.[38]

The private sector has also contributed. Many companies have established partnerships with universities to strengthen their black student recruitment and retention programs. In addition, companies have programs to assist technical education in elementary, middle, and secondary schools. One of the most important private initiatives is the strong industrial participation in the nonprofit National Action Council for Minorities in Engineering (NACME). The Council has been in operation for over a decade and has established several successful programs to increase minority participation in engineering. It also has served as a unique and timely data base on national trends in this regard.[39] Several private sector firms are also participating in the National Consortium for Graduate Degrees in Engineering, an effort designed to attract and support minority students in graduate engineering studies.[40]

Professional societies of engineers have developed programs as well. For example, the American Nuclear Society, whose membership includes a large number of nuclear engineers, established the Nuclear Engineering Education for the Disadvantaged (NEED) program two decades ago. It has significantly influenced black student participation in science and engineering in general through scholarships and motivation programs.

The federal government has established several initiatives to strengthen minority participation in engineering. The National Science Foundation (NSF) activities are particularly worthy of note, although the majority of the programs are so new that the probability of their future success is unclear. Foundation programs are directed toward precollege science education, undergraduate retention of engineering students, support for engineering programs at HBCUs, participation in research activities by black undergraduate students, scholarships and fellowships for black undergraduate and graduate students, and research support for black engineering faculty.[41] The NSF recently announced its Alliances for Minority Participation program, which is intended to "stimulate positive change in the participation of minorities in science and engineering."[42] Focused at the bachelor's degree level, alliances can involve colleges and universities, public school systems, government agencies, national laboratories, industry, foundations, professional societies, and others. Innovative approaches are sought for identification, encouragement, recruitment, academic assistance, financial support, retention, etc., in order to impact the numbers of successfully completing minority engineers.

Mission agencies of the federal government have also established programs to increase black participation in science and engineering. The Department of Energy and its national laboratories have been particularly aggressive. The Department's present and planned programs are comprehensive, including the establishment of "hands on" science programs for students of all ages, as well as high school science teacher enrichment efforts. The Department's HBCU program has seen a significant number of science and engineering students from historically black institutions participate in research programs at the laboratories. An example of such an alliance exists among Sandia National Laboratories, Los Alamos National Laboratory, Oak Ridge National Laboratory, and three minority institutions, one of which is the HBCU, North Carolina A&T State University. This alliance includes faculty development, curriculum development, and summer student exchanges among its programs.[43]

In addition to the above-mentioned major sectors of society, private citizens have been effective when galvanized in innovative programs. An excellent example is the Young Black Scholars program established and run by a group of black professionals and educators in Los Angeles, with the goal of increasing the number of black students eligible for four-year colleges and universities.[44] The program offers tutoring, college counseling, and personal attention to a selected group of eighth graders, and has followed the group through its high school years. Of the approximately 1,800 who have entered, almost 1,300 are now eligible to enter a four-year college or university. The program is unusual in that it was specifically designed for black students by black citizens who were requested to contribute $1,000 per year for four years to help start the program as well as to help tutor. The participating students were promised $1,000 scholarships if they graduated from their high schools within four years and obtained at least a 3.2 grade point average and high enough college entry test scores to be admitted. The program includes Saturday workshops on such subjects as chemistry and sessions in Scholastic Aptitude Test preparation.

CONCLUSIONS AND RECOMMENDATIONS

The history of black involvement in engineering is rich, including individuals who were forced to overcome major obstacles to fulfill their interests in invention and science. This legacy continues, as African Americans are active participants in today's engineering community.

The numbers are not encouraging, however, because black degreed engineers comprise fewer than two percent of the total practicing engineers. On the other hand, the large number of black high school graduates offers some hope for improvement. Nonetheless, intervention is needed to attract and retain more of these students in the quantitative fields in general, and in engineering in particular. Demographics indicate that over the next decade, the traditional source of engineering manpower—white males—will be unable to fulfill the needs of the U.S. Thus, blacks will increasingly be needed to overcome that shortage.

The future holds clear opportunities and a growing demand for engineers, coupled with a compelling need for new technologies. Technical innovation is needed for economic competitiveness, for better energy sources and more efficient energy use, for a cleaner environment, and for improvement in health care, to name a few key challenges. However, major obstacles exist to increasing black participation, obstacles that individuals from many sectors of American life are attempting to reduce, if not eliminate. What of their efforts? Are they comprehensive enough? Can more be done?

This article makes the point that the size of the challenge is immense, and, although a number of seemingly successful programs are in place, the rate of improvement is not substantial enough. Much more needs to be done. The congressionally chartered Task Force on Women, Minorities, and the Handicapped in Science and Technology[45] recommended a comprehensive set of actions to address the problems of increasing numbers of these groups in the technical professions. The suggested actions are addressed to the President of the United States, to federal agencies, to state and local governments, to educators, to parents, to professional societies, to the leaders of the media, and to American citizens in general. The Task Force particularly noted the importance of role models. The paucity of black engineers increases the burden on each of them to help solve this national problem. Many of the suggestions emerging from the Task Force report are outstanding, but, to date, little new seems to have been done to implement them. It is clear that full implementation will take considerable time, resources, and political will.

In addition to the Task Force report, the NACME study added significantly to the understanding of obstacles facing minority engineering students.[46] It indicated that some causes for low black participation in engineering are different, at least on the average, than obstacles faced by the general population. It found that a large portion of black engineering students have financial problems attending college. The popularly held notion that black engineering students are so highly sought after that financial aid is no problem needs to be revisited. Further, no qualified black engineering student should struggle through severe financial problems if the U.S. is to overcome its engineering manpower shortage.

The NACME study also indicated that cultural problems are still prevalent on campuses. Support systems apparently are spotty in their effectiveness, despite the many novel university programs. On predominantly white campuses, black engineering students too often lack effective support systems and are very rarely exposed to black faculty. The study results suggest that other faculty members can potentially be helpful in providing academic and psychological support, but few seem to be willing or able to do so effectively. Although not specifically addressed in the study, data indicate that a significant portion of black engineering students are graduated from the HBCUs, which have a better track record in providing academic, cultural, and psychological support systems, almost by their very nature.[47] However, engineering programs at these universities tend to have less financial support than the average. The effectiveness of their programs is evidenced by the fact that half of the black faculty at predominantly white research universities received their doctorates at

HBCUs.[48] Strengthening the programs at the HBCUs could greatly enhance their capability to respond to the need for engineers.

The NACME study, however, is not complete. The Council should seek support, perhaps from the National Science Foundation, for a truly comprehensive study of the financial and social situation in which black engineering students now find themselves. Questions must be answered that could greatly influence the development of minority student academic, financial, psychological, and cultural support programs. The specific differences in the situations at HBCUs and at predominantly white institutions need to be identified and better understood. The experiences of practicing black engineers need to be identified and relationships made with their education experiences, where appropriate. Better information on the effectiveness of various types of intervention efforts with black children at early ages needs to be developed. These are some of the issues that could be addressed by a thoroughly inclusive study of the situation faced by black engineering students.

The combination of the Task Force report[49] and the NACME study[50] indicates that much needs to be done over a long period of time. Some specific actions, however, can begin immediately while efforts are made to gather the political will to put in place the national, comprehensive program recommended by the Task Force. This article attempts to develop the arguments leading to the following set of recommendations, for immediate and *simultaneous* implementation by decision makers:

- Identify comprehensively and clearly the obstacles to retaining black engineering students and to recruiting black students to the quantitative fields, using the NACME study as a departure point. Experiences of students at both predominantly white universities and HBCUs must be included in the study.

- Increase significantly the number and size of scholarships and grants for attracting and retaining black students. It seems clear that the popularly held view that enough financial aid is available to black engineering students is at least open to serious question.

- Reevaluate minority academic, psychological, and cultural support programs on university campuses. Their effectiveness is apparently spotty. These programs, which are growing in number on campuses, need to be strengthened where necessary; the university campus must be a place where cultural diversity is nurtured.

- Widely disseminate information about the contributions of blacks to science and invention on college campuses and among the population as a whole. These historical success stories need to be shared with minorities and whites alike.

- The lack of engineering role models needs action on several fronts:
  — Sensitize the mass media to the negative images they sometime portray to young people about science careers.

- — Increase the number of black science and engineering role models at all levels—elementary schools through universities.
- — Engage black professional engineers in mentoring programs such as the Los Angeles Young Black Scholars effort.
- — Provide positive exposure to quantitative careers to black children at early ages.

- Strengthen the existing engineering programs at the HBCUs. These programs, although successful now, have substantial room for expansion in the quality of their engineering education programs and the quantity of student output.

Parity in engineering manpower for African Americans will not likely be reached soon. Poor inner-city schools, unsatisfactory health care for the poor, rampant crime, and readily available drugs are but a few of the important issues that must be addressed while the above recommendations are implemented. The Urban Marshall Plan recommended by the National Urban League[51] must be seriously evaluated and implemented.

On the other hand, rapid and substantial success of a national effort to increase the number of black engineers will contribute significantly to the economic future of America, thereby helping to provide the national resources to deal with these broader problems. From so many perspectives, the future of this country depends on action now!

It's The Thing That Counts, Or Reflections on The Legacy Of W.E.B. Du Bois

Gayle Pemberton, Ph.D.

> Do not at the outset of your career make the all too common error of mistaking names for things. Names are only conventional signs for identifying things. Things are the reality that counts. If a thing is despised, either because of ignorance or because it is despicable, you will not alter matters by changing its name. If men despise Negroes, they will not despise them less if Negroes are called "colored" or "Afro-Americans." [1]

In 1928 William Edward Burghardt Du Bois wrote those words in an article called "The Name 'Negro'" in *The Crisis* magazine. It was in response to a letter he had received from a young man named Roland A. Barton, who had taken umbrage at the designation "Negro." Barton had written from South Bend, Indiana:

> Dear Sir: I am only a high school student in my Sophomore year, and have not the understanding of you college educated men. It seems to me that since *The Crisis* is the Official Organ of the National Association for the Advancement of Colored People, which stands for equality for all Americans, why would it designate, and segregate, us as "Negroes," and not as "Americans."
>
> The most piercing thing that hurts me in this February *Crisis,* which forced me to write, was the notice that called the natives of Africa "Negroes," instead of calling them "Africans," or "natives."
>
> The word "Negro," or "nigger," is a white man's word to make us feel inferior. I hope to be a worker for my race; that is why I wrote this letter. I hope that by the time I become a man, that this word, "Negro," will be abolished. [2]

Barton would have no difficulty finding supporters for his position today, particularly as the debate continues about the terms "black" and "African American." As Charles V. Hamilton says, "This whole business of names has been a constant troubling issue in the history of African Americans." [3]

Du Bois was not particularly troubled by the problem with names. As he tells young Barton, black people by any other name would suffer the same oppressions. What Du Bois seeks to do is to engender a concern with larger issues than names, which certainly are important, but which have no substance of their own; they are fundamentally representative. He says, in other words, "Let's get our symbols straight and get to work."

Perhaps at no other time in recent memory has such advice been needed more than now. The late 1980s and the beginning of the '90s seem to be identified by a need to believe that the symbol is the thing: that sneakers are power, or that the flag is freedom and must never be burnt. The quality of public discourse these days on almost any subject is characterized by accusations from competing sides, with little concern for accuracy in arguments and even less regard for the complexities of the issues. There is invective and all too frequently an appeal to cheap emotions. All we need consider, to prove this, are the advertisements for politicians as they campaign. As June Jordan so effectively demonstrates in her poem, "A Short Note to My Very Critical and Well-Beloved Friends and Comrades," we seem locked into thinking in extremes, getting nowhere.

> First they said I was too light
> Then they said I was too dark
> Then they said I was too different
> Then they said I was too much the same
> Then they said I was too young
> Then they said I was too old
> Then they said I was too interracial
> Then they said I was too much a nationalist
> Then they said I was too silly
> Then they said I was too angry
> Then they said I was too idealistic
> Then they said I was too confusing altogether:
> Make up your mind! They said. Are you militant
> or sweet? Are you vegetarian or meat? Are you
> straight
> or are you gay?
>
> And I said, Hey! It's not about *my* mind.[4]

The Jordan volume is called *Naming Our Destiny;* Du Bois might have suggested *Creating Our Destiny* as an alternative.

I invoke the name of W.E.B. Du Bois in order to talk about the "thing" of him, his extraordinary prescience and intellectual bravery in the face of a hostile American world. He was born in 1868 and died the night before the March on Washington in 1963, nearly 100 years of living that witnessed some of the most magnificent and some of the most horrible moments in the history of mankind. Du Bois's words in the foreword of *The Souls of Black Folk,* published in 1903, characterize this century. He wrote, "The problem of the Twentieth Century is the problem of the color line."[5] And Black America entering the decade of the 1990s would be well served by not only remembering Du Bois, but also by reading him, studying him, arguing with him, and tasting some of his spiritual optimism, such as that which he vividly revealed when he wrote, "I want the colored people to have the right to develop according to their capacity and I certainly would be disappointed if they did not develop much higher things than the white race."[6]

I could be accused of hopeless idealism when I suggest that Du Bois and other great black thinkers and writers need to be studied and heard for the wisdom they can provide us now. But there have been danger flags raised over Black America for over a decade. Statistics abound revealing a dreadful state where black lives are being literally snuffed out by murder, disease, drug addiction, infant mortality, and poverty—and figuratively lost by homelessness, chronic mental and physical illness, poor education, nonexistent job opportunity, and despair. In some of our larger cities, it is as if the Four Horsemen of the Apocalypse and a few dozen more are knocking on Black America's door.

In the meantime, affirmative action programs and straw-man issues such as employment and educational quotas—issues that always appeal to America's racial psychosis—are being prepared as the campaign strategies for the 1992 presidential and congressional elections.[7] There are also signs throughout Black America that it certainly is fragmented, with much of the middle class perilously holding on to gains made over the last two decades, while a true underclass—out of the loop and separated from history—lives out a tortured existence with thirty-second sound bites and "film at eleven" on local and national news. Du Bois's final message to the world speaks to this problematic reality. He ended it with these lines:

> One thing alone I charge you as you live and believe in life. Always human beings will live and progress to greater, broader and fuller life. The only possible death is to lose belief in this truth simply because the great end comes slowly: because time is long.
> Goodbye.[8]

My father, Lounneer Pemberton, was a career Urban Leaguer, working in the twin cities of Minneapolis/St. Paul; Chicago; Dayton, Ohio; and Kansas City, Missouri. I remember him as being always under extreme stress, trying to negotiate with craft unions to open their doors to blacks, participating in the collective efforts for public accommodation, fair employment, and equal justice. He died in 1977, just a few months into his retirement.

He was a realist, but also I think he was a bit of a dreamer. Most of all, he was aware of the dangers of ignorance and self-delusion. My sister and I were taught from the cradle that one could never be simultaneously free and ignorant, because ignorance is tyranny, too.

People are fond of quoting George Santayana, who said, "Those who do not know their history are condemned to repeat it." In the face of the failure of a number of solutions to the many problems facing Black America, I am suggesting that we immerse ourselves in a reading of ourselves, that we actively read the great thinkers and writers of Black America. Du Bois said:

> I sit with Shakespeare and he winces not. Across the color line I move arm in arm with Balzac and Dumas, where smiling men and welcoming women glide in gilded halls. . . . I summon Aristotle and Aurelius and what should I will, and they come all graciously with no scorn nor condescension.[9]

What would it hurt to sit with Du Bois? At the least, it would protect us from accepting conclusions other people have made for us; and at the most, it might provide enough invigoration for a nationwide rehabilitation of bodies, souls, and neighborhoods.

KEEP THE SYMBOLS STRAIGHT

During the last few months, W.E.B. Du Bois has been mentioned in connection with two related and somewhat troublesome occasions. The first concerns his exclusion and that of other major African-American thinkers from the latest edition of *The Great Books*. The second has to do with the rumor that some people at Harvard have come up with the idea of exhuming Du Bois's bones from his grave in Ghana in order to bring them to the United States, perhaps to Cambridge, to lie in Mount Auburn Cemetery with the likes of Louis Agassiz—who most certainly would not have welcomed him—and William Ellery Channing, who probably would have. There has been a fairly loud outcry in the black American press and elsewhere against Mortimer Adler and others in charge of choosing *The Great Books*. The response to the disinterring of Du Bois has been more muted, largely because only a few members of the academic world know about it.

These two issues have much in common. First, they are representative of minds that are of a fairly exclusive turn—minds that are by no means exclusively white, either. The high priests of "Western culture" have made their point. The publishers of *The Great Books* in Chicago pronounced the finest efforts of African-American thinkers to elucidate the range of their experiences—to create art and philosophy from both the ravages and the wonderment of their lives—unfit to stand in a three-foot shelf with the Greeks, Romans, British, Germans, French, and white Americans. According to Adler, the three criteria for entrance into this august set of books are that the material must be "relevant to the contemporary world, be worth re-reading, and deal with the great ideas that confront mankind in every age."[10] Du Bois, with his scholarly books, his novels, his autobiographies, his poetry, his reviews, and his essays, certainly is the preeminent black American for this 60-volume set.

Harvard is having image problems. Currently, students are protesting the dearth of African-American faculty; efforts to find a successor to the late Nathan Huggins as chairman of the Afro-American Studies Program have fallen short. Some symbolism could help. Du Bois earned his first B.A. degree at Fisk and a second at Harvard; he was the first black American to earn a Ph.D. there. Harvard houses the W.E.B. Du Bois Institute, established in 1975, where scholars carry out pre- and postdoctoral research. Even the most virulent anti-Harvard person would have to admit that there are practically no better libraries or resources for scholarship than at Harvard. But that's not the point. Du Bois left the United States and "went home" to Africa, to Ghana. As yet, there is no news about a discovery of a codicil to his will revealing a suppressed and burning desire to be buried at Mount Auburn or anywhere else in the United States. Arnold Rampersad quotes him on the occasion of his becoming a citizen of Ghana: "I have returned that my dust shall mingle with the dust of my forefathers."[11] Risking audacity, I would also suggest that life for black Americans has not become what Du Bois envisioned—and, if it had, it would still not justify bringing his bones to this "home." To think that this would be an appropriate move for Du Bois is simply silly, and it follows with those in Chicago. It is more of the same old business, where the significance of African-American life is either trivialized by exclusion—and silenced—as with *The Great Books*, or—and perhaps worse—trivialized by a symbolic gesture that is preeminently insulting to the individual and, by extension, to the group.

Second, these two cases are centrally concerned with questions of what is worth learning and what is worth preserving. *The Great Books* are literally designed to be encased in shelves, to be displayed, physically preserved. They are not particularly comfortable books to read; the print is very small, the page size too large. Unlike the many editions of *The Great Books* authors used in colleges and universities, the translations are old; there are not enough notes with important supplementary information. There is a course one can take with these books; following the editors' instructions, one can work oneself through these greatest ideas of all time. But I have always suspected that people with such energy and desire are rarely the same ones who buy the books.

Du Bois wrote,

> Protest is for two purposes: first, for its effect upon your political enemies, and secondly for its effect upon yourself.[12]

Black Americans need not be surprised at their exclusion from *The Great Books*. It is almost inconceivable that the intellectual life of blacks would be upheld and made part of the mainstream when so many other facets of their lives have been kept on the margins and perceived to be at odds with the status quo. The fundamental assumption of *The Great Books* people is that there is nothing important to learn from black people. Du Bois's response was simply that the black American "would not Africanize America, for America has too much to teach the world and Africa. He would not bleach his Negro soul in a flood of white Americanism, for he knows that Negro blood has a message for the world."[13]

One need only consider the history of the music created by black Americans, the spirituals and jazz, to find a model for the omission of black artists from the mainstream. Du Bois, in *The Souls of Black Folk*, wrote of the sorrow songs:

> Little of beauty has America given the world save the rude grandeur God himself stamped on her bosom; the human spirit in this new world has expressed itself in vigor and ingenuity rather than in beauty. And so by fateful chance the Negro folk-song—the rhythmic cry of the slave — stands today not simply as the sole American music, but as the most beautiful expression of human experience

born this side of the seas. It has been neglected, it has been, and is, half despised, and above all, it has been persistently mistaken and misunderstood, but not-withstanding, it still remains as the singular spiritual heritage of the nation and the greatest gift of the Negro people.[14]

In 1903 Du Bois knew the standard for treating the artistic works of black Americans: it was either exclusion, derision, or frequently theft. American music, as taught and defined by our academic music departments, fails to recognize these paramount contributions. Indeed, I have been told by more than one assistant professor of music, contemplating the politics of his or her tenure review, that scholarly interest in jazz is a liability. I also remember reading a damning recommendation of a candidate for a music position that spoke of his great success in attracting black football and basketball players to his classes in jazz. The candidate was evidently serving as an important function on the campus by giving those perceived to be intellectually insignificant a course they would appreciate. It is interesting to note, too, that the American penchant for deferring to European tastes has not extended to an appropriate appreciation of jazz. During this century, this very valuable music has been championed in Europe and neglected at home by white and black alike. Perhaps the current revival of jazz in some quarters, prompted by today's young generation, and the durability of a number of older players and composers, may spark a new appreciation, but it is doubtful the academy will care much. American music is defined in other ways there. Nevertheless, a study of black music is impor-tant in charting the long history of the African-American experience; one need not have the nod of the academy to make such a study.

In short, if we are to protest against the sentinels at the gates of Western culture, we should be mindful of Du Bois's advice, and calculate the benefits of the protest to ourselves. If we protest his exclusion from *The Great Books* without re-reading him, we allow him to remain dead on a shelf with the other books and ideas, and not alive for us, or a part of the constant struggle for knowledge and freedom.

IDEAS SHOULD BE USEFUL

What is so vexing about this whole debate is that important questions about the great ideas themselves are never raised. There is no doubt about the brilliance and importance of the philosophers and playwrights and novelists and scien-tists and historians and economists and political theorists who make up *The Great Books*. My own study of literature and my devotion to it would be hollow if I were to suggest that these great ideas are unimportant. But what has hap-pened to them? Of course, freedom and democracy are great notions, and, for example, the rhetoric accompanying the lifting of the Iron Curtain last year pro-claimed the ascendancy of Western ideals of freedom and justice and so forth. But we have not conquered—or come close to conquering—the ravages of ignorance, disease, hatred, poverty, hunger, or despair that an actively engaged set of great ideas might challenge. American history suggests that, as a nation, we are ignorant, frightened, and combative when facing cultures and values that are foreign to our own, whether they reside in our cities or across the world. Centuries of great ideas have not kept us from babbling. After Chernobyl, after the forty-fifth anniversary of Hiroshima and Nagasaki, *The New York Times* can quote a citizen who thinks the use of nuclear weapons against Iraq might be a good idea.[15]

There are many people who argue against the suggestion that great ideas can or should be pressed into service in the real world. Allan Bloom, one of the most controversial opponents of multiculturalism in the academic curriculum, and a professor of philosophy at the University of Chicago, is one such person. For Bloom, the years in college are important, contemplative years away from the bitter realities outside the gates of many an institution. He writes:

> Men may live more truly and fully in reading Plato and Shakespeare than at any other time, because they are participating in essential being and are forgetting their accidental lives. The fact that this kind of humanity exists or existed, and that we can somehow still touch it with the tips of our outstretched fingers, makes our imperfect humanity, which we can no longer bear, tolerable. The books in their objective beauty are still there, and we must help protect and cultivate the delicate tendrils reaching out toward them through the unfriendly soil of students' souls. Human nature, it seems, remains the same in our very altered circumstances because we still face the same problems, if in different guises, and have the distinctively human need to solve them, even though our awareness and forces have become enfeebled.[16]

Apart from the fact that Bloom's argument aggressively omits women and "others," his point of view explains how many of its advocates are relatively untroubled by our inability to solve the gross injustices of our world. And it is not just a certain group of professors, or commentators from the political right, who share this cultural, romantic angst with Bloom. A friend told me recently that he had conducted a series of interviews with the "1990 Student." "They reject liberalism completely," he said, "and do not believe that government or society can solve these terrible problems."

Du Bois advanced the notion that black Americans were in charge of their own intellectual and political salvation. His long-running argument with Booker T. Washington about the tactics of the black struggle are a vital chapter of American history. Although he would disagree with the political implications of Bloom, he was a firm believer in the redemptive possibilities of study. He wrote:

> The foundations of knowledge in this race, as in others, must be sunk deep in the college and university if we would build a solid, permanent structure. Internal problems of social advance must inevitably come—problems of work and wages, of families and homes, of morals and the true valuing of the things of life; and all these and other inevitable problems of civilization the Negro

must meet and solve largely for himself, by reason of his isolation; and can there be any possible solution other than by study and thought and an appeal to the rich experiences of the past?[17]

What Du Bois offers is a sensibility and a vision devoted to the triumph of the soul, the body, and the body politic. Because his ideas are so broad in scope, even when they are at their most controversial or when expressive of his very 19th century tastes, they are supple enough to help us solve the real problems that the preservers of other great ideas have abandoned. Du Bois appeals to black Americans to do this work themselves.

Similarly, Ralph Ellison, author of *Invisible Man,* in a 1965 interview called "A Very Stern Discipline," mused about the fact that, at that time, much of Black America was being interpreted by others, but was not in the business of interpreting itself. He said:

> What is missing today is a corps of artists and intellectuals who would evaluate Negro American experience from the inside, and out of a broad knowledge of how people of other cultures live, deal with experience, and give significance to their experience. We do too little of this. Rather, we depend upon outsiders—mainly sociologists—to interpret our lives for us. It doesn't seem to occur to us that our interpreters might well be not so much prejudiced as ignorant, insensitive, and arrogant. It doesn't occur to us that they might be of shallow personal culture, or innocent of the complexities of actual living.[18]

Ellison's concerns are not dated; although the body of black scholarship has risen by quantum leaps since then, it is still insufficient to meet his demands. To illustrate the tenacity of his point, however, I will never forget the comment made to me by a young black woman who was hesitant to take a course from me because it required five papers. She said to me, without any irony, "I'm a minority. I can't write." She believed something she had heard about herself, as a generic black student, and she thoroughly internalized it. She accepted a ready-made scenario for her failure and was a star player in the role. How many other prepackaged scenarios will she accept before her life ends?

For Du Bois, great ideas had to be utilitarian; they had to feed the soul and the body. Washington, I fear, thought Du Bois placed too great a premium on the soul. But education for Du Bois was not an end in and of itself nor a temporary respite from life, as Allan Bloom would say. Rather, it was a springboard into life.

I have heard many people, who should know better, speak of "receiving an education." A received education is not worth having; an earned one is. Whites and blacks alike misunderstand this, but blacks more than whites are hurt by it. We need to cultivate a love of learning, in the sense of formal education. We need to recognize that education is not a commodity, or to use Du Bois's terms, a degree is not the "thing" any more than a flag is freedom. It must be an earned "thing," in use at all times, representative not of received knowledge, passively accepted, but actively lived and engaged in the quest for understanding. If we are serious about educating our children, for example, the next generation of black collegians will not be sitting in at administrative offices waiting for their schools to hire another black professor to save them. If we educate them well, there will no longer be a shortage of black professors.

CANONS AND SYMBOLS

In a recent edition of *The Chronicle of Higher Education,* Stephen S. Weiner wrote:

> To achieve an academic community that embraces diversity, we first have to learn how to talk about it. Issues involving race and ethnicity have emotional and political overtones, and many people feel uncomfortable discussing their perceptions, feelings, and aspirations.[19]

Weiner's point is not a new one, but it is precisely because people feel uncomfortable about speaking of race, ethnicity, and class that many people believe a fresh language, shorn of connotative ugliness needs to be created. But the issue is much more difficult than that, because when it comes to talking about the benefits of a pluralistic, democratic culture and the hope of a better future, most people believe that a language already exists—in the Declaration of Independence, in the Constitution, in Martin Luther King, Jr.'s "I Have a Dream" speech in August, 1963, in Emma Lazarus's lines at the base of the Statue of Liberty, and in any number of other places. In some ways, those who believe the language exists are right. The tragedy is the disparity between our words and our actions in the face of race and difference. The language for understanding diversity and pluralism is not so much uncreated as it is resisted.

Our language reveals the ways in which we think; every day, there appears evidence that there now exists an unbridgeable cultural chasm between people who all call themselves Americans, who have the same cultural aspirations, who buy the same goods, and who have the same fears. It is not comfortable being in America, and the future challenges us—as it should. Or, as Allan Gurganus put it in his eloquent "The Civil War in Us," an article that appeared just as "The Civil War" series on public television ended:

> We're still out here in the middle of a field. Face up and fearful of dawn's cannons, somehow aimed at us—by us. And chilled, we keep wondering: If we are alive right here on our native soil, then, beloved fellow citizen of our great saved Republic, why, oh why, do we still feel so far from home?[20]

In our universities and colleges, the battle over expanding the curriculum to include works by black, female, Latino, Asian, Native-American, and other "others" will carry us to the year 2000 and beyond. It has been my contention that some of this battle has to do with the impending millennium. A good portion of the population looks back, holds on to an idea of the familiar, and revises the past, in order to feel secure. Another portion says good riddance to the twentieth century and tries to envision a future that will be more politically and socially equitable. It would be impossible and useless to try to summarize here the many sides battling for control.

The *canon*—that body of works many consider indispensable to a higher education—is under siege, no doubt about it. Canons have existed for all societies. There are revered patriarchs and matriarchs, revered texts, revered ways of behaving that form the foundation of a society's values and mores. However, the United States is a different kind of society from those that have provided the pattern for our own canon construction. If we accept as our own a completely Eurocentric canon, the result of generations of various European societies writing about themselves, then we, in the New World, don't have to exist. The presence of blacks and others in the New World—those who have made it expressly different from the Old World—need not be taken into account. In other words, if the canon remains thoroughly grounded in Europe, all these "others," with profound effects on the lives of all Americans since the earliest explorations, do not have to be factored into the so-called "American experience."

A few white American writers have understood this terrible crisis of the American soul and have written about it. Blacks and some women writers have done the same; they all need to be read to enlighten us.

The converse exists among those thinkers who disapprove of the manner in which the lives of blacks and "others" do appear in works that are already in the American canon. Mark Twain, Harriet Beecher Stowe, Herman Melville, Edgar Allan Poe, and others created characters that in the least disclosed a realization of race and its effects on American history by its authors. In some cases, particularly Twain's *The Adventures of Huckleberry Finn,* the levels of cultural deception and illusion are painfully mapped out in the absurd journey of Huck and Jim.

Canons work well in closed cultural and religious systems. Salman Rushdie can be roundly condemned in Islamic quarters throughout the world, while being avidly read outside of those quarters. To see a rendition of Charles Dickens's *A Christmas Carol* in a London theater makes it positively a local story. But what does it mean to go hear a revival of *Porgy and Bess,* in New York, for example? Virgil Thomson, a celebrated white composer and music critic, in an early article on George Gershwin, composer of *Porgy and Bess,* raised an important point that is germane to issues of canons and systems. He wrote, "Folklore subjects recounted by an outsider are only valid as long as the folk in question is unable to speak for itself, which is certainly not true of the American Negro in 1935 [the year the opera was first produced]."[21] What the playgoer gets is a reading of black life, but nothing approaching the authenticity a liver of black life could provide. Or, to look at it another way, those who complain that the films "Glory," "Mississippi Burning," or "Driving Miss Daisy" are distortions of history seem to expect a black consciousness to come from white directors and producers. Filet mignon is not sold in fast food restaurants; the standard Hollywood film has never much concerned itself with authenticity.

Advertisers of beer and soda, rental cars, and airlines tell us what an open, free place the United States is, and that we must preserve that openness and freedom. Somehow, the idea of a closed canon seems peculiar and inappropriate for such a country. If we are going to hell, it will not be because we began teaching about the experiences of nonwhites in this vast and complex land.

We should also stop making lists of what is acceptable and what is not. Censors have always had field days with them. We have a passion for them and it is ridiculous. The problem is that the list becomes more important than what is on it, and then instead of fighting about real ideas, we fight about lists.

The other great assumption in this canon discussion is that the great thinkers and writers of all time, then and now, teach themselves. This is what I call the osmotic theory: reading *The Republic* of Plato will make one a better person; buying the complete works of Shakespeare and sitting in a class will guarantee that a student comes away with a love of the bard's moral philosophy, poetic genius, and universality; reading Karl Marx's *Das Kapital* will forever estrange a middle- or upper-class student from his or her parents; or reading about slavery from the perspective of one of its victims, instead of from one of its apologists, will somehow distort history.

But books do not teach themselves. A reading list filled with European classics, or the classics of any other continent, will not axiomatically cause a student to become any particular kind of person. How those classics or "renegade" texts are taught will matter more. No matter how multicultural a curriculum is, a teacher who has little knowledge of the context of a work or understanding of the tradition that work belongs to is not going to convey much insight to a classroom full of students. In both subtle and obvious ways, teachers deliver subtexts to their students. One of the most prevalent is something akin to: "We have to read this, so let's get it over with." Black students in predominantly white colleges have complained for years that when the subject matter turns to their lives, everyone in the classroom—including the professor—turns to the student for verification of the scholarship. It makes no sense, of course.

A fully Eurocentric curriculum cannot go very far in explaining the reality of the United States. A thoroughly Afrocentric one can fail to elucidate the thinkers and issues that those African and African-American writers are answering and challenging. Somewhere in the middle, without so much noise, there are answers.

In the meantime, the names of things change with great frequency. Within the last two years, we have watched the term "diversity in curriculum" change to "pluralistic curriculum" to "multicultural curriculum." It is as if the opposition to the name appears the night after the name appears for the first time in print. We are bedeviled by names again, when what we need is the "thing."

Du Bois said in 1922 that "the difficulty is that ignorant folk and inexperienced try continually to paint humanity as all good or all evil."[22] David Duke, the former Klansman, won 40 percent of the vote in the senatorial primary in Louisiana on a platform straight out of the 1890s. He managed to convince thousands and thousands of people that the words "affirmative action" were responsible for their economic woe and their feelings of emotional and cultural privation. This is in a country where businesses are increasingly owned by people from other countries who certainly will not be reinvesting all of their profits in helping Americans feel better about their country. Such demagoguery is allowed to persist in this country because people are unaware of their histories; they have not read the books they would ban. Such extremism can be fatal. When we pay attention to the swings of a pendulum only at its outermost points, we miss quite a bit of its movement. And we risk being deceived about its reality. This does not bode well for educating the citizens of the twenty-first century.

HISTORY VS. OSMOSIS

The following was written in 1968, about a generation of white youth:

> At some point between 1945 and 1967 we had somehow neglected to tell these children the rules of the game we happened to be playing. Maybe we had stopped believing in the rules ourselves, maybe we were having a failure of nerve about the game. Maybe there were just too few people around to do the telling. These were children who grew up cut loose from the web of cousins and great-aunts and family doctors and lifelong neighbors who had traditionally suggested and enforced society's values. . . . They are less in rebellion against the society than ignorant of it, able only to feed back certain of its most publicized self-doubts, *Vietnam, Saran-Wrap, diet pills, the Bomb.*[23]

Joan Didion was writing about the "flower children" of the Haight-Ashbury district of San Francisco. Her essay, "Slouching Towards Bethlehem," is a sardonic look at some pitiable lives and sordid underpinnings—those so frequently and glibly glossed over—of a 1960s generation. What is striking is the applicability of the substance of her comments now to both black and white American communities.

Many black students of college age are concerned about the mixed messages they receive from their society. In many cases, talented young blacks have gone to predominantly white colleges only to undergo enormous psychological and emotional stress due to insensitivity and racism on the part of white students and professors. Some of the black students' anxiety is generated internally, from a fear of failure, and sometimes from a fear of success. They have had difficult times balancing what they perceived to be the white values of the institution on the one hand, and the "counter-cultural" aspects of their black lives on the other. Attempts to create or maintain some equilibrium can easily sap a student's energy and make for some very confusing years.

Other students have rediscovered the traditional black college, hoping to find an implicit belief in their worth and a network of friendship that will protect them from a cold, corporate White America.

Similarly, white students, in facing a future much less financially secure than that which they had been raised to expect, have lashed out at blacks, women, and other people from religious, ethnic, and racial minority groups. The extreme atred displayed has surprised some, particularly those who believed the flower children were changing the nation or those who thought that the Civil Rights Movement of the 1950s through 1970s ended forever the sorry spectacle of active and violent racism in this country. Indeed, it is the children of the '60s flower generation who are now in college, impervious to the rhetoric of peace and understanding that so many earnestly, and perhaps many more faddishly, thought was the wave of the future.

What these white students share with their black counterparts is a lack of grounding, an immature or nonexistent sense of history, and a fear of each other and the world. Over the past few years, there have been many incidents of racial harassment at major and minor colleges and universities. In many of these incidents, black students were surprised by the events. (What surprised some older blacks was the response of black students to some of these incidents.) The students were shocked, some in tears at what happened, frightened and appalled that what they thought of as a safe place—this insular academic world—could be desecrated by such racism. Clearly their tormentors were not worried about being transformed through their readings of Plato and Shakespeare.

Many of these black students had not been told of a world that existed just figuratively minutes before their births, a racially segregated, discordant society posing as a haven of freedom. Their pain is quite real, but knowing more of the recent past might have helped mollify it. I have been told by black students and friends alike that many parents have chosen not to tell their children of the past because it was painful. Such selective amnesia ultimately serves the parent more than it does the child. Generations of blacks—out of shame, they say—historically have failed to pass on enough history. We should change that habit.

Eubie Blake, that fabulous ragtime and Broadway composer and pianist, was featured in a very late-night television program I saw in the 1970s. I remember seeing him play the piano, as he recalled his upbringing in Baltimore. At a totally unexpected moment, he abruptly stopped playing and looked straight into the camera, and tensely said, "Black people are the only people who throw away their culture." It was a poignant moment, hardly bearable, as Blake, then in his nineties, reflected, sadly and angrily, something he believed about Black America.

GETTING THE "THING"

The future is bleak, but we must believe that the work that needs to be done can be done if we are to avoid not only despair, but also tragedies whose proportions it is impossible now to calculate. It may not be too late to take counsel from Du Bois.

In 1934 Du Bois said of the black educated world, "This body of at least twenty-five million modern men are not called upon to commit suicide because somebody doesn't like their complexions or their hair. It is their opportunity and their day to stand up and make themselves heard and felt in the modern world."[24] In 1990, it would seem that a large percentage of Black America is making itself heard and felt, but that great numbers of them are also committing suicide.

One of the fallacies of history that my students believe is that the Civil Rights Movement began as a result of actions undertaken by Rosa Parks and Martin Luther King, Jr., in Montgomery, Alabama, in 1955. Certainly Parks and King were heroic. But the movement toward freedom—a word curiously out of fashion now—began generations before the fateful bus ride and boycott. There was always an intensity, a protest against discrimination by a people determined to become equal partners in the experiment called the United States. Along the way the roll call is filled with the names of leaders and followers, famous and forgotten, who did as much as they could for what was always called the "cause" or the "struggle."

We are at another terribly critical point in our history. In some ways, the United States is beginning to discover what it is like to no longer be that impetuous brazen child of the world. Even Du Bois sounds quaint and boosterish in some of his prose, a black George Babbitt convinced that the Black United States of America will be the best damn place and state of mind in the world. The face of the world is changing, the power and influences of the United States now resembling an aging society. The aging process is not going well. There is physical wreckage in our major cities that looks strangely like bombed cities of World War II Europe. But Europe is back. Are we?

Du Bois thought of Black America as messianic: somehow, he thought, the salvation of America was inextricably tied to the work of black hands. There can be no America—there never was an America—without the gifts of blackness. The narrator of Ralph Ellison's *Invisible Man* voiced a similar sentiment when he said:

> Must I strive toward colorlessness? But seriously, and without snobbery, think of what the world would lose if that should happen. America is woven of many strands; I would recognize them and let it so remain. It's "winner take nothing" that is the great truth of our country or of any country. Life is to be lived not controlled; and humanity is won by continuing to play in the face of certain defeat. Our fate is to become one, and yet many.—This is not prophecy, but description.[25]

Throughout history black Americans have shown themselves to be different from each other, and from White America. Paul Laurence Dunbar wrote of the "myriad subtleties" of black people; Du Bois saw the "Universal in the Particular."[26] This country has never been monolithically anything. As we approach the beginning of our fifth century, let us finally recognize that, and create a "thing," a culture befitting our many hues, beliefs, beginnings, and mores. If the struggle for freedom by black Americans, as expressed through the wonderful writings of Du Bois, cannot be thought to be "relevant to the contemporary world," or worth reading over and over again, or at the forefront of those that confront *humankind* in every age, then there are no great ideas.

According to many who knew him, Du Bois did not suffer fools gladly. He was not a cuddly grandfatherly type. Though he was not without humor, he was steely-eyed and deadly serious about the world and his beloved black brothers and sisters. At the end of his letter to Roland Barton, Du Bois wrote:

> Get this then, Roland, and get it straight even if it pierces your soul: a Negro by any other name would be just as black and just as white; just as ashamed of himself and just as shamed by others, as today. It is not the name—it's the Thing that counts. Come on, Kid, let's go get that Thing! [27]

Managing Employee Diversity: An Assessment

R. Roosevelt Thomas, Jr., D.B.A.

Much has been said recently about work-force diversity. In particular, corporate executives are seriously concerned about employee diversity in their companies, and are launching initiatives in pursuit of progress in this arena. As a result of their efforts and those of others, we are gaining in our understanding of this topic.

A significant learning has been the realization that managers have not failed at managing diversity, but rather that they have not gotten around to it. Also, results of interventions suggest that "way of life" changes will be required, if corporations, other organizations, and society in general are to be characterized by effective management of employee diversity. Stated differently, the traditional emphasis placed on enhancing relations between the genders and among the races will not be sufficient to assure quality management of a diverse work force. Additionally, major organizational "way of life" shifts will have to be encouraged through corporate culture and system changes.

In this article, I explore the evolving corporate managerial response to employee diversity and the results it has produced. I also look at implications of these efforts for other segments of society.

I write from the perspective of one who, over the past six years, has consulted with managers in pursuit of diversity objectives. In this role, I have spoken to hundreds of managers on the topic, conducted numerous workshops, and participated in major diagnostic research in several corporations. This experience will provide the foundation for my comments below.

Stimuli

The principal stimuli that have rekindled managerial interest in diversity have been the projections of *Workforce 2000,* a report prepared by The Hudson Institute and sponsored by the U.S. Department of Labor. In brief, this document indicated that the American work force will become increasingly diverse. This has led managers to conclude, "We must get ready."

Environmental Realities

Three factors in particular have formed the context for corporate preparation for diversity.

One, the diversity in the pipeline currently is different than what we have experienced before. Individuals who are "different" now are more likely to celebrate their differences and to resist losing what makes them unique. This reluctance to assimilate really is the driving force behind the urgency to "progress" with diversity. If individuals in the pipeline were open to assimilation, and if managers had the capability to assimilate new entrants, there would be no diversity issue, regardless of how much surface diversity might exist. Now that employees are reluctant to assimilate, managers will have to manage "unassimilated diversity," people who differ on and below the surface.

Two, the corporate environment is very competitive. Indeed, today's competitive dynamics are among the most intense and severe in the history of American industry. A major implication here is that managers can ill afford to underutilize any resource.

Three, the contextual realities of "unassimilated diversity" and intense competition, along with the changing work-force demographics, make diversity a business (viability) issue, as opposed to being primarily a legal, social responsibility or moral concern. Stated differently, a corporation's ability to tap the potential of employees—regardless of how different or similar they might be—will be a critical determinant of its competitive well-being.

PREPARING FOR DIVERSITY:
A REVIEW OF PAST PRACTICES

In the context of *Workforce 2000* and environmental realities, and as a means of setting the stage for future initiatives, a number of corporate managers have paused and reviewed past practices with respect to diversity. They have looked at three questions: How have we approached diversity in the past? What progress have we made? What issues remain to be addressed?

The traditional approach to diversity has been a combination of assimilation, "melting pot," and affirmative action (AA). Here, managers inform new employees that the corporation has a unique culture and that people who fit a certain mold tend to do better than others. To facilitate the individual's success, managers offer to help new entrants assimilate (adjust to the mold's specifics) by "melting" them in the melting pot.

Historically, managers and employees have found this approach acceptable. Only recently has this alternative been compromised by a growing reluctance on the part of individuals to be assimilated and also by an emerging belief on the part of managers that perhaps a diverse work force can offer benefits not available from a homogeneous group of employees. So, just as managers are preparing for a rush of diversity, they are beginning to question the capability of their traditional approach.

To compound matters, managers are learning that, while the traditional option has produced significant results, it also has manifested substantial limitations.

One manifestation has been the disproportionate clustering of minorities and women at the bottom of the corporate pyramid. While individual minorities and women may do well in a given corporation, as groups—collectively—they tend to stagnate disproportionately at the lower levels of the corporate hierarchy. From a managerial perspective, this clustering represents underutilization, the cost of which increases the more unfriendly the environment. I have heard expressions of concern about this clustering in corporations with excellent AA track records, and also in companies with less than outstanding AA histories. Managers are beginning to seek "progress" with diversity as a way of minimizing underutilization costs.

A second manifestation has been the frustrating cycle that corporations have experienced with affirmative action. The cycle begins with the recognition of a problem. Next, there is a burst of activity followed by apparent progress. After the celebration of the progress, there is satisfaction and relaxation. This state of bliss, however, is disrupted by an awareness that the apparent progress has disappeared and that the earlier symptoms are reappearing. Once again, a problem condition is recognized as the cycle begins anew. Over the years, I have yet to find a corporation not caught up in this cycle.

These manifestations of limitations have troubled these managers who are aware of them. Generally, they appreciate the progress that has been realized through the assimilation/affirmative action/melting-pot approach, but they also perceive that they may be up against the limits of this alternative. They are actively seeking ways to augment the traditional.

Among the issues that these managers see needing to be addressed are the following:

- How can a corporation's managers create a capability for naturally tapping the potential of a diverse work force? "Naturally" refers to a situation where no special interventions or efforts are required to assure that members of all groups experience equal opportunity.

- How can a corporation avoid the assimilation/affirmative action/melting-pot cycle? Stated differently, how can corporations make sustainable progress?

- How can white male backlash be avoided or minimized? How can the needs of the white male not be lost in the midst of increasing work-force diversity?

CURRENT PRACTICES

Current managerial approaches to diversity can be categorized as follows: (1) Traditional (affirmative action), (2) Understanding Diversity, and (3) Managing Diversity.

Traditional. By far, the most common approach is still the assimilation/affirmative action/melting-pot model, despite a growing awareness of its shortcomings. Among examples of interventions utilized are those listed below:

- Outreach efforts to increase the number of qualified minorities and women in the pipeline. Included here would be initiatives to influence individual selection of education and training opportunities, so that choices will be in line with projected occupational openings.

- Renewed recruitment efforts to increase the number of minorities and women in a given corporation.

- Programs to enhance minorities' and women's understanding of the requirements for corporate success. The thinking here is that this understanding will better prepare these individuals for assimilation.

- Mentoring programs for minorities and women. Where mentoring has been identified as a "success key," managers often establish special initiatives to assure that this avenue is available.

- Tracking of minorities and women viewed as having high potential for upward mobility. The intent is to assure that these employees remain visible and receive the necessary attention to ready them for promotions.

By and large, these interventions have been tried before and ultimately have not moved corporations beyond the cycle. Managers offer reasons as explanations for the revival of these initiatives:

- The status of women and minorities in corporations requires special attention and effort.

- Minorities and women expect, indeed demand, these thrusts.

- Managers often have little documentation of how successful an intervention was or was not in a previous cycle. Without this historical perspective, managers easily can find themselves repeating an intervention.

- Managers do not know what else to do. In this instance, little if any awareness exists of alternatives to the traditional approach; therefore, managers continue with what is familiar.

Understanding Diversity (UD). This approach represents a marked departure from the traditional. Historically, if an individual had difficulty accepting diversity, it has been assumed that he or she was racist or sexist. UD assumes that the difficulty flows from a lack of understanding, so the objective becomes that of enhancing the employee's ability to accept, understand, and appreciate differences among individuals. Examples of interventions under this rubric are the following:

- Establishment of caucuses that support the individual and foster understanding of the given group's "culture." Illustrations would be caucuses for women, blacks, and Hispanics.

- Designation of "cultural days," where specific cultures are highlighted. On "Hispanic Awareness Day," for example, the cafeteria may feature Hispanic food, and the Hispanic caucus may present an exhibit and a formal program reflecting the Hispanic culture.

- Presentation of educational and training programs to enhance participants' awareness of "cultural differences" and recognition of their personal feelings regarding individual differences.

While this alternative does differ from the traditional, it still subscribes to the assimilation assumption that the individual will adjust. Also, it offers little hope for breaking out of the cycle, primarily because it does not focus on variables such as corporate culture and people systems. I have seen instances where managers have made great progress with UD, only to find themselves still asking how they can get out of the frustrating AA cycle.

Managing Diversity. This approach is an emerging supplement to the traditional option. It calls for substantial variation from past practices. Below I offer highlights of the concept as it has evolved at The American Institute for Managing Diversity.

- Managing Diversity (MD) is a process, not a solution. MD is a vehicle for generating company-specific, research-based solutions for moving toward sustainable progress and breaking the cycle.

- MD defines managing as enabling or influencing as opposed to controlling. Hence, the fundamental question implicit in MD is the following: "As a manager goes about enabling his or her work force, and as it becomes increasingly diverse, are there things that must be done differently in managing a diverse work force?" Fundamentally, this is a question that has not been asked because managers have been focusing on creating a diverse work force. Demographic projections suggest that creating a diverse work force will be less and less of a challenge. The critical task will be that of securing from a diverse work force the required level of productivity.

- MD defines "diversity" as including the white male. So managing diversity does not mean the white male managing minorities and women, but rather any manager managing whoever is in his or her work force.

- MD relaxes the assimilation assumption and assumes that both the individual and the corporation will have to adjust, that the individual will not bear the burden of adjustment alone.

- A major distinguishing factor between affirmative action and managing diversity is that MD calls for corrective action. More specifically, MD focuses on correcting a system so that it works naturally for all employees, whereas AA only provides relief or an escape from dysfunctional aspects of a system.

- MD, unlike understanding diversity, calls for development of a managerial capability for creating a work environment that will naturally enable all employees—as opposed to enhancing an individual's ability— to accept, understand, and appreciate differences among people. The point made here is that a manager can be free of racism and sexism ˙and can accept, understand, and appreciate diversity without knowing how to *manage* diversity— without knowing how to create an environment that will work for all employees, regardless of how similar or dissimilar they might be. So when one inquires about how a corporation is doing with managing diversity, the focus is not on how the elimination of discrimination is coming, or on how race and gender relations are evolving, but rather on how the building of a *managerial capability* is developing.

- MD defines "diversity" broadly to include dimensions other than race, gender, and ethnicity. Other examples of diversity are age, tenure with the organization, lifestyle, functional and educational background, geographic origin, and diversity related to acquisitions and mergers—just to illustrate dimensions that could be included. The belief is that a manager cannot focus on one or two dimensions, while ignoring others without compromising progress with the factors being addressed. This breadth of diversity suggests that MD does not call for programs or initiatives, but a "way of life" change. Managers desiring to move forward with MD have to be prepared for fostering major change.

- MD requires recognition of the business (viability) motive. Managers cannot hope to implement "way of life" changes unless there is a clear grasp of the viability implications of MD, as well as the legal, moral, and social responsibility motives. Organizational participants must understand how MD can enhance the company's competitive posture.

MD is a viability issue in at least two ways. One, corporations increasingly will be required to burn a diverse fuel (human resources). Those burning the fuel better than their competitors will have a competitive advantage. Two, most of what is already on corporate America's plate for the purpose of enhancing viability either implicitly or explicitly calls for MD.

- Some companies are pursuing total quality. All approaches to quality that I have experienced call for empowering the total work force. Assuming a diverse work force, this requires MD capability.

- Independent of total quality, some corporations are seeking greater employee involvement and more participatory decision-making. In the context of a diverse work force, this cannot be done without MD capability.

- Other corporations are implementing "high commitment work teams." Given a diverse work force, the desired level of commitment cannot be achieved without MD capability.

- Others are running as lean as possible, thereby placing a premium on tapping the potential of all resources. With respect to human resources and with a diverse work force, MD capability is required.

- MD calls for cultural and systemic interventions as well as initiatives at the individual and interpersonal levels. Culture is defined as the basic assumptions underlying all activity in a corporation. They tend to be few in number and not immediately visible. These assumptions can be viewed as analogous to the roots of a tree. A key principle is that the roots *control* the branches. Nothing can be sustained naturally in the branches unless it is congruent with the roots.

  Given that the roots of most corporations were put in place when the work force was relatively homogeneous, now that the work force is increasingly diverse, MD suggests that it is managerially prudent to ask at least whether the old roots will work for the new circumstances. This explains, at least in part, the AA cycle experienced by corporations. Managers have not taken care to assure that the corporate roots (assumptions) are congruent with their diversity aspirations.

If a manager determines that the roots of his/her corporation are not appropriate for diversity, progress beyond the cycle and the disproportionate clustering cannot be made in a sustainable fashion without changing roots.

This same type of analysis has to be made with formal and informal "people" systems. Managers must understand how they work and then assess them to determine if they are appropriate for a diverse work force. Where systems are not congruent with diversity, they have to be modified. Examination and modification of culture (roots) and systems are at the heart of the MD process.

MD calls for all interventions to be grounded in a research-based diagnosis. Without research, a manager will have difficulty understanding and assessing the culture and systems of the company.

MD assumes parallel implementation with affirmative action and understanding diversity. In the long run, effective management of employee diversity will make AA and UD unnecessary. Unfortunately, given the current rate of change, long run means 20 or 25 years. Full utilization of human resources, in the meantime, will require the manager to implement MD, AA, and UD.

Only a handful of corporations has moved forward with managing diversity, and they are only in the initial stages of implementation. Much more widespread has been the adoption of the traditional AA approach and UD.

PROGRESS TO DATE

On the one hand, progress has been encouraging. As a result of AA and UD initiatives, recruitment of minorities and women has been enhanced; greater sensitivity exists regarding differences among people; minorities and women have experienced some increased upward mobility; and the morale and expectations of minorities have improved.

On the other hand, there is little to indicate that progress has been made toward a natural capability that will allow sustainable progress. Indeed, indications are that after substantial effort and movement with AA and UD, corporations are trapped in the cycle. I am seeing situations where corporations, after major AA and UD change efforts, are regrouping in hopes of finding a way to break the cycle. To date, the results have not been encouraging.

Managers involved in launching the MD process in their corporations remain optimistic about its potential to break the cycle; however, they have yet to generate hard data to support the logic behind MD's potential for moving a corporation beyond the cycle. This is simply because a lengthy time frame is required for implementation.

One reason these managers remain excited about the process is that they have yet to bump against its limits. Most of their implementation challenges have come from their colleagues being unable to make the culture and systemic changes called for by the process. As these managers and their colleagues learn more about the business (viability) rationale for MD, and as they gain experience with implementing and sustaining root (culture) change, more data will be available regarding the process's potential. This experience and learning are all part of the educational process implicit in MD.

The most discouraging aspect of MD is that too few companies have actually tried it. One encouraging indication is the tendency of corporations to be more willing to consider MD, after bumping against the limits of the traditional approach and UD.

A final note on progress to date is in order. It is becoming increasingly clear, regardless of the approach being utilized, that white male backlash will have to be addressed if meaningful progress is to be achieved. In all the talk about diversity, little attention has been paid to the uncertainties and needs of the white male. No true effort to manage diversity can advance without considering these issues.

RECOMMENDATIONS

Unless managers adopt a three-pronged AA, UD, and MD approach, I am not optimistic that they will generate sustainable progress and break the AA cycle. Unfortunately, as the corporate environment becomes more competitive, remaining in the cycle will become more costly.

If managers are to move beyond the cycle, they will have to broaden their perspective to include the tasks of creating a culture and creating a set of managerial systems that work for all employees. An initial requirement here is that managers approach diversity from a managerial posture. For most managers, this will require a major mindset shift, given the custom of viewing diversity as a moral or social responsibility or a legal issue. Breaking the cycle naturally must become a priority.

Indications for Other Sectors

The MD process essentially says that it is not enough to focus on relationships among people who are diverse, that a manager also must look at the factors that frame these interactions—such as culture (roots) and systems. If the manager does not expand the focus to include these elements, he/she will not likely be able to create an environment that will work naturally for all employees.

This reasoning also holds for other organizations in our society. For example, public schools increasingly experience conflicts among racial and ethnic groups, as do universities and colleges. Similarly, several American cities are struggling with racial and ethnic clashes. Typically, observers label these incidents as race relations incidents. The MD process suggests that they are symptoms reflecting the fact that these organizations have not moved to create an environment that will work for all participants.

It should be clear that these organizations and their administrators/managers have not failed in managing diversity, but rather that they have not gotten around to it. They have been preoccupied with creating a diverse set of organizational participants and fostering good interpersonal relationships between the genders and among the ethnic and racial groups. All of this is well and appropriate, and should be continued. However, these managers must simultaneously move beyond inclusion and race relations issues to the managerial tasks of crea appropriate cultures and systems. This holds for any organization with a diverse population. It also pertains to our society as a whole.

If we are unable to cope simultaneously with these conflicts and also to address the task of systemic and cultural change, we will assign ourselves to perpetual racial, ethnic, and gender conflict in our organizations and our broader society.

Cultural and systemic change will not be easy. An example is the current debate in some locales over an Afrocentric versus a Eurocentric focus in the core curriculum materials. The essential issue here is the nature of core knowledge that all students will be required to learn. How do we make the core sufficiently broad so that all groups will find it meaningful, yet also sufficiently focused to be congruent with the integrity of the country? Similar discussions within organizational contexts will be equally difficult, yet they will be absolutely necessary to develop environments that will work for all participants.

The Future

I have suggested in this article that effective management of diversity will require "way of life" changes for corporations, as well as for other organizations and society in general, and that these modifications will call for substantial alterations of corporate cultures and systems.

With respect to the future, I am optimistic that we will place managing diversity on our agendas. Until now, it has rarely been there. We have focused on implementing AA and enhancing relations among diverse groups. I think we are starting to see that if we cannot free ourselves of perpetual race and gender conflict, we will pay a heavy price in terms of organizational, societal, and economic viability. I am encouraged that we will move forward, now that we are beginning to realize fully that the stakes are high.

A Changing World Order: Implications for Black America

Donald F. McHenry

It is always difficult and risky to assess the importance of contemporary events in the great scheme of history. Events that are momentous in our time will become less important in perspective. Yet, one can safely predict that 1990 will more than hold its own over time. Probably no event since the attainment of nuclear weapons by the Soviet Union after World War II has had such a momentous effect on world affairs, and ultimately on the lives of individuals, as has had the end of the Cold War. Soviet attainment of the bomb ushered in an era of possible mutual destruction; the end of the Cold War opens up the kind of mutual cooperation that the architects of the post-war world saw wistfully disappear even before their plans were ratified.

THE END OF THE COLD WAR

International affairs have been revolutionized without the firing of a single weapon from the impressive and expensive arsenals that both sides accumulated. The doomsday clock, which moved relentlessly toward midnight in recent years, has not only stopped but also has actually been turned back. Only the most pessimistic of hard-liners would argue that the Cold War continues or, for that matter, that, aside from suicidal use of nuclear weapons, the Soviet Union remains in a position to wage major conflict.

The change in the relationship between the superpowers has meant a corresponding change in almost every aspect of foreign policy. The countries of Eastern Europe held democratic elections; began to break away from their military alliance with the Soviet Union; and, in an effort to modernize their economies, are moving away from the social economic structure that revolved around the bankrupt economic system of the Soviet Union.

Outside of Eastern Europe, there were also important changes. The United States and the Soviet Union worked closely together to resolve regional conflicts in Namibia, Cambodia, Angola, and Nicaragua. The decade is ending with the United States and the Soviet Union carefully coordinating policy aimed at turning back the effort of Iraq to annex Kuwait by force. The irony is that Soviet and American efforts have been coordinated through the United Nations, the most idealistic and ambitious result of World War II. Finally, after 45 years of semi-paralysis, the United Nations, no longer blocked by the veto of the superpowers, became a reasonably effective instrument for working to maintain international peace and security. The result was not without irony: the more the superpowers and other permanent members of the United Nations cooperated, as the drafters of the United Nations charter intended they should, the more the smaller countries began to worry about big country domination!

BEGINNING OF THE END OF APARTHEID

Events in the East-West conflict alone would have qualified 1990 as a remarkable year. However, the year will also stand out as the year of the decisive event that marked independence for Namibia and the beginning of the end of apartheid in South Africa. The embattled and isolated white minority government of South Africa finally concluded that peace and prosperity were not possible with internal division and strife, and that division and strife were the bedrock of apartheid. In an effort to persuade its internal and external critics that it was prepared to begin negotiations on a new South Africa, the government released Nelson Mandela, the black leader of the African National Congress, and opened the way for more normal political expression. Most of the world watched as Mandela—tall, dignified, and seemingly without bitterness—walked unbowed from a South African jail after having served almost 30 years in prison for having sought a basic human right.

The visit of Nelson Mandela to the United States in June, 1990, caught the imagination of the American public. The Mandela visit easily exceeded the attention paid to the visit of Gorbachev. Mandela toured the country, appeared at numerous large and small public and private events, generously thanked the American public for the assistance that his movement had received, and appealed to the American public and government to maintain pressure on the South African government until democratic rule was a reality in South Africa. Even for people who knew little about South Africa, Mandela's presence was a moving experience. For a nation that had grown all too cynical about such things, Mandela was a genuine hero.

Mandela had reason to thank the American public. Numerous churches, colleges, unions, and local and state governments had used their economic and political leverage to increase economic pressure on the South African government to end apartheid. The Anti-Apartheid Act of 1987 had passed the Congress and was then repassed over the veto of President Reagan. Only after South Africa had taken significant steps to end apartheid would normal economic relations between South Africa and the United States be resumed. The release of Nelson Mandela was one of those prerequisites.

As Mandela and his fellow citizens engage in the difficult process of negotiating a new constitution for South Africa, the problem facing Americans, and black Americans in particular, is how to play a constructive role. The white minority government must be encouraged to complete the positive changes that they have started; however, pressures for change must not be reduced prematurely. Similarly, those deprived of their rights in South Africa must continue to be supported, yet they must be encouraged to avail themselves of opportunities for reconciliation. Can these difficult roles be performed without getting them interwoven with domestic American politics? Can these difficult roles be performed while recognizing that the level of external involvement in the South African drama has fundamentally changed, and that more than ever the principal actors are the SouthAfricans themselves?

FOREIGN POLICY AND BLACK AMERICANS

What were the implications of these and other momentous events for the international community, for the United States, and, for purposes of this essay, for black Americans? This question has always had greater importance for black Americans than is usually assumed. It is an importance that extends beyond a superficial ethnic interest in African or Caribbean developments. Economic and political developments around the world affect the agenda, the priorities, and the resources of the United States. As was the case in Vietnam, and now in the Iraq situation, conflicts far away can draw on black Americans in disproportionate numbers.

ECHOES OF THE AMERICAN CIVIL RIGHTS MOVEMENT

It is worth noting that the political and social changes that took place in Eastern Europe and in South Africa were not unrelated to the social changes experienced in the United States during the sixties. The civil rights anthem, "We Shall Overcome," which was sung in joy and grief alike during the civil rights campaigns in the United States during the sixties, was sung spontaneously at the Berlin wall, in Wenceslas Square in Czechoslovakia, and in Tiananmen Square in China. The determination by citizens to participate in their government gained new momentum not only in Europe but also in Brazil, Argentina, and Chile in Latin America; and Zaire, Zambia, Gabon, Benin, and other countries in Africa. Entrenched military or one-party rule gave way to civilian governments or multiparty systems.

These changes came as the United States was about to come off of a self-inflicted high that bore no relation to the problems that the country faced. The Reagan administration had come into office with the apparent belief that the best government is that which governs least; that free enterprise ought to be free to pursue business with minimal regulation; that government had done all that it could or should to place the victims of slavery and discrimination on a competitive footing, and that, henceforth, those who had been disadvantaged could best benefit to the extent that society as a whole prospered; and, finally, that the United States had to strengthen itself militarily and had to turn back actively, even unilaterally, the "gains" of communism. Fiscally, this could be done while cutting taxes, maintaining entitlements, and spending whatever it cost on new weapons systems.

NO PEACE DIVIDEND—PERHAPS NO PEACE

Thus, it was widely expected that after 45 years of bearing an extraordinary portion of the defense of the free world, and after the spending binge of the Reagan years aimed at defense against a Soviet threat, there would be a "peace dividend." That is, that there would be large sums of money that would no longer be needed for defense and could be devoted to some of the pressing problems at home. For black Americans, the peace dividend was especially important, for areas of particular interest to those at the lower end of the economic spectrum might be addressed.

However, the peace dividend proved to be a mirage. In the first place, it was not military spending that stood in the way of addressing problems of pressing domestic importance. The problems simply were not important enough to cause Presidents Reagan and Bush to change their priorities and to push social problems higher on their list of priorities. Nor were these problems deemed to be important enough to walk away from the fiscal policies that made it almost impossible to take on additional programs. So long as entitlements were politically untouchable, taxes could not be increased, and military expenditures could not be cut; some, naively, looked forward to the peace dividend for relief.

Second, the very fiscal policies that enabled the administrations to pay for their extravagant lifestyles would consume whatever funds became available as a peace dividend. Unwilling to tax itself or to save, the United States had financed its spending binge by borrowing at home and abroad. With peace came the realization that interest payments, deferred maintenance, built-in expenditures for entitlements, and lower revenues from a sick economy consumed the peace dividend and additional taxes as well.

Third, most people underestimated the cost and dislocation of winding down defense expenditures. It is difficult and even unwise to terminate costly and long-term projects in midstream. Moreover, there was a price to pay in reorienting defense industries and their employees to nondefense-related activities.

Fourth, the changes in Eastern Europe were not without cost. Large-scale economic development was necessary, lest chaos move into the vacuum left by communism's failures. The United States was no longer in a position to undertake massive development programs in the area. However, it was necessary that assistance be provided and that the United States pay a share.

However, the fifth and final reason for the absence of a peace dividend was the sudden development of turmoil between Iraq and the international community over Iraq's invasion and annexation of Kuwait. Within days, the anticipated peace was shattered. Oil prices rose precipitately. The economy, already headed for recession, dropped more sharply. The new costs exceeded the peace dividend and the burden-sharing contributions from other countries combined.

As 1990 drew to a close, it was too early to determine the full extent of the effect of the Iraq situation on the future fiscal policies of the United States. Much depends on how quickly the situation can be resolved and, most importantly, on whether the withdrawal of Iraq can be accomplished peacefully. However, even a peaceful resolution to the situation will not end the cost. Even if Iraq were to withdraw from Kuwait, Iraq would remain a certain threat to the peace of the area, thus making it likely that some kind of continued force involving American troops or American support for regional forces would be required for the foreseeable future.

MILITARY CONFLICT, RACE, AND CLASS

Iraq's invasion of Kuwait brought most sharply into focus a question that ought to concern all Americans, but is of particular importance to black Americans. It is the disproportionate number of blacks in the military, and therefore, the disproportionate number of black lives at risk compared with the rest of the population should hostilities commence.

Some trace this situation to the absence of a draft, but similar situations existed in the Vietnam conflict where the draft was used. The military was populated by large numbers of blacks and whites who were unable to qualify for one of numerous deferments available. The common denominator was not so much race as it was socioeconomic status. Those well enough off to pursue a college education or profession could frequently qualify. (Or, as in the case of Vice President Dan Quayle, could legally avoid the draft by serving in a national guard unit.) The poorer, black or white, could not.

With the introduction of the volunteer army, the situation may be even more exaggerated. The military has based much of its recruitment on the opportunities the services offer for education, skilled training, and travel. With the opportunity, however, has come risk, a risk assumed by large numbers of blacks who see the military as an alternative—perhaps the only alternative—to the depression of the inner city and the large ranks of unemployed black youth. Ironically, the Iraq situation may have preserved the availabilty of the military to a broader portion of the population. Clearly, the ranks of the military were scheduled for sharp reductions with the end of the Cold War. Moreover, the military was becoming more highly selective as its manpower needs were reduced and the technical nature of its operations became more complex. Thus, the Iraq situation may have maintained the military as an outlet for the disadvantaged.

Inevitably, in the wake of possible hostilities in the Iraq situation, new questions have arisen about the fairness of the composition of the military in a democratic society. There appears to be no easy answer. Few would argue for the return to the draft unless manpower needs dictate. There will be new proposals for some kind of universal service in which all citizens participate.

The obvious solution would be to accelerate efforts to provide equal educational opportunity for all, regardless of race or economic circumstance. In the meantime, while no one doubts the willingness of black American military to serve patriotically if need be, there must exist nagging concern that opinion polls at the end of the year show less support among black Americans to undertake force to free Kuwait. Is it because most blacks and lesser educated whites, who show a similar reluctance, view the world from the same perspective? Or, do the numbers add up to a special concern?

PEACE AND THE DEVELOPING WORLD

The end of the Cold War may have unintended implications for the developing countries of the world, particularly African countries. Throughout the Cold War, developing countries had been able to benefit from and even to use superpower animosity to further their own ends. Non-alignment and third world status were sometimes an excuse to avoid choosing sides on either side of the dispute. When convenient, many of the same countries used the threat of advances by one of the superpowers to persuade the other to support a particular side in a regional dispute. Similarly, many developmental assistance programs were undertaken to buy loyalty or to prevent its sale to the opposing camp. Now the scenario has changed. Even the use of the terms "third world" and "non-aligned," always of questionable meaning, have become obsolete.

The post-Cold War Soviet Union has made it clear that it must concentrate on serious economic and political problems at home and can no longer take on the economic burden of large-scale assistance programs as it had in Cuba and elsewhere. Moreover, the terms of trade that the Soviets henceforth will use with developing countries and in Eastern Europe will be largely hard currency on market terms rather than the highly subsidized barter arrangements used previously.

The news for developing countries from the United States and Europe must be equally distressing. At the same time that developing countries must cope with economic dislocations resulting from increased oil prices, they must also face the likelihood that development assistance programs for them will be greatly reduced as the newly democratic countries of Eastern Europe not only compete for assistance but also become a higher priority. Germany, for example, will be preoccupied with the cost of Eastern Germany. Stripped of the East-West conflict as justification for assistance, there is a danger that Africa will receive fewer resources from the United States, despite initial efforts in the Congress to increase aid levels.

One benefit to the developing countries may not be initially greeted by them with enthusiasm. But, for all of those who worried about the possibility that great power rivalry in regional conflicts might cause the superpowers to back into a nuclear conflict they would have otherwise avoided, the restraint and superpower cooperation that resulted from the end of the Cold War is a welcome relief. Henceforth, developing countries will be less able to entice one of the superpowers to enter a fundamentally regional or internal conflict solely out of concern that failure to enter will allow the other superpower the opportunity to gain. At the same time, there is a benefit to the developing countries. Unable to attract the superpowers to confuse the issues, developing countries will be forced to come to grips with internal and regional conflicts on their merits. That is a welcome prospect, for it holds the possibility that conflicts in Angola, Mozambique, Cambodia, and elsewhere can be resolved more easily.

GLOBAL INTERDEPENDENCE

For some time students of international affairs have given lip service to the concept of interdependence. The theoretical concept has become the reality. Whether the issue is global warming, ocean pollution, or terrorism, it is increasingly obvious that the complex problems of modern society cannot be resolved within the boundaries of the nation state. That is also true of the economic well-being of the United States. As noted above, the United States, in part, was able to finance its wreckless fiscal policies of the eighties by borrowing from abroad. To the extent that German and Japanese investors lose confidence in the American economy or find it necessary to invest funds at home, the United States must reduce its expenditures or raise additional revenue. The budget bill passed in late 1990 did both. Still, the situation in Iraq places additional stress on an already stressed budget. Thus, not only is there no prospect for additional resources for starved domestic problems, but also there is the likelihood for additional budget reductions in domestic programs.

At the end of the year, a negotiation little known to most Americans but of significance to all Americans—the negotiation of the Uruguay Round of the General Agreement on Trade and Tariffs (GATT)—was at an impasse. At issue was the access of American goods to foreign markets. Access is important to American business and labor; in general, the relatively free access of foreign goods to the United States has meant the continued reduction of some American jobs, as foreign traders sell in the United States but erect barriers to similar sales in their markets by American producers. The classic examples are autos and agricultural products in Japan, agricultural products in Europe, and services and intellectual property in many developing countries. Unfortunately, each of these areas was strongly defended by powerful domestic constituencies that would be less able or unable to compete under conditions of free trade.

THE WAR ON DRUGS

One aspect of economic privation and turmoil elsewhere can be seen on the streets of the United States every day. It is the increased use of illegal, addictive substances and the crime that frequently accompanies their use and trade.

Most drugs are smuggled into the United States from countries in Latin America and Asia, where poor and impoverished farmers are paid small amounts of money for crops that are eventually processed and sold in the United States and other developed countries for astronomical sums of money. Illegal drug trade diverts scarce resources of the poor, further exasperates social problems, and leads to violent crime, including murder. The evidence points to widespread use of cocaine across the social spectrum in the United States. However, what is called recreational use in suburbia takes on monstrous proportions in the inner city. Moreover, in recent years, AIDS has grown more rapidly among blacks and Hispanics because of the use of drugs administered through contaminated needles. Thus, a problem that gets its start among the poor outside of the United States has its effect among the poor inside of the United States.

Although the problem of drugs can be attacked by a combination of education, treatment, and punishment of drug users, there must also be an effort to discourage the production of drugs at the source. Thus, in 1990, there were numerous efforts to capture drug cartel leaders in Colombia and Peru; to destroy crops in Colombia, Peru, and Mexico; and to interrupt the transport of drugs in the Caribbean. In late 1989, the United States invaded Panama in an effort to prevent the use of the country for drug trade and money laundering. Unfortunately, most of these efforts suffer from the tendency to emphasize intermittently one approach or another rather than the broadly based, coordinated, consistent, and long-term approach that is needed. Just as in the United States there tends to be a greater emphasis on punishment than on education and treatment, American programs abroad frequently place greater emphasis on interdiction and punishment rather than on economic development and trade programs that would provide opportunities for impoverished rural farmers. It was to bring coordination, coherence, and focus to the problem that Congress created the position of "drug czar." However, after two years, only the level of rhetoric has been raised.

THE OUTLOOK FOR 1991

The last decade of the twentieth century begins with hope and uncertainty. There is hope that a new spirit of cooperation has lessened the likelihood that man will destroy life as we know it in one brief moment of anger. But there is plenty of uncertainty. Will the international community stand together in the Middle East and thus discourage future aggressive acts such as Iraq's attempt to take over Kuwait? What will happen to the forces newly freed in Eastern Europe? Will balkanization take place as ethnic groups assert themselves, or will they see disadvantages in going in a direction opposite a uniting Eastern Europe? Will the nations of the world reach some agreement on trade, or will we repeat the chaos of the twenties and thirties? Will South

Africans come together to resolve the differences that divide them, or will the moment of goodwill be wasted and the situation return to the dark scenarios that had been previously forecast? Will the democratic and economic reforms of 1990 bear fruit early enough, or will discouragement tempt citizens to return to dictatorial ways? These are questions added to the agenda in 1990. They join such old questions as arms control, economic development, and the environment. The agenda remains formidable but more hopeful than at any time since World War II.

The Case of African Americans in the Persian Gulf: The Intersection of American Foreign and Military Policy with Domestic Employment Policy in the United States

Dianne M. Pinderhughes, Ph.D.

INTRODUCTION

The possibility that the United States might become involved in a war for oil in the Persian Gulf offers the opportunity to review the forces that shape career and employment choices of blacks in the larger society, and to evaluate the impact of affirmative action policies upon their success. In this article, I compare the participation of African Americans in the private and the public, especially military, sectors of the American economy. These are two distinctly contrasting sectors of economic opportunity for blacks. The military—especially the Army—shows higher concentrations of African-American men and women and somewhat different patterns of distribution than in any other sector of society for blacks in general.

What are the consequences of these patterns of representation for the U.S., and for the longer-term status of Black America if we fight a Persian Gulf war, and especially if we have a continuing policy of police intervention on an international basis? The combined foreign-military policy, which positions the U.S. as a world regulator, disproportionately jeopardizes the already perilous state of Black America, based on both socioeconomic and racial factors, quite distinctly from the white population. The socioeconomic factors are significant for the lower third of the white population, but the differences in the size of the white population group overall and its different economic status would insulate it from the intensity of impact felt by the black population. Because of racial discrimination in the private economy and because of the shift to the all-volunteer force (AVF), it is important to note that blacks are drawn into the military from all economic sectors. With the changed use of the reserves as part of the overall fighting force, significant numbers of older, well-educated, working and middle-class African Americans have already been, are being, or will be called to active duty during this Persian Gulf crisis.[1]

Policymakers have typically argued that the benefits outweigh the risks and the individual soldier can calculate and grasp those factors when he or she chooses to join. These asymmetrical racial occupational policy arenas, combined with American military interventionist policy, would have the effect of a racially unequal, significantly greater impact in lives lost, leadership lost, and overall costs upon blacks in comparison to whites. Black and white political leadership, policymakers, and intelligentsia have a responsibility to take note of these inequalities and to attack their sources in both domestic and foreign/military policy. In this chapter, I review the economic status of the black population in the private sector and the history of blacks and racial policy in the armed forces; evaluate the choices blacks can make between these two sectors; review the attitudes toward the military and war in general, as well as concerns about the current Persian Gulf crisis within the black population; comment briefly about the positions of black elected officials; and conclude with some policy recommendations.

THE ECONOMIC STATUS OF THE BLACK CIVILIAN POPULATION

I summarize black economic location in the private sector by reviewing the conclusions of several recent major studies on the status of black Americans, concentrating on their data on occupational distribution rather than on employment, income, or wealth, which are not useful comparisons when the military is involved. While there have been some improvements over the decades, all the studies conclude that serious race-based economic occupational inequalities remain.

Reynolds Farley and Walter Allen's study, *The Color Line and the Quality of Life in America,* reviews the long-term status of the black population and is based on analysis of 1980 census data. In evaluating occupational changes among blacks and whites between 1940 and 1980, they conclude:

> There have been improvements since 1940 in the occupational status of blacks, attributable in large part to the exodus of black men from farm labor and black women from domestic service. Racial differences in occupational distributions are declining, and differences are much smaller within specific educational groups than in the aggregate. Nevertheless, blacks are more concentrated at the bottom of the occupational hierarchy than whites, and the only blacks who have attained occupational parity with similar whites are college-educated women (Farley and Allen, 1987: 280).

A Common Destiny (Jaynes and Williams, eds., 1989), based on a series of studies commissioned by the National Research Council, reviews published research on blacks between 1940 and the late 1980s.

> Numerous studies. . . find that the proportion of employed workers in better jobs increased more rapidly for blacks than for whites and that this upgrading continued throughout the 1970s and 1980s. . . . Nevertheless, large occupational

differences remain and blacks are still greatly overrepresented in low-wage, low-skill jobs (Jaynes and Williams, 1989: 312).[2]

The Trotter Institute's multivolume *Assessment of the Status of African Americans* (Reed, ed., 1990) began as a critique of the National Research Council study; it includes an essay by economist William Darity. He argues that the

> black managerial class is heavily dependent on these same programs [social programs inaugurated in the 1930s and greatly expanded in the 1960s]; the earnings of black managerial class. . .can be traced directly to the expansion of social welfare programs under the rubric of the Great Society (64). Prior to 1960, black professionals and administrators were concentrated in education and, at the federal level, in the post office. The significant shift in the 1960s is that middle class blacks moved into noneducational social welfare agencies at the state and local level. . . . Between 1960 and 1976, the size of the black middle class roughly tripled (Brown and Erie, 1981: 308-309, quoted in Darity, 1990: 68).

Finally, David Swinton, Denys Vaughn-Cooke, and other economists have written in previous editions of the National Urban League's *The State of Black America* about the poor and declining economic status of the black population. In 1984, Vaughn-Cooke noted that a recovery from the 1982 recession had caused only a slight impact on the black population across a number of age cohorts; the Reagan administration tended to rely on the private sector to correct economic difficulties and was willing to accept "high rates of black unemployment as the price for this inflation control" (Vaughn-Cooke, 1984: 14). Toward the end of the decade, Swinton reported that "the evidence suggests that society has not been making any measurable progress in the last few years to ameliorate the high rates of poverty, low incomes, low levels of wealth, limited business ownership, and disadvantaged labor market positions that continue to characterize the economic status of the black population" (Swinton, 1988: 150).

In short, economic statistics show that blacks have made some gains in recent decades, but they have been relatively minor; in some cases, these gains are more related to the geographic and sectoral relocations blacks have undergone than to any significant redistribution in their occupational specializations. Even where there has been some increase—such as in that of the black middle class, it has been as a result of employment in public sector programs that service the black poor and working class. At the national level, the Reagan and Bush administrations have taken overtly oppositional postures toward continuation of even the moderate programs of affirmative action that were initiated during the Nixon administration and implemented during successive Democratic and Republican administrations until 1980. Most recently, of course, President Bush has vetoed the 1990 Civil Rights Act, which was constructed to overturn a number of U.S. Supreme Court decisions that had the chilling effect of weakening affirmative action policy.

The overall impact of these findings about occupational status is complicated by recent reports on the sharp drop in black life expectancy for the second year in a row (while that for whites has largely been stable or increasing) and by sharp increases (a two-thirds increase from 60.6 to 101.1 per 100,000) in the homicide rate among young black men.[3]

A BRIEF HISTORY OF AFRICAN AMERICANS AND RACIAL POLICY IN THE AMERICAN MILITARY

For most of American history, the participation of blacks in the military as part of the regular combat troops has been a politically controversial and highly volatile issue. Society consistently blocked long-term black participation in the armed forces until the post-World War II era.

National leaders typically chose to incorporate African Americans into the military because of white manpower shortages and/or because of the difficulties in winning the war; for the most part, even at the outset of most wars, the policy was to discourage rather than to encourage black participation (Dorn, 1989: 2). When their opponent was willing to use blacks (the British, for example, promised black slaves freedom if they fought against the American revolutionaries; even the South considered the possibility of using black slaves in the waning days of the American Civil War (Stillman, 1976: 893; Ploski and Williams, 1989: 836)), American leaders changed their posture on black participation. Even when military and political leaders chose to use blacks, they tended to direct them away from contact with the infantry and guns until they had no other choice.[4]

Five thousand blacks fought in the Revolutionary war; close to 400,000 during the Civil War, with fewer than half involved in direct combat; 371,000 in World War I; and approximately one million during World War II (Stillman, 1976; Ploski and Williams, 1989; Foner, 1974). Schexnider notes that the WWII Army was not only segregated, but it also "adopted a policy of *racial quotas* designed to ensure that the number of black troops would not exceed their proportion in the civilian population" (Schexnider and Butler, 1976: 422; emphasis in the original). The integration of the armed forces was planned by the late 1940s, but it was not implemented until the Korean War, when the rate of black enlistments in the Army rose to 25 percent, and military commanders found it increasingly difficult to maintain segregated understaffed white units and oversupplied black units. ". . . [T] Army was faced with a shortage of men in white units, especially those on the front lines in Korea. Military necessity therefore more or less forced integration of both training units and combat units" (Binkin et al., 1982: 29).

The integration of the military began with a shift from a quota on enlistments by race to a system using tests to regulate the entrance of blacks (Nalty and MacGregor, 1981: 264; Dorn, 1989: 2):

. . .Truman's secretary of the army, concerned that the elimination of quotas would cause too many blacks to enter the service, offered the president a way to restrict black representation indirectly:

> If, as a result of a fair trial of this new system, there ensues a disproportionate balance of racial strengths in the army, it is my understanding that I have your authority to return to a system which will, in effect, control enlistments by race.

Military personnel experts knew that blacks tended to score lower than whites on the services' standardized enlistment examinations and that therefore the number of blacks could be controlled by "the substitution of an achievement quota for the present racial quota." . . . Truman wrote "OK HST" on the secretary's memorandum (Dorn, 1989: 3).

Because of this, the proportions by race remained comparable to the overall population through the 1960s, although such percentages masked an increase in the draft, battlefield service, and death rates of blacks in Vietnam (Binkin, 1982: 43, 76). There was also variation by race among the services, with the Army having the highest proportion and the Navy the lowest proportion of blacks; that variation also existed between the enlisted and officer sectors.

The military has implemented successive generations of policies to facilitate racial integration. It integrated its personnel on base in the 1950s, sought to end discrimination in off-base housing and other services in the 1960s during the Kennedy administration, worked to discourage the race-based expressions of white racism and black militancy that arose in the Vietnam years as a significantly larger portion of blacks was drafted, and began to implement affirmative action plans beginning in 1970 (Binkin, 1982; DeFranco, 1987). In its comparatively swift actual implementation of integration in the 1950s, the military preceded the larger society by several decades.

Because of their full responsibility for their personnel, however, the armed forces have not limited their responsibility for racial integration to only a narrow area of life, such as public accommodations or schools, but have also designed policies that coerce nondiscrimination in a more comprehensive range of areas and in substantially stronger ways when compared to the formulation of public policies that apply to the private sector.

The Kennedy administration created the Committee on Equal Opportunity in the Armed Forces, which led to the creation of an Assistant Secretary of Defense for Civil Rights (Ploski and Williams, 1989: 854). During this era to reduce off-base housing discrimination, for example, the

> DoD has established Housing Referral Offices at every military installation . . . . The offices maintain listings of available rental and sale property, and are authorized to conduct preliminary investigations of housing complaints and report their findings to the local commander. By threatening to make discriminating landlords' property off-limits to all servicemen, local

commanders have been highly successful in eliminating what was once a severe hardship on black servicemen and their families (DeFranco, 1987: 78).

By contrast, a national civil rights housing law was not passed until 1968.

When federal contract compliance and affirmative action programs were implemented through Executive Order 11246 in 1965, the military was eventually covered by the same regulation in 1970. Local commanders had responsibility for implementation (DeFranco, 1987: 78), but even more importantly:

> Starting in the early 1970s, a new category appeared in the efficiency reports for officers and NCOs: race-relations skills. Filling out this section was *mandatory*, and the requirement was rigorously enforced. More blacks received promotions. Some officers with a poor record on race were relieved of command. All of this helped to set a tone. If only for reasons of self-interest, army officers and NCOs became highly sensitive to the issue of race (Moskos, 1986: 67; emphasis added).

In the early 1970s, as the proportion of blacks began to increase and as the Vietnam backlash combined to produce racial strife within the services, the Department of Defense (DOD) began to use social science to understand and manage its problems. It created the DOD Race Relations Institute (DRRI), which trained military personnel to "achieve racial harmony by inculcating all servicemen with a greater awareness of human relations, such as liberty, equality, prejudice, institutional racism, and cross-cultural problems" (DeFranco, 1987: 77). "By the time the DRRI came into existence, high-ranking military officials had proclaimed poor race relations as one of the worst problems that jeopardized the military's effectiveness and readiness" (Hope, 1979: 51).

It also involved existing research institutions such as the U.S. Army Research Institute for the Behavioral and Social Sciences in a five-year "study of the social psychology of race and gender relations in the U.S. Army" (Thomas, 1988: iii). While black soldiers in the 1980s reported, "You can still bump into an invisible shield of racism," or "The longer you stay in, the more you can see that racism knows how to hide itself. . ." (Moskos, 1986: 69), they were commenting on patterns that were not immediately visible, even after some considerable contact with the institution.

To summarize the current situation, after four decades of integration and several generations of policy, African Americans are represented in very significant numbers in most branches of the armed forces, as Table 1 shows. As of January, 1988, more than 400,000 African-American men and women were on active duty. (Ploski and Williams, 1989: 912). In 1986, the Army was approximately 27.2 percent black; the Navy, 12.8 percent; the Marine Corps, 19.0 percent; the Air Force, 15.1 percent; and the DOD overall, 19.1 percent.

Black women are represented in significantly higher proportions than men in all of the services; see Table 2. For example, among enlisted personnel, 28

Table 1
Blacks As A Percentage of the Armed Forces

Year	ARMY			NAVY			MARINE CORPS			AIR FORCE		
	Enlisted	Officer	Total	Enlisted	Officer	Total	Enlisted	Officer	Total	Enlisted	Officer	Total
1981	33.2	7.8	29.8	12.0	2.7	10.8	22.0	4.0	20.2	16.5	4.8	14.4
1984	29.6	10.4	27.2	14.2	3.1	12.8	20.5	4.4	19.0	17.0	6.3	15.1
1988	29.9	10.2		15.2	3.5		20.7	4.7		17.2	5.4	

Year	ALL SERVICES		
	Enlisted	Officer	Total
1981	22.1	5.3	19.8
1984	21.2	6.4	19.1

Sources: 1981 data are from Martin Binkin and Mark J. Eitelberg, *Blacks and the Military*, 1982, p. 42. 1984 data are from Alvin J. Schexnider and Edwin Dorn, *Who Defends America?*, 1989, p. 48. Data for 1988 are from Harry A. Ploski and James Williams, *The Negro Almanac*, 1989, p. 912.

percent of Army males are black, but 43.3 percent of females are. The respective percentages for the other branches are 13.4 percent black male and 21.8 percent black female for the Navy; 20.2 percent and 26.4 percent for the Marine Corps; 16.4 percent and 22.4 percent in the Air Force; and 20.1 percent and 30.5 percent DOD overall (Schexnider and Dorn, 1989: 48). Among the reserves, 17 percent of the enlisted personnel of the total selected reserves were black, as of 1986. Table 3 shows the distribution of blacks in the reserves and the national guard of the various branches of the armed forces (*Description of Officers, 1986*: 4–43, 4–49).

Table 2
Distribution of Black Women in the Active Duty Forces, by Service, 1986

		FEMALE	
	Total	No. Black	% Black
Army			
Enlisted	69,750	30,198	43.
Officer	10,946	1,959	17.
Navy			
Enlisted	45,602	9,948	21.
Officer	7,218	478	6.
Marine Corps			
Enlisted	9,246	2,439	26.
Officer	595	40	6.
Air Force			
Enlisted	60,694	13,914	22.
Officer	12,377	1,352	10.
DOD Total			
Enlisted[1]	185,292	56,499	30.
Officer	31,131	3,830	12.

[1]*Note:* This table omits warrant officers; 1,468, or 7.4 percent of the 19,931 warrant officers are black.

Source: Schexnider and Dorn, 1989, p. 48, based on Table 5.1.

Table 3
Total Selected Reserves* by Ethnic/Racial Background, 1986

Pay Grade/ Ethnic/Racial Background	ARNG	USAR	USNR	USMCR	ANG	USAFR	Total DoD	USCGR	Total Selected Reserve
				Reserve Component					
ENLISTED									
Total									
Black	16.7%	26.3%	10.3%	17.7%	8.6%	18.5%	17.8%	5.0%	17.6%
Hispanic	8.3	8.5	6.2	11.8	6.2	3.5	8.0	4.6	8.0
White	71.6	62.24	80.7	67.4	81.4	69.2	70.9	87.7	71.2
Other	3.4	2.8	2.8	3.1	3.8	3.9	3.2	2.7	3.2
Total	100.0	100.0	100.0	100.0	100.0	100.0	100.0	100.0	100.0
Number of Cases	18499	8877	4214	3185	4879	2727	42381	1952	44333
Total Personnel (In 1,000's)	321	191	88	31	70	46	747	11	758
OFFICERS									
Total									
Black	4.3%	7.56%	2.0%	4.4%	2.8%	2.9%	4.8%	2.7%	4.8%
Hispanic	4.2	3.8	1.6	2.2	3.4	2.1	3.3	2.0	3.3
White	89.2	85.8	93.3	91.9	91.1	93.0	89.2	93.6	89.3
Other	2.3	3.0	3.2	1.5	2.7	2.0	2.7	1.7	2.7
Total	100.0	100.0	100.0	100.0	100.0	100.0	100.0	100.0	100.0
Number of Cases	2179	2737	1516	701	864	626	8623	755	9378
Total Personnel (In 1,000's)	33	41	21	3	10	8	116	2	118

*Army National Guard, U.S. Army Reserve, U.S. Navy Reserve, U.S. Marine Corps Reserve, Air National Guard, U.S. Air Force Reserve, Total Dept. of Defense, U.S. Coast Guard Reserve.

Source: *Description of Officers and Enlisted Personnel in the U.S. Selected Reserve 1986*, Department of Defense Manpower Data Center, 1989, volume 4, pp. 4–43, 4–49. Based on a 1986 DOD Reserve Component Survey conducted in the spring of 1986 by the Research Triangle Institute for Defense Manpower Data Center.

Among officers, the proportions by race are not as dramatic, but black officers constitute a significant representation, especially in the Army, wher 10.4 percent of the officers and 7.3 percent of the generals were black in th mid-1980s (Schexnider and Dorn, 1989; Schexnider, 1988: 125). The othe services had considerably smaller proportions of blacks in their top leadershi positions, but the representation in the overall officer categories has increase significantly over the past decades.

The military is most distinct from the rest of society, because blacks such as General Colin Powell—the Chairman of the Joint Chiefs of Staff, makin him the nation's top military officer—have risen to the top of the bureau cracy, and because significant numbers of other black officers can be foun between Powell and the mass of blacks in the enlisted ranks. They include th commandant of West Point, and they operate at all levels of command in th Army, including the highest levels of command in Saudi Arabia (Moskos 1986; Schexnider, 1988). Alvin Schexnider notes, however, that changes i patterns of college attendance and changes in types of financial aid availabl to young blacks will reduce their numbers in college and their correspondin numbers available for officer candidacy. Moreover, ROTC programs are a uncertain source of new black officers because of the integration of highe education in recent decades. There are many new programs on black colleg campuses, but black students are less likely to participate in ROTC at pre dominantly white colleges and universities where most black students now matriculate. Schexnider notes, therefore, that "black colleges and universitie continue to produce about one-third of all black college graduates an approximately half of the ROTC commissions awarded to blacks" (Schex nider, 1988: 123). In its high levels of representation at the enlisted level, an in its proportional levels of representation and distribution among officer of some branches, the armed forces are unlike most other sector of society.

The military is most like other sectors of society in that, despite effort at affirmative action, the distribution of blacks in occupational position (especially at the enlisted level) is not radically different from that in othe sectors. Despite the fact that "the armed forces (especially the Army) have attempted to meet affirmative action goals for a more representative distri bution among major occupational groupings ... [and] the Army ... ha been successful in reducing the relative proportion of blacks assigned t those jobs, ... blacks are overrepresented in administrative and clerical job and in the relatively service and supply handler categories. This is nothing new" (Binkin et al., 1982: 55-57).

Nonetheless, after several generations of racial policies aimed at reducing the consequences of segregation, the military has progressed substantially and, in many ways, is quite distinctive from the rest of society.

BLACK RATIONAL CHOICES: COMPETITION IN THE PRIVATE AMERICAN ECONOMY VERSUS VOLUNTARISM FOR THE RACIALLY AND SEXUALLY INTEGRATED ARMED FORCES

"Though put far too crassly, an insight was given to me by a long-time German employee of the U.S. Army in Europe:

> In the volunteer army you are recruiting the best of the blacks and the worst of the whites" (Moskos, 1989: 79).

In this section, I evaluate the consequences of the existence of two very different economic sectors on the career choices for blacks as individuals and as a group, and I address the question of fairness when considering the benefits and burdens of military service as they have been discussed by academics and policymakers.

What are the consequences of integration/segregation in a society in which racial discrimination is still practiced, although to varying degrees in different sectors of it? Society has removed some racially based criteria, legal explicit forms of racial discrimination dealing with voting, entering public places, and education, but not others, such as those associated with jobs, housing, and wealth. The military sector has removed more of the racially based criteria than others and has taken steps to maximize the full use of a population group subject to discrimination in the other sectors of society; the military also has operating criteria within that sector that are most coercive in terms of discouraging discrimination and are strongly dependent upon and related to the personnel available to them. This occurred at the same time as it changed its entrance criteria from service coerced from a proportion of all young men to voluntary service with entrants not screened by race or gender.

The relatively high proportions of blacks in the military in general and in specific branches of the services are therefore a result of literally being pushed out of the private economy by several interactive factors: educational disadvantage, unemployment, discrimination, and economic difficulties in all black neighborhoods, and in many urban areas in the East and Midwest, as industrial production has migrated to other regions or other nations. Binkin and Eitelberg note the divergent patterns of male employment by race between 1955 and 1981: approximately 52 percent of white teenagers between 16 and 19 were employed in 1955, and after an increase in the 1970s, their employment levels fell to 51.3 percent in 1981. By contrast, 52.7 percent of black teenagers were employed in 1955 (a higher proportion than for whites of the same age), but rates fell steadily for black teenagers until, by 1981, only 24.6 percent were employed. Eighty percent of white males between 20 and 24 were employed in 1955, and 77 percent in 1981; comparable figures for blacks 20 to 24 were 78.6 percent in 1955 and 58.3 percent in 1981 (Binkin, 1982: 69).

Blacks have also been pulled to the military for several reasons. First, the shift to the all-volunteer force (AVF) meant that proportionately fewer whites, who had greater and more lucrative opportunities in the private economy, would apply. In 1981, civilian air traffic controllers earned $33,000, but only $13,000 in the military. Lawrence Korb, Assistant Secretary of Defense for Manpower, Reserve Affairs, and Logistics in the first Reagan administration, offered bonuses that exceeded their salaries to military controllers who would reenlist (Korb, 1989: 27-28).

Blacks have a somewhat greater chance of acceptance in the public than in the private sector. This is not the same thing as saying that the standards for entrance have fallen. Since the initiation of the all-volunteer army, "...the percentage of black high school graduates entering the Army has consistently exceeded that of whites. Thus today, the Army's enlisted ranks are the only major segment of American society where the educational levels of blacks surpass those of whites" (Moskos, 1989: 78). Moskos argues that "the black soldier has been fairly representative of the black community in terms of educational background" (Moskos, 1989: 79), but, in another work, he noted that "95.4 percent of black men joining the Army had high school diplomas, in comparison with 87.6 percent of whites" (Moskos, 1986: 67). Schexnider notes, however, that 50.9 percent of blacks completed high school in 1985 (Schexnider, 1988: 124). On the basis of education alone, black males entering the Army are not typical of their age cohort. They are disproportionately from among those who completed high school.

In order to fulfill its personnel needs, the Army was also required to offer an increase in pay, benefits, compensation, and opportunities for education to make the military more attractive. Binkin reports on the comparable earnings of all military personnel vs. black civilians (although without the risk of unemployment) in their early years; he shows a growing advantage in earnings of black military over black civilians for the black cohort beginning after the second decade of association with the military (Binkin, 1982: 72). Whites, by contrast, earn significantly more than the enlisted pay rates until their third decade in the military.

The issues of employment, opportunities for education, advancement, the reduction of the risk of unemployment associated with the private sector from which blacks suffer most severely, and active employment within a sector with significantly reduced patterns of race-based discrimination make the armed forces a considerably more attractive option for black men and women at all ages and occupational levels. A higher proportion of blacks employed in the private sector also supplemented their earnings in 1986 with continued attachment to the military reserves: 17.6 percent black for the total selected reserves, reaching a high of 26.3 percent in the Army reserves and a low of 5.6 percent of the Coast Guard reserves; see Table 3.

Policymakers have concluded that because the full range of choice about the decision to join the military is available to blacks, their calculations are rational and the representation issue is either moot or fair. Schexnider frames he question by arguing that debates about representation hark back to the Army's earlier policy of racial quotas on black enlistments, and that there are no barriers to blacks exercising their options. "Simply put, military service is employment, and at a time when jobs are exceedingly scarce, it is not unlikely that employers, in or out of the military, will favor whites over blacks as they have historically" (Schexnider and Butler, 1976: 429-30). While this was argued as the AVF was being implemented, Schexnider has not changed his position on this basic question (Schexnider, telephone conversation, December 10, 1990). Former U.S. Representative Shirley Chisholm (D-NY) expressed similar sentiments: "All this talk about a volunteer army being poor and black is not an indication of 'concern' for the black and poor, but rather of the deep fear of the possibility of a black Army" (quoted in Schexnider and Butler, 1976: 425).

Fullinwider argues that this issue of injustice, based on the choice between the risk of death in the military and the greater possibility of unemployment in the private sector, can be resolved:

> if the all-volunteer force increased its compensation package to a level that would attract middle-class whites. We could then be confident that the recruitment system did not exploit the presumed willingness of blacks to undervalue their lives (Fullinwider, 1989: 106).

Herein lies the heart of the problem. When confronted with differences in risk based on race, policymakers recommend that we restructure the incentives to enable the public sector to compete more effectively with the private sector for *whites*, rather than to shift the law to encourage more equitable competition for the labor of *blacks* in *both* the private and public sectors. In other words, why not make the private sector more attractive to blacks than to make the public sector more attractive to whites?

All assume that the issue is primarily one that is associated with or can be resolved by adjusting the incentives offered by the military. Because of the balance of benefits, the military is more attractive to blacks. The current balance of choice for blacks is rational and just, only if you accept the assumptions in the model, that discrimination is acceptable in the private but not in the public sector. It is not rational or fair if we step outside of the assumptions or make them clear.

We could, for example, make affirmative action policy the same in the public sector as it now is in the private, but we could not defend the country with an AVF because there would not be enough whites to make up the difference. We could also make affirmative action policy in the private sector the same as in the public sector, which would end higher-than-proportional representation of blacks in the military and also reduce the risk of exposure to war in the black community, because blacks could make choices that would more equitably distribute them in other less risky, economically more beneficial sectors of the economy. Finally, in either case, we could make our foreign policy less reliant on military intervention.

We could therefore make economic and energy policy more efficient, which would also mean we were not tied politically and economically to sexist, hier-archical, undemocratic regimes. Kuwait is probably only marginally less demo-cratic than Iraq; Iraq is certainly substantially less sexist than Saudi Arabia.

ATTITUDES AMONG AFRICAN AMERICANS
ABOUT THE MILITARY AND WAR

In writing this chapter, it has become clear to me that important internal contradictions exist within the black community about the participation of African Americans within the military, and that the depth of these has grown over the last two decades with the implementation of the AVF and the increased participation of blacks in the armed forces.

One source of the contradiction arises from the policy issues generated by the possibilities of segregation or integration. The segregation of most major areas in American life established its destruction (of segregation) as a primary racial goal for most African Americans. While there have frequently been disagreements about the value of integration as an end in itself and about the consequences of it, very few black political leaders opposed the end of racial segregation. Active integration or increased representation of blacks within major American institutions (or descriptive representation) has often been valued as an end in itself, apart from the substance of the policy for which these integrated blacks may be responsible. This separation of substantive policy issues and their consequences from the value assigned to increased descriptive representation leads to a very important contradiction.

This means that even though there has been *opposition* to war and to military service at times of war by blacks, these oppositionist views have tended to be obscured by the controversies about obstacles to participation in the military, to segregation in it, or, more recently, to the consequences of discrim-ination in the draft. In the 1960s and 1970s, for example, the Civil Rights Movement *both* strengthened the legitimacy of and increased the push toward integration in the public and private sectors—including the military—*and* sharpened the interests of the integrationist, Marxist, and revolutionary nationalist sectors of the movement in anti-regime critiques of the policies carried out by the U.S. military (Gill, 1991: 10-12).[5]

Gerald Gill has researched African-American opposition to war in the twentieth century:

> In arguing why blacks, for pragmatic and patriotic reasons, should support each of the respective wars, much of the traditional black leadership tried at first to ignore and later to rebut the arguments of black antiwar dissidents. . . .
> Each war witnessed "debates," often character attacks and often over ideological and philosophical differences, between critics and the supporters

over the rights and responsibilities of Afro-Americans during wartime.

Thus, black opponents often established their own criteria for a just war. Such criteria would entail only those wars with whose war aims blacks could identify as Americans in general and as Afro-Americans in particular. Thus, blacks as Americans were far more inclined to view a war as just if the nation's physical security were endangered. ... Moreover, for blacks to embrace a war as just they would have to perceive it as one in which they were fighting for freedom or fighting for justice for themselves or as one in which the United States, true to its revolutionary heritage, was firmly in support of a war of liberation (Gill, forthcoming: 559, 561).

Black attitudes on the Persian Gulf crisis remain fairly distinctive as usual. Gallup polls conducted in August of 1990 showed a majority of blacks offering support for a freeze on Kuwait assets; a boycott of Iraqi oil and a ban on Iraqi imports; and military action if Saudi Arabia is invaded (although often at substantially lower levels of support than whites; see Table 4). Otherwise, minorities of the African Americans polled supported sending the U.S. Navy to the Gulf, bombing military targets, sending U.S. ground troops, and taking immediate military action. This was somewhat different than whites, who supported some but not all of these actions with a majority. Black support for President Bush's handling of the situation in the Gulf shifted upward (see Table 5) from 41 percent on August 3-4, to 62 percent on August 9-12, and drifted back downward in the last two weeks of the month to 60 percent and 56 percent, respectively (*The Gallup Poll Monthly,* August, 1990: 4-6, 22-23).

The CBS News/*New York Times* poll for November 13-15, 1990, showed that support for the Bush administration's policies had just about evaporated among blacks. Support in the country in general had fallen significantly since August, but it had dropped the most among blacks. Black approval of Bush's handling of the invasion, for example, had fallen to 28 percent by mid-November, from majority support in August. Black support for Bush's decision in early November to send *additional* troops was supported by 41 percent of the total sample, only 30 percent of women (as compared to 52 percent of men), but only *17 percent* of blacks. Only 18 percent of blacks felt Bush had explained the situation well enough that they understood why the nation has sent troops, as compared to 41 percent of the total sample, 45 percent of the men, and 37 percent of the women. Ironically, the same proportions of the sample, as a whole, by gender and by race—approximately 50 percent—expected the military would end up fighting. Restoration of the Kuwaiti government and defense of the Saudi Arabian government were good enough reasons for a U.S. armed attack against Iraq for only 16 percent of the blacks, as compared to 35 percent of the sample, 40 percent of the men, and 30 percent of the women. The concern about nuclear weapons, expressed by a majority of the poll (54 percent of the total sample, 59 percent of men and 49 percent of women) as a reason for military action against Iraq was supported by only 36 percent of the blacks. Seventy percent of women, 71 percent of blacks, and

Table 4
Possible U.S. Responses to the Invasion, By Race and Gender

	Freeze Kuwaiti assets			Ban Iraqi imports			U.S. Navy to Gulf			No. of interviews
	Favor	Oppose	No opinion	Favor	Oppose	No opinion	Favor	Oppose	No opinion	
National	80%	10%	10%	72%	17%	11%	68%	22%	10%	810
Sex										
Male	86	8	6	79	14	7	77	17	6	405
Female	76	12	12	65	20	15	60	27	13	405
Race										
White	83	9	8	74	16	10	71	20	9	690
Black	67	17	16	55	25	20	45	39	16	73
Other	68	21	11	63	24	13	62	27	11	45

	Bomb military targets			Send U.S. ground troops			Allied oil boycott		
	Favor	Oppose	No opinion	Favor	Oppose	No opinion	Favor	Oppose	No opinion
National	31%	57%	12%	32%	56%	12%	76%	13%	11%
Sex									
Male	41	50	9	41	50	9	82	11	7
Female	23	63	14	25	61	14	71	14	15
Race									
White	33	55	12	32	56	12	79	11	10
Black	27	63	10	28	61	11	59	23	18
Other	25	71	4	47	44	9	70	17	13

QUESTION: As a result of the Iraqi invasion of Kuwait, would you favor or oppose the following actions the United States has taken, or could take (READ AND ROTATE): Freeze Kuwait's assets so that Iraq can't spend them; ban all imports from Iraq into the U.S., including oil; move U.S. naval vessels to the Persian Gulf as a show of force; use U.S. naval airplanes to bomb Iraqi military targets; send in U.S. Marines and Army ground troops to defend Kuwait; encourage all U.S. allies to boycott Iraqi oil imports?

Source: The Gallup Poll Monthly, August, 1990, pp. 4–5.

Table 5
Changes in Bush's Middle East Approval During August, By Race and Gender

	August 3–4				August 9–12			
	Approve	Disapprove	No opinion	No. of interviews	Approve	Disapprove	No opinion	No. of interviews
National	52%	16%	32%	810	80%	12%	8%	1227
Sex								
Male	60	15	25	405	88	7	5	607
Female	44	17	39	405	73	16	11	620
Race								
White	53	15	32	690	82	10	8	1037
Black	41	21	38	73	62	28	10	102
Other	49	23	28	45	77	17	6	77

	August 16–19				August 23–26			
	Approve	Disapprove	No opinion	No. of interviews	Approve	Disapprove	No opinion	No. of interviews
National	79%	14%	7%	1241	76%	17%	7%	1010
Sex								
Male	87	10	3	625	82	13	5	503
Female	72	18	10	616	70	20	10	507
Race								
White	82	12	6	1073	78	14	8	865
Black	60	33	7	102	56	36	8	85
Other	66	28	6	56	70	23	7	49

QUESTION: Do you approve or disapprove of the way George Bush is handling this current situation in the Middle East involving Iraq and Kuwait?

Source: *The Gallup Poll Monthly*, August, 1990, pp. 22–23.

67 percent of the total sample felt Congress should vote a declaration of war before American troops are sent into combat (Frankovic, 1990). A report on a December 9-11 poll by this same group in *The New York Times* showed that two-thirds of the whites felt sending troops to Saudi Arabia was the right thing to do, but only one-third of the blacks canvassed felt so. Whites were also evenly split between those who wanted to start military actions or wait for the embargo to work. Two-thirds of the blacks wanted to wait for the embargo to work (see Michael Oreskes, "Poll Finds Americans Divided on Sanctions or Force in the Gulf," *The New York Times,* December 14, 1990, pp. A1, A14).

The attitudes of blacks in the military, both about foreign and military policy, are presumed to be quite different from those of the general black population and especially from those of elected officials and political activists. "When the Congressional Black Caucus issued a formal condemnation of the U.S. invasion of Grenada, the reaction of one black general was, 'Why can't they support us just this once?' Another general explained, 'I just tune out the so-called black leadership when it comes to anything military'" (Moskos, 1986: 72). Senior black military leaders emphasize their success in a mainstream organization, their authority over whites as well as blacks, and go further: "Those who argue that affirmative action is necessary nevertheless believe that preferential treatment is inappropriate in the military. They draw manifest self-esteem from the fact that they themselves have not been beneficiaries of such treatment—rather the reverse" (Moskos, 1986: 72).

Yet, without the shift in the human resources available to the military produced by the transition to the AVF, and, simultaneously, without successive generations of integration, equal opportunity, and affirmative action policies, social science research, and retraining, black officers would not have been as successful as they now are. Although black military officers may not be able to explain fully the sources of their success, black leaders in the civilian world display their own inconsistencies.

Critical as black elected officials may be of military and foreign policy, they have certainly warmly embraced the crown jewel of racial achievement in the armed forces: General Colin Powell. The Chairman of the Joint Chiefs of Staff was recently the keynote speaker at the annual dinner of the Joint Center for Political and Economic Studies. General Powell has been asked to serve as honorary grand marshall for the annual King Week parade on January 21, 1991, in Atlanta. He was reported to have accepted the invitation (*Jet,* December 17, 1990: 18), but more recent reports suggest that the Gulf crisis may keep him from attending, which may also keep the King Center for Nonviolent Social Change from having to face the substantive issues associated with successful integration in the military. Dr. King was well-known for his advocacy of nonviolence as a means of social change; he maintained his position even when it became an extremely controversial issue within the Civil Rights Movement and when the Vietnam war became a major issue in national politics. Thus, the invitation from the King Center to General Powell is as vivid an example of the powerful philosophical attractions and contradictions incorporated within the drive for descriptive integration and the eventual formulation of substantive policy issues for blacks as one can imagine.

There are, in short, many conflicting strands of philosophical belief on the issue of black participation in the armed forces, the policies the military must execute, and questions about military expenditures. While some blacks, including elected officials and political activists, remain critical of military action, the proportion of participation by blacks in the military has risen significantly.

BLACK ELECTED AND PUBLIC OFFICIALS ON BLACKS IN THE MILITARY AND ON THE PERSIAN GULF CRISIS

Dellums et al. v. Bush is the name of the suit filed by 54 members of Congress to forbid the President "from going to war against Iraq without first seeking a congressional declaration of war." The federal judge who heard the suit ruled that Congress had not yet decided its position on the issue (and therefore rejected the plaintiffs' request). "He also said the history of Article 1 of the Constitution left no doubt that the framers intended that a President could not go to war without the explicit approval of Congress."[6]

This suit was led by Congressman Don Dellums: a black Democrat from California; a critic of the Vietnam war; and Chairman of the House Armed Services Subcommittee on Research and Development (and former chair of the Military Construction Subcommittee from 1983 to 1989), whose district includes the University of California-Berkeley—a major center of anti-Vietnam war protest—and a number of major military bases (Barone and Ujifusa, 1989: 100-103). The plaintiffs included most members of the Congressional Black Caucus, but as a group, it has not opposed the president on the specifics of the Persian Gulf case nor attacked the overall policy of military interventionism. Individuals such as Congressman Charles Hayes of Chicago have argued that Bush should return the troops with the release of the hostages: "Our need for health care, our need for housing—these are the kinds of things we need to do with our tight dollars," he said.[7]

Congressman Louis Stokes of Cleveland commented on this issue in a recent column in the Cleveland *Call and Post*; he captured the ironies and problems of the situation:

> When I think of these young black men and women stationed in Saudi Arabia, I am both proud and disturbed. Proud to know they are so willing to serve their nation even when our reasons for being over there are ambiguous at best. Disturbed because I recognize that after risking both life and limb, these young people will return to a country in which they are denied the very freedoms they defended abroad.

Just a couple of weeks ago, President Bush vetoed the 1990 Civil Rights bill. The President's veto was a blatant slap in the face to black and female military personnel he sent to the deserts of the Persian Gulf to fight and possibly die for the human rights of people in another part of the world. How does he explain to them that while fighting for the human rights of foreigners they are not entitled to their civil rights in America''?[8]

While individual political leaders may have raised the contradictions of African Americans fighting to protect Kuwaitis, the Caucus has neither criticized the strategy of war nor raised the issue of the impact of war on the black population as a whole.

THE FUTURE OF DOMESTIC, MILITARY, AND FOREIGN POLICIES: CONCLUDING OBSERVATIONS AND POLICY RECOMMENDATIONS

"Blacks occupy more management positions in the military than they do in business, education, journalism, government, or any other significant sector of American society. The armed services still have race problems, but these are minimal compared with the problems that exist in other institutions, public and private" (Moskos, 1986: 64).

The successful integration of the military was initiated in the late 1940s; it can be said to have achieved a significant measure of success by the late 1980s. It has taken almost a half century to achieve, along with persistent efforts and several generations of racial policy, including strong affirmative action policy, and a shift in the incentives for joining the military in order to transform successfully a highly segregated institution into an integrated one that also functions without obvious racism or racial violence on the part of either whites or blacks. The armed forces began to work on this well before the 1954 *Brown* decision; it is a relatively contained portion of the population with a different incentive structure. It has an authoritative chain of command, which accelerates the implementation of reform. We should understand, therefore, that we should not expect it to take any less time to effect comparable changes in the larger society.

The consequences of this shift for the black community—an increasing proportion of its population committed to the less lucrative, riskier military sector—amount to a political issue of considerable importance. While questions about it have been posed to General Powell and other military leaders, it is in fact a political issue that arises from discrimination in the private economy. Public elected officials in Congress, the executive branch, and policy analysts must address it.

Within the black community, efforts to attack segregation, exclusion, or subordination of blacks in the larger society and in the military have tended to take precedence over questions of substantive policy, once participation occurs. The shift in participation, combined with the end of the draft and the beginning of the AVF, means that the risks of protecting sources of American economic wealth abroad are borne increasingly by that sector of the population unable to enjoy it equally and—in the last two decades, having been pushed out of the economy altogether—at home. Blacks do share equally in the military more than in any other sector of society. The question that should be debated with the greatest intensity is when will we be able to share in the benefits of the private economy at home?

This crisis offers us the opportunity to consider a number of issues:

1. *Energy Use and the "American Lifestyle."* How much energy do we use daily in comparison to the rest of the world? It is better to invest in reinventing our economic bases than to continue to spend solely on polluting and other consumption-oriented inefficient uses. We should invest money in new technology and new procedures, educating some of the people now in the military in Saudi Arabia to deal with these new technologies.

What if negotiation fails, a war is begun, and the U.S. defeats Saddam Hussein in this Gulf war? We won WWII, and not having been challenged economically, we are still attached to an early 20th century industrial base that has been outstripped by our vanquished enemies. If we were to win this conflict, the U.S. would be politically tied to a reactionary and isolated elite in Kuwait and Saudi Arabia and be economically committed to continue to buy natural resources that commit us to continued use of aging, century-old technology.

2. *The Education of Our Population.* It is irrational to spend very carefully cultivated human resources that took 20 to 30 years or more to produce (and who cannot be reproduced in any less time) to protect very expensive energy use through warfare when there are energy alternatives. We literally cannot afford to use human beings in the way we are with some who are currently in the military in Saudi Arabia—when we cannot sustain quality of education at the lower levels, or the production of young, well-educated women and men within the U.S.[9] How do we begin to plan for other outcomes for blacks so that the "best and the brightest" do not end up in vulnerable labor sectors?

3. *The Impact of War on the Black Population.* Blacks in the AVF and in the reserves are drawn from among the better educated, economically more stable sectors of the black population. If we go to conventional ground war here and/or in some other region, with another dictator with an atomic weapon, we will have to pay for it with the lives of the best and brightest of a population group in the United States desperately in need of their leadership and their talent. The consequences are difficult to contemplate when we are already fighting and losing young blacks to deadly wars involving drugs and economic competition at home.

4. *Representation and Participation of Blacks in the Military.* In previous centuries, segregationists raised a number of issues with regards to blacks' qualifications: whether blacks could fight, whether they could command, whether they could fly airplanes, whether they could handle complex logistical

or leadership issues, etc. At the end of the twentieth century, with African Americans participating at literally every level of the military, there's nothing left for blacks to prove to the country.

What is left to prove: whether America can act wisely about its commitment to the lives of its black citizens and whether it is willing to value their lives and their economic potential as equal to those of whites, irrespective of peace or war, in both the public and private sectors. Until the nation faces the current inconsistencies in its economic employment policies and addresses the way in which it makes its energy, foreign, and military policies, Black America faces a very grim future.

A Portrait of Youth: Coming of Age in Harlem Public Housing

Terry M. Williams, Ph.D.
and
William Kornblum, Ph.D.

In the world laboratory of the sociologist, as in the more secluded laboratories of the physicist and the chemist, it is the successful experiment which is decisive and not the thousand-and-one failures which preceded it. More is learned from the single success than from the multiple failures. A single success proves it can be done. Thereafter, it is necessary only to learn what made it work. This, at least, is what I take to be the sociological sense of those revealing words of Thomas Love Peacock: "Whatever is, is possible."

Robert K. Merton[1]

PUBLIC HOUSING NEIGHBORHOODS: AN INTRODUCTION

High-rise housing projects can be good places to raise children and adolescents. They can also become centers for community building and bases for emergency efforts to enhance children's safety. We are so used to stereotypes of public housing as "drug infested war zones" that these may seem almost heretical notions. One important purpose of our research, however, is to break down stereotypes about people, about public housing, and particularly about teenagers growing up in public housing. We are also asking a number of questions: Can and to what extent do young people who grow up in high-risk environments become successful in spite of all the odds, and how do they do it? We want to account for successes at the individual as well as at the communal level.

This article and our forthcoming book are part of an ongoing community research project whose overall research aim is to explore the conditions that lead to successful and less successful housing projects. Our initial measure of "success" is how well the children coming of age in them seem to be doing—by conventional and less conventional standards of achievement. A year of field research in four housing projects is not sufficient to provide any definitive answers, but we begin to offer some explanations for the similarities and differences one observes among the projects. In comparison with the tenement neighborhoods that surround them, however, all these projects are more desirable environments in which to raise children.

187

Surrounding each of the housing projects there is severe urban blight, a condition that was addressed most effectively during the famous Harlem Youth Act period of the 1960s. During the 1980s, many of Harlem's neighborhoods, and especially those in the areas we discuss, have continued to lose population and to deteriorate. Violence associated with the drug trade and with alienated youth threatens to overwhelm everyone involved. Rates of infant mortality, teen pregnancy, homicide, rape, and other indicators have increased over the decade of the 1980s, despite major gains made during the previous two decades of social interventions.

In most discussions, public housing is equated with welfare dependency, segregation, the permanent "underclass," violence, neglect, and, in this epoch, with crack addiction or marauding adolescent "wolf packs." In New York City, these images do not universally apply to households in public housing. Yet, in describing relatively successful public housing environments, we do not seek to minimize the real dangers and risks to adolescents in the areas served by public housing.

The people who live in the neighborhoods we will describe are frustrated in their fight to protect their children from violence, addiction, disease, and death. The risks to adolescents who become enticed by deviant street life are worse than they have ever been before. Housing projects in Harlem and elsewhere in New York City are embattled neighborhoods, but they offer opportunities to establish bases of support for policies to address the threat of escalating violence and murder.

The children of Harlem and communities like it are imperiled. Whatever other goals it may have, the benefit of social science should be measured by how it equips neighborhood residents and local leaders to meet this severe and growing crisis.

RECORDS OF PUBLIC HOUSING IN THE U.S.: MIRROR, MIRROR ON THE WALL

Available social scientific studies of communal life in public housing projects tend to be out of date. Lee Rainwater's *Behind Ghetto Walls* or William Moore's *Vertical Ghetto*, two of the very best examples, reflect realities of Midwestern public housing projects during the 1960s or '70s when the studies were written.[2] Rainwater's study, still the most carefully researched view of life in racially segregated public housing, deals with the ill-fated Pruitt Igoe projects in St. Louis. Designed as a segregated community, with little connection between residential location and available jobs, and with inadequate investment in security and commons areas, Pruitt Igoe merited the poor reputation that led eventually to its intentional destruction.

William Moore, Jr.'s closely observed study (1964) of life in another Midwestern project largely supports the negative image of public housing environments one reads in *Behind Ghetto Walls*.

Moore agreed with other commentators of his time that the approximately 2.2 million residents of the nation's 3,500 public housing projects were living on segregated "islands of poverty." Moore believed he was seeing "a new matrix," one which "gave rise to our tragedy, the disadvantaged child and his new edifice of poverty, the public housing project (p. 8)."

Thirty years later, the reports from Midwestern big-city projects are not very different. William J. Wilson notes that the notorious Robert Taylor Homes on Chicago's South State Street include 28 sixteen-story buildings that house an official population of about 20,000, with another 5,000–7,000 living there outside the regulations. Chicago Housing Authority figures reveal that 93 percent of the Robert Taylor households are headed by a single parent, and that 83 percent of (non-elderly) households receive AFDC payments.

While comprising only about one-half of one percent of the city's total population, this racially segregated high-rise ghetto accounted for 11 percent of the city's murders, nine percent of rapes, and 10 percent of its serious assault cases.[3] For Wilson, as for Rainwater and others in an earlier period of writing on life in housing projects, such ill-planned and ill-fated housing projects add to the great burdens of the isolated African-American and Latino poor.

We do not dispute these assessments. But there are alternative and varied experiences in public housing in New York City.

Public housing was pioneered in New York; it is a proud if somewhat tarnished heritage of the city's social history. About 600,000 adults and children now reside in the city's public housing, a population equal to the nation's nineteenth largest city. These 600,000 people represent about 20 percent of the nation's total public housing population.

Among researchers at the federal Department of Housing and Urban Development, New York City public housing has the reputation of being better designed and constructed and generally better managed than that of most other U.S. cities.[4] In view of the significant total public housing population in the U.S., there has not been enough research on public housing to make such definitive claims.

Today there are about 3.5 million people living in 1.3 million public-housing rental units administered by about 3,000 public housing authorities. Sixty-three percent of all public housing units are occupied by families, but "76 percent of family households have a female head." Of the total number of units occupied by families, "75 percent are minority, and 59 percent receive welfare payments."[5] Over 10 years ago, in 1979, HUD researchers found that approximately seven percent of all public housing projects in the U.S. (containing about 180,000 people, or 15 percent of all units) were "troubled," either due to extreme physical deterioration or because of the kind of social ills that make projects like Robert Taylor in Chicago such difficult places to raise children.[6] There are no more recent assessments of social conditions in the nation's public housing neighborhoods to our knowledge, though there have been extensive assessments of physical conditions.[7]

In doing ethnographic research in 1979–81 to find out how boys and girls fared growing up in seven low-income communities (in New York, Cleveland, Louisville, and Meridian, Miss.), we spoke with many adolescents from public housing and nonpublic housing neighborhoods.[8] Although we had no systematic data with which to compare public housing with other housing environments, we noted wide variations in public housing quality and in the ways children and adolescents used and abused the facilities.

When invited by the MacArthur Foundation Committee on Successful Adolescence to submit a proposal for research that would continue our work on adolescence in low-income communities, we chose to work in public housing environments.

FOUR HOUSING PROJECTS IN HARLEM

Our contacts are adolescents, community activists, and parents in four New York City Housing projects, two in central Harlem and two in East Harlem. The housing projects were selected (in cooperation with Thomas Cook and Richard Jessor of the MacArthur Committee on Successful Adolescence) to hold constant most demographic and physical variables. This selection criterion increases the likelihood that differences among the projects with regard to adolescent outcomes like school performance and crime, for example, would be due to intervening social processes rather than to differences in population characteristics (such as the distribution and age grouping of children and adolescents).

Table 1 summarizes the characteristics of each of the four projects. The names of each are fictitious and the locations are purposely left somewhat unspecified.

Each is a high-rise project with roughly the same population and about equal proportions of children and adolescents, equivalent income distributions, and proportions of single-parent households. Table 1 indicates that two of the projects, Mission City Houses and Zion Hill Houses, are predominately populated by African Americans. Puerto Rican households predominate at Pepsi Market Apartments and Novarios Apartments, but in each of those is also a significant African-American presence (46 percent in Pepsi Market and 37 percent at Novarios).

Built in the 1950s or early 1960s, Harlem public housing buildings tend to be massive high-rise structures, not surprising given Manhattan land values. High-rise apartments have the distinct disadvantage of rendering child surveillance much more difficult than is true of lower buildings, but increasingly in Manhattan this is a problem faced by persons of all social

Table 1
Selected Demographic and Behavioral Characteristics,
Four Harlem Public Housing Projects, 1989

Location	Mission City Houses W. 141–144th Streets	Zion Hill Houses W. 112–115 Streets	Pepsi Market Apartments E. 112–115 Streets	Novarios Apartments E. 99–106 Streets
No. of Buildings	5	10	10	13
No. of Stories	19/21	13/14	6/10/14	6/15
No. of Apt. Units	1217	1379	1310	1246
Socio/Demographic				
Population	3125	3664	3376	3180
% Black	92.3	83.2	46.0	37.2
% PR	5.3	14.4	51.4	56.8
% White	0.4	0.4	0.9	2.7
% Other	0.2	2.0	1.7	3.3
Under 21	1215	1594	1392	1292
% of total population	38.9	43.5	41.2	40.6
% younger than 4	13.5	15.7	21.3	14.0
4–5	8.0	8.0	8.0	8.4
6–9	18.2	16.0	16.7	17.3
10–13	17.0	18.1	17.0	22.0
14–17	24.5	23.3	24.0	23.5
18–20	19.2	19.0	19.0	15.5
% over age 62	19.1	13.6	14.1	15.6
% Female Head	29.3	38.5	36.7	33.6
Mean Yrs. (residence)	15.9	20.7	20.4	19.4
Economic				
Av. Income	$11,418	$11,085	$10,865	$10,618
% AFDC	22.9	27.3	34.3	31.2
Social Indicators				
% Dropout 1980	33.0	7.2	22.0	17.0
1983 % <grade	70.0	32.4	69.2	25.4
1988 % <grade*	51.0	39.4	45.0	29.0
Crime Rates**				
1983	36.1	32.9	37.1	33.0
1984	50.1	28.6	48.6	40.1
1985	55.5	37.6	40.7	45.8
1986	56.5	49.9	39.2	44.8
1987	85.4	46.1	61.5	44.2
1988	81.0	52.4	50.9	50.6
All NY public housing projects 1988	46.0			
NYC 1988	98.2			

*Reading test for sixth graders, test and norms changed after 1987.
**Crime rates are for index crime complaints in the project per 1,000 residents.

Source: Calculations done by the authors, based on data from the U.S. Census Bureau, the New York City Police Department, and the New York Public Housing Authority records.

classes in elevator buildings. The upper classes, however, routinely channel their adolescent children toward after-school activities of all kinds, something parents in housing projects often attempt with less success.

Demographics in Harlem Housing Projects

The only significant demographic changes in Harlem housing projects over the past 15 years are increases in three-generation families and tenants who are over 65 years of age. The relatively long length of residence in the four projects (an average of over 19 years, Table 1), combined with the 40 percent average proportion of persons under 21, is a consequence of the aging of public housing households, the trend toward mothers and children doubling up with grandmothers, and the lack of housing alternatives.

There are also a great many demographic continuities in Harlem public housing. When Kenneth Clark and his associates drafted *Dark Ghetto* in 1964,[9] they noted that public housing households were at the lower end of the economic scale, that in about one-third there was "no husband present," and that one-third were "on welfare" (p. 109). Our figures for welfare households, single-parent households, and household income (see Table 1) suggest that a similar resident profile exists today. There are significant numbers of non-welfare, "working poor" households, and pensionnaires. On the average, about 29 percent of households in the four projects are receiving AFDC payments, far fewer than the 83 percent reported for Chicago's Robert Taylor Homes. Each project has roughly equal proportions of children and teenagers, with at least 500 girls and boys between ages 10 and 18.

School Achievement and Crime

Differences among the projects stand out in the school achievement of their children and rates of crime (see Table 1). In fact, these projects were initially chosen for variations in these dimensions so that there would be one predominantly African-American project with relatively positive outcomes and another with relatively less positive outcomes for schooling and crime. The same criteria were used to select projects with a majority of Puerto Rican residents. Thus, Zion Hill had a much lower rate of school dropouts (as indicated in the 1980 census), a lower percentage of children reading below grade level (an "ecological" measure based on performance of children in the local primary school, which serves mainly, but not exclusively, children from each project), and lower crime rates (as measured by New York City Housing Police figures on crime complaints per 1,000 residents) than did Mission City with which it was matched (see Table 1). Novarios also had relatively more successful school-performance measures than Pepsi Market Apartments, and a far lower jump in crime complaints between 1986 and 1987 than did Pepsi Market Apartments. We used 1986–87 crime data to make our initial selection, but when we obtained a longer series of crime data, only Mission City, among the four, continued to stand out as a project with consistently higher crime rates.

In comparison with the entire city, the overall crime rate is far lower in public housing. Table 1 shows that for the entire city in 1988, there were slightly over 98 index crime complaints per 1,000 persons, while the corresponding rate for all city public housing was 46.0. This difference would be entirely counter-intuitive except that when one breaks down the overall rate into crimes against persons (especially murder, rape, robbery, and aggravated assault), the rate for the entire city was 22.3, compared to 26.8 for public housing. The real difference in rates is explained by crimes against property, for which the city rate was 75.9 while it was 19.1 for public housing. Public housing environments are slightly more dangerous than the city as a whole, and there are far fewer automobiles and attractive possessions there to attract high levels of property crime.

Unfortunately, increases in crime within the city and housing authority since the crack epidemic began around 1983 are dramatic. Between 1987 and 1988, within New York City Housing Authority projects, rates of aggravated assault have increased 111.6 percent, murder and non-negligent manslaughter by 118.5 percent, and complaints of sales of heroin and cocaine by 370 percent. Also during this time, complaints of possession of dangerous weapons increased by 30 percent in the authority's jurisdiction, and 10 percent in the city. Similar increases in these crimes have occurred in the four projects we are working in. Significantly, between 1984 and 1988, Novarios and Pepsi Market Houses experienced almost a tripling in the number of complaints of sale of cocaine and heroin (from 0.5/1000 residents to 3.0), while at Mission City, the rate increased from 1.0 to 5.2. At Zion Hill, the rate dropped from 0.5 to 0.0.

That there were no recorded complaints of the sale of cocaine and heroin at Zion Hill in 1988, in the midst of a severe drug epidemic, may be the best indicator of the relative success of tenants and management there. However, the epidemic of adolescent violence and involvement in the drug industry gravely affects all the projects. A relatively small number of violent adolescents and young adults can terrorize entire neighborhoods. Successful and less successful projects may be equally threatened by gang violence and criminal victimization associated with the crack epidemic.

Before we turn to the informal efforts made by residents to create safe niches and our field research in the projects, it is worthwhile to note that all four are considered by personnel of the Housing Authority to be tough neighborhoods where children and adolescents are significantly "at risk." All are reputed to be challenging managerial assignments and difficult environments because they exist within larger neighborhood areas that are terribly run down and plagued by extraordinarily high crime rates.

Successful adolescence has as many meanings in Harlem as anywhere. Conventional success means achievement in school and community, progress through college or professional training—or career training, upward mobility, steady employment, and later forming a family. Less conventional success can mean coming back from trouble and failure, defeating the failure cycle, beating the risks of gang membership, avoiding the risks of adolescent pregnancy, overcoming a difficult homelife, educational delay, and social failure.

As elsewhere, the kids who "make it" in the most conventional ways despite all the odds have something special as individuals. They also tend to come from families that struggle to teach them "the right way." Yet they come from neighborhoods that would make some shudder to walk through, let alone live in. The tough, grim aspects of the neighborhoods may give the successful kids motivation to want to do better, often an unstoppable attitude. The plight of those they possibly leave behind in their mobility can also cause anguish in the young adults, a classic theme of coming of age in the ghetto. Marcus Bailey, one of the projects' extraordinary successes, expresses these themes and speaks for many of his Harlem peers, as we walk with him through his neighborhood of apartments and courtyards. "I always remember hearing, 'Don't forget where you came from.' I know people who should remember, but don't," he says. "Remembering your roots doesn't mean trying to chop down the tree. It does not mean getting away from the hood (neighborhood). Then again, that can depend on what your memories are. If all you remember is urine and garbage, you won't be back. If you remember your mentors and community programs, you'll be back."

Rosa Carrillo (a graduate student member of our research team) and I first met Marcus at a forum for elected officials. He was born and raised in the Novarios project and many of his relatives still live in neighborhood housing projects. As a twenty-year-old college graduate from a major private university, he is primed for a bright career. "It was either go to college or die," he laughs ironically. "It's what you call tough love. There were two extra special teachers, my fourth-grade and my sixth-grade teachers. Their emphasis was on teaching the history of people of color." He added that "teachers in the public system do not know very much about the people they are teaching, especially not about their history and experience in this country. Many teachers are alienated from their students, they finish with classes and they go home."

This comment takes us to the subject of mentors, a classic ingredient in the achievement of youth. "Mentors," says Marcus, ". . .were very important. They gave me blueprints. In the fourth grade, I had a teacher by the name of Shirley Graham DaBenny. She had that Malcolm/Tubman/Terrell-like love for her students. Mrs. D. was sharp. There was no half-steppin' in her class.

"My fourth-grade teacher, Mrs. D, died over the summer during childbirth. Our class was crushed. The fifth grade was a waste. I don't remember one positive thing from that year. I guess her memory is one thing that has kept me in the straight and narrow, for the most part. She was a beautiful sister. She was balanced, and focused. She was one hell of a mentor. She still is, she's with me now."

We spent much time talking, mainly about Marcus's beliefs, some of which are based on what he has been able to arrive at through his own reading as well as what he has learned from educators he has met. He claims that there are five foundations to his beliefs: spiritual development, community building, cultural principles, academic principles, and physical fitness. "I have been influenced by the writing of Garvey, Malcolm, Ida B. Wells, Adelaide Sanford, and W.E.B. Du Bois," he tells me.

Then he goes on to talk about the lack of autonomy and power in his community. "The projects are 'not our community.' Whites already know what you need. In our community there is a deficiency of role models and resources. The projects are 'not our community,'" he repeats. "The present educational system does not prepare you for life. Students are miseducated."

Marcus returns to his conflict over leaving the community and his sense that it is a kind of betrayal, feelings he had eloquently committed to paper.

> I was born out of a spirit of hope that refuses to be bound by despair. It is a spirit of hope that creates a better reality for all who come in contact with it. That is real. I was born out of the power of this spirit. So now we see there are some serious contradictions in our community. I guess the biggest contradiction is that the people we most easily recognize as successful are the ones who are the least help or use to their people.
>
> Check out this profile: A young black man, born in the "ghetto" of any large city. Strong fellow, good looking, good natured, articulate, but poor. He has learned the value of hard work from his family: not nuclear, but extended. He always did well in school. Now he proceeds to attend a prestigious university. Here begins his training to be a player in corporate America. His popularity carries over to college and he has friends who are black, white, and everything in between. His popularity keeps him from any realization about American racism. He knows that severe hardships are in black communities. He also knows racism must shoulder much of the blame. However, he knows "some good white people," so he theorizes that "all that radical B.S.U. (Black Student Union) s---" cannot be quite correct. For him, the bottom line is that each individual must be responsible for themselves and improve their condition. Therefore his career goals are centered around individualism and personal gain.[10]

As we walk down and through the projects, he talks for a few minutes about friends who have left and are afraid to come back to the community, others too embarrassed and/or hurt to return.

"My partner Jason and homeboy Freddy was born right here in these projects and we used to play all the time right on this corner and over there behind that building, kissing on girls and stuff. And when Jason came home last year from college in Kentucky, we both looked for Freddy and we found him all right, dealing on that corner selling that...(crack-cocaine). It just really hurt both of us, but especially Jason. He said, 'man I ain't coming back here. I can't stand to see all my friends wasted like this.' Well I tend to disagree with him. I am back and I'm gonna keep coming back. But I see the frustration and the hurt too. It hurts me to see the brothers, my friends like that. I know or I think I know the reasons why though, and I want to do something about it. The move here is to talk about the plans the white folks have for black men and how my life has come in contact with these plans. We gotta remember that there is more than one plan. Racism ain't easy no more. One minute this way, next minute that way. One minute the door is closed, the next minute it's open, but you can't get in. Next minute you're in, but you're stuck in the corner. Next minute you're at the table but can't speak. Next minute you can speak but no one is listening. Bottom line. Same deal."

Then we run into Marcus's friend Reuben. Reuben is also twenty years old and in his third year in Murray State University (Oklahoma). He has lived in the projects all his life and is a very close friend of Marcus. Both are regarded as neighborhood heroes, in part because they are excellent college-level basketball players and also because, although they attend college, they remain in the neighborhood over the summer. The same questions about mentors and doing well despite the odds creep up in our conversation.

"My mother," Reuben says, "was the person that influenced me the most. She would tell me to do what I thought was best. She would nag and push me to continue school. Now my nineteen-year-old brother goes to Union College and one of my two sisters is going to college too. But everything ain't peaches and roses around here. There is drug dealing and other crimes as an alternative to school; for example, at the back of the health center a lot of dealing goes on. We all know that drugs bring a lot of money, but there are risks involved. Many of these kids see it as a temporary thing. But they earn a certain amount and they can't quit.

"But I have a lot more to strive for. I'm going to try to get out. I want to go to the NBA or the professional leagues. And if all else fails I want to be a psychologist." He glances over at Marcus as if for confirmation. "I think it's pretty interesting how some children relate. Some of them repeat what their parents are doing."

Marcus makes a point about the amount of people who want to be part of the NBA, but how very few get in it. Reuben believes there are two factors that determine whether a male child of color continues through the educational system: financial aid and basketball. "The counselors in school have three or four pet students who are taken care of and the coaches have their pets. The other students are not pushed to do anything." Reuben says this is why he wants to stay in psychology and be a psychologist if the basketball doesn't work out.

"When I was at Murray State," Reuben says, "I studied with Native American Indians, Orientals, some blacks, and a whole lot of whites. All you see is country and a lot of cows. I went through a lot of discrimination and was arrested one time for having a bandaged finger." He holds up the finger that was once bandaged and explains. "They said I must be the one who broke into this place because there had been a window broken. They are really racist out there for real. That experience was very embarrassing for me but I know I have to stay for a little while longer because it's the only way I can get into the NBA. But I'll come back to Harlem and practice."

Most of the conventionally successful kids have had parents whom they have seen work all their lives to keep them comfortable in school and active in church, to involve them in the settlement houses, to keep them under supervision. Out of every cohort of teenagers coming of age in Harlem projects (and this is true of those in the Bronx and Queens and Brooklyn as well), there are a few like Marcus and Reuben who achieve conventional academic success despite the odds. The parents of these children always speak of having a close network of other parents and kin with whom they worked closely to protect the children and to give them opportunities for growth and learning. In addition to parental help, the most successful adolescents have had strong adult mentors.

Other teenagers whom we shall introduce are not always fortunate enough to have wise mentors and involved parents. Often their parents have too many troubles of their own, and too limited knowledge of how to help their children. This again raises the issue of what to do about the youth crisis, what to do to steer children away from the mobs and the crack scene toward positive activities and positive futures, and how housing projects can become centers of these efforts.

Everyday Life and Safe and Desirable Niches

The courtyards of Harlem public housing projects ring with the sounds of youth and neighborliness. One good time to watch the public life of a project's commons areas is in mid-afternoon when the children and teenagers are arriving home from school, and one can witness what Jane Jacobs might have called "the children's ballet in a public housing courtyard."[11]

There are few signs around the projects of the youth crisis mentioned before on a school-day afternoon or during the day on weekends. If one watches carefully, it is possible to spot a few clusters of teenagers that include some who are ready to steer customers toward a crack spot nearby. Or, in each of the projects—if one looks—it will be possible to find a teenage and young-adult crap game that attracts those longing for the faster tracks of street life. But these groups are small in number compared to the hundreds of children and teens who are doing just what their peers in any other American neighborhood do on a schoolday or weekend.

During the day there is ample evidence of the work parents and older siblings put into safeguarding the children. One person who understands and respects the young people's situation and indeed has a perspective on the world of the project is Mrs. Vasquez of the Novarios project. This stalwart parent and project leader is 64 years old, married, and has raised four children. They have all left the projects as everyday success stories, not superstars but, as she says, "regular everyday people living a normal life." One of her sons is an ambulance driver, another a police officer, the third a teacher, and her daughter works at the U.S. Census Bureau. Mrs. Vasquez has clear views on what works in parenting and what does not.

"The home is very important in the success of a child, I think," she says. "It's where respect is taught. If there is no respect, there is no dignity. You must have respect not only for oneself but for elders, and teachers and policemen and other people in general. The good seeds come from the home. . .and the troublemakers come from those who lack a home. In 1984, I had the opportunity of being a teacher's assistant and learned to teach. I find my role as a housewife important since it has allowed me to take care of my children. There was a time when it was not hard to make ends meet; now everything is expensive. Mothers are not in a position that they have to work in order to pay rent, food, and other necessities. In some cases, there are women who are alone, where their children suffer a lot. . ."

Mrs. Vasquez makes sure that in her building, there is no vandalism. "Youth hang out because there are not many things for them to do. But you take a place like Boys Harbor at 104th Street (an important settlement house in the community); they have recreation such as swimming. There are not that many activities for senior citizens. One reason has to do with their fear to leave their buildings."

Talking in the hallway where she regularly sits on house patrol for "her building," she informs the tenants as they enter that the elevators are not working. As tenants reacted to the news, I overheard several say that the elevators were experimental and they're being installed mainly in new projects. Some people reacted in anger and it seemed that those who were most affected were women with their shopping carts and those with children's carriages. Mrs. Vasquez says a petition is in order, and she wants the tenants to sign it because the elevators are very important to the senior citizens, and something should be done about them.

Collective Efforts for Good

Parents in public housing usually understand the risks their children face far better than any outsiders do—when their children are afraid to go to school because they are being bullied, or because they fear the pressure to join one or another gang, or because they fear their classmates will scorn them for not having proper clothes or sneakers. Their children may be anxious when the teenagers begin "hanging out" in an apartment in a troubled building within the project, or when the hanging-out spot is headed by adult drug abusers. All these and many more troubles the parents usually know about first. As with any other parents facing threats to their children's safety, project parents try in many ways to steer their children away from danger and to create safety zones for them.

In cooperation with project managers, the parents usually invoke a number of strategies to create safe and desirable niches for their children outside the schools, to which we earlier referred. Their broadcast collective efforts center on the selection of tenants and their own activism within the project's tenant organization. Tenant activists also usually reach out to institutions like the church or social welfare agencies that seek to help project residents. At a more informal level of organization, they often share responsibilities for surveillance in the project's public spaces and commons rooms.

Tenant Selection. The first line of defense for tenants of the housing projects is to seek some control over who becomes a tenant and who remains one. More than 20 years ago, Gerald Suttles[12] compared neighborhoods of low-rise tenements (Chicago "three-flats") with public housing, and found that housing project neighbors often felt they lacked control over their surroundings and could not express their own personalities and preferences through their physical environment. In our epoch of epidemic and violence, this complaint pales in comparison with tenants' needs to know whom to trust among their neighbors.

We continually hear tenants and managers speak of their desire to influence the tenant-selection process and to influence the way resources are marshalled to enhance public trust and safety. In New York public housing, as elsewhere, this influence is most often exerted through the activities of the Tenant Council and its tenant association in each project.

Tenant Activism. Tenant Councils in New York public housing tend to be extremely active organizations in a way almost unheard of in the surrounding neighborhoods, except those that have very active block associations. But block associations are voluntary groups that struggle to represent a smaller population in the forum of community politics or in the community meetings of the police department. The Tenant Council of a major project, in contrast, has a direct link to the resources of the Housing Authority, itself a powerful city agency, as well as all the access a block association might have to other community institutions. The Tenant Councils also have some degree of influence over common resources within the project; these may be considerable. In this sense alone, the housing project and its tenant organization represent a note of organization in low-income communities around which efforts to protect children and enhance their development can coalesce.

We do not see any obvious differences in the projects' tenant associations, due to the mix of African-American and Puerto Rican households and the most salient differences among the four are those discussed in terms of patterns of tenant activism and coordination with project management.

The Night as a Frontier

Night creates a social frontier in and around the projects. The problems of life in poor communities and the effects of the current youth crisis on housing project environments are far more evident at night. Kenya, a teenager from Pepsi Market, gives us a glimpse of nighttime behavior as he stands on the top part of the basketball court describing a scene he had witnessed when he tried to enter a project building in the middle of the night.

"I saw this girl sitting in the chair," he says, pausing to drink from the apple juice can. "She was in between that little corridor, the first door you come through and then the next door's locked. The other girl was doing her hair. It's right in between those two doors where you got to ring the intercom. It was late. It was about two o'clock in the morning. Sitting right there doing her hair."

I was curious to know about the buildings and floors where the tenants are very strong, where I'd hear them say things like: "put your garbage in bags"; "don't let the kids hang out in the hallways"; "no drugs can be sold here," and "every parent in the building make sure that your kids are in the house." I wondered if Kenya saw that kind of parenting going on. When I asked him, he didn't hesitate to say, "Yeah, you see it, but you know I don't really try to get into that yet. It's because I don't like it when they say . . . well I understand no dealing drugs and the garbage . . . but when it comes to not hanging in the hallway, and then when they're out on the street you don't want them on the street, and if it's in the house you might not want them in the house. Where else are they going to go? You're throwing them out and just pushing them off. Outside it's going to get worse for them. Sometimes, if I come back to my building early in the morning, I see people that's been out there all night. I mean these are not only kids, there are men and women that's out there too."

Kenya perceives a kind of hierarchy among the projects that operates along class lines when it comes to security. "There's some projects, most of them, where they don't have security, where at night it's the worst, going out for drugs and all of that."

Kenya's talk about the different kinds of projects points to some interesting questions. On the one hand, what a "good" project is from his point of view. But at the same time his observations suggest a larger issue. Where will our fears take us as we come to accept the whole panoply of security: guards, closed-circuit TV, ID cards to enter or leave buildings, electronic surveillance? Our fears, especially when they are played upon, may take us to accept as "normal" the maximum security that is taken for granted in our prisons. Under the guise of protection, we are going so far that we may be losing our basic rights.

Night in the streets around the projects becomes, in this time of crisis, the turf of the addicted and the dealers, the prostitutes and tricks and drug coppers and cops. The majority of parents in the projects are straight, early risers, trying to keep their children at home or in other safe places. They want to keep them out of the dark schoolyards and parks where the youth mobs gather. But this is extremely difficult. The kids have known each other since early childhood. Children do not always see the dangers as being so immediate as do their parents. This is especially true of the most impressionable pre-adolescents and young teenagers who crave older teenage role models. Besides, this is the big city, they complain; what good is it to stay shut up in the room? Thus, night also becomes the teenagers' and young adults' cover.

OVERCOMING CRISIS: FINDING SAFE PASSAGES

Wilding in Central Park

The course of our study has been dramatically shaped by events that occurred while our field research was underway. As we were beginning to expand our network of acquaintances with teenagers and young adults in the four Harlem projects, a series of violent events fixed a glaring spotlight on the city's youth crisis.

One night in the late spring of 1989, groups of 40 to 60 Latino and African-American teenagers rampaged through Central Park. A number of adults, most of whom were white, middle-class, Manhattan residents were wounded, many others were badly shaken, and one—a female jogger—was brutally beaten, raped, and left for dead. A few weeks later, three African-American young men were attacked in Bensonhurst, Brooklyn, and one was bludgeoned to death by racially enraged white young adults. The two events in Central Park and Bensonhurst have come to symbolize the dangerous climate of violence and conflicted race relations in New York City at the end of one decade and the beginning of another.

In the project neighborhoods where we were working, these events became the subject of intense reflection and bitter debate. And not just these events. During the same period, two children were abducted from a City Parks Department playground adjacent to Zion Hill. Two teenagers were killed in an apparent cocaine transaction in another of our projects. One teenage boy was killed and another remains comatose after a brutal episode of gang violence outside still another of the four projects. A gang of teenage girls (The Deceptor Cons) conducted a series of needle stabbings on Manhattan's West Side during much of the summer and fall.

One cannot talk to anyone in Harlem, in the projects, or in the surrounding neighborhoods, without hearing moving accounts of suffering and fear and courage. For it takes courage simply to lift the phone and call in a complaint about sales of narcotics, to say nothing of what it takes to organize tenants to drive out drug dealers. Nor is the situation that much different in the more privileged neighborhoods surrounding Harlem. The mood of the city's residents is deeply troubled. In the projects, we hear little hope expressed so far for promising solutions to the crisis. People hear warnings that "resources are limited" and the federal deficit is too high. Chances of strong initiatives from Washington are poor. In the meantime, the environment for adolescent development in Harlem, around the projects and in all the neighborhoods, becomes ever more risky.

Some of the boys who joined the so-called "wolf packs" in Central Park came from the projects where we are working. Some also came from more middle-class housing. Residents of one of the projects, a middle-income complex in Harlem, had been calling the police and other agencies, asking for help in dealing with a particularly violent group of 15 to 20 teenagers who were terrorizing the neighborhood for months prior to the violence in Central Park. They were told that there was nothing anyone could do because the incidents involved teenagers. Around this group and one or two of its violent leaders there coalesced a larger and more amorphous network of other teenagers who rampaged in the park. Some of those leaders went to trial for the Central Park rape, but no concerted steps have been taken to address the larger problem of youth violence in the neighborhoods we are describing. Indeed the situation is worsening.

The Writing Crew

In an effort to involve young people from the projects in our ethnographic research and in a small way to address the current crisis, we organized what we call the Writing Crew. They are a group of 10 to 15 teenagers who want to help us know their world from the inside. We generally reached them through our own social networks that were established prior to beginning our research. But in many instances, we also recruited writers whom we first met through "hanging out" in the projects and speaking to kids on housing-project benches.

Writing Crew members agree to write their own life histories and to keep diaries in notebooks that we supply and that we collect for copying. They are paid five cents per line of writing but must show up at our weekly Crew meetings where we discuss their work. They are told not to worry about spelling, punctuation, or style, unless they feel like making improvements in their writing a personal goal (something we gently encourage). Crew meetings turn into rap sessions or guided interviews, depending on what points are made in different writers' books. Very often the teenagers begin with cramped, limited descriptions, but they very quickly loosen up and find the writing coming more easily. Not all who express an interest in joining the Crew actually do so, but they usually remain interested outsiders and eager informants for those who continue with the writing.

A very diverse group of teenage young men and women, the Writing Crew includes some housing project residents who have dropped out of school and others who are rather high scholastic achievers. The Crew's informal leader is Kenya James. When we met him, he was a school dropout and a "lookout" and "counter" (of the day's receipts) in the cocaine trade. Through his involvement with the Crew, he has returned to an alternative school to study for his high school equivalency diploma (GED). He has made numerous appearances in public with us to discuss the youth crisis in the city, including lengthy interviews on National Public Radio, on television talk shows, and in articles in *The New York Times.* Recently, he has begun to publish his accounts of life in the Harlem streets in *Seventeen* magazine. He created the Crew's broadside publication known as *Underground Ballistics*, which now appears on bulletin boards and telephone poles outside the projects.

Other crews, unlike the one mentioned above, are also a part of the rites of passage in which some teenagers find it necessary to join in order to be accepted and protected in project neighborhoods. Where these other crews are engaging in antisocial behavior, we think it essential that youth workers be available to work with them to offer constructive alternatives.

Young people, some of whom are attempting to leave the projects, indicate to us their desire to do more with their lives than fight, deal drugs, and act out other antisocial behaviors. They have indicated a desire to change, but ask, "What do we do? Where else do we go to make a dollar?" They are counting on us for some answers. We must provide the answers to those questions or at least continue to support efforts to find solutions.

Sneaker Money: The Art of the Deal

Our discussion with the kids turns to youthful involvement in the drug trade. While most of the boys who consider themselves to be "street" have tried their hands at it, girls are minor players in the trade. The pressure seems to fall on the males to be "chill," to act and look a certain fashionable way in order to impress the girls.

The kids want to earn "sneaker money" (money for sneakers, a small sum) and if, as eighteen-year-old Kahlil explains it, "you do all right, then you stay in (the drug business) until something happens to you." He backs this up by adding that all the kids have a burning need for money: "Go to movies, buy sneakers, something like that, money in your pocket, buy pizzas, things like that. It's basically, you know, money, just money." And another chimes in, "You know, it's like feeling more independent than working part-time in a supermarket or something like that. All they have to do is just sit out there on the bench and sell these drugs. You go outside and sit on a bench anyway."

Attention turns to Kenya, who speaks eloquently about the roles his "homeys" (friends) play in the ever-present drug business. "They would rather be their own boss," he says. "But you gotta understand that not all of them be hustling. At least a handful of them work . . . . And when the drug business starts to boom, they leave the legit job and go to the dealing full-time. That's the part that is not understood, because with the drugs, they can make so much money. But even when they don't make big money, they keep trying to make it."

Territoriality, revenge, reputation, face, and honor are the five major factors accounting for most of the violence in the drug industry. Then, too, as other factors like manhood and the new street concept of "dising" (disrespecting) come into play, urban teenagers seem to find the contextual recipe for volatility. "You see how close everybody is in these spots," Kenya is saying. "When they first started it was tens and twenty-dollar bottles, and now it comes down to three-dollar bottles and two-dollar bottles."

This talk about money gets him back on the subject of how little money he has and coincidentally how little teenagers in the projects actually make by selling drugs.

Kenya spent his entire life around housing projects. He took his first plane ride, had his first foreign-restaurant experience at 18 with us. How he gained the attention of an adult mentor and expanded his horizons beyond his own neighborhood is both the story of his life and the accidental nature of mentoring for the vast majority of inner-city young people. We are coming to understand how individual characteristics (motivation and family background) for instance, help to influence the decision of a teenager to move in one direction or the other when confronted with the conditions and choices of street life. But we are also interested in how various structural factors (transportation systems, movement of jobs, housing opportunities) influence their choices and affect their outcomes as well.

The pressures on kids in the projects and the city more generally border on the absurd—at least for an adult outside this culture. But that is not the point. For both sexes, the pressures through which they must navigate to reach manhood or womanhood (with self-esteem and the approval of their peers) must be taken seriously, because they are codes of behavior that are defined as necessary and desirable by the others, their peers. Take, for example, the pressure Sheena received from her friends about her non-use of slang.

"I got into an argument with a girlfriend of mine about using slang. Okay? Because I don't like to use it all that much and she told me I was acting white because I wasn't using slang. I looked at her like she had two heads instead of that one big one she's got. I said, 'girl you and the rest of your girls are 'cah-ray-zy' (crazy) and better get back some smarts if you want to make it out here."

Yet, it is this kind of ethnic conformity that causes many of the kids to seek safe passages through an entirely different ecology than many middle-class kids. The idea that one is acting "proper" or "white" means that the kids not conforming to the street-kids culture are betraying their friends and indeed their "race" by their acts. This conformity is not gender-specific. In the case of Kenya, for example, he was told to rejoin the crack-cocaine crew he left and not take a regular job or be considered a "punk," a "chump," or a "sissy." These everyday pressures force the kids with little social support or weak egos to never quite reach their potential.

CONCLUSION: PUBLIC HOUSING AND A RESPONSE TO THE YOUTH CRISIS

If there could be only one new policy response to the present youth crisis, we would assign experienced youth-gang workers to each project. Based in the projects where the greatest numbers of children at risk are found, they would work the streets afternoons and nights. Their difficult job would be to help steer the kids away from drugs and violence. They would try to get the kids into constructive activities and wean them away from violence. Violent children would be introduced to people who could build on their athletic talents. If they turned out to be incorrigible sociopaths, this would become known, and other steps could be taken to isolate them from the others. Boys and girls who think their lives are fatally marred by arrest records would be coaxed into education and work programs. The street workers would try to foster a new sense of pride in Harlem's most troubled and street-jaded adolescents and young adults. The goal would be for young adults and adolescents to begin to "speak strongly" against drugs, especially to the younger ones, and to rekindle young people's interest in the great African-American and Latino heritage in New York and the world.

Street-gang workers were deployed during the gang and heroin epidemics of the 1950s and early 1960s with considerable success. They do not work alone, but serve as outreach workers to link kids with the existing agencies of the community. Their efforts are no panacea. Still they can save lives and prevent some of the senseless violence that now has the city in its grip. It would cost less than $50,000 per worker per year (including training and overhead support) to serve the immediate population of a project (the average population, ages 10 to 18, is at least 500) and the adjacent neighborhoods (where even more of the mob youth are recruited).

Of course, there needs to be not just one measure taken to meet the youth crisis, but many. Some could be short-term measures, such as a program to get the kids to turn in their guns, while others need to be based on longer-term approaches to structuring opportunities for mobility in poor neighborhoods. Public housing was never intended to become the final, permanent household residence for as high a proportion of its residents as it has in New York and other large cities. The rising tide of economic mobility was supposed to lift families continually out of public housing and into the housing market. Instead, we have been witnessing the opposite trend; for the past 10 years or more, families have been bringing in their children (often reluctantly) and doubling up in existing apartments. Salaries have remained stagnant, buying power has diminished, rents have soared.

So what is to be done? Why not renew efforts to make the projects the nodes of upward mobility they were originally intended to be; if not for the adult residents, then at least for the children? This will entail enhanced community centers in the projects where adults and children can learn new skills and where they can become aware of the array of opportunities and programs that already exist to serve them. It will mean expanded networks to link employers with young people and older adults in the projects who have been gaining needed skills. It will require expansion of the public housing stock through rehabilitation of apartment units in the abandoned blocks adjacent to the projects.

Selling off the original public housing resource is clearly something that should *not* be done unless one wishes to encourage homelessness and profiteering. Even the most seemingly enlightened of these policies, such as encouraging tenants to buy their apartments, forecloses the possibility that the housing stock can serve as a base of mobility for future generations. Far more desirable are policies that build outward from existing public housing projects into immediately adjacent neighborhoods where satellite public housing in rehabilitated buildings provides additional low-cost housing. Where initiatives are underway that promise to add to the apartment stock, there is no reason why mixed rental and ownership plans might not be desirable. In this context, the specific case of Harlem is a good policy test for plans to expand public housing initiatives.

According to the recent "Public Housing Resident Empowerment Act" introduced in Congress by Rep. John Porter (April, 1989), "It's time to stop thinking of public housing residents as the problem, and start thinking of them as the solution." So far, so good. But the proposed bill goes on to "effectively authorize sale of public housing indefinitely" and "eliminates restrictions on resale of public housing units, and invests buyers with full rights of home-ownership at the end of five years." Novarios Apartments, for example, begin at 99th Street on Manhattan's East Side, where apartments sell for about $10,000 a room, if they sell at all. Below 96th Street, apartments sell for over $100,000 a room. Did Congress, in the Housing Act of 1937, which created the federal initiative for public housing, intend that tenants who happen to be on the spot when a purchase offer is made should reap windfall profits from the sale of a public property? If there are tenants at Novarios or any other public housing projects who can afford to buy property, they would better be encouraged to invest in the neighborhoods adjacent to the projects where they now live. In Harlem that would also be a good investment, and one which would free apartments in existing public buildings for new generations of tenants. Tenant ownership, through a variety of means—including sweat equity—is a welcome idea, but not if it promises to diminish the precious supply of lower-cost housing located within a short subway ride from the most densely concentrated labor market in the nation.

Mrs. B., the manager at Zion Hill, talks freely about the progress and setbacks she and her tenants experience in trying to build a good environment in which to raise children. They are proud at Zion Hill of the way the project has "shaped up." There is much more to say of their efforts to build a neighborhood where originally, as she puts it, "they just piled so many poor strangers on top of each other." For our part, we hope we have begun to show that once one comes to know the projects and the struggles people are waging there, it becomes somewhat more evident how social science can be of assistance.

CONCLUSIONS AND RECOMMENDATIONS

Conclusions

The preceding articles are more than a powerful indictment of the status quo; they provide guidance in helping America to solve the problems which beset Black America. Inherent in the scholarship and the pointed analyses is a belief in the possibility of positive change.

Today's Urban League holds fast and true to the vision of our founders—a legacy of interracial cooperation and bold advocacy. Those principles are unchangeable and unchanging. They have laid the foundation for our goal of racial parity by the year 2000.

Although racism persists, African Americans must be on guard against allowing white racism to provoke racist feelings in themselves, because any form of racism dehumanizes and brutalizes.

The heroic Nelson Mandela has said, "I have fought against white domination, and I have fought against black domination. I have cherished the idea of a democratic and free society in which all persons live together in harmony and with equal opportunities."

That is also the credo of the Urban League. We must remind a forgetful nation that racism has no place in any society and a world speeding toward a new century. This is not only a moral imperative, but also an economic necessity.

America has only one hope of entering the 21st century as a world power and a global economic force. That hope lies in its ability to achieve racial parity and to make full use of African Americans and other minorities it has so long rejected.

White America looks at how the cup is half full, while Black Americans, having less than 60 percent of the income of whites, know that the cup is half empty.

African Americans today remember that their roots are in the ghetto and that black society remains vulnerable. We know that it takes two earners to be middle class and that all it takes to fall out of the middle class is a spell of sickness or unemployment.

The new African-American middle class knows that the system must change to accommodate its needs and aspirations and those of the less fortunate black majority. While taking some solace in the successes that they have earned, African Americans are dissatisfied with the slow pace of progress. Positive change is not driven by failure, but by success. Alexis de Tocqueville wrote over two centuries ago that a grievance can be endured so long as it seems beyond redress, but it becomes intolerable once the possibility of removing it crosses men's minds.

Middle-class African Americans with professional status and valued skills are not looking back to see how far they have come—they are looking ahead to see how far they, and their poorer brothers and sisters, can go.

We will always remind America that fairness, justice, and equal rights are neither liberal nor conservative. They are American constitutional principles that must be protected.

Never before has America faced so clear a choice in its treatment of African Americans and minorities. It can continue to ignore our needs and allow more and more of us to sink deeper into poverty and dependence. Or it can invest in our human resources, assure quality education and job training opportunities, and bring neglected minorities into the productive mainstream.

History teaches us, however, that America has often allowed racism to dictate wrong choices. But history also teaches that vested interests drive America's actions. Racial parity is in our country's self-interest.

It is time now to get back to basics. Instead of wasting resources, we have to start investing in our future. America is going to lose the economic war with Japan and Europe unless it finds a way to use the underestimated and underserved minority that is the core of the future work force. Getting them off unemployment rolls and onto payrolls is the way America can overcome its labor and skills shortages.

The National Urban League's concept for an Urban Marshall Plan is an essential part of the solution. It is an economic program; an investment program, not a social program. But it will take working partnerships of government, education, business, labor, and the community-based voluntary sector to get the job done.

We have called on President Bush to convene a national Workforce 2000 summit meeting of leaders from the community, government, education, labor and industry. The goal of that summit meeting would be to devise a national workforce strategy to assure that every American—and especially today's excluded minority youth—has the education and the skills to succeed in our changing society.

The Urban League has made its choice. It is a choice consistent with our history and our strengths—a choice for racial parity and for black economic progress.

The National Urban League will target its resources on education, career development, employment, and job training programs that can win social and economic equality for African Americans, while we will continue to advocate on the key issues affecting African Americans.

The following recommendations address critical policy areas that must be addressed in order for us to move toward the goal of racial parity in this society.

Recommendations

RACE RELATIONS

With racial incidents regrettably on the increase since 1989, we must stand as one in not only condemning racism, but also in committing to make the American dream of freedom, justice, and opportunity real for all of us.

As America enters the last decade of the twentieth century, we renew our unerring call for leadership in both the public and private sectors to place the elimination of racism at the top of the national agenda.

FEDERAL BUDGET

Enactment of the Omnibus Reconciliation Act of 1990 (P.L. 101-508) brought changes in the budget process that will have dramatic implications for domestic, defense, and international public policy decisions. These decisions must reflect the reality that our nation will not prosper if its urban communities continue to decay, its children under-educated, its work force unskilled, its physical infrastructure falling apart, and the health of its people deteriorating.

Therefore, our federal budget choices must include a domestic agenda that funds the rebuilding of our infrastructure and the expansion of job training and education programs. Attacking these issues aggressively will strengthen U.S. capability to compete effectively in the modern economy.

ECONOMIC DEVELOPMENT

The difference between the average incomes of African-American and white families has been steadily growing, raising the prospect that the attainment of parity in this area under current conditions would not occur until the year 2151. The observed rate of relative progress would have to increase by more than 11 times to reach parity by the year 2000.

While full employment will ultimately help to close the wage gap, we continue to call for a national program of African-American economic development, supported by the federal government and the private sector, that assists in creating jobs for the African-American community. African Americans must meet the employment needs of our changing economy by increasingly being trained in technical careers. There must be a combined effort by both the public and private sectors if African Americans are to continue to strive for parity by the year 2000 in the economic development arena.

We urge Congress and the Bush administration to continue minority set-aside programs that enhance business opportunities and employment and that foster economic development in African-American communities.

EMPLOYMENT

With African-American and other minority populations comprising an increasingly larger share of labor force growth, the adverse employment conditions they face, relative to those of the white working population, could seriously impact the nation's productivity and economic competitiveness.

The National Urban League will continue its call for parity in the work force by the year 2000. To achieve parity, we urge the private sector and federal government to use all of their resources to provide equitable employment opportunities for African Americans.

The 101st Congress failed to amend the Job Training Partnership Act. Lawmakers in the 102nd Congress, First Session, should amend the JTPA to ensure better access for the truly disadvantaged. Additionally, Congress, with the support of the Bush administration, should enact legislation that will close the gap between unemployed African-American workers and others.

CIVIL RIGHTS

When President Bush vetoed the Civil Rights Act of 1990, he failed the African-American community miserably.

In a speech before the National Urban League's 79th annual conference on August 8, 1989, in Washington, DC, President Bush declared, "My administration is committed to reaching out to minorities, to striking down barriers to free and open access. We will not tolerate discrimination, bigotry, or bias of any kind— period."

By vetoing the Civil Rights Act of 1990, the president let a political decision prevail over his commitment to fairness and justice. He was advised that the bill was a "quota bill." The League disagrees and believes that the president should put politics aside and do what is right.

The Civil Rights Act of 1990 will be reintroduced when the 102nd Congress convenes this month. Congress should overwhelmingly pass this critical legislation, and President Bush should live up to his word by not blocking legislation to end discrimination in the workplace but be fair. We urge President Bush to sign it.

EDUCATION

1991 marks a historic year for the National Urban League and its Education Initiative. In September, 1986, the League committed its human and fiscal resources to improving educational outcomes for African-American students by launching a National Education Initiative. Since then, more than 300,000 students and parents have participated in educationally oriented activity in the 114- affiliate Urban League network. This activity has one goal: to increase the academic achievement of African-American students.

The League remains committed to the Education Initiative and invites others who are equally committed to improving African-American students academically to join our advocacy.

We call upon Congress and the Bush administration to create educational policies and programs that will enhance the opportunities for African-American students.

We were strongly disturbed by the U.S. Education Department's recent decision to discontinue financial aid targeted for minority students in federally supported colleges. We applaud the president for reviewing this insensitive directive and urge him to restore the policy to where it was prior to the Education Department's attempt to change it.

CRIME AND CRIMINAL JUSTICE

With the continuous surge in violent crimes, especially homicides, urban communities are leaving our young people with environments that are becoming increasingly difficult in which to survive. Guns and drugs are holding African-American communities hostage.

The National Urban League calls upon Congress and the president to get all guns, particularly military assault weapons, out of the hands of criminals. These weapons should not be accessible to anyone involved in illegal drug activity and should be banned—period—from the public.

HEALTH

National momentum for developing a universal health care plan offers the 102nd Congress the opportunity to go down in history as the Congress that transformed words into action on affordable, quality health care access for all Americans.

The well-documented disparity in the health status of African Americans at every stage of human development and the disparity in the health care delivery system's response to the health needs of African Americans point to a national crisis in public health policy.

Therefore, the National Urban League calls upon the 102nd Congress to enact a universal health care plan that includes provisions for closing the health gap between African Americans and whites in four key areas:

1. In critical indexes of health status, such as life expectancy and infant mortality;

2. In lethal health problems, such as cancer, cardiovascular disease and stroke, diabetes, homicide and legal intervention, chemical dependency, and HIV/AIDS;

3. In access to quality health care, such as access to quality health insurance and a comprehensive system of health care; and

4. In the health professions, where African Americans are severely underrepresented.

HOUSING

Homeownership continues to be only a dream for many African-American families, as housing costs remain high and the availability of financial loans become more difficult to obtain. The nation's financial institutions continue to be troubled by bank failures, which are affected by the state of the economy. Because the economy is near recession levels, it, in turn, could provoke an additional rash of bank failures, further exacerbating the situation.

Congress must appropriate funding in Fiscal Year 1992 for the Cranston-Gonzalez National Affordable Housing Act of 1990. This measure, signed into law by President Bush (P.L. 101-625), is the most significant revision of national housing policies since 1974. Once funded, it will preserve, produce, and renovate affordable housing for low-income people.

We also call upon local governments to recognize and financially support the hard work of community-based organizations that have created effective model housing development programs.

ENERGY

With oil prices increasing or remaining at high levels, African-American consumers are forced to pay higher prices for fuel. For those on fixed budgets, any increase in the cost of home heating oil or gasoline can place extreme hardships on families. With gasoline prices on the rise, due to the Persian Gulf situation and the new five-cent tax per gallon of gas for deficit reduction, low- to moderate-income families are disproportionately feeling the crunch.

We call on the federal government to increase funding of the Low-Income Home Energy Assistance Program (LIHEAP), which has received drastic cuts in the past few years. As fuel costs continue to rise, funding levels should be increased proportionately. Joint efforts on the part of the federal government and the private sector are needed to assist low-income African Americans who pay increasingly higher utility bills.

INTERNATIONAL AFFAIRS

The Middle East conflict presents yet another problem that this nation must address amidst growing and ever-demanding domestic concerns. While there are no easy solutions to war and conflict, the National Urban League endorses a peaceful resolution to the Middle East unrest.

We support the bipartisan congressional call for the United Nations-endorsed economic sanctions. In essence, all of the necessary strategies to save lives first and financial resources second should be fully exhausted.

While we celebrate the release of Nelson Mandela, apartheid still has not ended in South Africa. We support all efforts, especially the continuation of economic sanctions, to end apartheid in that nation.

Post-apartheid South Africa will require significant educational and financial support so that black South Africans are prepared to govern effectively a nation where their participation has been systematically denied. We call upon public and private institutions to assist black South Africans as they move toward liberation and greater political empowerment.

APPENDICES

Economic Costs of American Racism

Billy J. Tidwell, Ph.D.
Director of Research
National Urban League, Inc.

INTRODUCTION

The question of the costs of racism has slowly but inexorably moved toward the center of public consciousness and concern. The reference here is not only to the recognized human hardships the phenomenon visits upon its victims. Nor is it limited to the nebulous notion of moral degeneracy. The costs also include what society has had to pay in social instability, in impairment of its capacity to produce and progress, and in constraints on its role as a purveyor of democratic principles in the developing world. Of course, there are the economic costs; i.e., the adverse effects of racism in dollar terms.

As the 21st century approaches, bringing new demands and challenges, it is essential that there be more public understanding and appreciation of the costs of racism — past, present, and future. It is important that policymakers conduct more hard-nosed benefit-cost analyses of the problem in assessing what is in the best interest of the general welfare. Under present conditions, the problem of racism goes well beyond the moral imperative to "do the right thing." It has become an urgent matter of national security. Consequently, we must decide as a nation whether we can continue to bear the costs. We must decide as a nation whether it is time finally to balance the ledger of racial justice.

While the cost issue has commanded serious attention in the past, it must be treated even more seriously as a contemporary concern. There are two key considerations in this regard. First, the racial demography of the nation is changing rapidly, with African Americans and other minorities comprising a growing share of the total population. Between now and the year 2000, the African-American population is expected to increase by 12.8 percent, compared to a 5.2 percent growth rate for whites.[1]

Corresponding changes are occurring in the composition of the civilian labor force. By the year 2000, African Americans will account for 17.4 percent of all new workers, up from 15 percent in 1988. The proportion of new white workers is projected to decline by 7.5 percent during this period.[2]

Thus, African Americans could be the critical human resources of the future. However, they must be prepared and allowed to contribute their talents, unencumbered by the race-based constraints on development and access that have been endemic to their experience in White America. The cost of racism in this respect could quite literally bring the nation to the brink of bankruptcy as a competitor in the changing global marketplace.[3]

Second, the recent movement toward democratization in Eastern Europe and other parts of the world is widely applauded as a positive development that is in the geopolitical self-interest of the United States to promote. Although the changes appear irreversible, the incipient democracies are nonetheless fragile systems whose futures are very much hanging in the balance. The degree to which this country is able to provide moral as well as material support could be decisive in some cases. In this connection, the continuing specter of racism in America and the persistence of racial conditions that contradict the nation's most fundamental democratic principles limit its ability to exert moral influence in the international community. Here, too, racism and discrimination are severe liabilities.

These observations simply underscore the importance of coming to grips with the costs of racism and investing the nation's collective energies in more progressive directions. The price of the status quo is too high, and could go even higher unless the right kinds of commitments are made to settle the racial inequality account.

This paper seeks to advance understanding of the racism problem by examining some of the economic costs it involves. Although our focus is on the "bottom line" issue, it is recognized that there is a high degree of interplay between economic costs and the other types of costs mentioned above.

For context, we first provide an overview discussion of American racism in concept and practice.

AMERICAN RACISM

Whatever perspective one adopts and the historical period to which it is applied, racism or racial discrimination against African Americans denotes one overriding condition—subordination. Generically, racial discrimination can be viewed as ". . .differential treatment by members of a dominant race which functions to deny or to restrict the choices of members of a subordinate race."[4] Under slavery, the differential treatment of African Americans was systematic and all-encompassing. The slaves were regarded as chattel and did not share, therefore, in the protections, rights, and privileges the Constitution conferred on all American citizens. Indeed, slavery in the United States was unique in the efficacy and completeness of the subordination process.[5] The system was driven by a singular purpose, human exploitation, and was anchored in an ideology of white biological and spiritual superiority for its justification.

Emancipation brought very little relief to the subjugation of African Americans. Except for a brief period during Reconstruction, the freedmen continued to occupy a caste-like status. Their subordinate condition was affirmed by the Supreme Court's infamous "separate but equal" decision in *Plessy v. Ferguson* and codified in an elaborate framework of segregationist laws and practices that prevailed for nearly four generations.[6] Jim Crowism was virtually as effective as slavery itself in denying to African Americans the choices and opportunities experienced by the white majority. Further, the doctrine of white supremacy was reinvigorated during this period, penetrating deeply into the value system of the larger society and sharply regulating relations between the races. Also, African Americans continued to be exploited for the monetary benefit of whites—as sharecroppers, tenant farmers, etc.

It is worth pausing here to emphasize three salient points in this brief account. First, for most of their history, African Americans have been discriminated against as a matter of official government policy. Thus, the government's role has gone well beyond merely condoning mistreatment. Government institutions created, implemented, and enforced the rules of racial oppression. This circumstance vividly distinguishes the historical experience of African Americans from that of other racial and ethnic groups that have been the objects of discrimination and prejudice.[7]

Second, the generation and maintenance of structured inequalities in quality of life has been a hallmark of American racism. There have always been clear standards in this society as to what constitutes individual and family well-being and what it means to be "successful." In terms of basic subsistence needs, the enjoyment of amenities, prestige, emotional and physical health, etc., the American conception of "the good life" is universally shared. By the same token, the mechanisms for social mobility and the "pursuit of happiness" have been well-defined and functional. The effect of racism, however, has been to restrict systematically the quality of life for African Americans by denying them access to these mainstream vehicles for socioeconomic advancement, and otherwise limiting their rewards from personal initiative. The upshot is that African Americans have been relegated to a much lower standard of well-being in all vital areas of life than that enjoyed by the white majority. The durability of these disparities attests to the potency of racism as a force in American life.[8]

Third, and related to the preceding comments, American racism and the systemic processes associated with it have operated to promote the interests of the white majority. Through their blatant economic exploitation of African Americans and privileged, if not exclusive, position in the society's opportunity structure, whites have gained advantages that may be impossible to overcome.

Resuming the chronology, the legal status of African Americans was fundamentally altered in 1954 by the Supreme Court's *Brown* decision, which overturned the "separate but equal" ruling in *Plessy v. Ferguson*. Declaring that separation was inherently unequal, the Court ushered in an era of radical restructuring of American race relations. Further court decisions, the 1964 Civil Rights Act, the 1965 Voting Rights Act, and a series of executive orders redefined the federal government's attitude toward equal opportunity and its constitutional obligation to ensure racial equality. There is no doubt that the larger spate of judicial, legislative, and executive actions commenced in 1954 brought profound improvement in the African-American condition. But have they eliminated racism? Have they eradicated racial inequality? Have they resolved the perennial American dilemma? Such questions continue to dominate public debate. Those who believe racism has been overcome often cite the positive changes in racial attitudes that have occurred over the years. Indeed, a substantial body of survey research suggests that the prevalence of racially hostile and unaccepting sentiment among whites has declined sharply.[9] On the other hand, the recent upsurge of racially motivated violence against African Americans (e.g., the killing of Yusuf Hawkins in Bensonhurst, New York) suggests that racism in its basest form is still very much a part of the American scene.[10]

Just as the evidence concerning racial attitudes is mixed, so, too, are assessments of the socioeconomic status of African Americans. On the one hand, the long-term progress of African Americans, in both absolute terms and relative to the condition of whites, has been impressive. For example, in terms of income level, a basic measure of economic well-being, African-American families averaged $19,329 in 1988, compared to $1,986 in 1947. In 1988, the ratio of African-American to white median family income was .57, up notably from 0.51 in 1947. Similarly, the median earnings of African-American workers climbed from $79 per week in 1947 to $314 in 1988, closing the earnings gap with white workers by 11.9 percent. In occupational mobility, only 6.0 percent of African-American workers held positions as professionals and managers in 1940. By 1980, this percentage had grown to 14 percent, narrowing the racial disparity by 69.0 percent.

In educational attainment, the median years of schooling for African Americans in 1940 was 5.7, compared to 8.8 years for whites. By 1980, African Americans were averaging 12.0 years, as against 12.5 years for whites. Likewise, in 1940, fewer than two percent of African-American females or males had completed college, while 5.0 percent and 7.5 percent of their respective white counterparts were college graduates. In the four ensuing decades, the proportion of African-American females completing four years of college increased to 12.0 percent; 11.0 percent of African-American males were in this category. The corresponding figures for whites were 22.0 percent and 25.5 percent.[11]

Similar long-term gains have been observed for other important status indicators. On balance, the cumulative data document empirically what one might intuitively expect: African Americans are generally much better off today than they were half a century or even one generation ago.[12]

On the other hand, the long-term progress is counterbalanced by the persistence of deep racial inequalities in key areas of individual and family well-being. Moreover, the relative advancement of African Americans has slowed and, in some cases, even reversed, in recent years. In 1970, for example, the median income of African-American families was 61.3 percent of the median for whites. In 1989, the percentage ratio was considerably lower at 56.2. In 1972, African-American workers were 2.0 times more likely to be hit by unemploy-

ment than their white counterparts. In 1989, the racial unemploym~
2.5:1. In 1980, the African-American poverty rate was 2.8 times the ~
for whites. By 1989, African Americans were more than three tir~
to be poor.

The overall wealth status of African Americans is a minuscule nine percent of the wealth of whites. African-American families average about $3,400 in wealth or net worth, compared to $39,000 for white families. African Americans own barely two percent of the nation's businesses and account for less than one percent of the U.S. total in gross receipts. In the health area, the racial disparity in infant mortality rates has widened during the past decade, and life expectancy among African-American males has declined.[13]

The list could go on. However, it suffices to say that racial parity in critical areas of socioeconomic well-being remains a highly elusive goal. Indeed, the author has projected elsewhere that, at current rates of change, parity status in most instances will not be achieved for an inordinate amount of time into the future, if ever.[14] The evidence of continuing racial inequalities cogently demonstrates that racism is still operative in the body politic and that the effects of the historical oppression of African Americans have not been overcome. The evidence also confirms the operation of contemporary racism in much more subtle, institutional ways, as compared to the blatant exclusionary forms of the phenomenon that existed in the past. "Modern prejudice," writes Pettigrew, "is subtle and indirect. It is a part of widely and deeply held values, and it is reinforced institutionally. Old-fashioned bigotry can still be found throughout the nation, but confusion between it and modern prejudice obscures the current phenomenon. In fact, it is its careful separation from the older, cruder types of bigotry that helps to distinguish these new patterns of racism."[15]

THE COST ISSUE

From the early days of slavery to more recent times, social analysts and commentators have propounded the cost of racism and discrimination in heavily moral terms. Gunnar Myrdal is rightfully credited as having formulated the most influential conceptualization of racism as a moral issue. In introducing his seminal study of the problem, Myrdal states:

> The American Negro problem is a problem in the heart of the American. It is there that the interracial tension has its focus. It is there that the decisive struggle goes on. This is the central viewpoint of this treatise. Though our study includes economic, social, and political race relations, at bottom our problem is the moral dilemma of the American. . . .The "American Dilemma". . .is the ever-changing conflict between. . .the valuations preserved on the general plane which we shall call the "American Creed," where the American thinks, talks, and acts under the influence of high national and Christian precepts, and. . .the valuations on specific planes of individual and group living, where. . .group prejudice against particular persons or types of people. . .dominate his outlook.[16]

Thus, Myrdal's perspective highlights the departure between the abject status and treatment of African Americans and the society's avowed democratic ideals. The viewpoint conjures up related notions of "equity," "fairness," and "justice." Contemporary students of race relations have retained this focus on morality, even as they give it a pragmatic slant. A representative articulation is offered by Silberman, who admonishes that America ". . . must accept the Negro as an equal and participating member of society because it is the only right thing, the only decent thing, to do. In the long run, the greatest threat to the United States is not political or military, but moral. . ."[17] Even in the popular culture, the morality factor remains a commanding preoccupation, as illustrated by the public response to the recent movie, "Do the Right Thing."

Except on the most metaphysical level, it is virtually impossible to disentangle the premium on moral rectitude from more practical considerations of cost and consequence. Morality is serviceable, while immorality can seriously disserve the interests of a society and the welfare of all of its members. As Knowles and Prewitt argue in their analysis of American racism, ". . . it adversely affects whites as well as blacks."[18] In *Beyond Black and White*, psychiatrist James Comer summarizes the concern this way:

> The white mind has cost white people, black people and the nation dearly. It is impossible to calculate the price in dollars and cents. . . . It has meant the loss of an enormous amount of human talent. The number of black lives snuffed out by violence is beyond counting. The number of black lives crippled and maimed is even greater. The psychological and social development of America's children—white as well as black—has been stunted. As a result, the nation is not prepared for an advance scientific and technological age.[19]

The economics of racism and discrimination is without doubt the overriding factor in any assessment of costs. In American society, where the free enterprise system reigns supreme, the general welfare is defined and pursued in terms of economic interests. This observation is not intended to be an indictment. Free enterprise is most compatible with our democratic precepts and, for the most part, has afforded Americans an exceptionally high standard of living. Hence, the primacy of economics is not in dispute here. To the contrary, our aim is to demonstrate that racism has been a serious hindrance to economic performance and well-being. In this sense, there is little question that we can no longer afford the price.

The analysis addresses two interrelated concerns—the economic price that African Americans themselves have had to pay and the price that racism has cost the general economy. The first concern is the more straightforward and obvious of the two. White America has clearly recognized the economic deprivations suffered by African Americans, even though there continues to be substantial disagreement regarding the extent to which African Americans themselves are responsible for their current economic problems. The cynical sentiments are expressed most vocally in popular discussions of the so-called "black underclass." Nevertheless, white Americans have evinced through the years a more supportive attitude toward the principle of equal opportunity and compassion for the difficulties African Americans on the whole have experienced in realizing economic well-being.

It is necessary to stress, however, that White America generally has approached this subject from a moral standpoint; that is, from the standpoint of the "American dilemma" as originally conceived. There has been relatively little appreciation of the interface between the economic well-being of African Americans and that of the society at large. Thus, in considering the need to eradicate racism in the economic area, the question "What's in it for me?" has not been treated as a priority issue, the operative answer being "Very little." This view is misguided.

The second objective of our analysis, then, is to examine how the economic conditions of African Americans impact the nation's economy and, thus, the individual economic self-interests of the white majority. There is some indication that a more enlightened perspective on this topic is beginning to take hold. For instance, *Money* magazine, the highly respected periodical on financial affairs with a predominantly white readership, recently published a major article on "Race and Money." One of the most cogent assertions of the article was that "While blacks bear the brunt of racism, the resulting inequalities cost all Americans enormously."[20] We estimate some of this cost in the second part of the analysis.

Costs to African Americans

The economic costs of racial inequality to African Americans are examined according to four basic indicators of group economic status—income level, unemployment rate, occupational representation, and earnings. In each case, the condition of African Americans is compared to that of the white majority. Hence, any reference to racial equality or parity involves the relative positions of these two groups.

1. *Income.* Income is the most basic measure of economic status, and per capita income is used here to estimate the cost of racism. Table 1 shows African-American and white personal income data for the years 1980-1989, adjusted for inflation. In columns a and b, we see how the two races compare in terms of actual per capita income for each year. The personal income of African Americans is consistently far less than that of whites. In proportional terms, the level of African-American to white income ranges from a low of 56.3 percent in 1982 to a high of 59.5 in 1988. For the period as a whole, then, African Americans averaged less than 60 cents to each dollar of income received by whites.

The instructive data for our purposes are contained in columns c to e. Column c shows the actual aggregate income of African Americans for each year, while column d indicates what this amount would be under the condition of

Table 1
Comparison of African-American and White Per Capita Income and Estimated Costs of Racial Inequality 1980–1989, in 1989 Dollars

Year	(a) Per Capita Income Afr. Amer.	Wht.	(b) Ratio AA/Wh (%)	(c) Total AA inc. (actual) in bils.	(d) Total AA inc. (with parity)	(e) Cost est. in bils.
1989	$8,747	$14,896	58.7	$266	$453	$187
1988	8,271	13,896	59.5	242	421	179
1987	7,961	13,686	58.2	234	401	167
1986	7,779	13,332	58.3	226	385	159
1985	7,520	12,832	58.6	214	366	152
1984	7,147	12,455	57.4	202	361	149
1983	6,803	11,957	56.9	188	331	143
1982	6,571	11,679	56.3	179	319	140
1981	6,675	11,686	57.1	179	314	135
1980	6,897	11,820	58.4	183	312	129

Source: Based on data in U.S. Department of Commerce, Bureau of the Census, Current Population Reports, *Money Income and Poverty Status in the United States: 1989*; and *Trends in Income, by Selected Characteristics: 1947 to 1988*.

racial parity; i.e., if African Americans had the same per capita income as whites. The figures in column e represent the difference between African Americans' actual total income and their total as determined from the parity computation. This difference is the "cost" of racial inequality in income. The order of magnitude is immediately apparent. The personal income loss for African Americans ran as high as $187 billion in 1989. The grand total for the 10-year period is a mind-boggling $1.5 trillion! This is a staggeringly large number by any standard.

It is also worth noting that the size of the estimated income loss figure increases progressively from one year to the next. Between 1980 and 1989, the amount went up by $58 billion, a growth rate of 45 percent.

Of course, the parity and cost estimates are subject to a number of caveats. For example, a more rigorous analysis would take into account the different age distributions of the African-American and white populations. African Americans are the younger group, and are therefore more likely to have persons who are not yet old enough to produce income. Assuming that African Americans should have the same per capita income as whites might generate inflated parity estimates. Likewise, any number of determinants may operate to sustain the personal income gap between African Americans and whites. What proportion of the problem to assign to racism as opposed to some more race-neutral cause(s) is a vexing question that is not easily answered.

Even allowing for the technical limitations of this type of analysis, there should be no doubt that massive amounts of personal income are denied to African Americans by racism and discrimination. One cannot help but contemplate what such added consumption power would mean to the economic welfare of African Americans themselves and to the nation's commerce.

2. *Unemployment Rates.* One of the principal constraints on the income of African Americans is their inordinately high level of unemployment. Indeed, severely disproportionate unemployment rates distinguished the economic status of African Americans throughout the 1980s. The severity of the problem is detailed in Table 2, which presents overall African-American and white unemployment rates from 1980-1989. As the table shows, African Americans were more than twice as likely as whites to be hit by unemployment in each year. One should bear in mind that the economy experienced two major recessions in the early part of the decade, which had a devastating impact on the work force as a whole. In particular, the respective jobless rates for 1982 and 1983 reflect the gravity of the economic downturn. Since 1983, the jobless rate among both groups has declined progressively, concomitant with the economic recovery. However, the racial unemployment gap has not abated. To the contrary, African Americans were more likely than whites to be jobless in 1989 than they were in 1980. In good economic times and bad, then, disproportionate unemployment dominates the labor market experience of African Americans.

Table 2
African-American and White Unemployment Rates
and Unemployment Ratios, 1980-1989

Year	Afr. Amer. (%)	White (%)	Ratio Afr. Amer. to White
1989	11.4	4.5	2.5
1988	11.7	4.7	2.5
1987	13.0	5.3	2.4
1986	14.5	6.0	2.4
1985	15.1	6.2	2.4
1984	15.9	6.5	2.5
1983	19.5	8.4	2.3
1982	18.9	8.6	2.2
1981	15.6	6.7	2.3
1980	14.3	6.3	2.3

Source: U.S. Department of Labor, Bureau of Labor Statistics, *Handbook of Labor Statistics,* August, 1989; *Employment and Earnings,* January, 1990.

One gains a more direct understanding of the impact of disproportionate African-American unemployment in cost terms by focusing on the actual number of jobs lost in a given year. Swinton provides such an assessment:

Even without looking at the impact on discouragement and labor-force dropout, the higher unemployment rates experienced by blacks cost blacks hundreds of thousands of jobs every year. . . . During 1988, on average, the unemployment parity gap was over 1 million jobs. Black men experienced a 379,000 job shortage due to lack of parity in unemployment while black women suffered even more, experiencing a 425,000 job shortfall. Black teenagers lost 182,000 jobs due to lack of parity in unemployment.[21]

Finally, it is important to observe that the phenomenon of disproportionate African-American unemployment occurs across occupations and industries and irrespective of educational achievement levels. For example, one study found that the racial unemployment gap among certain categories of administrators and managers was 4.5:1 in 1985; i.e., African Americans in these occupations were four-and-one-half times as likely as their white counterparts to be jobless.[22]

3. *Occupational Representation.* Not only are African Americans much more likely than whites to be unemployed, but they are also much more likely to be employed in lower status, lower paying occupations, and are correspondingly less likely to hold the more prestigious and rewarding positions in the occupational structure. Racism and discrimination in economic life continue to cost African Americans dearly in these respects, as is indicated by the data in Table 3.

The first two columns in the table show what percentage of all workers in each occupational category African Americans and whites represent. The third column shows the degree to which African Americans are overrepresented or underrepresented in a given category, relative to their proportion of the employed work force. In 1988, the latter figure was 10.1 percent versus 86.8 percent for whites.

The pattern is clear: African-American workers are overrepresented in the lower status occupations and underrepresented at the upper end of the occupational scale. For example, while they comprised just 10 percent of employed workers in 1988, African Americans accounted for 15 percent of all operators, fabricators, and laborers, an overrepresentation of five percent. Similarly, they were overrepresented by 12.5 percent among private household workers. On the other hand, African Americans accounted for only 5.6 percent of all executives, administrators, and managers, and just 6.7 percent of all professional workers. Whites were overrepresented in both of these categories. While the occupational status of African Americans has improved considerably over time, one can only infer that racism and discrimination continue to limit their advancement.[23]

4. *Earnings.* The most obvious effect of the occupational disadvantages of African Americans is found in their earnings levels. Overall, the earnings of full-time African-American workers in 1989 were just 78 percent of the earnings of their white counterparts. (See Table 4.) African-American males fared much worse than did females. The percentage of African-American to white earnings among males was .72, compared to .90 among females.

These earnings differentials have changed very little in the past 10 years. They, too, suggest the continued operation of racial discrimination in the labor market, and the data help to clarify the economic costs African Americans incur as we

Table 3
Occupational Representation of African
Americans and Whites, 1988

Occupation	% Afr. Amer.	% White	Diff. between AA % for occup. & % of empl'd
Mgrs & profs.	6.2	90.5	−3.9
Exe., admin., managerial	5.6	91.6	−4.5
Professional	6.7	89.4	−3.4
Tech., sales, admin. support	9.1	87.8	−1.0
Technicials & related support	9.3	85.7	−0.8
Sales	6.1	90.9	−4.0
Adm. support	11.3	85.5	1.2
Service	17.6	79.0	7.5
Private hh'd.	22.6	75.6	12.5
Protective serv.	16.7	81.5	6.6
Other service	16.7	78.8	7.3
Precision prod., craft, & repair	7.5	980.1	−2.6
Oper.'s, fabricators, & laborers	15.0	82.1	4.9
Farming, forestry, fishing	6.6	91.7	−3.5

Source: U.S. Bureau of Labor Statistics, *Handbook of Labor Statistics, August 1989,*
  Table 17.

Table 4
Median Weekly Earnings of African-American and
White Workers, by Sex, 1989

	Afr. Amer.	White	Ratio
Total	$319	$409	.78
Females	301	334	.90
Males	348	482	.72

Source: U.S. Bureau of Labor Statistics, *Employment and Earnings, January, 1990,*
  Table 54.

approach the 21st century. The earnings variable figures prominently below in our analysis of the economic cost to the society as a whole.

Cost to the National Economy

Historically, the American economy was the envy of the western world. There seemed to be no limit to the ability of the capitalist, free enterprise system to generate income, wealth, and a progressively higher standard of living for the American people. This stature as a leader in economic development continues. However, it has been seriously challenged in recent decades by economies that have proved to be highly competitive. Japan, West Germany, and South Korea are exemplary among the countries that have made impressive progress in developing their economies over the past 40 years or so. As a result, the world marketplace has changed dramatically. Americans have experienced the ramifications of this development in painful ways. There is growing concern that the erosion of America's position in the global economy will continue unless forthright actions are taken to reverse the trend.

The central issue is how to improve the nation's economic productivity and efficiency in the face of the changing demands on performance. In this connection, there is broad consensus on the need to undertake progressive structural and technological initiatives, even as there is disagreement concerning specific actions. At the same time, there is an increased emphasis on the importance of removing existing constraints on economic progress. This is the context in which the contemporary role of racism and discrimination must be critically examined. This is the context in which the issue of the economic costs of racism takes on far-reaching significance.

Economists and other social scientists have debated for years the question of whether and how racial discrimination militates against the nation's economic interests. The question is exceedingly complex, and the divergent scientific literature reflects the difficulty of getting a handle on it.[24] However, the preponderant body of opinion asserts that racism is indeed a major hindrance to the overall functioning of the economy.

> . . . [D]iscrimination will be costly to society, since it results in a clear and potentially serious loss of efficiency. When society's rewards and penalties are distributed to its members in a manner not consonant with their relative productivities, then at least some scarce resources are bound to be overallocated to relatively unproductive members of the "favored" race. . . and underallocated to more productive members of the race being discriminated against. . . . Society's aggregate real output, therefore, will fall below its potential. . .[25]

Another writer puts the issue squarely in terms of the utilization of human resources. "Discrimination on the basis of gender or race," he writes, "is not only harmful to its victim, it wastes important resources. When talented people are denied access to jobs commensurate with their potential, productivity and economic competitiveness suffer."[26]

As to the economic dysfunctions of discrimination against African Americans, in particular, Perlo's conclusion accords with our own judgment:

> . . . [E]conomic discrimination at Blacks is the nation's number one economic problem. No economic problem affecting the majority of the population can be solved or significantly eased unless the solution includes a vast improvement in the economic situation of Black people and substantial reduction of the discrimination against them.[27]

The data in the previous section illustrate that "vast improvement" in the condition of African Americans remains to be achieved. Most notably, African Americans continue to be disproportionately unemployed and underemployed, both of which circumstances bespeak a counterproductive underutilization of human resources. What does it cost the economy? The data in Table 5 provide a partial but revealing answer.

The table shows (1) the ratio of African-American to white per capita earnings in 1989, (2) the actual aggregate earnings of African-American workers during the year, (3) what the aggregate earnings of African-American workers would have been under the condition of racial parity (i.e., if their per capita earnings were equal to that of white workers), (4) the difference between the actual and parity aggregate earnings estimates, and (5) the proportion of the year's overall gross national product (GNP) this difference represents."[28] Items 2, 3, and 4 interest us the most.

In 1989, the aggregate earnings of African Americans were about $219 billion. If racial parity in earnings had prevailed, however, the total would have been $311.9 billion. Since labor is a principal component of GNP, the absence of earnings parity cost the American economy nearly $93 billion in 1989. Put differently, racial equality would have boosted the GNP for the year by about 1.8 percent. In fact, for each year between 1980 and 1989 (data not shown), the GNP would have been close to two percent higher had there been earnings parity between the races. Thus, the total loss to the economy during this period is in the hundreds of billions of dollars.

Table 5
Estimated Effect of Racism on the Economy, as Measured by the Difference Between Actual African-American Earnings and Earnings Under Parity
1989

% of AA to white earnings	Total AA earnings (actual)	Total under parity	Diff. between actual & parity	% of GNP
.70	$219.1 bil.	$311.9 bil.	$92.8 bil.	1.8

Source: Computed by author from data in U.S. Bureau of Labor's *Employment and Earnings, January, 1990.* GNP data are from the Bureau of Economic Analysis.

CONCLUSION

This paper has examined some of the economic costs of racism in American society. Of course, such analyses can be very problematic. The issues are inherently elusive and terribly complex. Cause-effect relationships are difficult to conceptualize and even more difficult to determine empirically.

Despite the caveats, the upshot of the analysis can be stated simply: American racism is a profoundly costly problem. Thus, the failure of this nation to come to grips with the existence of racism and discrimination should be a matter of deep concern to us all. We all pay a heavy price. To be sure, reasonable people will disagree over various cost estimates and the overall magnitude of the problem. However, there should be consensus that the costs are too high and that the problem must be solved.

It is important to underscore the policy considerations set forth in the opening. Profound changes in the demography of the country, coupled with the emergence of an increasingly competitive global marketplace, have altered drastically the framework within which we must assess our needs as a nation and set our national priorities. In addition, the momentous political developments in Eastern Europe and other parts of the world, which have brought resurgent movements toward democracy, are vitally linked to our own self-interests. To this mix of dynamics, one also must add the nation's worsening fiscal crisis, spearheaded by a huge budget deficit and an unprecedented calamity in the savings and loan industry, whose severity still has not been fully disclosed. In the context of these exigencies, the continued presence of racism in our national life is much more than a nuisance, embarrassment, or moral outrage. It is a liability of immense proportions.

American society has, therefore, reached a critical point of departure that could have decisive implications for her long-term future. Whether we will pursue the right course toward strength and vitality or continue to endure the failures of the past is uncertain. What is certain is that the future is ours to control. What is certain is that action based on enlightened self-interest holds the greatest promise. What is certain is that lowering the costs of racism is a key prerequisite to progress.

Toward Development of a National Drug Control Strategy

Robert McAlpine
Director of Policy and Government Relations
National Urban League, Inc.

NOTE: In September, 1990, the National Urban League submitted to the Office of National Drug Control Policy recommendations for development of the nation's third annual drug control strategy. This paper is based on those recommendations, with information added where appropriate.

RECOMMENDED DRUG CONTROL POLICIES

In 1989, the National Urban League issued a comprehensive report, *Public Policy Empowerment Mandate: The Drug Trafficking Issue,* in which a set of strategies for combating drug trafficking and substance abuse was outlined in three distinct categories: (1) supply efforts, (2) demand efforts, and (3) African-American approaches. The League has reiterated these recommendations for consideration by the Office of National Drug Control Policy (ONDCP). Drug trafficking and substance abuse continue to impact disproportionately the lives and communities of African Americans.

Key recommendations that we believe have not been given utmost priority include: declaration of the drug crisis as a **national emergency** by the president, and **drug treatment on demand** for all in need, whether voluntarily, through outreach, or through incarceration.

The need for drug treatment services is especially acute among addicted pregnant women. A June, 1990, report by the General Accounting Office (GAO), *Drug-Exposed Infants, A Generation At Risk,* documents this tremendous need. For example, the report notes that:

- Many programs that provide services to women, including pregnant women, have long waiting lists. Treatment experts believe that unless women who have decided to seek treatment are admitted to a treatment facility the same day, they may not return. However, women are rarely admitted the day they seek treatment.

- Nationwide, drug treatment services are insufficient. A 1990 survey conducted by the National Association of State Alcohol and Drug Abuse Directors, Inc. (NASADAD), estimates that 280,000 pregnant women nationwide were in need of drug treatment, yet fewer than 11 percent of them received care. Hospital and social welfare officials in each of the five cities in the [GAO] review also told [GAO] that drug treatment services were insufficient or inadequate to meet the demand for services of drug-addicted pregnant women.

- In addition to insufficient treatment, some programs deny services to pregnant women....One of the primary reasons treatment centers are reluctant to treat pregnant women relates to issues of legal liability. Drug treatment providers fear that certain treatments using medications and the lack of prenatal care or obstetrical services at the clinics may have adverse consequences on the fetus, and thereby expose the providers to legal problems.

- Other barriers to drug treatment for women include the lack of child care services...[and] fear of criminal prosecution. Drug treatment and prenatal care providers told [GAO] that the increasing fear of incarceration and losing children to foster care is discouraging pregnant women from seeking care.

Providing timely drug treatment to addicted pregnant women can simultaneously help prevent and/or minimize the related risks of HIV infection for both the mother and the newborn, as well as the increasing phenomenon of the "boarder baby" crisis.

Additionally, our survey of 17 Urban League affiliates with funded substance abuse programs reveals that nine of the affiliates reported that *treatment* was one of the substance abuse services most needed in the community.

GUNS MUST BE ERADICATED
AS A TOOL OF THE DRUG TRADE

Eliminating unlawful possession and use of guns must be an integral component of this nation's anti-drug policy. The National Urban League has a long-standing policy of supporting a curb on the sale of guns. Relative to the drug wars occurring in the African-American communities of this nation, the League continues to call on the Congress and the president to get all guns out of the hands of criminals, especially military assault weapons. These weapons should be banned period for any public use.

According to the National Center for Health Statistics (1988), after a significant decline in the early 1980s, the number of 15–24 year olds killed by firearms in the U.S. increased more than 16 percent, from 6,765 to 7,852, between 1984 and 1986. Among black males in this age range, firearm fatalities increased more than 20 percent during these two years.

The Office of National Drug Control Policy must take heed of the call from communities, hospitals, physicians, and local police to curb the role of handguns and assault weapons in: the mounting drug-related homicides; the severe public health-related problems, costs, and social impact on individuals and families who suffer from the devastation of gun-related injuries. The evidence is overwhelming:

- In a September 10, 1990, news conference held in Washington, DC, the police chiefs of New York (Dr. Lee P. Brown) and the District of Columbia (Isaac Fulwood) jointly called for legislative action to curb guns. Both cities have suffered from a rash of gun-related murders and injuries.

- *The Washington Post* (9/11/90) reported on mounting gun-related violence in Chicago. *The Post* stated that "Police recorded 75 shooting incidents, resulting in 13 deaths, in a rampage of violence (in Chicago) last weekend marked by gang warfare and drive-by shootings." This type of carnage is not limited to Chicago, as we know it is being repeated in many cities throughout this country.

- According to Martin et al., in the *Journal of the American Medical Association* (1988), firearm injuries cost an estimated $429 million a year in hospital expenses alone; 85.6 percent of that is borne by taxpayers. Total annual medical costs for firearm injuries, including physicians' fees, ambulance service, rehabilitation and follow-up care are estimated to exceed $1 billion. The percentage of costs paid for by public sources is substantially greater for firearm injuries than for all hospitalizations considered together.

- According to the Pediatric Trauma Registry, National Institute for Disability and Rehabilitation Research (1989), in fiscal year 1988, two percent of the pediatric inpatients admitted for injuries were gunshot victims, a 70 percent increase from the 1.3 percent rate in FY 86. Forty percent of these injuries occurred at home.

- According to unpublished data, Trauma Center, DC General Hospital (1989), gunshot wounds were the most frequent injuries among 10-18-year-old trauma victims reporting to that hospital in 1988. These wounds accounted for more than 43 percent of the trauma cases (37 of 85 cases) in this age range. Overall, gunshot-wound trauma cases at the hospital increased by 228 percent to 551 cases between 1986 and 1988.

Clearly, this nation's third annual National Drug Control Strategy would be unrealistic and not reflective of the severe crisis occurring in our communities if it did not address the issue of gun control.

THE OFFICE OF NATIONAL DRUG CONTROL POLICY MUST COORDINATE WITH CHILD WELFARE EXPERTS ON DECISIONS PERTAINING TO CHILDREN IN DRUG ENVIRONMENTS

The Office of National Drug Control Policy must ensure that policies governing families and children at risk in drug environments be consistent with the laws and reform efforts that have been under way in the child welfare system. Because of the special impact of this system on African-American children and their families, the ONDCP must consult fully with African-American experts in this field. For example, according to a recent study by the National Black Child Development Institute, *Who Will Care When Parents Can't? A Study of Black Children in Foster Care* (1989), despite the attempt at child welfare reform through enactment of the 1980 Adoption Assistance and Child Welfare Act (P.L. 96-272):

- Black children continued to be represented disproportionately in the foster care population;
- Black children continued to remain in foster care for long periods of time; and
- Black children were not being offered services that would reunite them with their families as soon as possible.

The National Urban League strongly recommends that the ONDCP coordinate its efforts with such experts as:

- The National Black Child Development Institute (contact Evelyn K. Moore, Executive Director, Washington, DC, (202) 387-1281).
- Black Administrators in Child Welfare, Inc. (contact Joyce Johnson, Staff Director, c/o the Child Welfare League of America, Washington, DC, (202) 638-2952).
- Ella S. McDonald, Executive Director, Richard Allen Center On Life, Inc., (New York, NY, (212) 862-7160).

ANTI-DRUG TRAFFICKING AND SUBSTANCE ABUSE ACTIVITIES OF THE URBAN LEAGUE MOVEMENT

In response to National Urban League President and Chief Executive Officer John E. Jacob, the Council of Executives' Public Policy Empowerment Mandate on Drug Trafficking, the Urban League Affiliate Movement, and our National Office have undertaken various anti-drug activities.

As of July 31, 1990, seventeen Urban League affiliates had established funded substance abuse programs that provide a variety of services based on the needs of their respective communities (such as aftercare, education, intervention, prevention, and treatment). Another 25 Urban League affiliates who do not have funded substance abuse programs provide services to substance abusers in their respective communities through other programs. Of these 25, 14 affiliates are in the process of planning for the implementation of funded programs.

Urban League affiliates in Baltimore, Winston-Salem (NC), Phoenix, Dallas, and St. Louis have been working with the National Institute on Drug Abuse (NIDA) in hosting NIDA's regional conferences to examine substance abuse and AIDS issues in African-American communities throughout the country. The National Urban League's Director for Program Development, Ann Hill, has coordinated this effort with our participating affiliates.

In December, 1990, IBM and the National Urban League announced the formation of "Drugs Destroy Dreams—A Youth Drug Intervention Program" that is being implemented in Baltimore and seven other cities, effective January 1, 1991. The $1.4 million pilot program is aimed at alcohol and substance abuse by youth at risk. Working with Urban League affiliates across the country, IBM employees and retired volunteers will work as instructors and mentors to teach drug prevention and early intervention to youngsters aged 12 to 16. The substance abuse curriculum will be taught in three-month sessions; besides Baltimore, these include Detroit; Columbia, SC; Providence, RI; Tucson, AZ; Tacoma, WA; Akron, OH; and Tampa, FL. The program will also involve parents, school officials, business leaders, and community groups.

Further, the National Urban League has established a "Stop the Violence Clearinghouse." In 1989, an all-star line-up of rap artists joined together to express their concern over the growing number of black homicides and violence sometimes linked to their concerts. They produced a hit—"Self Destruction"—that has become the unofficial anthem in the crusade against violence. Proceeds from the record and its videotape have been used to establish the League's Stop The Violence Clearinghouse. It collects, develops, and shares programmatic and resource information on youth programs aimed at preventing teen violence and destructive behavior. To date, more than half a million copies of "Stop the Violence" have been sold. Ruth Terrell, Director of the League's Youth Resources, should be contacted for further information on the clearinghouse.

For any additional information about Urban League anti-drug programmatic activities, contact William J. Haskins, Vice President, Programs, National Urban League, 500 East 62nd St., New York, NY, 10021, (212) 310-9000.

RECOMMENDED STRATEGIES

The National Urban League recommends strategies in three distinct categories: (1) supply efforts, (2) demand efforts, and (3) African-American approaches.

These recommended strategies are a beginning process to initiate public policy debate and formulation. While these strategies may not solve the entire problem, they present a starting point from which efforts can be made by community-based organizations and others. The Urban League will begin to advocate these strategies immediately and invites other African-American organizations and interested parties to join in the fight to get drugs out of our communities. This drug crisis should not be a jurisdictional issue, where bureaucratic agencies struggle as to who should control or have the greater responsibility in solving the problem. We all must work together. As such, the

League is willing to meet with the Bush administration's drug czar to provide technical assistance from the African-American perspective in the development of the National Drug Control Strategy. We make this request in accordance with P.L. 100-690, Section 1005.

The League will urge all of its affiliates to implement local plans that conform with the policy recommendations in this initiative. It will implement a plan of continued review and monitoring of this policy initiative. The League will commit the necessary manpower to assist in the promotion of this Public Policy Empowerment Mandate on Drug Trafficking. We hope everyone will join.

SUPPLY STRATEGIES

While it is recognized that the federal government and experts are taking the position that the war on interdiction (i.e., stopping the importation of illegal drugs through U.S. borders) is being lost, the National Urban League feels that efforts should be made to continue the fight. This nation should not simply give up the fight; we must not concede.

1. The federal government should declare an all-out war against international and national drug smuggling/trafficking.
    A. The president should declare the drug crisis a national emergency.
        — The president has statutory authority to do so.
    B. The Congress should urge the president to declare the drug crisis a national emergency.
2. The Congress and the president should commit the necessary funds to implement fully the recently passed Anti-Drug Abuse Act of 1988 (P.L. 100-690).

    — Passage of the act is a major step in the right direction; however, without the necessary money, the law will never be effective. The facts are clear. The amount of money currently appropriated to fight the war on drugs is minimal when considering the impact that the crisis is having on this nation.
3. Harsh economic sanctions should be implemented against countries who are suppliers of illegal drugs to the U.S. and who do not assist in stopping illegal drugs from leaving their countries.

    —P.L. 100-690 provides inter-country agreements; however, other countries need to be punished severely if they do not cooperate fully.
4. The federal government should allow for the *military* to be used as a major resource to assist in efforts to cut off the importation of illegal drugs through U.S. borders.

    — P.L. 100-690 allows for the Defense Department to be an active force in the efforts of interdiction. This nation's defense buildup has been tremendous over the past eight years. Use of the military is a common-sense approach, since the purpose of a military/defense buildup is to defend this nation's borders and freedom. The war on drugs just may be this nation's greatest threat to freedom and liberty. It makes no sense to have a military buildup and not use it to fight a war. The war on drugs is real.

DEMAND STRATEGIES

To make significant strides towards ending the drug crisis, we must balance supply efforts with an equal commitment to reducing demand. Demand strategies are recommended with the firm belief that these approaches can and must work.

- Education and Prevention

    Federal, state, and local governments should take the leadership in developing and promoting education and prevention programs to be targeted primarily at youth.

    A. The Drug-Free Schools and Communities Act (DFSCA), amended by P.L. 100-690, should be strongly supported with the necessary funds to assist schools and communities in their efforts to educate young people on the risk and dangers of drug use and abuse.

    B. In addition to the Drug-Free School programs, the National Urban League recommends that every school district in this nation adopt a mandatory curriculum on the use and danger of drug abuse. It is best that our young people learn in the classroom the dangers of using or involvement in drugs rather than out in the streets.

- Treatment

    Federal, state, and local governments should make every effort to create and ensure the availability of programs that will deliver the services needed to help drug abusers. Treatment on demand must be available.

    A. Adequate funding must accompany the treatment and prevention programs as provided in the Anti-Drug Abuse Act of 1988 (P.L. 100-690). These programs can be successful only with adequate resources and proper accountability to ensure that objectives of the programs are met.

    B. For those who are incarcerated for drug related crimes/criminal behavior, mandatory treatment programs should be made available. It does no good to lock up people and not treat them and send them back into society without any cure. By not giving the proper treatment to incarcerated addicts, we will simply send renewed drug abusers back to the streets. This activity is critical and could reduce the problem of illegal drugs entering penal institutions.

C. For those whose criminal behavior (i.e., misdemeanors) would not require extended incarceration, treatment programs should be mandatory alternatives. After one brush with the law, where property or life has not been seriously threatened, the drug abuser should be allowed to have access to rehabilitation. This would be a sensible alternative, especially where jurisdictions experience prison overcrowding. Instead of just turning the drug abuser away from jail where there is no space, a therapy-treatment program that will help the drug abusers with their immediate problem is needed.

AFRICAN-AMERICAN APPROACHES

As proposed by Dr. Wade W. Nobles and Dr. Lawford L. Goddard, three strategic components are critical if the problem of substance abuse is to be solved by the African-American community:

1. The first component is to consciously reclaim, evaluate, apply, and institutionalize our own traditional techniques of development, socialization, and enculturation.

2. Second, develop an authentic Afrocentric theory and practice (therapy and education). This focus would require the establishment and support of African-American think tanks and research and development centers, charged with the responsibility for developing:

   • Afrocentric theories of human development and transformation;

   • Culturally consistent intervention and prevention treatment methods; and

   • African-American-based development and training programs in response to the concrete conditions impacting upon the viability of African-American people.

3. Third, undertake a systematic program of "community inoculation through cultural immunology." This would require that we develop and formally (re)introduce into the African-American community cultural mandates, functions, and expectations designed to stimulate the community's production of indigenous processes that have the capacity to resist negative agents and/or prevent the development of attitudes, ideas, and/or behavior antithetical to the African-American community's own well-being, welfare, and viability. This represents a radically new and different perspective on what needs to be done in the African-American community.

NATIONAL URBAN LEAGUE AFFILIATE ACTION

The following action steps illustrate supportive activites and policy initiatives that can provide a vehicle for immediate affiliate activity. These local activities, along with the national focus, will begin the process of placing the National Urban League on record in attacking drug trafficking in African-American communities throughout the United States.

Suggested Action Steps

1. Document the nature and extent of drug sales in the community.
2. Develop a detailed assessment of ongoing activities by local institutions designed to curtail the sale of drugs.
3. Determine what policies and resources exist for eliminating neighborhood drug sales.
4. Identify the main gaps and barriers to effective policy implementation.
5. Hold strategy sessions with key individuals in institutions that can help solve the problem of drug sales.
6. Develop a community-wide consortium of black organizations and neighborhood groups to support and advocate for drug-free communities.
7. Arrive at a community consensus regarding the specific policy and action priorities to be addressed.
8. Develop a detailed work plan with clear quantitative benchmarks and objectives.

Illustration of Supportive Activities and Policy Initiatives

1. Hold rallies and demonstrations involving as many African-American organizations as possible to demonstrate support for the effort. Put pressure on authorities, and make it socially acceptable to speak out about drug sales in African-American neighborhoods.
2. Support ongoing efforts of other anti-drug groups in African-American neighborhoods.
3. Pressure local governments, law enforcement agencies, chambers of commerce, and others to place a priority on eliminating neighborhood drug sales.
4. Advocate for, and support the enforcement of, tougher penalties and prison guidelines for persons convicted of drug-related offenses and the seizure of assets.
5. Support the establishment of alternative incarceration sites.
6. Initiate and/or participate in efforts to review and revise existing juvenile statutes relating to criminal activities and punishment guidelines.
7. Advocate and support the strict enforcement of both drug use and drug sale laws.

SUZANNE BERGERON, RONALD JACKSON, and LISA BLAND MALONE of the National Urban League's Department of Policy and Government Relations contributed to this appendix, as well as A. KIMBERLY JOHNSON of the League's National AIDS Minority Information and Education Project, who compiled the affiliate survey information cited in this paper.

Community Mobilization for Education in Rochester, New York: A Case Study

David Wirschem
Manager of Program Planning and Research
Urban League of Rochester, New York, Inc.

Rochester, New York, is the central city in an urban county of a little over 700,000 people. Its City School District enrolls 32,000 students in 50 schools; 71 percent are minorities, mostly African American, some Hispanic American; 73 percent are below the poverty level. The district's educational problems are not unlike those of most other urban communities around the nation. Rochester, however, has been in the forefront of the movement to articulate and address what is now acknowledged to be a national education crisis.

Dramatic reforms in the Rochester City School District have attracted national attention, particularly since 1987, when a headline-grabbing, collective-bargaining agreement between the district and its teachers' union was unveiled. Significant reform activities were well underway before that time, having derived major impetus from a 1985–86 community mobilization campaign by the Urban League of Rochester. Following is an overview of that campaign, Rochester's reform activities, and their results.

AN URBAN LEAGUE COMMUNITY-MOBILIZATION CAMPAIGN

The Urban League of Rochester has been a leading advocate for educational improvements since its inception. Yet, when the organization celebrated its 20th anniversary in 1985, it found little evidence of educational parity between blacks and whites or between city and suburban schools in the Rochester area. In the city's 1984 graduating class of 1,273 students, there were but 35 African Americans with grade averages of B or higher. That year, 725 students, nine percent of the senior high enrollment, dropped out, and the rate was rising rapidly.[1]

The severity of the problem moved the Urban League, under the leadership of its President, William A. Johnson, Jr., to undertake a community-wide education initiative. It would inform the community of the magnitude of the crisis and attempt to make every segment of the community a part of the solution. A year-long agenda of promotional activities was laid out, including (1) meetings to solicit the support of key individuals and groups and to involve them in the planning; (2) three public "speakouts" to hear the concerns, respectively, of students, parents, and educators; (3) a major conference of 150 key community leaders, cosponsored by the League and the University of Rochester, to begin to identify

243

reform strategies; and (4) at the end of the year, "town meetings" held simultaneously at 12 sites throughout the city, to bring the public into the movement en masse.

With each event, coverage by the news media increased. Rochester's educational television station, WXXI, taped the speakouts and produced a highly effective video, which helped to dramatize the problem for participants in subsequent events. By the time of the town meetings in the fall of 1985, the local media were virtually saturated with stories on public education, and national network television began to take an interest in Rochester.

From that first year of promotional activity, two parallel developments emerged that would eventually begin to bring about substantive changes in the schools. First, at the conclusion of the town meetings, the 1,000 or so people in attendance were invited to serve on school action committees at the schools of their choice. Approximately 600 of them agreed to do so. Each committee was co-convened by a community volunteer and the school principal, and was charged with defining and implementing a project that would *improve academic achievement.* By the end of the academic year, 35 of the city's 45 schools had begun implementing such projects.

The second development was a result of the community leadership conference at the University of Rochester, which had concluded with the appointment of a high-level task force of community leaders to identify specific educational improvement strategies. In March, 1986, the task force issued its report, *A Call to Action.* The report was a compendium of recommendations to all segments of the community that have a stake in public education—the school district, teachers, students, parents, businesses, community organizations, human service agencies, cultural and religious institutions, colleges, libraries, the media, etc. The document acknowledged an education crisis, but refrained from assigning blame, proclaiming, "all of us share responsibility for the problem, and all of us can contribute to finding solutions."[2] The *Call to Action* attracted great attention and was printed in its entirety in the daily newspaper, the *Times Union.* Interest within the business community was heightened at the same time by a separate business task force report, which carried in-depth recommendations for actions by business and industry to help the schools.

Following the report, there was a general outpouring of community support for education throughout Rochester. Businesses announced new jobs and scholarship programs for city students; churches and colleges began expanding their tutoring and mentoring programs; abundant advertising support was forthcoming to promote community attention and to motivate students through the media; and service agencies sought to bolster their youth intervention programs. All of this began at a time when, at the building level, school action committees were implementing changes geared to individual schools, and the central administration was implementing the *Call to Action*'s checklist of recommendations to the district. The burden of managing all of these responses inevitably fell on the school district administration.[3]

SHAPING THE REFORMS

The notion that Rochester's schools were undergoing "reform" undoubtedly sprang from the sheer volume of projects being advanced to improve education—hundreds of them during the three years following the *Call to Action*. Amidst the vast array of activities, several key changes within the district have shaped the reforms.

Toward School-Based Management

One such change has been the decentralization of school management decisions and responsibility for school improvement from the district's central office to its individual schools. The Urban League's school action committees had been devised with the idea of hastening the identification of specific problems and the design of strategies tailored to each school. The committees also had the advantage of expediting the involvement of large numbers of people in school reform. The only centralized aspect of the school action committees was a city-wide steering committee, which the Urban League convened periodically throughout 1987 to promote information sharing among schools.

The school action committees were not the first attempt to decentralize responsibility for school improvement, nor would they be the last. The Superintendent of Schools, Peter McWalters, had long been a proponent of greater school-level decision-making, and during the 1986-87 school year, he sought to advance the concept by implementing a "Management Model for Improved School Performance." The model was held to be the district's "first coordinated effort to raise student achievement through the vehicle of school-based planning."[4] While activities under this new model gradually replaced the school action committees, they progressed unevenly; some schools forged ahead with energetic improvement agendas while others did little. The basic concept of "school-based planning," however, was retained, and in 1987, it was embodied in the new three-year teachers' contract, where the parties agreed "to cooperatively participate in the development of school-based planning at each school location."[5]

Since then, school-based planning has evolved, slowly, as the locus of school improvement activity. Its driving rationale is simply that better results are obtained when the people closest to the problems are involved in designing solutions. The school-based planning teams in Rochester now involve over 1,000 teachers, parents, administrators, and high school students. Each team prepares an annual improvement plan, presents it publicly, and reports on results at the end of the year. In time, school-based planning will be transformed into full school-based management, with the transfer of greater budget authority to the schools. Several schools were selected to develop their own budgets on a pilot basis for the 1990-91 school year.

Excellence in Teaching

Another key "reform" in Rochester has been the attempt to promote higher teaching standards through an aggressive program of professional development, coupled with higher pay and expanded teacher responsibilities. This program, too, was initiated under the 1987 teachers' contract, which provided that "A Career in Teaching Plan" would be developed for implementation the following year. The plan provided a progression of career levels that enable top teachers to receive top pay while remaining in the classroom. A "Peer Assistance and Review Program" was established to provide intervention for teachers who performed unsatisfactorily. However, with the new contract's record pay increases, which, by 1990, brought the average teacher's salary to over $44,000 and starting pay to over $28,000, Rochester now has the means to recruit the best new teachers available—when there are openings.

Some issues addressed in the 1987 contract have yet to be fully resolved. One sticking point in particular carried over into 1990 contract negotiations—the idea of tying teacher pay raises to student performance. Lack of agreement on a way to do that resulted in teachers returning to work in the fall of 1990 without a contract.

Secondary School Restructuring

During the 1987–88 school year, then, much energy went into the development of mechanisms to implement school-based planning and higher teaching standards. However, during that same period, even greater energy was going into plans for a massive restructuring of the district's secondary schools. The district had experienced gradually declining secondary enrollments and growing disenchantment with curriculum options in the city's mixture of junior highs (grades 7–8), senior highs, and combined junior-senior high schools. Consequently, the decision was made to regroup into middle schools (grades 6–8) and high schools (9–12), requiring a massive relocation of students, teachers, and administrators in 1988–89. Furthermore, the newly organized schools were established as "schools of choice," to better engage students by allowing them to choose which schools they wanted to attend.

The restructuring would likely have occurred in some manner with or without the broader reform movement. Yet, it occurred smack in the middle of the movement and, for a while, overshadowed other reform items. The district treated it as a central part of the reform agenda. While it delayed progress on other reform initiatives, the restructuring was probably both necessary and inevitable.

Overcoming Disadvantage

Early in the reform movement, the School Board adopted Superintendent McWalters' proposed new mission statement, which asserted bluntly that "all children can learn; it's up to the school to overcome any socioeconomic or pre-school disadvantage." Getting everyone in the system to accept this premise has been an ongoing challenge, entailing nothing less than "cultural change," as the superintendent calls it. Moving teachers to accept responsibility for student outcomes was a key objective of the 1987 union contract. One device in particular, "home base guidance," was adopted in most secondary schools: in the homerooms, teacher responsibilities were expanded to include ongoing guidance for each student, including appropriate contact and communication with parents.

Other important strategies to help overcome economic and ethnic disadvantage have included expansion of early childhood education programs; an effort to reduce the number of elementary student transfers from school to school during the academic year; and the creation of Rochester New Futures Initiative, Inc., a central coordinating agency for services to troubled students, now working with several schools on a pilot basis. Many school improvement projects initiated by school-based planning committees, as well as many of the business/community partnership programs that have been established, are also specifically geared toward overcoming disadvantage.

The emphasis on overcoming the disadvantages of poverty and minority status has become the essence of Rochester's reform movement.

THE COSTS

The district has been quick to point out that educating disadvantaged children costs more. Its expenditures have risen 44 percent since 1985–86, to a total of $255 million—about $7,900 per pupil—in 1990–91. Fortunately, during the same five-year period, the district enjoyed an 80 percent increase in state aid, budgeted now at $147 million, offsetting most of the increased costs. New York State aid to urban schools, in fact, has increased steadily throughout the past decade; Rochester's has tripled.[6]

Unfortunately, New York State has increased spending in many areas over the past decade, and now, to the consternation of many and the surprise of few, the state faces a fiscal crisis. At this writing, serious cuts in school aid are being considered in the state capital for the current year and beyond.

THE RESULTS

What started as a project to commemorate the 20th anniversary of the Urban League of Rochester was still going strong when the League celebrated its 25th. The community has waited anxiously for results for five years while reform after reform was being unveiled. While no one expected dramatic results overnight, neiyther did anyone really foresee the volume of work or the amount of restructuring that would be deemed necessary just to get the ball rolling. Improved student performance, it appeared, would have to wait until major institutional changes were in place and had a chance to operate for awhile.

However, the changes outlined above are now largely in place, and indications of whether or not they are working should be available soon. The first signs of encouragement appeared in the district's annual reports for 1988–89 and 1989–90.[7] Positive results were noted in the elementary grades, where there were modest improvements in reading and math test scores and significant increases in the numbers of children promoted to the next grade. These gains were made, furthermore, at the same time fewer new referrals were being made to special education classes. If these trends continue over the next few years, there will be good reason to celebrate.

Results in the new middle schools were not yet evident in existing measures of student performance. Grades in core subjects for 7th–8th graders had begun to show gradual improvement from 1985–86 through 1987–88, but stood still during 1988–89, when the new middle schools were in the throes of implementation. While comparable information had not yet been compiled for 1989–90, the administration felt strongly that the desired changes were progressing well in the middle schools and that the impacts on student performance will follow.[8]

The high schools, which were also undergoing traumatic reorganization in 1988–89, have shown no tangible improvements in student performance. The institutional changes have met with greater resistance there than at the other grade levels; school-based planning committees have struggled for consensus, teachers have been slower to embrace such concepts as home base guidance, and large numbers of students have had to adapt to new schools, albeit "schools of choice."

It is at the high school level that the crisis conditions heralded five years ago are still seen in full force. Data for 1989–90 are now available that show a dropout rate of 14 percent (1,054 students), as compared to 13 percent, in 1985–86 (expressed as percentages of total 9th–12th grade enrollment). There are almost as many dropouts as there are graduates: 1,168 seniors graduated last year, and only 17 percent of them received the college preparatory "Regents Diploma," down from 25 percent five years earlier.[9] At the end of 1988–89, over 20 percent of 9th–12th graders were retained in their grades, as compared with 11 percent at the end of 1985-86.[10]

The most painful comparisons are in relation to the suburban school districts in the Rochester area, 17 of them, enrolling over two-thirds of the metropolitan student population. The highest dropout rate in any of the suburban districts is a little over four percent, less than a third of the city's rate, and while 56 percent of the city's graduates go on to college, the rates in the suburban districts range from 63 percent to 94 percent. While those districts are wealthier than the city, only two of them had higher per pupil expenditures in 1988-89.[11]

Clearly, there have been major changes in Rochester. The community has been mobilized; people care about education. The school district has responded admirably with far-reaching institutional changes. There is hope.

But, no, we are not yet finished.

Chronology of Events
1990*

Jan. 1:   **David Dinkins** is sworn in as the first black mayor of New York City. Dinkins declares "We are all foot soldiers on the march to freedom, here and everywhere."

Jan. 1:   **John C. Daniels** is sworn in as the first black mayor of New Haven. The former Connecticut state senator repeats his campaign theme: "We must move, and I will move us, to a point at which the maximum number of citizens are involved in our major decisions." The 57-year-old politician promises to focus on poverty in the city of 127,000—the seventh poorest city in the nation among cities of its size.

Jan. 3:   Rev. **Jesse Jackson** calls on the Bush administration to offer a reward for the capture of whoever is responsible for the bombings that killed a federal judge and a civil rights lawyer in the South. *The New York Times* quotes Jackson, at the inauguration of Atlanta Mayor **Maynard Jackson,** as saying, "Just as President Bush is willing to issue a bounty for Noriega, it must be done for this."

Jan. 3:   Atlantic City (NJ) Mayor **James Usry** and three others are indicted on bribery and corruption charges stemming from a wide-ranging probe of influence-peddling in the seaside gaming resort, as reported in *The New York Daily News.* Usry is the gambling mecca's first black mayor and president of the National Conference of Black Mayors.

Jan. 5:   Black leaders in Boston demand an apology from police, politicians, and the news media for accepting at face value the story of a white suburbanite who said he and his wife were attacked by a black man. New details suggest **Charles Stuart** plotted the murder of his pregnant wife, **Carol.** Stuart committed suicide Jan. 3rd, after his brother told police of Charles' involvement in the attack. A grand jury is investigating the case.

Jan. 6:   New York City Schools Chancellor **Joseph Fernandez** announced a sweeping reorganization of his central headquarters staff that will eliminate 14 bureaus and 218 jobs. In his first days as Chancellor,

*This chronology is based on news reports. In some instances, the event may have occurred a day before the news item was reported.

Fernandez says he wants to show Mayor David Dinkins that he is serious about the new Mayor's austerity efforts.

Jan. 8:   The U.S. Supreme Court orders a federal appeals court to take first crack at deciding whether Louisiana's system of higher education must undergo sweeping changes to help desegregate its public colleges and universities. The justices said they do not have the authority yet to review the case, which has been in the courts since 1974.

Jan. 8:   The NCAA votes overwhelmingly to alter Proposition 42, a rule critics charge is racist because it prevents schools from providing any financial aid to academically deficient freshmen athletes. The amended proposal allows freshmen who do not meet NCAA academic guidelines to receive non-athletic aid without affecting the school's team-scholarship limit.

Jan. 8:   Dancer-choreographer **Judith Jamison** is named artistic director of the Alvin Ailey American Dance Theater. Jamison, who won fame as a principal dancer with the company from 1965-80, succeeds Ailey, who died last month of a rare blood disorder.

Jan. 9:   The National Urban League calls for a $50 billion Urban Marshall Plan that would assist inner-city blacks much like the original aid program helped rebuild Western Europe after World War II. League President and Chief Executive Officer **John E. Jacob** charged, in releasing *The State of Black America 1990*: "America will become a second-rate power unless we undertake policies to ensure that our neglected minority population gets the education, housing, health care, and job skills they need to help America compete successfully in a global economy." Jacob added that an Urban Marshall Plan could be the lever that "closes the black-white economic gap by the year 2000."

Jan. 9:   College enrollment among black students declined during the 1980s, partly because growing numbers of middle-class blacks chose the military instead of higher education. The American Council on Education, an umbrella organization of higher education groups, found that lower enrollment of middle-class students accounted for almost half of a widely reported drop in black students entering college. Other reasons: a shift of financial aid from grants to loans and higher entrance requirements.

Jan. 9:   The Nation's Report Card, released by the U.S. Department of Education, shows students are still "dreadfully inadequate" in reading and writing skills. *The Washington Post* quotes Education

Secretary **Lauro Cavazos** as noting "one bright spot: minorities—blacks in particular—were largely responsible for the reading achievement gains of 17-year-olds."

Jan. 9: For the first time in more than a century, the share of blacks living in the South is increasing. The Census Bureau reports the proportion of blacks living in the South grew from 52.2 percent in 1980 to 55.9 percent in 1988, reversing a decline that had been underway for more than 100 years.

Jan. 9: President **Bush** meets with NAACP Chairman **Benjamin Hooks** to assure him that the administration will "not let up" in investigating the recent wave of bombings aimed at civil rights figures. A federal judge and a lawyer involved in civil rights cases were killed last month by mail bombs. Other mail bombs, sent to the courthouse in Atlanta and to an NAACP office in Florida, were intercepted by authorities.

Jan. 9: **Joe Morgan** is voted into baseball's Hall of Fame in his first year of eligibility. Regarded as the premier second baseman of his era, he was the National League's MVP in 1975 and 1976. His team, the Cincinnati Reds, won the World Series both years. The induction ceremony will be August 5th in Cooperstown, New York.

Jan. 13: **L. Douglas Wilder** takes the oath of office as the first black elected governor of Virginia before a crowd of 30,000. With dignitaries from around the world witnessing the historic moment, Wilder proclaims that he, too, is a "son of Virginia . . . proud to carry on in the tradition of . . . Jefferson, Madison, and Mason."

Jan. 13: *The New York Times* reports that Louisiana Republicans have endorsed a New Orleans state senator for the party's nomination for the U.S. Senate, decisively rejecting a former Ku Klux Klan leader, **David Duke.** Duke pledges he will run in the state's open primary October 6th.

Jan. 15: Bells ring out in all 50 states and 144 other countries and a moment of silence is observed to honor **Martin Luther King**'s 61st birthday. The New York Stock Exchange pauses, and the Liberty Bell rings in Philadelphia. Forty-six states and the federal government mark the holiday, which—for the first time—falls on King's birthday. The four states not recognizing the federal holiday are Arizona, Montana, Idaho, and New Hampshire. Wyoming is observing the holiday this year only.

Jan. 15: Black activists in Boston mark **Martin Luther King**'s birthday by starting a seven-day boycott of the city's two daily newspapers for their coverage of the racially divisive **Charles Stuart** murder case. The activists say the coverage of the bizarre crime contributed to the "polarization" of the city.

Jan. 15: Massachusetts' powerful banking community announces its $400 million investment plan to help revitalize Boston's inner-city neighborhoods. Coming in the wake of three separate studies showing racially biased lending patterns in the city's home-mortgage market, and on the heels of the Stuart murder case, the plan could be a healing message for a community smarting from months of negative press and decades of institutional neglect.

Jan. 15: **William Burrus** is reelected executive vice president of the 365,000-member American Postal Workers Union. The Wheeling, West Virginia, native will now serve as the union's second highest elected officer for another three years.

Jan. 15: **Jerry Hunter** is confirmed by the U.S. Senate to a four-year term as the General Counsel of the National Labor Relations Board. As General Counsel, Hunter will have final and independent authority to investigate unfair labor practice charges filed with the agency.

Jan. 15: *Jet* magazine reports the Houston Endowment has pledged one million dollars to help establish the **Mickey Leland** Center for World Peace and Hunger at Texas Southern University. The center at Leland's alma mater will house the archives of the late congressman, who was killed along with 15 others—including National Urban League trustee **Patrice Yvonne Johnson**—while on a famine relief mission in Africa last August.

Jan. 16: Cancer death rates for blacks and other minorities are increasing much faster than those for white Americans, sometimes as much as 20 to 100 times more. The striking figures are published in a new atlas of cancer mortality statistics by the National Cancer Institute.

Jan. 16: Two Library of Congress employees have charged the library's management with racial discrimination, reviving allegations more than 15 years old. The employees contend that management has taken away responsibility and prestige from blacks in midlevel positions through discreet reorganizations.

Jan. 16: Col. **Marcelite Harris** is selected to be a brigadier general, the first black woman to reach that rank in the U.S. Air Force. The Houston native is the commander of the 3300th Technical Training Wing at Keesler Air Force Base near Biloxi, Mississippi.

Jan. 18: Washington, DC, Mayor **Marion Barry** is arrested and charged with possession of crack cocaine at a local hotel. Barry's arrest is the result of an FBI sting operation. The bust comes three days before Barry had planned to announce his reelection campaign.

Jan. 18: In an unprecedented action, Health and Human Services Secretary **Louis Sullivan** asks R.J. Reynolds Tobacco Company to withdraw a new cigarette brand called "Uptown" that is specifically targeted at black smokers. The government's top health policymaker, who is black, maintains higher smoking rates among blacks, especially males, are a major reason why blacks experience higher rates of lung cancer, other cancers, heart disease, and stroke compared with whites.

Jan. 19: The R.J. Reynolds Tobacco Company, stung by the public attack from the nation's top health official, cancels its plans to market a brand of cigarette aimed at blacks. The company's marketing executive tells reporters, "We regret that a small coalition of anti-smoking zealots apparently believes that black smokers are somehow different from others who choose to smoke." Health and Human Services Secretary **Louis Sullivan** says he is "elated by the news."

Jan. 22: Dr. **Lee Patrick Brown** is sworn in as Commissioner of the New York City Police Department, marking him as head of the nation's largest police force. *The New York Times* quotes Brown as pledging to make the department "a part of the community, not apart from the community."

Jan. 22: DC Mayor **Marion Barry** enters a drug rehabilitation program in West Palm Beach, FL. Barry's spokeswoman says he will be treated for alcoholism, but others insist the mayor has an equally serious problem with cocaine abuse, according to *The Washington Post*. Barry turned over most of his duties to City Manager **Carol Thompson**.

Jan. 23: **Craig Washington** is sworn in as the newest member of Congress by House Speaker Tom Foley. The 48-year-old lawyer from Houston says he could "never replace Rep. **Mickey Leland**," that he is "merely his successor." Leland was killed in a plane crash last August during a hunger mission near the Ethiopian-Sudanese border.

Jan. 24: *The New York Times* reports that the Rockefeller Foundation will spend $15 million over the next five years to expand a program that seeks to better the educational performance of poor children, especially from minorities. The program, developed by Yale University professor **James Comer**, promotes a shared belief in the value of education among teachers, parents, and pupils. The program, begun 20 years ago in New Haven, CT, has been adopted by more than 70 schools in nine districts nationwide. It will be tested by special National Urban League programs in five others, based on the experiences of the League's affiliate in Rochester (NY), which began its program in the mid-'60s.

Jan. 24: Louisiana Governor **Buddy Roemer** rejects the State Pardon Board's recommendation of clemency for Gary Tyler, a black civil rights advocate who says he was framed for killing a white student in Destrehan, 25 miles northwest of New Orleans. Serving a life sentence with no possibility of parole, the 31-year-old Tyler has waged a long fight for freedom that has been supported by Amnesty International and other groups.

Jan. 24: A Hispanic police officer is sentenced to seven years in prison for manslaughter in the deaths of two unarmed black men in an incident last January that inflamed ethnic tension and became a symbol of Miami's troubled racial past. Officer **William Lozano** will remain free on $10,000 bond while appealing his conviction.

Jan. 25: President **Bush** nominates New York lawyer **John Dunne** to the nation's top civil rights post. The announcement comes nearly six months after Congress refused to confirm **William Lucas** for the job of Assistant Attorney General for Civil Rights.

Jan. 26: California Congressman **Augustus Hawkins**, Chairman of the House Education and Labor Committee, announces he will retire at the end of the year. The 82-year-old Democrat has served in Congress 28 years, longer than any other African American; he is the oldest member in the House of Representatives. Hawkins tells reporters that after 56 years in politics, "I believe I can do a better job outside than inside Congress."

Jan. 26: Yale University announces a five-year plan to recruit minority professors. Responding to a report that sharply criticized Yale's record on affirmative action, university president **Benno Schmidt** said that Yale will increase the number of minority visitors to campus, hire and promote qualified minority professors, and create summer fellowships for Yale undergraduates who may be attracted to academic careers.

Jan. 26: The family of **Carol Stuart**, the woman apparently killed by her husband in an attack in Boston that he blamed on a black mugger, announces a scholarship fund for residents of the inner-city area where the shooting took place. The DiMaiti family contributed $10,000 to the fund; $132,600 has been donated to date.

Jan. 30: Several civil rights and minority groups write eight major national environmental organizations, charging them with racism in their hiring practices. *The New York Times* reports they are demanding that the environmental groups take steps within 60 days to assure that 30 to 40 percent of their staffs are minority. Dr. **Benjamin Chavis, Jr.**, of the United Church of Christ's Commission for Racial Justice, claims the national environmental movement is isolated from the poor and minority communities that are the chief victims of pollution. Spokesmen for the environmental groups agree they have a poor record of hiring and promoting minorities but deny that racism is involved.

Feb. 1: Former Charlotte (NC) Mayor **Harvey Gantt** announces he will seek the Democratic nomination for the U.S. Senate seat held by Republican Jesse Helms. Describing Helms as "immovable, rigid even in the face of change," Gantt hopes his twice having been mayor of the largest city in the state will help him to become the first black to win statewide office.

Feb. 1: The four black college students who helped launch the civil rights movement in the '60s re-enact their lunch counter sit-in at Woolworth's in Greensboro (NC), to mark the 30th anniversary of their protest. They are greeted by a black Woolworth vice president who noted that 30 years ago, he would have been denied service, too.

Feb. 3: **Sidney Barthelemy** is reelected Mayor of New Orleans. The second black to hold the city's top elected post, Barthelemy calls on "all New Orleanians to come together...rich and poor, black and white" after a divisive campaign that focused on racial prejudice.

Feb. 5: **Barack Obama**, a 28-year-old graduate of Columbia University, is elected president of the *Harvard Law Review*, the nation's most prestigious student legal journal.

Feb. 5: *Jet* magazine quotes General **Colin Powell**, the black Chairman of the Joint Chiefs of Staff, as saying the military deserves praise as an equal opportunity employer. Interviewed on ABC-TV's "This Week with David Brinkley," the nation's highest ranking uniformed officer said the armed forces offer black Americans equal opportunity "more so than any other form of endeavor in our society."

Feb. 5: *Jet* magazine reports producer-entertainer-musician **Quincy Jones** has received two of France's highest honors: the Legion of Honor award and "Man of the Year."

Feb. 5: **Joel Fluellen,** an actor who protested black stereotyping in Hollywood and who played the brother in "The Jackie Robinson Story," dies at the age of 81.

Feb. 6: A federal appeals court rules that Mississippi's public universities are insufficiently desegregated, overruling a lower-court judge. As reported in *The New York Times*, the court said that, with few exceptions, the state's five historically white and three historically black universities remain virtually as segregated as when black citizens sued the state in 1975.

Feb. 7: Public schools in Selma, AL, are shut as several hundred blacks chanting "soul power" and "I am somebody" march through the streets to protest white leadership of the city's mostly black schools. The crowd, according to published reports, is also protesting the recent firing of **Norward Roussell**, the first black school superintendent in this 1960s battleground of the Civil Rights Movement. Amid protests, Roussell was reinstated.

Feb. 7: Lawmakers of both parties introduce legislation to overturn U.S. Supreme Court decisions that restricted the legal tools available to challenge job discrimination. The Civil Rights Act of 1990 puts the Bush administration on notice to live up to the president's State of the Union call for all Americans to combat bigotry and bias wherever they find it.

Feb. 8: CBS News suspends humorist **Andy Rooney** for three months without pay after a gay magazine prints racial remarks attributed to him—and denied by Rooney. The Los Angeles-based *Advocate* quotes Rooney as saying that "most people are born with equal intelligence, but blacks have watered down their genes because the less intelligent ones are the ones that have the most children. They drop out of school early, do drugs, and get pregnant."

Feb. 8: Sources tell *The Washington Post* the Bush administration will challenge the constitutionality of a Federal Communications Commission plan giving preference to minorities and women in awarding broadcast licenses. The pair of cases to go before the Supreme Court will mark the justices' first look at the legality of affirmative action plans since they struck down a Richmond set-aside plan for minority contractors last year.

Feb. 8:   *The Christian Science Monitor* reports suburban middle-class parents are upset that the Los Angeles school board has adopted a year-round school schedule. The board maintains that it is necessary to house the soaring number of students, primarily inner-city minorities who are bused to the suburbs. The parents insist they are being punished because the scheduling creates summer vacation and extra-curricular conflicts.

Feb. 8:   Former Washington Bullets **Dave Bing**, **Elvin Hayes**, and **Earl Monroe** are elected to the Basketball Hall of Fame in their first year of eligibility. The trio will be inducted May 15th in Springfield, Massachusetts.

Feb. 9:   The high rate of premature deaths among black Americans — two-and-a-half times greater than among whites in some age groups—is the result of so many different causes that even if high-quality health care were equally available to both races and incomes were equal, a significant portion of the gap would remain. That's the finding of a 13-year survey of 8,806 black and white adults by the federal Centers for Disease Control in Atlanta.

Feb. 10:   Houston Oilers quarterback **Warren Moon** is named the NFL Man of the Year. He donates the $25,000 check from the League to the Crescent Moon Foundation to finance college scholarships.

Feb. 11:   **Nelson Mandela** is released from prison after more than 27 years. The 71-year-old lawyer—the world's most famous political prisoner—tells a crowd of 100,000 in Cape Town, South Africa, that the "factors which necessitated the armed struggle [in the '60s] still exist today." In a dramatic speech broadcast around the world, Mandela vowed to seek a democratic and free society, an ideal for which he says he is still "prepared to die" for, echoing his famous remarks when he was convicted of high treason in 1964 and sentenced to life in prison.

Feb. 12:   The nation's largest law firms have failed to recruit, retain, and promote minority lawyers in representative numbers. The *National Law Journal* study of the nation's 250 largest law firms finds that the number of women who are partners or associates grew steadily in the '80s. But black, Hispanic, Asian-American, and American Indian lawyers saw no significant increase in opportunities.

Feb. 12:   About 150 black teenagers end their five-day occupation of Selma High School, part of an ongoing protest brought on by the firing of the city's first black school superintendent [see Feb. 7].

257

Feb. 13:   The Boston School Committee fires the city's first black school superintendent. *The New York Times* reports the 13-member committee voted to buy out the remaining 18 months of **Laval Wilson's** two-year contract, saying it was management style, not race, that prompted the firing. The committee's four black members and one white member walk out in protest.

Feb. 13:   Public schools in Selma, AL, reopen under heavy security by city police, state troopers, and members of the National Guard. The school board closed all schools six days ago when a long-simmering racial dispute erupted.

Feb. 13:   The most popular colleges for the nation's outstanding African-American students are Harvard, Stanford, Yale, and Florida A&M, says the National Merit Scholarship Corporation. *USA Today* reports Florida A&M's publicist wants it known that his 102-year-old historically black college in Tallahassee is "up there in that elite company."

Feb. 14:   *USA Today* reports Rev. **Al Sharpton** and two other New York City black activists were sentenced to 45 days in jail and imprisoned immediately for their roles in the 1987 "Day of Outrage" protest against purported racism in the city. A judge found them guilty of obstructing government, trespass, and disorderly conduct. Sharpton, Rev. **Timothy Mitchell**, and **Charles Barron** led more than 70 protesters into the subway system, where they stalled evening rush-hour service.

Feb. 15:   DC Mayor **Marion Barry** is indicted on eight counts of cocaine use and possession and lying to a federal grand jury about it. The U.S. District Court alleges the three-term DC chief executive used cocaine on at least five occasions during the past two years. Barry claims the charges are not surprising, saying they represent "a continuation of the political lynching and excesses of the Justice Department." [See also January 18.]

Feb. 16:   *The New York Times* reports the New York City school system, whose student population is 80 percent nonwhite but whose staff of teachers and principals is 70 percent white, is preparing a detailed plan to recruit more black, Hispanic, and Asian employees. The proposal is the first affirmative action plan in the system's history and will use numerical goals and timetables in cases of persistent inequality, both for minorities and for women.

Feb. 19:   In the largest U.S. housing discrimination settlement ever, a Los Angeles apartment complex agrees to pay $450,000 to a black airline customer service agent, a white express mail handler, and others involved in an unsuccessful effort to share a two-bedroom apartment. NAACP Legal Defense and Educational Fund attorneys say the award represents a major victory showing apartment managers and owners throughout the U.S. that "blatant racial discrimination is not only illegal and morally intolerable, [but] from now on, it will also be extremely costly."

Feb. 23: President **Bush** selects **Arthur Fletcher** to be chairman of the U.S. Civil Rights Commission. The 65-year-old black Republican has held top federal posts under Presidents Nixon, Ford, and Reagan. *The New York Times* reports civil rights leaders are lauding the appointment, viewing it as a signal that the Bush administration is taking the troubled commission more seriously than the Reagan administration did.

Feb. 23: Prominent African-American businessman **Comer Cottrell** purchases bankrupt Bishop College, once the largest black college in the Western United States, in a liquidation auction. The 58-year-old owner of Pro-Line Corporation—the nation's 18th largest black-owned company—purchased the entire 130-acre campus and 22 buildings in Dallas (TX) for $1.5 million.

Feb. 23: *The Washington Times* reports that blindness and other sight problems are twice as common among blacks than whites, according to a first-of-its kind study by Johns Hopkins University researchers. The researchers also found that, among those with vision problems, more than half could improve their sight with correction but had not.

Feb. 25: The Roman Catholic's only black archbishop in the U.S., the Rev. **Eugene Marino**, breaks a silence of more than seven months by challenging black Catholics who have left the church to come home. Speaking to a mostly black audience in Washington, Bishop Marino insists that "breaking from the unity of the church is...divisive and regressive." Marino does not mention the name of Rev. **George Stallings**, who formed an independent Catholic congregation last July, but it was clear whom Marino meant in his remarks.

Feb. 25: *The New York Times* reports a fence separating poorly tended graves of blacks from neatly kept graves of whites must come down in Lebanon, KY. A U.S. district judge has ordered the Ryder Cemetery Company to provide equal care to all sections of the private cemetery.

Feb. 26:   Rev. **Jesse Jackson** announces he will not run for mayor of the District of Columbia this year. *The Washington Post* quotes the former Democratic presidential candidate as saying he prefers to concentrate on national issues and the fight for District statehood. Jackson's announcement ends weeks of speculation as to whether he would challenge a crowded field of candidates seeking to replace **Marion Barry**.

Feb. 26:   Nearly one of every four young black males is behind bars or on probation or parole. The report by the Sentencing Project, a nonprofit organization that promotes alternative punishments and sentencing reform, calls for changes in the criminal justice system to make first-time lawbreakers less likely to become repeat offenders. The author of the study said its findings "should be disturbing to all Americans," that unless something is done, "we now risk the possibility of writing off an entire generation of black men from leading productive lives."

Feb. 27:   The death penalty is more likely to be the sentence when a white is killed than when a black is killed, according to the General Accounting Office. *The New York Times* reports the congressional agency also found in its review of 28 studies of death sentences since a 1972 U.S. Supreme Court decision forced states to review their capital punishment laws that, in cases involving the death penalty, the race of the victim was more important than the race of the defendant.

Feb. 27:   *The Christian Science Monitor* reports the African National Congress is facing mounting pressure to suspend its "armed struggle" as **Nelson Mandela** visits the ANC's headquarters in exile—in Lusaka, Zambia—for the first time. The leaders are expected to discuss the question of a cease-fire and to choose a 10-person delegation to travel to South Africa to meet with President **Frederik de Klerk**.

Feb. 27:   *The Washington Post* reports **J. Kenneth Blackwell**, the former Cincinnati mayor who served as deputy under secretary at the Department of Housing and Urban Development, is resigning to run for Congress in his native Ohio. Blackwell, a Republican, was the highest ranking black official at HUD; he was urged to seek the post by President **Bush**.

Feb. 28:   The six leaders of Africa's so-called front-line states that rim South Africa appeal to other nations to maintain economic sanctions against the white-governed country, at least until the United

Nations considers whether President **Frederik de Klerk's** reforms are sufficiently irreversible to warrant lifting the punitive measures. Their appeal comes as Zulu Chief **Mangosuthu Buthelezi** urges President **Bush** to lift sanctions against Pretoria as soon as possible. After that Oval Office meeting, Buthelezi told reporters he had a "gut feeling" Bush would lift them as soon as he legally can.

Feb. 28: DC Mayor **Marion Barry** pleads not guilty in U.S. District Court to three perjury and five cocaine possession charges. His lawyer, **R. Kenneth Mundy**, vows Barry will not plea-bargain nor resign. The 53-year-old mayor is free pending his trial set for June 4th.

Feb. 28: Hundreds of thousands of dollars in bank loans to Rep. **Harold E. Ford** (D-TN) were nothing more than a "shell game" to hide political payoffs, Assistant U.S. Attorney Gary Humble charges in opening arguments at Ford's trial for conspiracy, bank fraud, and mail fraud. *The Washington Post* quotes Ford's attorney as saying the loans were legitimate and that Ford fully intended to repay them and has done so.

Feb. 28: More than 40 percent of the 339 black members of the U.S. Capitol Police sign up to establish a "pressure group" inside the force that one of the organizer's says would work "for fair and equal treatment" and seek an end to "discrimination, cronyism, and nepotism" in assignments and promotions. *The Washington Post* reports the group finds it "an insult" that only one black captain and three black lieutenants are among the 65 top officers of the Capitol Police.

Feb. 28: *USA Today* reports the winners of Britannica Awards for communicating valuable knowledge include Soviet scholar Grigory Tunkin and three U.S. citizens—physicist Freeman Dyson, African-American historian **John Hope Franklin**, and evolutionary biologist Stephen Jay Gould. Each receives $25,000 and a gold medal.

March 1: Five white supremacists who called themselves the Confederate Hammerskins are convicted in Dallas, TX, for conspiracy to violate the rights of minorities. The defendants, ranging in age from 19 to 25, face a maximum of 20 years and fines up to $500,000.

March 1: Three youths convicted of riot in the 1986 Howard Beach (NY) racial attack are arraigned on the same charge, two months after an appeals court overturned their prior convictions because of trial judge error.

March 1:   **Martin Luther King, III**, apologizes for saying "something may be wrong" with homosexuals, and meets with angered gay rights leaders to learn more about their concerns. King made what he called "uninformed and insensitive remarks" before middle-school students in Poughkeepsie, NY, on February 27. Gay rights leaders praise King for his candor and say they are satisfied with his apology.

March 2:   **Carole Gist** becomes the first black "Miss USA." She downplays her skin color, saying "There is so much more to me than my blackness." The six-foot, 20-year-old college student will compete April 15 in the Miss Universe pageant.

March 3:   DC Delegate **Walter Fauntroy** announces he is giving up the seat he has held for 19 years as the District's nonvoting delegate to Congress to run for mayor. *The Washington Post* reports the 57-year-old Baptist minister pledges to "restore the tarnished image of our city."

March 3:   President **Bush** salutes publishing tycoon **Walter Annenberg** for setting a "significant and marvelous example" by donating $50 million to the United Negro College Fund, the largest gift ever to black colleges. Annenberg tells reporters at his Palm Springs (CA) estate that the UNCF colleges are a "major force for positive change for their role in giving thousands of young blacks an opportunity to realize their full potential."

March 4:   Thousands of civil rights veterans march through Selma, AL, to re-enact the aborted March 7, 1965, demonstration that ended with the "Bloody Sunday" clash at the Edmund Pettus Bridge. Afterwards, they re-enact the 50-mile march led two weeks later by Dr. **Martin Luther King, Jr.**, from Selma to Montgomery. Out of the violence and turmoil of that first march came passage of the historic Voting Rights Act.

March 4:   CBS humorist **Andy Rooney** apologizes to the American public for his alleged racist remarks [see February 8]. Rooney says it is "demeaning" to defend his record on racism, but that he had "learned a lot" about how damaging it can be to articulate opinions so ineptly about an entire class of people.

March 5:   The South African government sends troops into the Ciskei homeland to suppress riots by mobs that burned factories and looted shops after the territory's authoritarian president was ousted in a military coup.

March 6:   **Clarence Thomas** is confirmed by the U.S. Senate as a judge on the U.S. Circuit Court of Appeals for the District of Columbia. The 41-year-old black conservative has been head of the Equal Employment Opportunity Commission since 1982. The Yale Law School graduate's nomination was challenged because he opposes quotas and affirmative action to fight hiring discrimination.

March 6:   In an agreement with the **NAACP**, a shopping mall in Columbia (SC) pledges to hire more blacks and to stop detaining black teenagers under a 1960s trespassing law. NAACP national chairman **William Gibson** says the pact is the first of its kind reached with a shopping mall on the hiring and treatment of blacks, and he is encouraging other chapters nationwide to negotiate similar agreements, according to *The New York Times*.

March 7:   The American Bar Association reports that, after years of efforts to recruit more minority students, law schools are beginning to make progress. *The New York Times* quotes from the ABA report, which finds that 22 percent more minority students are enrolled in the current school year than three years ago. From 1988 to 1989 alone, there was a 10 percent jump in minority enrollment, the largest one-year increase to date. Asian Americans had the largest increase — up 49 percent.

March 7:   Twelve-year-old **David Aupont** is tied up, beaten with a bat, doused with gasoline, and set on fire by a teenager in Brooklyn (NY) because David refused to smoke crack. He suffered second- and third-degree burns over 55 percent of his body.

March 8:   **Florida Atlantic University**, in affluent Boca Raton on the Gold Coast, announces it will offer free tuition next fall to every black freshman who meets admission standards. In what is regarded as a dramatic attempt to attract top black students, the school—one of nine public state universities—was told by the Board of Regents to increase the size of its next freshman class by 50 percent, according to published reports.

March 12: The Commerce Department, in a move that stirred deep anger and disappointment among officials of big cities, establishes strict tests that must be met before it will adjust the 1990 census figures to compensate for any undercounting of minority groups and poor people in inner cities. *The New York Times* quotes New York City Mayor **David Dinkins** as saying that the guidelines represent "nothing more than a continuation of [the department's] longstanding hostility to the idea of correcting an almost certain undercount."

March 12: *USA Today* reports David Aupont, the 12-year-old New York boy set ablaze during a robbery attempt, received get-well wishes from across the country and an offer from the Vietnam Veterans of America to donate skin from its skin bank [see March 7]. The 13-year-old who allegedly set David on fire is charged as a juvenile with attempted murder, assault, kidnapping, and weapons possession.

March 12: A vital witness in the impending Bensonhurst murder trial deals the prosecution a major blow by telling the Brooklyn District Attorney that he will not keep his pledge to testify in New York City's most notorious racial case since Howard Beach. *The New York Times* reports the witness, **John Vento**, was immediately charged with second-degree murder in the death of **Yusuf Hawkins**, the black teenager whose slaying ignited a citywide furor last summer. **Vento**, who is white, had been denounced by other whites for agreeing to cooperate with the prosecution in exchange for immunity from prosecution in the controversial case.

March 15: *The Washington Post* reports the state of Maryland is justified in setting aside government building contracts for blacks and women to make up for past discrimination, according to an independent study by Big Eight accounting firm Coopers and Lybrand. However, the consultants say, Asians, American Indians, native Alaskans, and Pacific Islanders should be excluded from the minority set-aside program to ensure that it is constitutional.

March 17: Church crusaders against alcohol and cigarette billboards in minority neighborhoods in New York City have scored a major victory that will change the look of neighborhoods in Chicago, Detroit, and Oakland. *The Washington Post* reports that on two Saturdays, a group of 50 people from Abyssinian Baptist Church, led by Rev. **Calvin Butts**, spraypainted billboards all over Harlem, resulting in one of the nation's largest billboard advertisers announcing that it will remove all such billboards within five blocks of schools, play areas, and churches in those cities.

March 17: *The Washington Post* reports the **World Council of Churches** is adding racism to its list of top concerns. At the council's "Justice, Peace, and Integrity of Creation" convocation in Seoul, black delegates from the U.S. and Africa pressured the leaders to adopt racism as an element of priority, along with economics, security and militarism, and care of the environment.

March 18: *The New York Times* reports **Shauna Jackson** has been elected president of the *Law Review* of Stanford University, one of the most prestigious law journals in the nation. A second-year law student, Jackson is the first black female to head the law review.

March 18: Comedian/actor **Robin Harris** is found dead in Chicago, just hours after performing at a sold-out theater. The 36-year-old performer, who apparently died in his sleep, appeared in the movies "Do the Right Thing," "Harlem Nights," and "House Party."

March 20: **George Haley** is sworn in as chairman of the U.S. Postal Rate Commission in Washington, DC. The 64-year-old former Kansas state senator is the first African American ever in the post. Brother of *Roots* author **Alex Haley**, he will be responsible for hiring staff and making contract and procurement decisions.

March 20: *The Star-Ledger* reports the FBI is having little success attracting more blacks and Hispanics two years after stepping up its efforts to recruit minority agents. By contrast, the percentage of minority agents at other federal law enforcement agencies that traditionally have welcomed minorities—the Drug Enforcement Administration, the Bureau of Alcohol, Tobacco, and Firearms—is twice the FBI's. California Congressman **Don Edwards**, whose subcommittee oversees the agency's affirmative action policies, insists he will hold a hearing to find out why the results are not better.

March 20: *The New York Times* reports that 400 minority students in Pennsylvania will have the opportunity to attend graduate school at no cost under a new program to encourage postgraduate work. The $15 million endowment program is a way to address the declining enrollment of minorities in professional and graduate schools. The endowment effort will be the second in the U.S.; it is patterned after one in Florida, which has financed 142 scholarships for minority students to attend graduate school since 1984.

March 21: Boxer **Sugar Ray Leonard** announces he will donate $250,000 to TransAfrica Forum of Washington, DC, to help develop a research and education institute on Africa and the Caribbean.

March 21: Namibia becomes an independent African nation, marking the end of colonialism in Africa. With the lowering of the South African flag, President **Sam Nujoma** and his SWAPO-dominated government inherit a country with a 70-percent illiteracy rate and an economy totally dominated by a small white minority.

March 22: Secretary of State **James Baker** tells South African officials they must end a nearly four-year-old state of emergency before the U.S. lifts sanctions against the white-led government. Baker, the first U.S. secretary of state to visit South Africa in 12 years, meets with President **Frederik de Klerk** over the objections of African National Congress leader **Nelson Mandela.**

March 22: Most Americans are living longer and getting sick less often, but the gap between the health of blacks and whites continues to widen. The annual report on the nation's health, conducted by the Department of Health and Human Services, cites the major reasons for the disparity are AIDS, homicide, and lack of access to care, as reported in *The Washington Post.*

March 27: The U.S. Supreme Court agrees to decide whether school systems that were once segregated and were ordered to undertake busing or other integration efforts may abandon those efforts once courts have determined that the original segregated system has been eliminated. The case involving the Oklahoma City Board of Education is expected to answer what *The Washington Post* calls "the most important unresolved question in desegregation law": what efforts formerly segregated school districts must make to maintain integrated schools.

March 28: The U.S. Supreme Court hears arguments on whether the Constitution permits the federal government to favor blacks and other minority members in the awarding of licenses to operate radio and television stations [see Feb. 8]. *The New York Times* reports the cases have wide ramifications for all government affirmative action programs.

March 28: **Barbara Jordan**, the first black woman elected to Congress from the South, is selected to join the National Women's Hall of Fame. The 54-year-old professor at the University of Texas served on the House Judiciary Committee during the Watergate hearings. The induction ceremony in Seneca Falls (NY) is set for August 26th, the 70th anniversary of the ratification of the 19th Amendment, which gave women the right to vote.

March 28: *The Washington Post* reports a new study is challenging the theory that the increased concentration of poverty in inner-city neighborhoods over the past generation is the result of a mass flight of the black middle class. The study, published in the current *American Journal of Sociology*, found that most upper-income black families have been unable to escape inner-city neighborhoods because of housing discrimination. As a result, both high- and low-income blacks tend to live in proximity in the nation's major cities.

March 28: **Ruth Owens**, widow of Olympic track legend **Jesse Owens**, is presented the Congressional Gold Medal by President **Bush** for her husband's "humanitarian contributions in the race of life," according to *The Washington Post*.

March 29: New York's highest court becomes the first in any state to rule that lawyers for criminal defendants cannot dismiss prospective jurors because of their race. *The New York Times* reports that in issuing the unanimous decision, the court also upheld the manslaughter convictions of three young men in the Howard Beach racial attack case. The ruling represents a major curb on the ability to use peremptory challenges to exclude certain people from sitting on juries.

March 29: An assistant prosecutor in the Bensonhurst racial slaying case has resigned from the Brooklyn District Attorney's office. *The New York Times* reports **Bruce McIntyre**, a 36-year-old Yale Law School graduate, is stepping down amid reports that he felt he was to be a "token black at the prosecution table" in the trial [see March 12].

March 30: Sister **Thea Bowman**, a 52-year-old nun who devoted her life to educating and evangelizing blacks and promoting the cause of women in the Roman Catholic Church, dies of cancer at her home in Canton, MS. The granddaughter of a slave, Sister Thea was a lecturer, evangelist, poet, and singer. She was to receive the Laetare Medal—the oldest and most prestigious award given to U.S. Catholics—at the University of Notre Dame on May 20. The award will be presented posthumously.

March 31: *The Washington Post* reports that the **Republican National Committee** is planning to join forces with civil rights groups around the country to bring court cases aimed at creating scores of new black and Hispanic congressional and state legislative seats. The plan is part of a 1990 GOP redistricting proposal. "I guess you could call it an unholy alliance," quips **Frank Parker**, who heads up the voting rights project of the Lawyers' Committee for Civil Rights Under Law.

March 31: *The Washington Post* reports that the African National Congress is putting off its first meeting with the South African government, dealing a setback to efforts to negotiate a settlement to the country's racial conflict. ANC leader **Nelson Mandela** says the April 11 meeting is being postponed to protest police action last week during which 11 demonstrators were shot to death and more than 400 wounded in a township south of Johannesburg.

April 1:   Dr. **Franklyn Jenifer** succeeds Dr. **James Cheek** as president of Howard University. The 50-year-old Washington, DC, native is former chancellor of higher education in Massachusetts. Jenifer is the first Howard graduate to serve as its president. As head of what is widely regarded as the "black Harvard University," Jenifer will face gnawing budget problems and campus divisions that still are healing from last year's student unrest.

April 2:   Former DC Police Chief **Maurice Turner** announces he will run for Mayor. In light of **Marion Barry**'s indictment for cocaine possession and perjury charges, Turner asserts that Washington "is in a governmental crisis and in need of new leadership."

April 2:   *The New York Times* reports that a new survey shows little increase this year in the percentage of U.S. newspaper reporters, editors, and photographers who are minority members. The survey, by the American Society of Newspaper Editors, says minorities comprise 7.8 percent of the newsroom work force, up from 7.54 percent last year. When the annual survey was launched in 1978, minorities made up only 3.95 percent of that work force. That figure has risen each year.

April 3:   Jazz legend **Sarah Vaughan** dies of lung cancer at her San Fernando Valley (CA) home. The 66-year-old vocalist, known at the "Divine One" and "Sassy," won one Grammy during her spectacular five-decade career.

April 4:   President **Bush** predicts a black man or woman will soon be president of the U.S. Speaking at the 20th anniversary banquet of the Joint Center for Political and Economic Studies in Washington, Bush said he is "heartened by the increased growth in the number of black elected officials nationwide"—from 200 in 1968 to 6,000 two decades later.

April 4:   *The Washington Times* reports President **Bush**'s approval rating among blacks hit 74 percent in a recent national poll. The newspaper cites the president's appointing 47 blacks to top government jobs and unmatched black access to the White House as reasons for his surge in popularity among African Americans.

April 4:   The **Congressional Black Caucus** recommends that President **Bush**'s new defense spending plan be cut by $23.7 billion. Chairman **Ron Dellums** (D-CA) says the savings could be used for vitally needed domestic programs.

April 4: The **Bush** administration is threatening to veto the 1990 Civil Rights Act. *The Washington Post* reports the president prefers its own bill that would reverse some but not all of the U.S. Supreme Court decisions that sharply restrict the reach of federal employment discrimination laws. Attorney General **Dick Thornburgh** calls the congressional bill "unacceptable," charging it will lead to racial quotas in the workplace.

April 5: President **Bush** honors pop superstar **Michael Jackson** at the White House as "Entertainer of the Decade." While in Washington, Jackson was also honored by the Capital Children's Museum as Humanitarian of the Year for his work with children.

April 5: African National Congress leader **Nelson Mandela** and South African President **Frederik de Klerk** meet for the first time since Mandela's release from prison [see February 11]. *The Christian Science Monitor* reports that, as a result of the meeting, three days have been set aside for exploratory talks from May 2 to 4.

April 6: *The Washington Times* reports the FBI will announce a $500,000 reward to help solve the rash of mail bombings in the South. The newspaper quotes Justice Department officials as saying the reward, which is being financed in part by a wealthy Southerner, will be given for the bomber's arrest and conviction.

April 7: The Rev. **Harold Flowers**, a patriarch of the Civil Rights Movement in Arkansas, dies of cancer at the age of 78 in Little Rock. Flowers was the oldest practicing black attorney in the state.

April 10: Idaho governor **Cecil Andrus** signs a bill making the third Monday in January **Martin Luther King Jr.-Idaho Human Rights Day**. Proponents added human rights to get enough votes for it to pass. King's birthday is not a state holiday in Arizona, Montana, and New Hampshire.

April 12: Playwright **August Wilson** wins the Pulitzer Prize for drama for his play, "The Piano Lesson." The 44-year-old writer joins an exclusive group of playwrights with two Pulitzers to their name. His other Pulitzer was awarded in 1987 for the play "Fences."

April 12: New Jersey Governor **James Florio** calls for calm after a night of racial violence in Teaneck. No one was seriously hurt in the rampage, which included looting, rock throwing, and car burning. The melee began during a candlelight service for **Phillip Pannell**, a black teenager shot by a white police officer during an armed confrontation on Tuesday. A grand jury is investigating.

April 15: *The New York Times* reports black enrollment in colleges and universities reached record highs in the late '80s, largely because the schools developed extensive recruiting programs to tutor, counsel, and provide financial aid to prospective students. The newspaper quotes educators and sociologists who assert that efforts to stress to black students the importance of higher education had found an increasingly receptive audience, mostly among young black females.

April 15: *The New York Daily News* reports federal prosecutors have concluded that Mayor **David Dinkins** set a fair price for stock he transferred to his son, and they expect to close their probe without filing tax-evasion charges. Dinkins' holdings in the Inner City Broadcasting Corporation and their value had been a major issue during his campaign for mayor.

April 17: The Rev. **Ralph David Abernathy**, the right-hand man of Dr. Martin Luther King, Jr., dies of a heart attack at age 64 in an Atlanta hospital. Abernathy, a leader in the civil rights movement and former head of the Southern Christian Leadership Conference, was accused of betraying King in his controversial autobiography. President **Bush** said he joins all Americans in mourning the loss of a "tireless campaigner for justice."

April 18: The U.S. Supreme Court rules 5-to-4 in a Kansas City (MO) case that judges may order school boards to raise taxes to achieve racial desegregation.

April 18: Former tennis star **Arthur Ashe** warns that schools that exploit black college athletes should beware that they might end up on a "hit list" and be subject to boycotts by student athletes. Ashe issued the warning at a televised forum titled "The Black Athlete: Winners or Losers in Academia?" Ashe, along with 10 other panelists including sports sociologist Dr. **Harry Edwards**, says the list would be circulated among parents of prospective recruits; its intent is to change, not damage, schools.

April 19: *The Washington Times* reports that the **Congressional Black Caucus** wants the Pentagon to cut its ranks by 200,000 personnel in one year, a move that could severely affect blacks who joined the armed forces in large numbers during the past two decades. The Caucus wants billions of dollars from President Bush's arms budget diverted to social programs. Critics of the plan charge that blacks who are very prominent in support, supply, and administration positions in the military will be the ones most likely to lose their jobs first.

April 20: More than 50,000 people cross the Brooklyn Bridge, pour into lower Manhattan, and surround City Hall to protest a U.S. Food and Drug Administration (FDA) ban on blood donations from Haitians and black Africans. *The Washington Post* reports the FDA prohibits any Haitian immigrants or those from certain African countries from giving blood as a precaution against spreading AIDS. New York mayor **David Dinkins** told the crowd: "The FDA is wrong. I predict they're going to reverse themselves. I recognize that the Haitian community has been discriminated against." The newspaper also reports a federal AIDS advisory committee is recommending that the blood ban be eased for people who have been screened for the deadly virus.

April 21: Chanting, "Teaneck, Teaneck, have you heard, this is not Johannesburg," 900 demonstrators marched a mile and a half to the Teaneck (NJ) Police Headquarters to protest the fatal shooting of a black 16-year-old boy, **Phillip Pannell**, by a white police officer 11 days ago [see April 12]. *The New York Times* reports a state grand jury will meet next week to sort out conflicting accounts of how Pannell was shot in the back by Officer Gary Spath. For decades, Teaneck has been known for a spirit of cooperative race relations.

April 22: *The New York Times* reports repeated written and verbal racial attacks, varying from epithets scrawled around her dormitory room to death threats sent through the campus mail, have rendered an Emory University freshman almost mute. **Sabrina Collins**, a premed student on the dean's list and a varsity soccer player, has spoken little since her April 11 hospitalization. She is being treated at the Medical College of Georgia for "emotional traumatization."

April 22: Blacks are more likely than whites to be victims of rape or aggravated assault and are more than twice as likely to be robbery victims. The Justice Department's National Crime Survey finds that the rate of such violent crimes against black Americans age 12 or older was 44 per 1,000, compared with 34 per 1,000 among whites in the same age group, according to data collected between 1979 and 1986.

April 22: Former Maryland state senator **Verda F. Welcome**, the first black female state senator in the U.S., dies after a long illness in Baltimore at the age of 83. She sponsored bills to establish equal pay for equal work and voter registration by mail.

April 23: *The New York Times* reports Professor **Derrick Bell** of Harvard Law School has requested an unpaid leave of a year or more to protest the lack of diversity on the school's faculty. He vows not to return until the school hires and tenures a woman of color.

April 23: President **Bush** signs a law ordering a study of crimes motivated by racial, ethnic, or sexual prejudice. *The New York Times* quotes the president, who told an audience that included liberal Democrats, conservative Republicans, and the first homosexual rights advocates invited to a White House ceremony, that "The faster we can find out about these hideous crimes, the faster we can track down the bigots who commit them."

April 23: **Clifton Reginald Wharton**, the first black American to attain the rank of ambassador in the Foreign Service, dies in Phoenix at the age of 90. Wharton was also the first black to be assigned as minister of a nonblack country; President **John F. Kennedy** named him ambassador to Norway in 1961.

April 24: Former Atlanta Mayor **Andrew Young**, a Democrat, formally enters the race to be Governor of Georgia.

April 25: Tenor saxophonist **Dexter Gordon** dies of cancer in Philadelphia at age 67. Gordon helped define the bebop style of jazz begun in the 1940s by Lester Young, John Coltrane, and Charlie Parker. His playing influenced future generations of musicians. He was nominated for an Oscar for his performance in the 1986 movie "Round Midnight."

April 25: The U.S. Justice Department declares illegal Georgia's method of electing more than a third of its superior court judges, saying that at-large voting in the state's judicial circuits makes it impossible for black judicial candidates to win office.

April 25: The **Congressional Black Caucus'** proposal that the Defense Department cut its payrolls by 200,000 in one year could hurt blacks who have recently swelled the armed services' ranks. *The Washington Times* quotes several black enlisted men who question the Caucus' proposed cuts, which are five times the rate proposed by the Pentagon, saying the deep cuts would cause a lot more unemployment in the black community.

April 25: *The New York Times* reports the U.S. Justice Department has ended a 15-month investigation of DC Delegate **Walter Fauntroy**'s employment of a colleague's son in the U.S. House of Representatives. Fauntroy is a mayoral candidate whose campaign had been plagued by uncertainty about the inquiry's status.

April 25: **Lee Eric Smith** is named the editor of the University of Mississippi school newspaper, becoming the first black to hold the post in the paper's 50-year history.

April 25: The administration at Bernard M. Baruch College and a group of black and Hispanic graduates who want their own alumni association have ended a long court battle over the school's refusal to recognize such an organization. *The New York Times* reports the two sides came to terms on allowing the seven-year-old Black and Hispanic Alumni Association to add the name of the New York college to its name, something the administration had resisted.

April 27: Vandalism and violence aimed primarily at blacks moving into white neighborhoods accounted for about half of the nation's racial hate crimes last year, a survey by a group that monitors such activity shows. *The New York Times* reports the Klanwatch Project's study found most incidents in the survey involved vandalism, like the scrawling of "K.K.K." on doors and walls or harassing phone calls and letters.

April 28: **Robert "Bob" Ellison** takes over as president of the White House Correspondents Association. An eight-year veteran of the group and White House reporter for the Sheridan Broadcasting Network, Ellison is the first black person to head the group.

April 28: *The Washington Post* reports the federal government plans another bank fraud trial for Rep. **Harold Ford** (D-TN), quoting a prosecutor who says he may try to move the case out of the African-American congressman's home district. The 44-year-old lawmaker went on trial earlier this year in U.S. District Court in Memphis, but a mistrial was declared April 27 when jurors said they were deadlocked [see Feb. 28].

April 29: The Rev. **Henry C. Gregory III**, senior minister of Shiloh Baptist Church in Washington, DC, dies of lung cancer in White Sulphur Springs, WV; he was 54. Gregory's historic church was founded by slaves 127 years ago and is nationally known for its social and political activism.

April 30: The growing diversity of college students has led to mounting racial tension and diminished the overall sense of community and quality of life on America's campuses, a new survey reveals. One out of every four presidents surveyed for "Campus Life: In Search of Community," a report by the Carnegie Foundation for the Advancement of Teaching, calls racial tension a problem on campus.

April 30: A former top aide to **Samuel R. Pierce, Jr.**, tells Congress how the former Secretary of Housing and Urban Development was directly involved in the political manipulation of federal housing programs. **DuBois Gilliam** is serving an 18-month prison sentence for manipulating housing grants; his credibility has been questioned repeatedly by Pierce's lawyers, who say their client has done nothing wrong.

May 1: **Marguerite Ross Barnett** becomes the president of the University of Houston (TX), with a student population of 32,000. The 47-year-old author and political scientist is the first black and the first woman to hold the top administrative post.

May 2: The South African government holds its first formal meetings with the **African National Congress** in Cape Town. The talks, according to *The Washington Post*, are designed to lead to negotiations toward a new constitution and an end to apartheid in South Africa.

May 7: Selma's first black school superintendent has accepted a $150,000 settlement from the city's white-controlled board of education. In exchange, **Norward Roussell** has dropped a $10 million racial discrimination suit against the city and is resigning, according to published reports. His ouster earlier this year sparked student boycotts and marches [see Feb. 7].

May 8: **Harvey Gantt**, the former black mayor of Charlotte (NC), tops the six-man field in the Democratic primary for the U.S. Senate seat held by Republican **Jesse Helms**. Gantt does not receive enough votes, however, to avoid a runoff. He will face **Michael Easley**, a drug-busting district attorney, on June 5th.

May 8: Atlantic City (NJ) mayor **James Usry** will have to face a June 12th runoff for the top city seat with white City Councilman **James Whelan**. The black mayor has pleaded not guilty to bribery charges against him [see Jan. 3].

May 11: Despite the effect of a flat economy, the nation's leading black-owned companies posted a small gain in 1989. Total revenues reached $8.81 billion, up 0.3 percent from 1988 revenues of $6.79 billion, according to *Black Enterprise* magazine. Heading the *BE* 100 firms: **TLC Beatrice International Holdings Company** of New York City, with revenues of $1.5 billion.

May 12: Virginia Governor **L. Douglas Wilder** orders state agencies and institutions to divest themselves of financial holdings in companies doing business in South Africa. *The Washington Post* reports the order primarily affects Virginia's employment retirement system, which has nearly $10 billion in investments for state employees and pensions. The state pension fund holds the largest block of stock with South African ties—between $400 million and $700 million worth.

May 14: The White House announces President **Bush** would like to sign a civil rights bill, and has only minimal differences with pending legislation. The announcement comes after Bush meets with a dozen black civil rights leaders, including National Urban League President **John E. Jacob,** the appointed spokesman for the group. Bush earlier threatened to veto the 1990 Civil Rights Act.

May 14: **Dorothy Thomas** becomes the first African-American female to serve as chief of Pennsylvania's Capitol Police. The 117-member force provides security at the gold-domed Capitol complex in Harrisburg and at state office buildings in Philadelphia, Pittsburgh, and Scranton.

May 14: **Terence Todman**, ambassador to Argentina, is awarded the rank of career ambassador by Secretary of State James A. Baker III. The veteran Foreign Service officer joins only 11 other U.S. diplomats who have been nominated by the president and confirmed by the Senate for this august rank, in recognition of especially distinguished service, since it was created 10 years ago.

May 16: Legendary entertainer **Sammy Davis, Jr.**, dies of throat cancer in his Los Angeles home; he was 64. Known as the "Candy Man," among other superlatives, Davis was a dancer, musician, impressionist, actor, vaudevillian, and a star of theater, nightclubs, and television. Davis, whose career began at age three, never spent a day in school, yet he coauthored three books.

May 16: Blacks were rejected at more than twice the rate of whites for home loans in the first half of 1989, a Treasury Department official testifies on Capitol Hill. *The Washington Times* quotes **Jerald Kluckman** as saying from the second half of 1988 to the first half of 1989, the rejection rate for blacks rose from 23 percent to 29 percent, while rising from only 11 to 13 percent for whites. Kluckman testified before a Senate Banking subcommittee examining discrimination in the mortgage lending industry.

May 16: *The Washington Times* reports that Michigan Congressman **John Conyers** believes there is a "deepening concern" among black officials that the U.S. Justice Department is harassing them. At a House Judiciary Committee hearing, the black congressman cited for Attorney General **Dick Thornburgh** the recent prosecution of Tennessee Congressman **Harold Ford** and the current investigation of District of Columbia Mayor **Marion Barry** as examples of federal abuse. Thornburgh angrily replied that it is "totally and absolutely false" to say federal prosecutions of blacks or other minorities are based on racial prejudice.

May 17: A jury finds **Joseph Fama** guilty of second-degree murder in the Bensonhurst racial slaying, one of several violent racial incidents that have polarized New York City. Accused of being the trigger-man in the murder of 16-year-old **Yusuf Hawkins** last August, Fama faces 25 years to life in prison [see March 12].

May 18: *The New York Times* reports the saddened Brooklyn neighborhood of Bensonhurst and East New York is struggling to return to normal in the wake of the racially charged murder trial that ended in an outburst of raw emotion. Some 500 black demonstrators, led by the Rev. **Al Sharpton**, marched into predominantly white Bensonhurst to protest the acquittal of **Keith Mondello** on all murder and manslaughter charges in the shooting death of **Yusuf Hawkins**. Mondello was convicted of a series of lesser charges that prosecutors say could bring a prison sentence of eight to 24 years [see March 12].

May 20: **Betti S. Whaley**, president of the Washington Urban League, dies at Howard University Hospital; she had diabetes and septicemia. The 60-year-old activist was the first female to head the Washington Urban League, and was highly regarded as a tenacious, outspoken, and shrewd administrator. Her 37-year career with the League included top positions within the national headquarters, where she was credited with increasing the participation of women throughout the Urban League Movement.

May 20: **Franklin Hall Williams**, a civil rights activist who served as the United States' first black ambassador to the U.N. Economic and Social Council, dies of lung cancer in his home in New York City. A founder of the Association of Black American Ambassadors, he was ambassador to Ghana from 1965 to 1968. Williams, who helped found the Peace Corps, was president of the Phelps-Stokes Fund, an organization that promotes education, at the time of his death; he was 72.

May 21: **Cernoria D. Johnson**, one of the highest ranking females in the Urban League's successful drive to become the premier social service and civil rights organization in the U.S., dies in Washington, DC. She began her 45-year-long career with the League as the first Executive Director of the Fort Worth and Oklahoma City affiliates.

May 22: **Conrad Harper** is elected president of the New York City Bar Association. He is the first African American to head the 120-year-old association, one of the nation's most prestigious legal fraternities.

May 25: *The Christian Science Monitor* reports that 59 percent of corporate boards surveyed seated women in 1989, compared to 11 percent in 1973. The Korn/Ferry International survey also finds that ethnic minorities were found on only nine percent of boards in 1973, but 32 percent last year.

May 28: *The Washington Times* reports that eight California blacks are suing the state for the right to have their nine children take an IQ test. Since 1986, state educators have been barred from administering intelligence tests to black children because a federal judge ruled they were culturally and racially biased. But the parents contend that they want their children tested to prove that they should not be in classes for the educable mentally retarded.

May 31: *The New York Times* reports federal district judge **Arthur Garrity, Jr.** has issued his final order in Boston's 16-year-old desegregation case. Garrity bars "creating, promoting, or maintaining racial segregation in any school or other facility in the Boston school system."

May 31: A national organization that studies incidents of bigotry is urging college presidents to take stronger steps to confront rising racial and ethnic tensions on campus. *The New York Times* quotes **Adele Dutton Terrell**, the program director for the National Institute Against Prejudice and Violence, as saying "We feel unless the chief executive is willing to make a public commitment to the value of diversity and to maintaining a harmonious campus, none of the other efforts can come to fruition."

May 31: *The New York Times* reports that what had been depicted as racial harassment that left a black student at Emory University traumatized and mute was instead apparently a hoax [see April 22]. Local and state prosecutors reviewing the case of **Sabrina Collins** say the overwhelming evidence suggested that she had staged the episode herself. Collins' attorney denounced the finding, saying, "It is apparent that the person who inflicted this pain and suffering is not only free to do it again but has also succeeded in evading the investigation."

May 31: President and Mrs. **Bush** honor Soviet President **Mikhail Gorbachev** at a White House state dinner, more evidence in the thaw in U.S.-Soviet relations. Among the distinguished invitees are National Urban League President and Chief Executive Officer **John E. Jacob** and his wife **Barbara**.

June 1: U.S. District Judge **W. Arthur Garrity** signs written orders bringing to an end Boston's 16-year school desegregation case. *The Christian Science Monitor* quotes Judge Garrity as saying racial quotas must still be maintained when teacher layoffs are involved.

June 4: Sister **Cora Billings** becomes the pastoral coordinator of St. Elizabeth's Roman Catholic Church in Richmond, VA, and the first black nun to head a parish in the U.S.

June 4: African National Congress leader **Nelson Mandela** begins his six-week tour of 13 countries, including Britain, Canada, and the United States, where he is scheduled to address the United Nations and the U.S. Congress.

June 5: Former Charlotte (NC) Mayor **Harvey Gantt** defies history and becomes the state's first black U.S. Senate nominee this century [see May 8]. Gantt won 57 percent of the vote in the Democratic runoff; he faces a daunting foe in November against the incumbent GOP arch-conservative, Sen. **Jesse Helms**.

June 11: A Brooklyn judge sentences two white men to maximum prison terms for their roles in the killing of black teenager **Yusuf Hawkins** last August. **Joseph Fama** was sentenced to 32 years and eight months to life in prison [see May 17]. **Keith Mondello** was sentenced to five years and four months to 16 years [see May 18].

June 11: *Jet* magazine reports the Commission on Minority Business Development was recently established by Congress through the Business Opportunity Development Reform Act of 1988. The commission, which met recently in Chicago to hear testimony from business owners, will review and assess the operations of all federal programs intended to foster and promote the development of minority-owned business to determine their effectiveness.

June 13: **Joe Wright**, one of the original members of the "Wilmington Ten" whose arrests and jailing for the firebombing of a grocery store became a rallying point for the Civil Rights Movement, dies of sarcoidosis in Wilmington at the age of 37.

June 15: **St. Clair Drake**, a pioneer in black studies who was the first permanent director of Stanford University's African and Afro-American Studies Program, dies of a heart attack in Palo Alto (CA) at age 79. His works included *Black Metropolis: A Study of Negro Life in a Northern City*, which was hailed by reviewers as a landmark of objective research and one of the best urban studies produced by American scholarship.

June 17: A coalition of black college students holds a march and rally in the nation's capital, hoping to rekindle student movements of the 1960s, according to *The Washington Post*. The demonstration kicks off a week of events aimed at focusing the nation's attention on issues such as education and racism. The group bonded together largely because of the dwindling federal funds for student financial aid and an increase in racially motivated incidents on and off college campuses.

June 19: The drug and perjury trial of DC Mayor **Marion Barry** begins with the jury hearing prosecution and defense versions of the case. Barry admits smoking crack but says he was entrapped. The jurors will be sequestered for the duration of the trial.

June 24: National Urban League Guild founder and president **Mollie Moon** dies peacefully in her sleep in New York. A trained pharmacist and prominent New Yorker, Moon launched what has become a tradition in the nation's largest city each February: the black-tie Beaux Arts Ball. She received the League's highest honor—the Equal Opportunity Award — last year. President **Bush** also awarded her the President's Volunteer Action Award, which was presented to her in a ceremony in New York by Mayor **David Dinkins**.

June 25: African National Congress leader **Nelson Mandela** tells President **Bush** that he cannot completely renounce the use of violence and armed struggle to achieve racial equality in South Africa. *The New York Times* quotes Mandela as saying that the ANC will consider ceasing hostilities once the Pretoria regime accepts all conditions for talks on a new constitution. At the White House meeting, the President assured Mandela that U.S. sanctions will not be lifted until all of the conditions set by Congress have been met. The White House visit is part of Mandela's 10-day itinerary in the U.S. Tomorrow, Mandela will address a joint meeting of Congress; he was welcomed with a ticker-tape parade in New York City upon his arrival in the U.S. five days ago.

June 26: The U.S. Supreme Court upholds two federal affirmative action programs aimed at increasing minority ownership of broadcast licenses [see March 28]. *The New York Times* reports the five-to-four decision rejects the **Bush** administration's arguments that the programs are unconstitutional.

July 1: Florida Supreme Court Justice **Leander Shaw** becomes chief justice, the first black ever promoted to that post in the state, and the first black to head any of Florida's three branches of government. The 59-year-old jurist has served on the Supreme Court since January, 1983.

July 3: The third trial in the Bensonhurst racial killing ends with jurors acquitting **John Vento** of intentional murder charges [see June 11]. The jury does not reach a verdict on a second murder charge and on a riot charge.

July 4: Dr. **Gwendolyn Calvert Baker** is elected president of the New York City Board of Education. Among her priorities, the 58-year-old educator tells *The New York Times*, are lengthening the school day to keep youngsters productively engaged, involving parents more in decisions, and having children graduate from high school knowing two languages.

July 10: *The Washington Post* reports **Eugene Marino**, the 56-year-old black Roman Catholic Archbishop of Atlanta, has resigned, citing mental and physical health problems. Appointed to head the archdiocese in 1988, Marino is America's highest-ranking black Catholic priest. He underwent treatment for alcoholism 12 years ago, and now says he needs "an extended period of spiritual renewal, psychological therapy, and medical supervision."

July 18: The U.S. Senate passes the **Civil Rights Act of 1990** in a form that President **Bush** has already threatened to veto. The 65 to 34 vote is two short of the amount needed to override a presidential veto.

July 20: Most women prosecuted for using illegal drugs while pregnant have been poor members of racial minorities, even though drug use in pregnancy is equally prevalent in white middle-class women. *The New York Times* quotes experts who say poor women are more likely to be prosecuted because public hospitals—where they go for care—are most vigilant in their drug testing and more likely than private hospitals to report women whose tests show drug use.

July 29: National Urban League President and Chief Executive Officer **John E. Jacob**, citing projections that members of minorities will comprise a larger and larger part of the nation's work force, says the United States must grant them equality not merely out of a moral imperative, but for "its own economic self-interest." In his keynote address opening the League's 80th anniversary conference in New York, Jacob declared that the nation has only one hope of entering the 21st century as a world power and a global economic force: "[T]hat is its ability to achieve racial parity and to make full use of the African Americans and minorities it has so long rejected."

Aug. 2: California Democratic Congressman **Pete Stark** apologizes to Health and Human Services Secretary **Louis Sullivan**, saying he should not have called the former head of the Morehouse Medical School "a disgrace to his race." Stark had challenged Sullivan's positions on abortion, health care, and civil rights. Sullivan, who demanded the Stark apology, told reporters that "I don't live on Pete Stark's plantation."

Aug. 3: The U.S. House of Representatives approves the 1990 Civil Rights Bill, despite threats by President Bush to veto the measure. Bush contends the legislation would lead to job quotas for women and minorities. The Senate passed a similar bill last month.

Aug. 3: The PGA Tour announces a new policy intended to make sure that none of its 120 yearly tournaments will take place at private clubs that discriminate by race, religion, or sex. *The New York Times* reports the move is the PGA Tour's response to the recent controversy over the membership practices at Shoal Creek Country Club in Alabama, site of the PGA Championship. The controversy started in June when **W. Hall Thompson**, founder of Shoal Creek—a club outside of Birmingham—said his club would "not be pressured" into admitting black members.

Aug. 3: *The New York Times* reports New York Congressman **Floyd Flake**, pastor of one of the largest black churches in the city, was indicted on charges of misappropriating $75,200 from a federally subsidized housing complex built by his church and with evading taxes on $66,700 of the church's money that he and his wife put to personal use. Flake strongly denies any wrongdoing.

Aug. 8: A black FBI agent who charged in civil suits that he was racially harassed by white agents will receive full pay and pension benefits, possibly worth more than $1 million under a settlement of the case. *The New York Times* reports attorneys for **Donald Rochon** and the FBI have signed an agreement this week that settles the three-year-old legal battle arising from the black agent's charges that he was harassed by white colleagues when he worked in the FBI's Chicago office.

Aug. 10: DC Mayor **Marion Barry** is convicted of one misdemeanor count of drug possession and acquitted of another misdemeanor drug charge. The jury failed to reach a verdict on the 12 remaining charges, including the most serious ones [see June 19]. Judge **Thomas Penfield Jackson** declares a mistrial on those 12 counts, and federal prosecutors say they are uncertain whether they will seek a new trial on those charges.

Aug. 10: The U.S. Justice Department has filed a lawsuit challenging Georgia's runoff election system, which it says discriminates against black candidates. *The New York Times* reports the suit attacks a requirement that a candidate must win a majority of the vote in a multi-candidate election or face a runoff. Civil rights activists hail the suit, while some white Democrats warn the move could cause some whites to become Republicans.

Aug. 11: *The Washington Post* reports former Atlanta Archbishop **Eugene Marino** has been admitted to a hospital psychiatric unit. Marino, the first African-American Roman Catholic Archbishop, resigned last month [see July 10th]. Church officials confirmed last week that an intimate relationship with a former lay minister, led to Marino's resignation last month.

Aug. 11: Thousands of black families find it difficult, if not impossible, to make the leap from renting to owning a home. *The Washington Post* cites a Harvard University Joint Center for Housing Studies report which found that 3.5 percent of black renters in the U.S. are able to buy homes now, compared with 16.9 percent of whites. Researchers say lower incomes than whites and racial discrimination in buying and borrowing are the major barriers to black home ownership.

Aug. 16: The Florence (SC) *Morning News* reports a Vietnam veteran was denied membership in an all-white American Legion post last month because he is black. The rejection of **Thurmond L. Thompson**, who works for General Electric, has led the organization's national headquarters to call for an investigation.

Aug. 17: More than 100 black groups hold a "Summit Conference of Black Organizations" in Washington, DC, to lay a foundation for an organization that would duplicate across the country programs that have been successful in battling social ills plaguing the black community. *The Washington Post* reports the groups were invited to participate by the NAACP, signaling a new focus for the 81-year-old civil rights organization. The newspaper quotes Executive Director **Benjamin Hooks** as saying, "We're here to talk about what we can do to help lift ourselves...but we're not going to let the government off the hook, and we're not going to let the large, white-owned corporations off the hook."

Aug. 18: Legendary entertainer **Pearl Bailey** dies in Philadelphia at the age of 72. The dynamic and irrepressible singer, actress, comedian, and author collapsed at a downtown hotel. A star of stage and screen, Bailey had suffered from a heart ailment for many years. She served the nation as a diplomat, wrote several books, and received a bachelor's degree from Georgetown University at the age of 67. Her throaty-voiced performance in "Hello Dolly!" was one of the monuments of the musical stage.

Aug. 21: FBI Director **William Sessions** names the agency's highest-ranking black field agent to investigate allegations that evidence of widespread racial discrimination within the bureau was covered up by white supervisors. **Paul R. Philip**, head of the FBI office in San Juan, Puerto Rico, and a team of eight investigators will study the charges made by **Donald Rochon**, a black agent whose case has become a symbol of lingering discrimination in the bureau [see Aug. 8].

Aug. 23: The State of Mississippi has been ordered to pay more than $4.7 million in the final ruling of a 20-year-old discrimination suit against the state's employment agency. *The New York Times* reports the ruling was the first victory against a state employment agency accused of engaging in a pattern of racial or sexual discrimination on a class basis.

Aug. 24: An all-white American Legion post in Florence, SC, that refused membership to a Vietnam veteran because he is black has now agreed to let him re-apply and has adopted a bylaws change that virtually insures he will be accepted. The rejection of **Thurman Thompson** earlier this month prompted the organization's national headquarters to investigate the incident [see Aug. 16].

Aug. 25: *The Washington Post* reports the plane crash in Ethiopia that killed Rep. **Mickey Leland** (D-TX) and 15 others last year was probably caused by pilot error. A probe by the Ethiopian Civil Aviation Authority finds the pilot may have felt pressured to fly in bad weather because of the "importance of the mission" to inspect relief efforts in the Ethiopian famine.

Aug. 27: Blacks and whites agree to rotate control of the troubled Selma school system in an effort to end months of racial tension, protests, and lawsuits. *The New York Times* reports that under the compromise approved by the City Council, the school board will have 10 voting members, five blacks and five whites, with the chairmanship rotating racially each year.

Aug. 27: Veteran film and television actor **Raymond St. Jacques** dies of cancer of the lymph glands in Los Angeles at the age of 60. He appeared in numerous prime-time television series, including "Rawhide," and received acclaim for his roles in "Cotton Comes to Harlem" and "The Evil That Men Do," among others.

Aug. 29: CBS names **Johnathan Rodgers** president of its television stations divisions. The 44-year-old former vice president and general manager of the CBS affiliate in Chicago becomes the highest-ranking black executive in network television and the first black to be named president of a division at any network.

Sept. 2: Amid strong counterprotests, the police cancel a march that was planned in downtown Washington, DC, by Ku Klux Klan members. *The New York Times reports* 40 Klansmen in robes and hoods are allowed to hold a rally on the U.S. Capitol grounds. One arrest was made for inciting to riot, and several injuries, all among protesters, are reported.

Sept. 6: A federal judge in Newark (NJ) rules that it is racially discriminatory for communities to require police officers, fire fighters, and other municipal employees to live in the towns that they serve. The case at issue involved the 99-percent white town of Harrison, which had the residency requirement that the judge found violated the federal Civil Rights Act.

Sept. 9: Miss Illinois, **Marjorie Judith Vincent,** is crowned "Miss America 1991." The black abortion rights advocate says she "wants it all," according to published reports, and will use her reign to help battered women.

Sept. 12: The Ford Foundation awards $1.6 million to 19 institutions to help diversify the ethnic and cultural content of their curriculums. *The New York Times* reports the grant program is the latest move in an effort by the foundation and education associations and officials to address ethnic tensions on American campuses.

Sept. 12: Reebok International Ltd. appoints Denver Nuggets co-owner **Bertram Lee** to its board of directors. The 51-year-old African-

American entrepreneur joins Reebok as the athletic shoe industry comes under fire from civil rights group Operation PUSH. The organization called last month for a boycott of Nike, Inc., because of what the group calls Nike's poor record of minority employment and business dealings with black-run firms and banks. Nike says it plans to appoint a minority director by June, 1991. Lee maintains he was asked to join the Reebok board before PUSH took on the industry.

Sept. 13: **Althea T.L. Simmons,** the head of the Washington branch of the NAACP since 1979 and the organization's chief lobbyist in the capital, dies of respiratory failure in Washington; she was 66. Simmons spent more than 35 years with the civil rights agency, holding posts as national education director, national training director, director of special voter registration drives, and associate director of branch and field services. She successfully lobbied for the extension of the Voting Rights Act in 1982, the creation of a holiday honoring **Martin Luther King, Jr.**, sanctions against South Africa, and the subsequent congressional override of President Reagan's veto.

Sept. 17: Federal prosecutors announce they will not retry DC Mayor **Marion Barry** on the 12 drug and perjury charges that a jury was unable to resolve last month. *The New York Times* reports that the announcement means the government—after spending several years and several million dollars investigating and prosecuting the mayor—achieved only a single misdemeanor conviction, possession of cocaine, for which he might receive little more than a suspended sentence [see Aug. 10].

Sept. 24: **Harold L. Trigg,** one of the first doctors to use methadone in treating heroin addiction, dies in New York of lung cancer; he was 66. Dr. Trigg helped establish Beth Israel Hospital's methadone maintenance program, which has become one of the largest drug treatment programs in the world.

Sept. 25: Members of the **Congressional Black Caucus** react angrily to a racial slur by Japan's Justice Minister, who drew a parallel between blacks and prostitutes. The members call on President **Bush** to protest, saying that blacks in the United States armed forces are helping to protect Japan. In Tokyo, Justice Minister **Seiroku Kajiyama** formally apologizes for telling reporters after an undercover trip to a red-light district, "Bad money drives out good money, just like in America where the blacks came in and drove out the whites."

Sept. 28: The **Congressional Black Caucus** declares it is time to stop talking and start doing something about the mounting list of black officials who have been investigated, indicted, or convicted in what many black leaders view as a clear pattern of government harassment and selective law enforcement. *The Washington Post* reports Michigan Congressman **John Conyers** announced he will hold hearings next year on the harassment issue.

Sept. 28: The Texas system of electing district judges by county-wide voting is upheld by a federal appeals court that said protections against diluting minorities' voting power have no bearing because judges are not public servants. *The Washington Post* reports the decision is expected to be appealed before the U.S. Supreme Court.

Sept. 28: The state of Mississippi has done enough to erase years of discrimination and compensate the state's three historically black universities. *The Washington Post* reports a federal court handed down the ruling, which reverses a decision by a three-judge panel that Mississippi illegally operates separate universities for blacks and whites and that opening admissions in 1962 did not go far enough.

Oct. 3: Civil rights activist and Off-Track Betting Corporation chief **Hazel Dukes** fends off cries of racism after she complained on radio that waiters "who can't even speak English" are filling jobs that should go to black people. In a prepared statement published in *The New York Times,* Dukes said she has devoted her life "in the fight for equal justice and opportunities," that she welcomes "all races and nationalities and will continue to work hard until we obtain freedom and equal opportunity for all."

Oct. 3: **Charles L. Sanders**, managing editor of *Ebony* magazine since 1968, dies in Chicago at the age of 58; the cause of death was not reported. During his 20-plus years with Johnson Publishing Company, he opened the firm's first overseas bureau, in Paris, where he wrote a weekly column, "Paris Scratchpad," for *Jet* magazine, a sister publication.

Oct. 5: The U.S. House of Representatives passes a major crime bill after approving an amendment that would permit prisoners under death sentences to seek reversal of their sentences if they could produce evidence suggesting a pattern of racial discrimination in prior state cases. *The New York Times* reports the antidiscrimination measure would apply retroactively to existing death-penalty convictions and could have a profound effect on the country's 2,400 death-row inmates, most of whom are black.

Oct. 8: Efforts to improve race relations by increasing the number of black police officers in Denver (CO) have generated ill feelings among whites and blacks alike. *The New York Times* reports that blacks do not want standards and scores on the qualification exams lowered for blacks because they are competent enough to pass any qualification. Whites, in turn, say they are angry that black candidates for police training do not have to score as high as white applicants on the exams.

Oct. 12: The attorney for DC Mayor **Marion Barry** is asking for a retrial in the mayor's drug and conspiracy case. Defense attorney **R. Kenneth Mundy** claims U.S. marshals may have influenced jurors in the case, telling them that alternate jurors who were excused just before deliberations began would have voted "guilty, guilty, guilty" to the 14 charges against the mayor.

Oct. 15: The South African government scraps its laws against blacks using the same toilets, movies, parks, swimming pools, and beaches as whites. As it eliminated the Separate Amenities Act—one of the cornerstones of apartheid—the government warned local municipalities against pulling any legal "funny tricks" to return to segregation, according to published reports.

Oct. 16: Drummer and band leader **Art Blakey** dies of lung cancer in New York at the age of 71. Blakey and his Jazz Messengers had an enormous influence on the jazz and cultural life of America.

Oct. 22: President **Bush** vetoes the 1990 Civil Rights Act, which was drafted as a response to a series of recent U.S. Supreme Court decisions curbing federal civil rights protections [see April 4, May 14].

Oct. 22: *Jet* magazine reports public school officials in Milwaukee have approved a plan to create two schools next year that will cater to the needs and experiences of young black male students. The school board voted to designate an elementary school and a middle school as African- American Immersions Schools, with a specific curriculum for black males. The project is believed to be a first for a public school district in the U.S.

Oct. 22: **John F. Davis**, a former deputy executive director of the Department of Planning and former executive editor of *The New York Amsterdam News*, dies of lung cancer in New York at the age of 50. In 1963, at the age of 22, he became the youngest full-fledged member ever appointed, until that time, to the board of directors of the NAACP. He was also a founder of the New York City Black Convention.

Oct. 24: The U.S. Senate falls one vote short of overriding President **Bush**'s veto of the 1990 Civil Rights Act, giving a victory to those who contended the legislation would have led to the widespread use of quotas in hiring and promotion. The measure's supporters insist that it was not a quota bill, that it explicitly ruled out quotas as a remedy for discrimination; they vow to reintroduce it in the 102nd Congress next January.

Oct. 26: Federal District Judge Thomas Penfield Jackson sentences DC Mayor **Marion Barry** to six months in prison and a year of probation for his cocaine possession conviction. The judge refused Barry's suggestion that community service would be a more appropriate punishment than jail, noting that the three-term mayor had "given aid, comfort, and encouragement to the drug culture" by using cocaine for five years and lying about it. Barry is appealing both the conviction and the sentence.

Oct. 28: During the mid-'80s, the number of black-owned businesses in America grew at a much higher rate than that of other businesses. Black-owned firms increased 38 percent, from 308,000 in 1982 to 424,000 in 1987, according to a Census Bureau report, *1987 Survey of Minority-Owned Business Enterprises—Black*. The report also finds, however, that black enterprises averaged only $47,000 each in annual receipts, compared to $146,000 for all small and mid-sized firms.

Oct. 29: *Jet* magazine reports **Leatrice McKissack**, chief executive officer of McKissack and McKissack Architects and Engineers, has been named National Female Entrepreneur of the Year. The former math teacher was honored at a White House ceremony during Minority Business Week. Since becoming head of the country's oldest and largest black architectural firm, which extends back four generations of a family, the firm has grown from a staff of 10 to 28, with construction projects up from $15 million to $100 million.

Oct. 29: *Jet* magazine reports **Carmen Turner**, the first black Metro rail system general manager in Washington, DC, has resigned to become the first black under secretary at the Smithsonian Institution. Second in command, she will handle the day-to-day operations of the Institution with 5,600 employees and a $550-million budget.

Oct. 29: **Spelman** and **Morehouse Colleges** in Atlanta are ranked third and seventh, respectively, in the latest *U.S. News and World Report*'s annual survey of American institutions of higher learning in the South. The results were based on the colleges' selectivity in admissions, quality of faculty, financial resources, student satisfaction, and reputation among peers.

Oct. 30: Sixteen years after the U.S. Justice Department accused the state of Louisiana of running a dual system of higher education—one for blacks and one for whites, a federal judge has reluctantly dismissed the government's case. *The New York Times* quotes Judge **Charles Schwartz, Jr.** as saying that there are no disputed material facts left for the court to resolve. The ruling was welcomed by some state officials and educators who told reporters that it is "great news that Louisiana is not operating a segregated university system." Civil rights officials say they may appeal the ruling to the U.S. Supreme Court.

Nov. 3: President **Bush** signs bills to expand the Head Start preschool program and to provide money for childhood immunization. The Head Start legislation authorizes $20 billion over the next four years for the program — enough to serve all eligible poor children for the first time in its history. At current budget levels, the program serves only 20 percent of the eligible children.

Nov. 5: Pianist and composer **Bobby Scott** dies of lung cancer in New York City at the age of 53. He was a jazz prodigy who made his first album, toured with Gene Krupa, and had a hit single—"Chain Gang"—before turning 20. He produced records for performers such as Aretha Franklin and Johnny Mathis. Some of his best-known compositions are "A Taste of Honey" and "He Ain't Heavy, He's My Brother."

Nov. 6: Attorney and former utility executive **Sharon Pratt Dixon** wins the DC mayoral race. Garnering a spectacular 85 percent landslide, she promises to "clean house," repeating her campaign theme, according to published reports. Her victory comes as **Marion Barry** is defeated in a bid for a seat on the DC Council.

Nov. 6: North Carolina Senator **Jesse Helms** defeats former Charlotte Mayor **Harvey Gantt** in the race for the U.S. Senate seat Helms has held for the past three terms. The incumbent had trailed in polls in the final days but won handily after he ran a series of negative ads that unfairly equated Gantt's support of affirmative action with quotas.

Nov. 6: Voters in Arizona reject a measure to honor slain civil rights leader **Martin Luther King, Jr.** with a state holiday. King's birthday is recognized by Arizona by an executive order from former Governor Evan Mecham, but it is a nonpaid holiday celebrated on a Sunday.

Many communities within the state, however, celebrate King's birthday by district mandate.

Nov. 6:   A black-led boycott of Miami-area schools cripples the school district's transportation system and keeps 30 percent of students out of classes. About 2,500 teachers and most school bus drivers honor the boycott, called by black leaders to protest the appointment of a white Hispanic as superintendent.

Nov. 7:   NFL Commissioner **Paul Tagliabue** says he will ask the league's owners to take the 1993 Super Bowl to be played in Arizona away because of the state's rejection of a paid King holiday on the third Monday in January. House Minority Leader Art Hamilton says a King Day bill will be introduced in the next session of the legislature to prevent the NFL move from Phoenix.

Nov. 8:   DC Mayor-Elect **Sharon Pratt Dixon** names former National Urban League President **Vernon Jordan** chairman of her 28-member transition team.

Nov. 8:   *The Washington Post* reports **Walter Leroy Moody, Jr.**, refuses to enter a plea after being charged in the race-related mailbomb killings of a federal judge and civil rights lawyer. In a hearing before a federal magistrate in Atlanta, lawyers for the 56-year-old Rex, GA, resident say the fact that a federal judge was one of the victims damages impartiality of all federal judges; they are trying to bar *any* federal judge from hearing the case. They have asked the Senate Judiciary Committee to appoint an independent officer to hear the case. A plea of not guilty was entered automatically because of Moody's refusal to plead.

Nov. 9:   **Harold A. Stevens**, the first black to sit on New York State's highest court and a former State Assemblyman, dies of a heart attack in New York at the age of 83. He received the Papal Pro Ecclesia et Pontifice medal in 1954 from Pope Pius XII for his interracial work.

Nov. 9:   Scholars assembling a multivolume work on the papers of **Martin Luther King, Jr.**, have found evidence that the slain civil rights leader borrowed heavily from the works of others in his doctoral dissertation and some other student essays. Jon Westling, the acting president of Boston University where King studied, told reporters he is assembling a board of scholars to investigate the charges, which "merit close scrutiny." A spokesman for **Coretta Scott King** had no immediate reaction.

Nov. 12: Dillard University in New Orleans announces that it will establish a National Center for Black-Jewish Relations. Dr. **Samuel Du Bois Cook**, the university's president, says $100,000 will be given as seed money to establish the center, with a goal of raising upwards of $10 million for the center. Cook says the center is intended to heal a rift that has developed between blacks and Jews since they worked side by side during the Civil Rights Movement in the '60s.

Nov. 14: **Guichard Parris**, a noted scholar, historian, and communications pioneer, dies of a heart attack in New York at the age of 86. Parris created the National Urban League's Department of Public Relations in 1946 and led it for 25 years until his retirement. He coauthored with **Lester Brooks** *Blacks in the City*, the official history of the National Urban League.

Nov. 17: A skeleton exhumed from a New York cemetery is that of Haitian slave **Pierre Toussaint**, who is a candidate to become the first black Roman Catholic saint from the U.S. Cardinal **John O'Connor** says a team of archaeologists, forensic scientists, and anthropologists confirmed the identity of Toussaint, who died in 1853 at age 87.

Nov. 19: Concern is expressed by leaders of minority journalist organizations that hiring freezes and budget cuts may have an effect upon hiring and promoting black, Hispanic, Asian, and Native American journalists. *The New York Times* quotes **Thomas Morgan**, president of the National Association of Black Journalists and a reporter at the newspaper, as saying, "We see the recession as an excuse not to keep the commitment made through the years to vastly increase the number of minorities in newsrooms."

Nov. 19: Broadway tap dancer **Ralph Brown** dies of congestive heart failure in New York at the age of 76. His most recent Broadway engagement was in "Black and Blue," which he left because of failing health. After his debut at the Cotton Club in 1934, he traveled for several decades with band leader **Cab Calloway**.

Nov. 20: An 11:00PM curfew on weekdays and a midnight one on weekends goes into effect for teenagers in Atlanta, prompting mixed reactions to the new law. Some residents are hoping that it will reduce drug-related violence, while others charge that it is aimed at poor black children and their parents.

Nov. 20: **W. Montague Cobb**, a professor emeritus of anatomy at Howard University and a past president of the NAACP, dies at the age of 86 at George Washington University Hospital in Washington, DC.

He had heart ailments and pneumonia. A professor at Howard for more than 40 years, he was also a persistent and eloquent spokesman in behalf of many civil rights causes, an author, an editor, a historian of blacks in medicine, a member and officer of numerous societies, a violinist, and the recipient of many honors. *The Washington Post* eulogizes Cobb as a leader who "will be remembered as a special figure in the history that he first studied and then helped to shape significantly."

Nov. 20: The U.S. Bureau of Engraving and Printing agrees to end practices that black workers say kept them in low-paying jobs. The federal agency that prints money and stamps also agrees to pay $1.4 million in back wages.

Nov. 20: A group of Harvard Law School students files suit in Boston, charging that their school—long seen as a bastion of liberal thinking—discriminates against women and minorities in its hiring of professors. Second-year law student **John Bonifaz** told reporters: "Today we use the only instrument of power Harvard Law School seems to understand." **Derrick Bell**, the first tenured black professor there who took an unpaid leave to protest the lack of a woman of color on the faculty [see April 23], applauded the students: "They've done the right thing.... [B]ut the chance of any civil rights suit these days is not good." Dean **Robert Clark** rebuts, saying the complaint "does not have merit."

Nov. 21: **Maudine R. Cooper**, DC Mayor **Marion Barry's** staff director and a longtime civil rights leader in the District, is appointed president of the Washington Urban League. Cooper succeeds **Betti S. Whaley**, who died in May [see May 20]. Cooper has worked in the District government for seven years, first as the director of the DC Office of Human Rights and more recently as the top staff official in the mayor's office. Before that, she was a top official with the National Urban League.

Nov. 21: Federal judge **David Hittner** of Houston approves the settlement of a class-action lawsuit that accused **State Farm Insurance Companies** of discriminating against minorities and women in its Texas region. The settlement allows $12 million to be distributed among the seven named plaintiffs and qualified blacks, Hispanics, and women who were not hired, recruited, or promoted in agent or representative trainee jobs prior to 1984.

Nov. 24: Waterbury (CT) Alderman **Gary A. Franks**, elected November 6 as the first black Republican to win a voting position in the U.S.

House of Representatives since President Franklin Roosevelt's "New Deal" lured blacks away from the party of Lincoln, is called a "new star" for the GOP and considered to be the nation's highest-ranking black Republican elected official.

Nov. 24: A radical black rival to **Nelson Mandela**'s organization says he is ready to join him in a united front to work for a multiracial democracy in South Africa. *The New York Times* quotes **Clarence Makwetu**, acting president of the Pan-Africanist Congress of South Africa, as saying he favors a joint approach between his group and the African National Congress to President **Frederik de Klerk**'s program of political change.

Nov. 26: *The Washington Times* reports contributions totaling $150,000 from the National Endowment for the Humanities, the National Endowment for the Arts, and the Reader's Digest Association, Inc., will support the creation of a monument to the nation's first peacetime black regiments. The monument, to be located at Fort Leavenworth (KS), will honor the Buffalo Soldiers, or the Ninth and Tenth Cavalry regiments, which helped settle the West and Southwest during the late 1880s.

Nov. 26: Howard University should toughen admission requirements, offer early retirement to the entire tenured staff of the medical school, and eliminate or merge some of its schools, according to a commission that President **Franklyn Jenifer** appointed to assess the university after he assumed the top post at the "black Harvard" [see April 1]. *The Washington Post* says the report's harshest criticism was directed at the College of Medicine, whose faculty is described as "totally out of touch with the latest trends in teaching equipment, technology, and methods."

Nov. 27: Novelist **Charles Johnson** becomes only the second black male to win the National Book Award, taking the fiction prize for his historial novel, *Middle Passage*, about the voyage of a freed slave. The 42-year-old English professor at the University of Washington is the fourth black writer to win the prestigious award in its 40-year history. **Ralph Ellison** is the only other black male to earn it for his novel, *Invisible Man*, in 1953. The two black female recipients are **Gloria Naylor** *(The Women of Brewster Place)* and **Alice Walker** *(The Color Purple)*.

Nov. 28: Life expectancy for black people in the United States has dropped substantially, continuing a four-year decline, say health experts at the National Center for Health Statistics. *The New York Times* reports the drop was large enough that it helped reduce the overall life expectancy for all Americans. Blacks' life expectancy fell to 69.2 years in 1988; for whites, the rate was 75.6, unchanged from the previous year. Because of the decline in the black rate, overall life expectancy dropped from 75 years in 1987 to 74.9 years in 1988. The data also show a further widening of the gap between the life expectancy for whites and blacks, a trend the health and federal experts described as alarming.

Nov. 29:   The International Association of Insurance Fraud Agencies switches its 1991 convention from Phoenix to St. Louis. The shift results from Arizona's failure to adopt a state holiday honoring slain civil rights leader **Martin Luther King, Jr.** Association executives add, according to *USA Today*: "Too many members would skip seminars to play golf." Meanwhile, Episcopal Church leaders say they will keep their summer convention in Phoenix, but will protest by spending less money there.

Nov. 30:   DC School Superintendent **Andrew Jenkins** is fired by the school board during a tumultuous three-hour meeting. *The Washington Post* reports the board voted 8-3 to dismiss Jenkins without specifying a cause and placed him on 30-day leave. Jenkins had been at odds with most of the board since his hiring in 1988 as head of the 81,000-student school system.

Dec. 1:   The National League of Cities cancels its 1991 convention in Phoenix because Arizona does not recognize **Martin Luther King, Jr.**'s birthday as a state holiday. The group, which has 9,000 members, says it will take its annual convention to Phoenix in 1995, provided the state adopts the holiday to honor the slain civil rights leader.

Dec. 2:   A tactic used to uncover housing discrimination will be expanded to prosecute illegal employment bias, Equal Employment Opportunity Commission Chairman **Evan Kemp, Jr.**, tells reporters. Civil rights groups will use minorities and women to pose as job seekers, just as they posed in the past as prospective renters or home buyers. Their testimony can be used to prosecute offenders. The tactic extends the use of testers to the federal employment bias arena for the first time.

Dec. 3:   Ceremonies in Montgomery (AL) mark the 35th anniversary of the city bus boycott that helped launch the Civil Rights Movement.

Dec. 4:   Former heavyweight boxing champ **Muhammad Ali** arrives in New York after a mission to Baghdad in which he won the release of 15

American hostages. *The Washington Times* quotes from Ali's prepared statement in which he declares that he is "on the side of Al-Islam which means peace."

Dec. 7: *The Washington Post* reports **Daniel T. Blue** is chosen as the Speaker of the NC House of Representatives. The 41-year-old attorney is the first black Speaker of a southern legislature since Reconstruction.

Dec. 9: Former congresswoman **Barbara Jordan** accepts the Ellis Island Medals of Honor in New York in behalf of 95 of the nation's outstanding citizens of immigrant backgrounds. The awards are given by the Statue of Liberty-Ellis Island Foundation. Jordan, a professor of public affairs at the University of Texas, recently agreed to be the unpaid counsel on ethics to **Ann Richards**, the incoming Governor of Texas.

Dec. 9: **Yolanda King**, daughter of the late civil rights leader, cancels her scheduled appearance in a musical play in Tucson, AZ—one of three states with no paid holiday honoring her father. King had stated earlier that she would perform in "Stepping Into Tomorrow" with the daughter of the late **Malcolm X, Attallah Shabazz**. King's publicist declined to say what prompted the last-minute reversal.

Dec. 10: The U.S. Supreme Court asks the Justice Department for its views on whether a post-Civil War law applies to racially based firings, an issue left undecided by its 1989 ruling in *Patterson v. McLean Credit Union*. The *Patterson* decision narrowed the reach of the 1866 antidiscrimination law, ruling that it did not apply to job-related harassment. If the high court does agree to hear the case next term, it could prompt a revival of the Civil Rights Act of 1990, which passed Congress easily, but the Senate failed to override President **Bush**'s veto [see Oct. 24].

Dec. 10: Nearly half—46.5 percent—of America's black children live in poverty, and the youngest are the worst off. The findings, disclosed by the **Joint Center for Political and Economic Studies**, confirm what many poverty analysts already knew. Children under the age of three in families led by single mothers who have never married have the highest poverty rate: 87 percent in 1984, up from 76 percent in 1979. Nearly two-thirds of the mothers were in their twenties.

Dec. 10: South African musician **Hugh Masekela** receives the Humanitarian Award at the United Nations for his 30 years of work in human rights.

Dec. 12: *The New York Times* reports that a Chicago research group established by the American Bar Association found that white men who bargained with salespeople over the price of a new automobile were able to get significantly lower prices than could blacks or women. The findings question whether civil rights laws are adequate to protect African-American and women consumers against discrimination.

Dec. 14: **Jean-Claude Baker**, one of several children adopted by legendary entertainer **Josephine Baker**, buys columnist **Walter Winchell**'s files on her in Los Angeles. Baker and Winchell had an angry public disagreement over an incident in 1951 at the Stork Club. Winchell was sued by Baker, but she lost the lawsuit.

Dec. 14: A food bank and a Seattle youth symphony are the beneficiaries of a court settlement brought on by ticket buyers who sued **Michael Jackson** for canceling a series of concerts in Tacoma (WA) in October and November, 1988. Jackson said an illness kept him from performing. Ticketmaster, the City of Tacoma, and Jackson agreed to contribute $32,500 each to Northwest Harvest, the food bank, and to the symphony.

Dec. 17: President **Bush** moves swiftly to staunch a political hemorrhage at the U.S. Department of Education by intervening in what he called the "very disturbing" ban on minority scholarships. On Dec. 12, the department's Assistant Secretary for Civil Rights, **Michael Williams,** issued an order barring schools that receive federal funds from offering scholarships that exclude whites from consideration. The scholarship order will be halted for at least two years and perhaps canceled entirely.

Dec. 18: The 1963 murder case of civil rights leader **Medgar Evers** is being reopened. **Byron De La Beckwith**, a 70-year-old white supremacist twice tried for the crime, will face a third murder trial, prosecutors say. De La Beckwith was jailed outside of Chattanooga after Governor Ned Ray McWherter signed a warrant for his extradition at the request of Mississippi officials.

Dec. 18: Boston police violated individual civil rights in using stop-and-search tactics and appeared to have coerced witnesses to testify in the **Stuart** murder case, the attorney general claims [see Jan. 5].

Dec. 24: The only black to gain prominence in stock-car racing, **Wendell Scott**, dies in Danville (VA) from spinal cancer at age 69. Scott had competed in more than 500 Grand National races, finishing in the top-five standings 20 times. Actor **Richard Pryor** portrayed Scott in the movie "Greased Lightning," which focused on Scott's career.

Dec. 27: **Henry Steeger, III,** president of the National Urban League from 1960 to 1964, dies of bone cancer in New York City at the age of 87. Steeger, cofounder and president of Popular Publications, Inc., warned at the League's 1961 annual conference that a social explosion was probable unless something was done to give blacks equal rights and opportunities.

Dec. 29: **Reginald F. Lewis,** chairman and chief executive officer of Beatrice International Holdings, donates one million dollars to a number of organizations, particularly medical school scholarships for minority youth.

Dec. 30: **Hall Thompson,** founder of the Shoal Creek Country Club in Birmingham (AL), resigns as chairman of the club's board. He touched off a major controversy concerning the racial membership of the club as it was preparing to host the PGA championship [see Aug. 3]. The *Birmingham News* reports that Thompson's resignation is unrelated to the controversy.

NOTES AND REFERENCES

The Elusive Quest for Racial Justice: The Chronicle of the Constitutional Contradiction, *Derrick Bell*

Editor's Note. The stylistic conventions in the following footnotes are reprinted here as they appeared in *And We Are Not Saved*—JD.

FOOTNOTES

Introduction

¹Derrick Bell, *And We Are Not Saved: The Elusive Quest for Racial Justice* (New York: Basic Books, 1987).

Chapter

¹Samuel Eliot Morison, *The Oxford History of the American People* (1965), p. 305.

²See J. Miller, *The Wolf By the Ears* (1977), p. 31.

³Donald Robinson, *Slavery in the Structure of American Politics: 1765-1820* (1971), p. 92, quoting from Thomas Jefferson, *Notes on the State of Virginia*, T. Abernethy, ed. (1964).

⁴*Ibid.*

⁵Staughton Lynd, *Class Conflict, Slavery, and the United States Constitution* (1967), pp. 181-82, (quoting Max Farrand, ed., *The Records of the Federal Convention of 1787* [1911], vol. I., p. 533).

⁶See, for example, Lynd, *Class Conflict*, p. 182.

⁷Robinson, *Slavery in the Structure of American Politics*, p. 185.

⁸Farrand, *Records*, vol. I, p. xvi.

⁹William Wiecek, *The Sources of Antislavery Constitutionalism in America: 1760-1848* (1977), pp. 63-64.

¹⁰Robinson, *Slavery in the Structure of American Politics*, p. 210.

¹¹*Ibid.*, pp. 55-57.

¹²Charles Beard, *An Economic Interpretation of the Constitution of the United States* (1913), pp. 64-151. See also Pope McCorkle, "The Historian as Intellectual: Charles Beard and the Constitution Reconsidered," *American Journal of Legal History* 38 (1984): 314, reviewing the criticism of Beard's work and finding validity in his thesis that the Framers primarily sought to advance the property interests of the wealthy.

¹³Morison, *Oxford History*, p. 304.

¹⁴Dumas Malone, *Jefferson and the Rights of Man* (1951), p. 172 (letter from Washington to Jefferson, 31 August 1788).

¹⁵W. Mazyck, *George Washington and the Negro* (1932), p. 112.

¹⁶*Ibid.*

¹⁷Derrick Bell, *Race, Racism and American Law* (2d ed. 1980), pp. 29-30.

¹⁸James Madison, quoted in Farrand, *Records*, vol. I, p. xvi.

¹⁹Malone, *Jefferson*, p. 167 (letter written in 1788 from James Madison to Philip Mazzei).

²⁰*The Records of the Federal Convention of 1787* (rev. ed. 1937), vol. II, p. 222.

[21]Gouverneur Morris, quoted in Robinson, *Slavery in the Structure of American Politics*, p. 200.

[22]*The Records of the Federal Convention of 1787*, p. 222.

[23]See Edmund Morgan, "Slavery and Freedom: The American Paradox," *Journal of American History,* 59 (1972), 1, 6.

[24]See Wiecek, *Sources of Antislavery Constitutionalism*, pp. 62-63.

[25]A. Leon Higginbotham, *In the Matter of Color, Race and the American Legal Process: The Colonial Period* (1978), p. 380.

[26]Wiecek, *Sources of Antislavery Constitutionalism*, p. 42.

[27]Luther Martin, quoted in David Brion Davis, *The Problem of Slavery in the Age of Revolution, 1770-1823* (1975), p. 323.

[28]In the Northern states, slavery was abolished by constitutional provision in Vermont (1777), Ohio (1802), Illinois (1818), and Indiana (1816); by a judicial decision in Massachusetts (1783); by constitutional interpretation in New Hampshire (1857); and by gradual abolition acts in Pennsylvania (1780), Rhode Island (1784 and 1797), New York (1799 and 1817), and New Jersey (1804). See L. Litwack, *North of Slavery* (1961), pp. 3-20.

[29]Broadus Mitchell and Louise Mitchell, *A Biography of the Constitution of the United States* (1964), pp. 100-101.

[30]Morgan, "Slavery and Freedom." The position taken by the Colonel is based on the motivation for American slavery set out in Professor Morgan's paper; he developed the thesis at greater length in his *American Slavery, American Freedom* (1975).

[31]Morgan, "Slavery and Freedom," p. 22.

[32]Morgan, *American Slavery, American Freedom*, pp. 380-381.

[33]Morgan, "Slavery and Freedom," p. 24.

[34]Morgan, *American Slavery, American Freedom*, p. 381.

[35]Tilden LeMelle, "Foreword," in R. Burkey, *Racial Discrimination and Public Policy in the United States,* 38 (1971). The quote is reprinted in *Race, Racism*, supra note 17 at 41.

The Economic Status of African Americans: "Permanent" Poverty and Inequality, *David H. Swinton, Ph.D.*

REFERENCES

Swinton, David H. 1990. "The Economic Status of Blacks 1990," *The State of Black America 1990*, ed. Janet Dewart. New York: National Urban League, Inc.

_____ . 1988. "The Economic Status of Blacks 1988," *The State of Black America 1988*, ed. Janet Dewart. New York: National Urban League, Inc.

_____ . 1987. "The Economic Status of Blacks 1987," *The State of Black America 1987*, ed. Janet Dewart. New York: National Urban League, Inc.

_____ . 1986. "The Economic Status of the Black Population, 1986," *The State of Black America 1986*, ed. James D. Williams. New York: National Urban League, Inc.

U.S. Department of Commerce Bureau of the Census. 1990. *Money Income and Poverty Status of Families and Persons in the United States: 1989* (advance data from the March 1990 Current Population Survey). Washington, DC: U.S. Government Printing Office.

_____. 1990. *Money Income and Poverty Status in the United States: 1989.* Washing[ton, DC: U.S.] Government Printing Office. (Data from this annual report are cited in this chapter for th[e years] 1987-1990; the facts of publication are unchanged except for the year of publishing.)

_____. 1990. *Survey of Minority-Owned Businesses: Black, 1987,* MB87-1. Washingt[on, DC: U.S.] Government Printing Office.

_____. 1988. *Money Income of Households, Families, and Persons in the United States: 1986.* Washington, DC: U.S. Government Printing Office.

_____. 1986. *Household Wealth and Asset Ownership: 1984.* Washington, DC: U.S. Government Printing Office.

_____. 1986. *Statistical Abstract of the United States: 1986.* Washington, DC: U.S. Government Printing Office.

U.S. Department of Labor Bureau of Labor Statistics. 1990. *Employment and Earnings, January and October 1990.* Washington, DC: U.S. Government Printing Office. (Data from this annual report are cited throughout this chapter for the years 1986-1989; the facts of publication are unchanged except for the year of publishing.)

_____. 1990. *Employment Situation: November 1990.* News Release, Table A-3, December, 1990.

_____. 1990. *Geographic Profile of Employment and Unemployment, 1989.* Washington, DC: U.S. Government Printing Office.

_____. 1988. *Geographic Profile of Employment and Unemployment, 1987.* Washington, DC: U.S. Government Printing Office.

_____ 1985. *Handbook of Labor Statistics, June, 1985.* Washington, DC: U.S. Government Printing Office.

===

Budgets, Taxes, and Politics: Options for the African-American Community, *Lenneal J. Henderson, Ph.D.*

FOOTNOTES

[1]John W. Wright (ed.), *The Universal Almanac 1991* (Kansas City and New York: Universal Press Syndicate Company, 1990), p. 108.

[2]*Ibid.,* p. 220.

[3]John L. Mikesell, *Fiscal Administration: Analysis and Applications for the Public Sector* (Chicago: The Dorsey Press, 2nd Edition, 1986), p. X.

[4]Frank Sacton, "Financing Public Programs Under Fiscal Constraint," in Robert E. Cleary and Nicholas Henry (eds.), *Managing Programs: Balancing Politics, Administration, and Public Needs* (San Francisco: Jossey-Bass Publishers, 1989), pp. 147-166.

[5]Lenneal J. Henderson, "Budget and Tax Strategy: Implications for Blacks," in Janet Dewart (ed.), *The State of Black America 1990* (New York: National Urban League, Inc., 1990), pp. 53-54.

[6]Wright, *op. cit.,* pp. v, vi.

[7]Georgia A. Persons, "Blacks in State and Local Government: Progress and Constraints," in Janet Dewart (ed.), *The State of Black America 1987* (New York: National Urban League, Inc. 1987), pp. 167-192; Georgia A. Persons, "Reflections on Mayoral Leadership: The Impact of Changing Issues and Changing Times," *Phylon,* Vol. 41, No. 3 (September, 1985), pp. 205-218; and Hanes Walton, *Black Politics: A Theoretical and Structural Analysis* (Philadelphia: J.B. Lippincott, Inc., 1972).

[8]Henderson, *op. cit.,* p. 55.

ne Congressional Black Caucus, *The Quality of Life, Fiscal 1991 Alternative Budget* (Washington, DC: U.S. Government Printing Office, 1989), p. 1.

[10]Children's Defense Fund, *Children's Defense Fund Budget FY 1989* (Washington, DC: Children's Defense Fund, 1989), p. 12.

[11]For example, see Congressional Task Force on Federal Excise Taxes, *Analyzing the Possible Impact of Federal Excise Taxes on the Poor, Including Blacks and Other Minorities* (Washington, DC: Voter Education and Registration Action, Inc., July, 1987).

[12]*State of Small Business, 1989* (Washington, DC: U.S. Government Printing Office, 1989).

[13]Persons, "Blacks in State and Local Government: Progress and Constraints," *op. cit.*

[14]Hanes Walton, *When the Marching Stopped: The Politics of Civil Rights Regulatory Agencies* (Albany, NY: State University of New York Press, 1988), p. 59.

[15]Lenneal J. Henderson, "The Impact of Military Base Shutdowns," *The Black Scholar,* September, 1974, pp. 56-58.

[16]"The Peace Economy: How Defense Cuts Will Fuel America's Long-Term Prosperity," *Business Week,* No. 3137, December 11, 1989, p. 51.

[17]*Ibid.*, p. 52.

[18]Marshall Kaplan, "Infrastructure Policy: Repetitive Studies, Uneven Response, Next Steps," *Urban Affairs Quarterly*, v. 25, n. 3 (March, 1990), pp. 371-388.

[19]Children's Defense Fund, *op. cit.*, p. 12.

[20]District of Columbia, *Operating Budget, 1990 Fiscal Year.*

[21]Section 641, 42 USC 7141.

[22]*Functional Interrelationships of the Office of Minority Economic Impact* (Washington, DC: U.S. Department of Energy, 1989).

[23]William W. Ellis and Darlene Calbert, *Blacks and Tax Reform 1985-86* (Washington, DC: The Congressional Research Service, 1986).

[24]Fiscal *progressivity* increases the burden of deficit reduction or taxation as taxpayer capacity to pay them increases; *regressivity* burdens those most who are least able to pay.

[25]Paul Leonard and Robert Greenstein, *One Step Forward: The Deficit Reduction Package of 1990* (Washington, DC: Center on Budget and Policy Priorities, 1990), p. 5.

[26]Mikesell, *op. cit.*, p. 487.

[27]Lenneal J. Henderson, "Fiscal Strategy, Public Policy, and the Social Agenda," *The Urban League Review,* v. 13, nos. 1 and 2 (Summer 1989/Winter 1989-90), pp. 9-22.

[28]*Ibid.*

[29]Leonard and Greenstein, *op. cit.*, pp. 12-14.

[30]*Ibid.*, pp. 16-17.

[31]Henderson, "Blacks, Budgets, and Taxes," *op. cit.*, p. 84.

FOOTNOTES

[1] Children's Defense Fund, *Children 1990: A Report Card, Briefing Book, and Action Primer* (Washington, DC: Children's Defense Fund, 1990), p. 10.

[2] Opinion expressed by John E. Jacob in an address ("Leadership for Responsible Change") delivered to the Association for Supervision and Curriculum Development, Distinguished Lecture Series, 1990, p. 4.

[3] Children's Defense Fund, *op. cit.*, p. 26.

[4] *Ibid.*, p. 27.

[5] *Ibid.*, p. 92.

[6] *Ibid.*, p. 24.

[7] *Ibid.*, p. 26.

[8] *Ibid.*

[9] *Ibid.*

[10] Niara Sudarkasa, "African and Afro-American Family Structure," *Anthropology for the Nineties,* ed. Johnnetta Cole (New York: The Free Press, 1980; reprinted 1988), p. 193.

[11] *Ibid.*, p. 197.

[12] *Ibid.*, p. 204.

[13] Jawanza Kunjufu, *Countering the Conspiracy to Destroy Black Boys* (Chicago: Afro-Am Publishing House Co., 1983); Kunjufu, *Countering the Conspiracy to Destroy Black Boys Vol. II* (Chicago: African American Images, 1986).

[14] Kunjufu, *op. cit.*, 1983, p. 3.

[15] *Ibid.*, p. 5.

[16] *Ibid.*, p. 7.

[17] *Ibid.*, p. 18.

[18] *Ibid.*, p. 23.

[19] It's been said, just because you're paranoid doesn't mean that you're not being followed.

[20] Committee on Policy for Racial Justice, *Visions of a Better Way: A Black Appraisal of Public Schooling* (Washington, DC: Joint Center for Political Studies Press, 1989), p. 31.

[21] *Ibid.*

[22] John Henrik Clarke, "African-American Historians and the Reclaiming of African History," *African Culture: The Rhythms of Unity,* eds. Molefi Kette Asante and Kariamu Welsh Asante, (Trenton: First Africa World Press, Inc., 1985, reprinted 1990), p. 170.

[23] Frances Fitzgerald, *America Revised: History Textbooks in the Twentieth Century* (Boston: Atlantic-Little, Brown Books, 1979), p. 98.

[24] Fernand Braudel, *On History* (Chicago: University of Chicago Press, 1980), p. 122.

[25] St. Clair Drake, *Black Folk Here and There* (Los Angeles: Center for Afro-American Studies, University of California, Los Angeles, 1987), p. 34.

[26]*Ibid.*, p. 35.

[27]Often the Caucasian or majority culture person fails to understand the force of Anglo-American hegemony in the contemporary United States.

[28]Drake, *op. cit.*, p. 114.

[29]Dorothy Holland and Naomi Quinn (eds.), *Cultural Models in Language and Thought* (New York: Cambridge University Press, 1987), p. 4.

[30]*Ibid.*, p. 7.

[31]Gerald D. Berreman, "Race, Caste, and Other Invidious Distinctions in Social Stratification," *Anthropology for the Nineties,* ed. Johnnetta Cole (New York: The Free Press, 1972; reprinted 1988), p. 504.

[32]John Ogbu, *Minority Education and Caste: The American System in Cross-Cultural Perspective* (New York: Academic Press, 1978).

[33]Norris Brock Johnson, "Schools and Schooling: Anthropological Approaches," *Issues and Theories in Development,* eds. Michael J. Begab, H. Carl Haywood, and Howard L. Garber (Baltimore: University Park Press, 1981), p. 290.

[34]*Ibid.*, p. 291.

[35]Jean Piaget, "The Right to Education in the Present World," *To Understand Is To Invent: The Future of Education* (New York: Grossman Publishers, 1973), pp. 69-71.

[36]*Ibid.*, pp. 51-52.

[37]*Ibid.*, p. 56.

[38]*Ibid.*, p. 140.

[39]Margaret Beale Spencer, "Risk and Resilience: How Black Children Cope with Stress," *Social Science*, 71:1 (1986), 24-25.

[40]*Ibid.*, p. 30.

[41]"The children tested in Atlanta in 1982 differed significantly from the other groups on only about two dozen of the 116 measured stress indicators. Compared to other youths, they exhibited more immaturity, dependence, and masochism, and they had more nightmares, more physical problems without knowing etiology, and a greater fear of animals." The data also show that the differences "become even less distinctive after controlling for social class. Further, an Afrocentric racial identity appears to be correlated with the presence of fewer clinical symptoms. That is, a greater own-group acceptance is associated with fewer observed clinical symptoms of stress." Spencer, *op. cit.*, pp. 25-26.

[42]Spencer, *op. cit.*, p. 26.

[43]James P. Comer, "Black Family Stress and School Achievement," *Educating Black Children: America's Challenge,* eds. Dorothy Strickland and Eric J. Cooper (Washington, DC: Bureau of Educational Research, School of Education, Howard University), 1987, p. 77.

[44]*Ibid.*, p. 81.

[45]*Ibid.*, p. 83.

[46]Stephen S. and Joan C. Baratz, "Early Childhood Intervention: The Social Science Base of Institutional Racism," *Harvard Educational Review,* 40:1 (1970), 31-50; Ronald Edmonds, "Effective Schools for the Urban Poor," *Educational Leadership,* October, 1979.

[47]Comer, *op. cit.*, p. 84.

[48]Committee on Policy for Racial Justice, *op. cit.*, p. 32.

⁴⁹Children's Defense Fund, *op. cit.*, p. 10.

⁵⁰Kunjufu, *op. cit.*, 1986, p. 1.

⁵¹*Ibid.*, p. 30.

⁵²W.E.B. Du Bois, "Education and Work," *The Education of Black People: Ten Critiques 1906-1960,* ed. Herbert Aptheker (New York: Monthly Review Press, 1973), p. 38.

⁵³*Ibid.*, p. 79.

⁵⁴Piaget, *op. cit.*, p. 85.

⁵⁵Taylor and Dorsey-Gaines, *Educating Black Children: America's Challenge,* eds. Dorothy Strickland and Eric J. Cooper (Washington, DC: Bureau of Educational Research, School of Education, Howard University, 1987), p. 87.

⁵⁶Holland, *op. cit.*, p. 6.

⁵⁷Paul T. Hill, Arthur E. Wise, and Leslie Shapiro, *Educational Progress: Cities Mobilize to Improve Their Schools,* Report #R-3711-JSM/CSTP (Santa Monica: Center for the Study of the Teaching Profession, the RAND Corporation, 1989), p. 11.

⁵⁸*Ibid.*, p. 12.

⁵⁹*Ibid.*, p. 20.

⁶⁰*Ibid.*, p. 23.

⁶¹*Ibid.*, p. 29.

⁶²Josie G. Bain and Joan L. Herman, *Community Mobilization Plan for Action* (Los Angeles: UCLA Center for Research on Evaluation, Standards, and Student Testing, 1989).

⁶³Hill, Wise, and Shapiro, *op. cit.*

⁶⁴*Ibid.*, p. 20.

⁶⁵Children's Defense Fund, *op. cit.*, p. 10.

REFERENCES

Hansen, Judith Friedman. 1979. *Sociocultural Perspectives on Human Learning.* Englewood Cliffs: Prentice-Hall, Inc.

Hawkins, Darnell. 1986. "Black Overimprisonment: South and North," in *Social Science* 71:1.

Ogbu, John. 1982. "Cultural Discontinuities and Schooling," in *Anthropology and Education Quarterly* 13:4.

Developing Untapped Talent: A National Call for African-American Technologists, *Warren F. Miller, Jr., Ph.D.*

FOOTNOTES

¹John E. Jacob, "Black America, 1989: An Overview," in Janet Dewart (ed.), *The State of Black America 1990* (New York: National Urban League, Inc., 1990), pp. 5-6.

²See, for example, J. Naisbitt, *Megatrends* (New York: Warner Books, Inc., 1982).

³See, for example, *Ebony Pictorial History of Black America* (Chicago: Johnson Publishing Company, Inc., 1971).

[4]S. Massie, "And the Beat Goes On . . ., The African-American Legacy in Science and Engineering," *Journal of the National Technical Association,* Vol. 64, No. 1 (Summer, 1990), p. 22.

[5]R.C. Hayden, "The Inventive Genius of Granville T. Woods," *Journal of the National Technical Association,* Vol. 64, No. 1 (Summer, 1990), p. 44.

[6]Massie, *op. cit.*

[7]*Ibid.*

[8]The Task Force on Women, Minorities, and the Handicapped in Science and Technology, *Changing America: The New Face of Science and Engineering* (Washington, DC: U.S. Government Printing Office, 1989), pp. 1-46.

[9]*Ibid.*

[10]*Ibid.*

[11]R.A. Ellis, "Minorities in Engineering," *Engineering Manpower Bulletin No. 102* (Washington, DC: American Association of Engineering Societies, Inc., 1990), pp. 1-6.

[12]*Ibid.*

[13]"Report of the Committee on the NSF Role in Attracting Minorities to Careers in Science and Engineering" (Washington, DC: National Science Foundation, 1989), pp. 1-16.

[14]Ellis, *op. cit.*

[15]*Ibid.*

[16]*Ibid.*

[17]"Report of the Committee . . .," *op. cit.*

[18]*Ibid.*

[19]D.L. Friedman and N.W. Kay, "Keeping What We've Got: A Study of Minority Student Retention in Engineering," *Engineering Education,* April, 1990, pp. 407-422.

[20]Engineering Manpower Commission, *Engineering and Technology Degrees 1988, Part II—By Minorities* (Washington, DC: American Association of Engineering Societies, 1989), pp. 37-65.

[21]Ellis, *op. cit.*

[22]E. Alterman, "Black Universities: In Demand and In Trouble," *The New York Times Magazine,* November 5, 1989.

[23]A. Murray and U.C. Lehner, "Strained Alliance," *The Wall Street Journal,* June 25, 1990.

[24]*Ibid.*

[25]M.L. Dertouzos, R.K. Lester, R.M. Solow, and the MIT Commission on Industrial Productivity, *Made In America: Regaining the Productive Edge* (Cambridge: MIT Press, 1989).

[26]E. Denison, *Accounting for United States Economic Growth, 1929-1969* (Washington, DC: Brookings Institution, 1974).

[27]W.E. Massey, "Science Education in the United States: What the Scientific Community Can Do," *Science,* Vol. 245 (September 1, 1989), p. 915.

[28]Testimony of S.S. Hecker, Los Alamos National Laboratory, "Science Making a Difference in the 21st Century," before the U.S. Senate Committee on Energy and Natural Resources, Subcommittee on Energy Research and Development, July, 1990.

[29]Interim Report, "National Energy Strategy," DOE/S-0066P (Washington, DC: U.S. Department of Energy, April, 1990).

[30]*Ibid.*

[31]S.S. Hecker, *op. cit.*

[32]Engineering Manpower Commission, *Engineering Salaries: Special Industry Report* (Washington, DC: American Association of Engineering Societies, 1990), p. 19.

[33]W.E. Massey, *op. cit.*

[34]*Changing America, op. cit.*

[35]R. Pool, "Who Will Do Science in the 1990's?," *Science*, Vol. 248 (April, 1990), p. 433.

[36]*Ibid.*

[37]"Report of the Committee," *op. cit.*

[38]Minority Engineering Program Office, *Striving Towards the 21st Century: Building for Tomorrow* (Ann Arbor: The University of Michigan, 1990).

[39]*NACME Statistical Report 1988* (New York: NACME, Inc., 1989).

[40]*Changing America, op. cit.*

[41]"Report of the Committee," *op. cit.*

[42]"Alliances for Minority Participation," Draft Program Announcement (Washington, DC: National Science Foundation, March, 1990).

[43]"Memorandum of Understanding and Intent," Science and Technology Alliance, Fundacion Educativa Ana G. Mendez, New Mexico Highlands University, North Carolina A&T State University, Los Alamos National Laboratory, Oak Ridge National Laboratory, and Sandia National Laboratories, November 4, 1987.

[44]M.N.K. Collison, "Unique Program Guides Black Eighth Graders Out of High School and On to College," *The Chronicle of Higher Education,* Vol. 26, No. 43, July 11, 1990.

[45]*Changing America, op. cit.*

[46]Friedman and Kay, *op. cit.*

[47]Alterman, *op. cit.*

[48]*Ibid.*

[49]*Changing America, op. cit.*

[50]Friedman and Kay, *op. cit.*

[51]Jacob, *op. cit.*

It's The Thing That Counts, Or Reflections on the Legacy of W.E.B. Du Bois, *Gayle Pemberton, Ph.D.*

FOOTNOTES

[1]W.E.B. Du Bois, *W.E.B. Du Bois: Writings,* "The Name 'Negro'," in *The Crisis*, March, 1928 (reprint edition, New York: Library of America, Literacy Classics of the United States, 1986), p. 1220.

[2]*Ibid.,* pp. 1219-1220.

[3]Charles V. Hamilton, quoted in Michael Specter, "Men and Women of Their Word: But Should That Word Be 'Black' or 'African American'?," *The Washington Post National Weekly Edition,* October 28-November 4, 1990, p. 10.

[4]June Jordan, *Naming Our Destiny* (New York: Thunder's Mouth Press, 1989), p. 98.

[5]Du Bois, *The Souls of Black Folk,* in *W.E.B. Du Bois: Writings, op. cit.,* p. 359.

[6]Du Bois, quoted in Elliott M. Rudwick, *W.E.B. Du Bois: Propagandist of the Negro Protest* (1960; reprint edition, New York: Atheneum, 1968), pp. 148-149.

[7]See "Issue of Job Quotas Sure to Affect Debate on Civil Rights in the 90's," *The New York Times,* December 10, 1990, pp. A1, A16.

[8]Arnold Rampersad, *The Art and Imagination of W.E.B. Du Bois* (Cambridge: Harvard University Press, 1976), p. 291.

[9]Du Bois, *The Souls of Black Folk, op. cit.,* p. 438.

[10]Mortimer Adler, quoted in "'The Great Books of the Western World' Is Revised for the First Time Since Its 1952 Original Publication," *The New York Times,* October 25, 1990, p. C26.

[11]Rampersad, *op. cit.,* p. 289.

[12]Du Bois, "Protest," from *The Crisis,* October, 1930, reprinted in *W.E.B. Du Bois: Writings, op. cit.,* pp. 148-149.

[13]Du Bois, *The Souls of Black Folk, op. cit.,* p. 365.

[14]*Ibid.,* pp. 536-537.

[15]*The New York Times,* November 15, 1990, p. A1: "'I wouldn't even hesitate to use the big bomb—whatever's necessary to get the job done.'—Myron Gregory of Charles Town, WV."

[16]Allan Bloom, *The Closing of the American Mind: How Higher Education Has Failed Democracy and Impoverished the Souls of Today's Students* (New York: Simon and Schuster, 1987), p. 380.

[17]Du Bois, *The Souls of Black Folk, op. cit.,* p. 437. Even though he is speaking of a black population thoroughly segregated, who among us would claim that black Americans are completely integrated into American society?

[18]Ralph Ellison, "A Very Stern Discipline," in *Going to the Territory* (New York: Random House, 1986), p. 229.

[19]Stephen S. Weiner, "Accrediting Bodies Must Require a Commitment to Diversity When Measuring a College's Quality," *The Chronicle of Higher Education,* Vol. XXXVII, No. 6 (October 10, 1990), pp. B1, B3.

[20]Allan Gurganus, "The Civil War in Us," *The New York Times,* October 8, 1990, p. A17.

[21]Virgil Thomson, *A Virgil Thomson Reader* (Boston: Houghton Mifflin, 1981), p. 26.

[22]Du Bois, "Again, Lincoln," from *The Crisis,* September, 1922, *in W.E.B. Du Bois: Writings, op. cit.,* p. 1199.

[23]Joan Didion, "Slouching Towards Bethlehem," in *Slouching Towards Bethlehem* (New York: Simon and Schuster, 1979), p. 123.

[24]Du Bois, "Counsels of Despair," in *The Crisis,* June, 1934, in *W.E.B. Du Bois: Writings, op. cit.,* p. 1255.

[25]Ralph Ellison, *Invisible Man* (New York: Random House, 1952), pp. 435-436.

[26]Paul Laurence Dunbar, "We Wear the Mask," *Lyrics of Lowly Life* (New York: Dodd, Mead and Company, 1986), p. 167; W.E.B. Du Bois, "President Harding and Social Equality," in *The Crisis,* December, 1921, in *W.E.B. Du Bois: Writings, op. cit.,* p. 1194.

[27]Du Bois, "The Name 'Negro'," *op. cit.,* p. 1223.

The Case of African Americans in the Persian Gulf: The Intersection of American Foreign and Military Policy with Domestic Employment Policy in the U.S., *Dianne M. Pinderhughes, Ph.D.*

FOOTNOTES

[1]See, for example, the article in *The New York Times,* November 25, 1990, pp. 1 and 6, which describes the 719th Transportation Company of the 369th Transportation Battalion of the New York National Guard, otherwise known as the "Harlem Hellfighters" (from its service with the French Army in World War I). It is composed of black and Hispanic soldiers, "80 percent of whom are New York City civil servants, including transit employees, sanitation workers, and police officers like the 719th's commander, Capt. Dennis Bush" (p. 6). See also the article in *The Washington Post,* November 28, 1990, p. 1, which features young black men (from the University of the District of Columbia) for whom enlistment and training as Naval Reserve medics was "their only ticket to advancement in a society where they feel civilian opportunities are limited." Ironically, one young man's father is a retired Army sergeant who "couldn't afford to send him [his son] to college, and he wanted to go to school, and this was the only means he had to go to school," said Frye's father [who now, at 56, is a fire fighter at Fort Bragg, NC].

[2]Jaynes and Williams report that the "major sources of black gains in earnings and occupation status from 1939 to 1965 were South to North migration and concurrent movement from agricultural employment to nonagricultural industries" (p. 296). Even so, these "economic gains from migration ended during the late 1960s" (p. 297).

[3]See Philip J. Hilts, "Life Expectancy for Blacks in the U.S. Shows Sharp Drop," *The New York Times,* November 29, 1990, pp. A1 and B17; see also Seth Mydans, "Homicide Rate Up for Young Blacks," *The New York Times,* December 7, 1990, p. A26.

[4]This pattern of use of blacks during times when white labor was unavailable or in short supply parallels that found in the private sector; it occurred in northern industry during World War I, when European immigrants were unavailable, and during labor unrest and strikes (see Pinderhughes, 1987: 16-24).

[5]Gill notes that, in 1967, NOW leaders were adverse to suggestions that the organization come out against the war. Such narrowness, according to activist-lawyer Flo Kennedy, would be one of the reasons for her departure from the organization (Gill, 1991: 14). In the current Persian Gulf crisis, NOW came out early (November 27, 1990) with a press release opposing the possible use of force (National Organization for Women Press Release, November 27, 1990).

[6]See Neil A. Lewis, "Lawmakers Lose A Suit on War Powers," *The New York Times,* December 14, 1990, p. A15.

[7]See the *Champaign-Urbana News-Gazette,* December 9, 1990, p. A-5.
Dellums' district includes a number of military personnel and employees as well as military installations. His work on the House Armed Services Committee generated a study on defense policy that concentrated on military hardware, nuclear strategy, and budgetary issues rather than on the personnel questions associated with the increasing numbers of blacks in the AVF (Dellums, 1983).

[8]See Rep. Louis Stokes, "The Black Veteran: Defender of the American Dream," Cleveland *Call and Post,* November 22, 1990, p. 5A.

[9]Significant demographic changes in the graduate student population in systems of higher education have been showing up for several years (see *The New York Times,* November 29, 1990, pp. A1, A24). Too few Americans are interested in or qualified to fill out graduate enrollments, especially in the sciences, but this is also true in many fields in American higher-education institutions. Eventually, this will affect the faculties of these institutions, and we will increasingly have an internationalized intellectual class. This may not be undesirable, but it will produce significant political problems. The increased use of blacks in the military, in light of this development, makes for an even more ironic contrast.

REFERENCES

Barone, Michael and Grant Ujifusa. 1989. *The Almanac of American Politics 1990.* Washington, DC: The National Journal.

Binkin, Martin and Mark J. Eitelberg, with Alvin J. Schexnider and Marvin M. Smith. 1982. *Blacks and the Military.* Washington, DC: The Brookings Institution.

Darity, Jr., William. 1990. "Race and Inequality in the Managerial Age," *Assessment of the Status of African Americans: Social, Political, and Economic Issues in Black America,* ed. Wornie L. Reed. Boston: William Monroe Trotter Institute, University of Massachusetts.

DeFranco, Joseph J. 1987. "Blacks and Affirmative Action in the U.S. Military." Unpublished Master of Arts in Public Administration thesis, University of Illinois.

Dellums, Ronald V. 1983. *Defense Sense: The Search for a Rational Military Policy,* ed. Patrick O'Heffernan. Cambridge: Ballinger Publishing Company.

Description of Officers and Enlisted Personnel in the U.S. Selected Reserve, 1986, Volume 4. 1989. Arlington, VA: Defense Manpower Data Center.

Dorn, Edwin, ed. 1989. *Who Defends America? Race, Sex, and Class in the Armed Forces.* Washington, DC: Joint Center for Political Studies.

Farley, Reynolds and Walter R. Allen. 1987. *The Color Line and the Quality of Life in America.* New York: Russell Sage Foundation.

Foner, Jack D. 1974. *Blacks and the Military in American History, A New Perspective.* New York: Praeger Publishers.

Frankovic, Kathy. 1990. "CBS News/*New York Times* Poll," November 19 and December 14, 1990.

Fullinwider, Robert K. 1989. "Choice, Justice, and Representation," 97-110, *Who Defends America? Race, Sex, and Class in the Armed Forces,* ed. Edwin Dorn. Washington, DC: Joint Center for Political Studies.

The Gallup Poll Monthly. August, 1990.

Gill, Gerald. Forthcoming. *Dissent, Discontent, and Disinterest: Afro-American Opposition to the United States, Wars of the Twentieth Century.*

_____ . 1991. "From Maternal Pacifism to Revolutionary Solidarity: African-American Women's Opposition to the Vietnam War," *Sights on the Sixties,* ed. Barbara Tischler. New Brunswick: Rutgers University Press.

Hope, Richard O. 1979. *Racial Strife in the U.S. Military, Toward the Elimination of Discrimination.* New York: Praeger Publishers.

Jaynes, Gerald David and Robin M. Williams, Jr., eds. 1989. *A Common Destiny: Blacks and American Society.* Washington, DC: National Academy Press.

Jet, "General Powell's Invitation to Lead King Week Parade Stirs Ideological Dispute," 79 (December 17, 1990) 10, p. 4.

Korb, Lawrence J. 1989. "The Pentagon's Perspective," 19-32, *Who Defends America? Race, Sex, and Class in the Armed Forces,* ed. Edwin Dorn. Washington, DC: Joint Center for Political Studies.

Moskos, Charles C. 1989. "The All-Volunteer Force and the Marketplace," 75-95, *Who Defends America? Race, Sex, and Class in the Armed Forces,* ed. Edwin Dorn. Washington, DC: Joint Center for Political Studies.

_____ . 1986. "Success Story: Blacks in the Army." *The Atlantic,* 257 (May, 1986), 64-72.

Nalty, Bernard C. and Morris J. MacGregor, eds. 1981. *Blacks in the Military Essential Documents.* Wilmington, DE: Scholarly Resources.

Pinderhughes, Dianne M. 1987. *Race and Ethnicity in Chicago Politics: A Reexamination of Pluralist Theory.* Urbana-Champaign: University of Illinois Press.

Ploski, Harry A. and James Williams, eds. 1989. *The Negro Almanac: A Reference Work on the African American.* New York: Gale Research, Inc.

Reed, Wornie L., ed. 1990. *Assessment of the Status of African Americans: Social, Political, and Economic Issues in Black America.* Boston: William Monroe Trotter Institute, University of Massachusetts.

Schexnider, Alvin J. and Edwin Dorn. 1989. "Statistical Trends," 41-54, *Who Defends America? Race, Sex, and Class in the Armed Forces,* ed. Edwin Dorn. Washington, DC: Joint Center for Political Studies.

Schexnider, Alvin J. 1988. "Blacks in the Military: The Victory and the Challenge," 115-128, *The State of Black America,* ed. Janet Dewart. New York: National Urban League, Inc.

Schexnider, Alvin J. and John Sibley Butler. 1976. "Race and the Ail-Volunteer System: A Reply to Janowitz and Moskos." *Armed Forces and Society,* 2 (May, 1976): 421-434.

Stillman, II, Richard J. 1976. "Black Participation in the Armed Forces," 889-926, *The Black American Reference Book,* ed. Mabel M. Smythe. Englewood Cliffs: Prentice-Hall, Inc.

Swinton, David H. 1988. "Economic Status of Blacks 1987," 129-152, *The State of Black America 1988,* ed. Janet Dewart. New York: National Urban League, Inc.

Thomas, James A., ed. 1988. *Race Relations in the U.S. Army in the 1970s: A Collection of Selected Readings.* U.S. Army Research Institute for the Behavioral and Social Sciences.

Vaughn-Cooke, Denys. 1984. "The Economic Status of Black America—Is There a Recovery?," 1-23, *The State of Black America,* ed. James D. Williams. New York: National Urban League, Inc.

A Portrait of Youth: Coming of Age in Harlem Public Housing, *Terry M. Williams, Ph.D., and William Kornblum, Ph.D.*

FOOTNOTES

[1] Robert K. Merton, in a personal communication with the authors, 1990.

[2] Lee Rainwater, *Behind Ghetto Walls: Black Family Life in a Federal Slum* (Chicago: Atherton-Aldine, 1970); William Moore, Jr., *Vertical Ghetto* (New York: Random House, 1969).

[3] William J. Wilson, *The Truly Disadvantaged* (Chicago: University of Chicago Press, 1987), p. 25.

[4] John Goering, in a personal communication with the authors, 1989.

[5] A report to the U.S. Department of Housing and Urban Development on the state of public housing, compiled by Abt Associates, Boston, MA, 1988, p. 8.

[6] Ronald Jones et al., 1979.

[7] Abt, *op. cit.*

[8] Terry M. Williams and William Kornblum, *Growing Up Poor* (Lexington, MA: D.C. Heath and Company, 1985).

[9] Kenneth Clark, *Dark Ghetto: Dilemmas of Social Power* (New York: Harper & Row, 1965), p. 109.

[10] Excerpt from "Writing Crew Journal," Saturday, August 12, 1989, Graham Court, 116th Street, West Harlem.

[11]Jane Jacobs, *Death and Life of Great American Cities* (New York: Random House, 1961).

[12]Gerald Suttles, *The Social Order of the Slum* (Chicago: University of Chicago Press, 1969).

Economic Costs of American Racism, *Billy J. Tidwell, Ph.D.*

FOOTNOTES

[1]U.S. Department of Commerce Bureau of the Census, Current Population Reports, *Projections of the Population of the United States by Age, Sex, and Race: 1988 to 2080* (Washington, DC: U.S. Government Printing Office, 1989).

[2]U.S. Department of Labor Bureau of Labor Statistics, "Outlook 2000," *Monthly Labor Review,* Vol. 112, No. 11 (November, 1989).

[3]For relevant arguments, see William B. Johnston and Arnold H. Packer, *Workforce 2000: Work and Workers for the 21st Century* (Indianapolis: Hudson Institute, 1987). See also the Prepared Statement of John E. Jacob, President and Chief Executive Officer of the National Urban League, Inc., "Change, Challenge, and Choice: African Americans and Workforce 2000," submitted to the U.S. House Committee on Education and Labor, June, 1989.

[4]Richard M. Burkey, *Racial Discrimination and Public Policy in the United States* (Lexington, MA: D.C. Heath and Company, 1971), p. 9.

[5]Stanley M. Elkins, *Slavery: A Problem in American Institutional and Intellectual Life* (Chicago: University of Chicago Press, 1959); and Kenneth M. Stampp, *The Peculiar Institution: Slavery in the Ante-Bellum South* (New York: Vintage Books, 1956).

[6]C. Vann Woodward, *The Strange Career of Jim Crow* (New York: Oxford University Press, 1966).

[7]See Billy J. Tidwell, "Racial Discrimination and Inequality," *Encyclopedia of Social Work, Vol. 2* (Silver Spring, MD: National Association of Social Workers, 1987), pp. 448-455. See also Melvin Steinfield, *Cracks in the Melting Pot: Racism and Discrimination in American History* (New York: MacMillan Publishing Company, 1970).

[8]Gunnar Myrdal, *An American Dilemma* (New York: Harper, 1944); Gerald David Jaynes and Robin M. Williams, Jr. (eds.), *A Common Destiny: Blacks and American Society* (Washington, DC: National Academy Press, 1989); and Billy J. Tidwell, *Stalling Out: The Relative Progress of African Americans* (Washington, DC: National Urban League Research Department, 1989).

[9]Thomas F. Pettigrew, "New Patterns of Racism: The Different Worlds of 1984 and 1964," *Rutgers Law Review,* Vol. 37, No. 14 (Summer, 1985), p. 686.

[10]Dionne J. Jones, *Racially Motivated Violence: An Empirical Study of a Growing Social Problem* (Washington, DC: National Urban League Research Department, 1988).

[11]Jaynes and Williams, *op. cit.*; see also Reynolds Farley and Walter R. Allen, *The Color Line and the Quality of Life in America* (New York: Russell Sage Foundation, 1987).

[12]*Ibid.* See also James P. Smith and Finis R. Welch, *Closing the Gap: Forty Years of Economic Progress for Blacks* (Santa Monica, CA: Rand Corporation, 1986).

[13]Jaynes and Williams, *op. cit.*; Tidwell, *Stalling Out, op. cit.* See also 1988 Commission on the Cities, "Race and Poverty in the United States—and What Should Be Done," *Quiet Riots: Race and Poverty in the United States,* eds. Fred R. Harris and Roger W. Wilkins (New York: Pantheon Books, 1988), pp. 172-184.

[14]Tidwell, *Stalling Out, op. cit.*

[15]*Op. cit.,* p. 692.

[314]*Op. cit.,* p. xxi.

[17]Charles E. Silberman, *Crisis in Black and White* (New York: Vintage Books, 1964), p. 16.

[18]Louis L. Knowles and Kenneth Prewitt (eds.), *Institutional Racism in America* (Englewood Cliffs: Prentice-Hall, Inc., 1969), p. 127.

[19]James P. Comer, *Beyond Black and White* (New York: Quadrangle Books, 1972), pp. 119-120.

[20]Walter L. Updegrave, "Race and Money," *Money,* December, 1989, p. 154.

[21]David H. Swinton, "Economic Status of Black Americans," *The State of Black America 1989,* ed. Janet Dewart (New York: National Urban League, Inc., 1989), pp. 31-32.

[22]Billy J. Tidwell, "Topsy Turvy: Unemployment among Black Administrators and Managers," *The Forum,* National Forum for Black Public Administrators, Vol. 3, No. 1 (February, 1987), pp. 1-3.

[23]Billy J. Tidwell, *Black Unemployment in the Private Sector: A Twenty-Year Assessment* (Washington, DC: National Urban League Research Department, 1988).

[24]For a relevant discussion, see Frederick Stirton Weaver, "Cui Bono? And The Economic Function of Racism," *Review of Black Political Economy,* Vol. 8 (Spring, 1978), pp. 302-313; and Michael Reich, "Who Benefits from Racism? The Distribution among Whites of Gains and Losses from Racial Inequality," *Journal of Human Resources,* Vol. 13 (Fall, 1978), pp. 524-544. See also Michael Reich, *Racial Inequality: A Political-Economic Analysis* (Princeton: Princeton University Press, 1981).

[25]Thomas F. D'Amico, "The Conceit of Labor Market Discrimination," *Economics of Discrimination Thirty Years Later,* AEA Papers and Proceedings, Vol. 77, No. 2 (May, 1987), p. 310.

[26]Joseph Duffey, "Competitiveness and Human Resources," *California Management Review,* Spring, 1988, p. 98.

[27]Victor Perlo, *Economics of Racism U.S.A.: Roots of Black Inequality* (New York: International Publishers, 1975), p. 3.

[28]Limiting the base to those in the work force avoids the problem of including transfer income in the estimate. Such income, of course, does not contribute to GNP.

REFERENCES

U.S. Department of Commerce Bureau of the Census. 1990. Current Population Reports. *Money Income and Poverty Status in the United States: 1989.* Washington, DC: U.S. Government Printing Office.

_____ . 1989. *Trends in Income, by Selected Characteristics: 1947 to 1988.* Washington, DC: U.S. Government Printing Office.

U.S. Department of Labor Bureau of Labor Statistics. 1990. *Employment and Earnings: January 1990.* Washington, DC: U.S. Government Printing Office.

_____ . 1989. *Handbook of Labor Statistics, August, 1989.* Washington, DC: U.S. Government Printing Office.

Toward Development of a National Drug Control Strategy, *Robert McAlpine.*

REFERENCES

"Children and Guns: A Fact Sheet." 1989. Washington, DC: U.S. House of Representatives, Select Committee on Children, Youth, and Families.

"Deadly Chicago Weekend Blamed on Gangs, Drugs." 1990. *The Washington Post.* September 11, 1990, p. A3.

Drug-Exposed Infants, A Generation at Risk. 1990. Report to the Chairman, U.S. Senate Committee on Finance. Washington, DC: General Accounting Office, pp. 8-9.

"NRA Loses Court Challenge to California Assault-Gun Ban." 1990. *The Washington Post.* September 11, 1990, p. A5.

Public Policy Empowerment Mandate: The Drug Trafficking Issue. 1989. Washington, DC: Policy and Government Relations Department, National Urban League, Inc.

Who Will Care When Parents Can't? A Study of Black Children in Foster Care. 1989. Washington, DC: National Black Child Development Institute, Inc.

Community Mobilization for Education in Rochester, New York: A Case Study, *David Wirschem*

FOOTNOTES

[1] *1985-86 Year-End Statistical Data,* City School District, Rochester, New York, September, 1986.

[2] *A Call to Action: A Report from the CED/Urban League Community Task Force on Education,* Urban League of Rochester, NY, Inc., and Center for Educational Development, Rochester, NY, March, 1986, p. 1.

[3] For a detailed description of Rochester's community mobilization campaign and responses to it, see William A. Johnson, Jr., Betty Dwyer, and Joan Z. Spade, "A Community Initiative: Making a Difference in the Quality of Black Education," *Urban League Review,* Summer, 1987, National Urban League, Inc. Research Department, Washington, DC; and Desmond Stone, *Continued Commitment: The Call to Action Three Years Later* (Rochester, NY: Center for Educational Development, 1989).

[4] *Guidelines for School-Based Planning, 1988-1989,* City School District, Rochester, NY, p. 3.

[5] "Rochester City School District/Rochester Teachers Association Contractual Agreement," July 1987-June 30, 1990, p. 14.

[6] *1985-86 Rochester* and *1990-91 Budget,* City School District, Rochester, NY.

[7] "1988-89 Annual Report of the Rochester City School District, November, 1989"; and Peter McWalters, "Superintendent's Report to the Rochester School Board," December 12, 1990.

[8] *Ibid.*

[9] *1989-90 Year-End Statistical Data,* City School District, Rochester, NY, September, 1990.

[10] *Revised Rochester City School District Budget, July 1, 1990-June 30, 1991,* p. 56; and *District Data Report, 1986-87,* City School District, Rochester, NY, December, 1986, p. 23.

[11] *Times Union,* Rochester, NY, February 16, 1990.

Acknowledgments

The National Urban League acknowledges with sincere appreciation the invaluable contributions of the authors of the various articles in this publication.

We give special thanks to associate editor Paulette J. Robinson, whose exemplary skills, insight, and commitment add greatly to this effort.

We also acknowledge Johnnie Griffin, proofreader; Michele Long Pittman, project assistant; and the special contributions of National Urban League staff, including Leslye L. Cheek, Ernie Johnston, Jr., B. Maxwell Stamper, Farida Syed, Faith Williams, Ralph Faust, and Denise Wright of the Public Relations and Communications Department; Daniel S. Davis and Betty Ford in the Office of the President; Dr. Stephanie Robinson, Director, Education Department; Washington Operations; Department of Policy and Government Relations; the Research Department; and the Program Departments.

Order Blank

National Urban League Publications
500 East 62nd Street
New York, N.Y. 10021

	Per Copy	Number of Copies	Total
The State of Black America 1991	$19.95		
Recent Volumes in series:			
The State of Black America 1990	$19.00		
The State of Black America 1989	$19.00		
The State of Black America 1988	$18.00		
The State of Black America 1987	$18.00		
Postage and handling: Individual volumes—$2.00 each Book Rate			
$3.00 each First Class			
Amount enclosed			

- -

"With Honors" Lithograph

Limited edition, numbered lithograph of "With Honors" by Synthia Saint James, signed by the artist. "With Honors" is the fourth in the Great Artists series created for the National Urban League through a donation from the House of Seagram. Proceeds benefit the National Urban League.

Unframed lithograph 26¾" × 36". Full color. $1,000 each, includes postage and handling.

Also available as a poster in celebration of the League's 80th anniversary. 28½" × 35". Full color. $35.00 each, plus $5.00 postage and handling.

For information and to order, contact:

> National Urban League, Inc.
> Office of Development
> 500 East 62nd Street
> New York, New York 10021

Please make check or money order payable to:
National Urban League, Inc.

Order Blank

National Urban League Publications
500 East 62nd Street
New York, N.Y. 10021

	Per Copy	Number of Copies	Total
The State of Black America 1991	$19.95	_____	_____
Recent Volumes in series:			
The State of Black America 1990	$19.00	_____	_____
The State of Black America 1989	$19.00	_____	_____
The State of Black America 1988	$18.00	_____	_____
The State of Black America 1987	$18.00	_____	_____
Postage and handling: Individual volumes—$2.00 each Book Rate		_____	_____
$3.00 each First Class		_____	_____
Amount enclosed		_____	

"With Honors" Lithograph

Limited edition, numbered lithograph of "With Honors" by Synthia Saint James, signed by the artist. "With Honors" is the fourth in the Great Artists series created for the National Urban League through a donation from the House of Seagram. Proceeds benefit the National Urban League.

Unframed lithograph 26¾" × 36". Full color. $1,000 each, includes postage and handling.

Also available as a poster in celebration of the League's 80th anniversary. 28½" × 35". Full color. $35.00 each, plus $5.00 postage and handling.

For information and to order, contact:

National Urban League, Inc.
Office of Development
500 East 62nd Street
New York, New York 10021

Please make check or money order payable to:
National Urban League, Inc.